Breakaway

AN AUTOBIOGRAPHY

DAN MURPHY

DEDICATION

To all hoops enthusiasts and all those engaged in life. May you always get a lucky bounce.

The proceeds from this book will benefit the Bairo Pite Clinic in Dili, Timor-Leste. To find out more about the BPC's mission and how you can contribute, visit www.bairopiteclinic.org.

FOREWORD

My dad asked me to write a little something to introduce his memoirs and I agreed mostly because that's the sort of things sons do for fathers, if their fathers are the memoir-writing type. When sitting down to do it, I found that writing about my dad is like writing about the sun. I could describe the chemical composition, diameter and circumference, life phases, etc., but capturing the significance and import of the sun to our existence on Earth is daunting. Each step attempted is hesitant because a writer never risks being trite more than when he attempts to be profound. On the other hand, what the hell. If my dad had wanted some tepid pabulum, he would have given me a wide berth in the first place. So here you go, Daddio…

My dad would have been a great soldier but you blew it, Vietnam "police action." By being such a calamitous, trumped-up farce, you turned a lot of honorable warriors against you. My dad is strong, fast, smart, courageous, and determined. He would have used these assets to significant effect in a military conflict. Instead, galvanized by the wanton turpitude of your prolonged aggression, he rose against you and your moral sequelae. And yes, Dad, that last bit was for you.

I've played a lot of basketball with and against my dad. People who don't play sports sometimes make the mistake of simplifying

1

them but intelligent people who happen to be athletic are just as likely to participate as stupid, athletic people. To the former type, sports are battle ballets played out on chessboards by civilized savages. For my dad, basketball was the enduring physical outlet that medicine was for his spirit. To you, reader, it may seem strange that he has chosen to weave these two themes into the narrative of his life but it is distinctly appropriate. The forms of this world are not as solid as they seem. We are shadows commingling, and our natures prove out the same way however we opt to play upon the cave wall. Too, we are storytellers, all of us, but we can only spin our yarns if they are fundamentally unbroken from beginning to end. Basketball and medicine have been lifelong strands for my dad and, as such, their constituents have combined.

I know my dad better than just about anyone else. I'm very familiar with his strengths and his shortcomings as some of both are mine as well. The most difficult thing for me to accept about him has been that he cannot be truly mine. He is Doctor Dan more than he is "Dad" and this is how it had to be, how it should be, because no matter how much I would have liked to have him around throughout my life, accessible whenever it was convenient for me to visit, he has had and will continue to have more important things to do. I write that last without any resentment. Finally, I can do that. You have cast your prodigious gifts back onto the suffering world, Dad, as is right and proper. Like everybody else, I would do well to make measure of your accomplishments and follow suit.

Liam Alexander Murphy

BREAKAWAY

One night in the dead of winter in 1925, the town of Coleraine in frigid northern Minnesota was brought to life by the heroics of a seventeen-year-old basketball player, Cornelius B. Murphy. Using an assortment of nifty inside moves, both right and left hooks, and a deadly two-handed set shot, Murphy single handedly outscored the entire visiting Hibbing squad, netting sixteen points for Greenway High in a 23-15 upset victory. At 5'10", Con also jumped center after each made basket, and never lost a tip.

This was the same Con Murphy who first made the paper at age eight when he delighted onlookers by chasing a bull moose down the main street of this young Irish town. My father was a very quiet, studious boy who, by the age of twelve, had read every book in the town library. He was the oldest of six brothers who, along with two sisters, helped fill the Murphy home.

Grandfather Cornelius M. Murphy was the seventh son of a seventh son, which besides being a most portentous Irish omen, also graphically exhibits a powerful genetic propensity for prolific scoring. All the boys worked in the iron mines as did nearly everyone else in this tax rich, model, company town. Coleraine was reserved for the English and Irish elite of the mining community, while bohunks, Slavs, and other southern Europeans stayed just down the road in the frontier-like wide open settlement, Bovey.

C.M. was the master mechanic during those boom years when high grade ore traveled from Duluth to Pittsburgh via the Great Lakes, supplying Mr. Carnegie's steel mills.

Great grandpa's family emigrated from County Cork during the potato famine, settling in Ishpeming, U.P., Michigan where mining also thrived.

Grandma Murphy was of German extraction and had worked as a maid in C.M.'s home until his mother died. Because her cooking was so good, he married her. As the new mines developed in the Mesabi, the family trekked across Wisconsin to Itasca county Minnesota.

Con, my father, went on to medical school at the university in Minneapolis. When his younger brother Joe came down to begin medicine two years later, Con knew his way around well enough to be able to sneak a cadaver into Joe's bed while he slept. Joe almost went back to mining the next morning but later thanked his mentor for providing him with the pivotal experience influencing his specialty choice away from both pathology and psychiatry in one poignant lesson.

Dad stayed on at Hennipen County for three years after finishing his MD degree gaining valuable experience treating victims of the teamster labor battles and extracting bullets from Machine-gun Kelly's banking associates.

Mother, Ethel Koelzer, grew up in Jordan, Minnesota. German was her first language as it was for many before WWI. Her nickname was "schimmel" or white stallion for her beautiful blonde hair. She flunked fourth grade but with a good eye check and glasses, the next year she successfully negotiated not only fourth but also fifth grade. And she played basketball. At 5'10" and good coordination she was quite formidable. Local lore has it that she once beat one of the

Pollard boys one on one. After high school, Ethel went on to get her nursing degree and worked at the county hospital in Minneapolis where she met Con.

During The Depression, however, jobs were scarce even in the medical profession. Dad found an opening in Alton, Iowa, a booming metropolis of one thousand people. Ethel followed or chased a year or two later, and they were married in 1941.

While WWII ravaged the globe, taking fifty million lives, my parents worked overtime in an attempt to make up the difference. Before the decade was out, five scrappy sibs occupied the good doctor's abode on the north edge of town. I, the middle child, was delivered by my father on the auspicious autumnal equinox of '44. On day one, the borders of my character were powerfully tested as the sweet satisfaction of mother's milk feebly attempted to blunt the rage of the fashionable dorsal slit ritual.

My first memory of basketball came one summer day when, against rules, I ventured across the street and up the block two houses to Dud's backyard. There I watched as the older neighborhood guys made the dust swirl as they gracefully worked the ball around, periodically arching it high in the air toward the chains hanging from the black metal circle with the flat wood behind. Yells punctuated the action as everyone seemed to get excited especially when the ball fell through the chains.

Presently, as I observed the furious action, the ball came bouncing past me and rolled onto the adjoining yard. I gleefully ran to retrieve it, oblivious to the screams behind me, thrilled to be a part of the action. What I didn't know was that the ball had entered the red zone, an area whose perimeter was known to the inch by every player. Then, out of the corner of my eye, I saw it coming. This was the yard of Ted, the town cop. Slavering and bounding full tilt, his atavistic canine, bee-lined toward his innocent prey. Instinctual terror narrowly provided the necessary adrenaline as I retreated rapidly, barely crossing the tether-defined circumference as the snap of the rope rendered futile that of the powerful mandible. I heard the guys laughing as I ran back home to more comfortable security. My first lesson in teamwork came a few days later as I watched one of the guys divert the monster while another darted in for the ball. What fun!

Northwest Iowa wasn't settled until after the Civil War in the later part of the nineteenth century because of the tenacious resistance put up by the Sioux. The military action following the disastrous Little Bighorn encounter, secured the rich black loam for the waves of new immigrants.

To the east of Alton came the Luxemburgers escaping the ravishes of European wars. These people were industrious, catholic, beer drinking polka dancers. My mother's German came in handy with this group.

West of our beloved river town was all Dutch. Economic opportunity along with the search for religious freedom motivated their departure from northern Europe. Extreme industriousness, teetottling, and an exacting moral code characterized these "Hollanders," members all of the Reformed faith. Having stated this, I must mention that, at an early age, I had to learn to use a few classic expletives like the ubiquitous "hou je bek," the more emphatic "kippen strunt," and the in-your-face provocative "klootzak." More apropos to the subject matter at hand, these people were tall, strong, and athletic, not to mention stubborn and competitive; especially those whose surnames ended in "a," the Freislanders.

Being Irish-German, our family wasn't intimately tied to either side. Con, as the only physician in town, attended the needs of all, and as far as I can tell, was universally loved and respected.

The meandering Floyd River served as a moat separating the two disparate ethnic groups except in the few municipalities straddling its banks where some inevitable mixing occurred. Naturally, someone had to run the bakery and someone else the tavern. Sgt. Floyd, a member of the Lewis and Clark expedition, was the first Caucasian to die on the banks of the unforgiving stream, succumbing to acute appendicitis. At age eight, after nine inches of rain, I watched houses float over the nearby bridge as frantic phone calls went unheeded downstream where twenty six perished that same day.

In the town of Alton, baseball was king. Several local boys even had brief stints in the biggies during the thirties playing for St. Louis. We too were the Cardinals, passing away the beautiful summer days playing America's game. How clearly I can remember sailing toward the diamond, Richie Ashburn glove swinging on the handlebars, my cap with the meticulously coifed brim tilted into the breeze, singing the latest Everly brothers' hit.

We had Peewees, Midgets, Junior Legion, and finally Town Team. Our coach, Dave, not only knew the game inside out but also gave us an edge with the strategic use of his uncanny ability to place an oyster on an umpire or an opposing coach's shoe from as far as ten feet away. Just a quick "ptt" from him and suddenly you've got to react. Do you say something foolish, wipe it off, pretend to ignore it, or worst choice of all, attempt to match it? Any way, you look bad and we go one up psychologically.

We had tons of fun and we could play. Fundamentals and practice were the keys. I'm still amazed to see so many major leaguers not able to lay down a bunt.

I, myself, was on my way to becoming the next Stan Musial or maybe Mickey Mantle. By age eleven, I was batting cleanup for teams at three levels and hitting .500. What a glorious feeling to be called "you little fart" by the next town's ace right hander after going three for three off him in a big Jr. Legion game. My only regret was that my older sister never thanked me for boosting her social position by such exploits.

Two things then happened dramatically altering my life. First, almost overnight, my eyes went bad, and second, my mother died. She had battled with breast cancer for five long years, undergoing bilateral mastectomies, radiation, and finally multiple thoracenteses done by my father drawing fluid from her disease-filled chest allowing more air to enter her progressively failing lungs. I can only imagine the anguish she felt, realizing the futility of her condition, as she instructed dad to stop the painful procedures. None of us will ever forget the priest coming to our home for the Extreme Unction sacrament, the way she sent five small kids to the movies that night, and then the frantic run back home after the call. Father, although accustomed to being in such situations, was barely able to lead us through the rosary huddled in that dimmed bedroom. Each of us, in turn, kissed her goodbye.

From then on, I found myself more and more, alone on the basketball court, quietly shooting hoops.

7

BREAKAWAY

Every Saturday morning, during the school year, the public school gym was open for basketball. This was only a block from our house, but the prevailing politics of the time was that catholic kids, who attended their own school, were not welcome. This was just plain not acceptable to me. These were my buddies and this was where the action was, so I stubbornly, and quite creatively, re-entered the building any way I could. Once I came through a window and climbed down a chain to gain access, or a Protestant friend would sneak me in the back door. Maybe it was because my father was the good Dr. Murphy and on the bank board or that I had such a pitiful look on my face when discovered that made the difference, but, after a time, the janitor gave up and I was never bothered again.

Being picked for a real game was something else. You watch, dribble on the sidelines, shoot while no game is going on, try to look tall, until finally, one day, they need one to play, and, the critical decision is made. Even though you're just a little brat, at least you might not ruin the game for the real players and you're chosen. Of course, you don't see the ball for the longest time but you are in the mix.

By the sixth grade, I was in lots of games. One Saturday, there was a blizzard, and not too many regulars showed up at the gym. Consequently, I got into a hot game with mostly high school players. I remember for the last basket of the game, my neighbor Donny, who was five years older than me, dribbled between my man and me, turned, handed me the ball and said "shoot it." It was just a fifteen foot set shot, but with the big guys, and for the game, it was special. Donny did it just because he was automatically nice and always thinking of how someone else would feel.

That same afternoon, I grabbed my sled and went to the school hill to take advantage of the new snow. On my first run down the hill, I thought I felt something scrape my runner as I sped past the school. As I pulled the sled back up the hill, I looked closely at the tracks I had made. Suddenly I saw something shiny in the snow partly uncovered by the fresh track. You can imagine my surprise as I reached down and picked up a perfect, new silver dollar. Some days are just like that!

Alton High School had a graduating class of four kids that year. Our school, St. Mary's Academy, had a class of thirteen. There was

8

never any doubt where we Murphy's would go. Only a rare Catholic would cross the line to attend public school and it was frowned upon within the church and in society.

St. Mary's had been built in the 1880's. We had no indoor toilets; had to go out back to another small building if the need presented. There was a huge bell hanging in a cupola atop the school with a rope hanging down through two floors to ground level. Sports teams would traditionally enter the school whenever they returned with a win to "ring it up." The faculty consisted of one nun for seventh and eighth, and three nuns for high school. This was all considered as expected by everyone. But, what seems impossible even now is that we had no coach, and no gym!

Beginning in seventh grade, St. Mary's did have an official basketball program. The parish priest coached the Jr. High and the High School teams. Practices were held in the parish hall which originally was the settlers first country church now moved into town. The sidelines were within inches of the walls while the top of the key intersected with the center circle. The lights were poor, the ball bounced differently off each board, and the building couldn't hold heat. Still, we played there hour after hour. Our workouts usually followed the same pattern; lay-ups, the weave up top, scrimmage, then free throws.

As a freshman, I played some varsity. Our games were at the public school gym. Most memorable was the game where I found myself with the ball with four seconds left trailing by one. Not wanting to miss, I held the ball as the clock ran out. The remarks directed toward me afterward put me irrevocably on the pathway to becoming a gunner. That year we finished with a perfect 0-18 record.

Academically, I did fine. Algebra seemed so logical, and what's Latin to "the perfect acolyte?" English was a bit more challenging as I hardly ever read unless it was "Who is Elgin Baylor?" in Sport magazine, or anecdotes in Boys Life. Bottom line was that, in addition to being endowed with above average native intelligence, I had a raging demon inside whispering "Don't lose! Don't ever lose!" This all-encompassing imperative included everything from tiddlywinks, Chinese checkers, and Ping-Pong, to long distance spitting, calling in crows, and who can say the alphabet backwards the fastest. Stubbornness was not my short suit!

All of this was severely tested at my freshman initiation when I was forced to propose to Clara Sue. This poor classmate, all through elementary school, had been tortured unmercifully because of a certain immutable aspect of her physical appearance. I was "the best" at this barbaric taunting. Twenty years later, when I was a doctor, I assisted her in the delivery of a beautiful baby girl. Afterward, as we chatted, she told me how the tears soaked her pillow every night during those school years. Yet she held no rancor; her life had turned out fine. I muttered an apology as I left, amazed once again, at the perplexing nature of human behavior.

Summer was a time for lots of interesting activities. Not just the swimming, fishing, and golf, but the highly creative games like "kick the can," "seven steps," and the somewhat naughty "stop the car." There were several ingenious versions of the latter. Before dusk, we would stretch the rubber string from the innards of a K-28 golf ball across Highway 10 as it ran past the long line of thick hedge highlighting our yard. We always hung a piece of paper with a clever provocative ditty on it in the middle of the band. A more perverse methodology was in order after dark. Utilizing crab apples in various stages of decay from our big old tree, hiding stealthily behind the hedge, as many as twenty of us delinquents would rise up to pelt the unsuspecting passerby with our aromatic offerings. The screech of tires signaled our frenetic scurrying into the shadows of the neighborhood like rats in a sewer. On special occasions, some of the more demented of the group would execute the old, feces in the lit paper bag ring doorbell and hide, trick.

Basketball games were a constant. The dust never settled on the smoothly worn court across the street. Even guys from the surrounding towns arrived to challenge in. I began to understand the subtle use of expletives and observed directly how various players navigated the minefield separating aggressive play from criminal assault.

One picture perfect Sunday afternoon, we regulars were enjoying ourselves with a nice non-threatening little game, when a strange car pulled up. A momentary pause in the action accompanied a collective gaping of mouths, as five big newcomers exited the vehicle and sauntered toward the court. Three of them had to be at least 6'5" or above. They spoke English with a smattering of Dutch thrown in. For a moment we felt as if we were at the O.K. Corral. "We got winners." one of them informed us. They then proceeded to decimate all opponents, holding court for two hours, before driving off into the sunset laughing like Sinter Klaas. Lessons learned: there is no good answer for bulk in the half-court game, and, more importantly, nonchalance and raw swagger can get you a big edge.

That August, the buzz of the town was that St. Mary's had hired a coach. Sure enough, young Mr. Potts arrived week before school began, fresh out of college. His mandate was to bring respectability back to "Bluejax" athletics, teach all P.E. and social sciences, and drive the school bus. Pay was four thousand dollars. Years later he told me that all those chores paled when compared to the stress provoked by the added responsibility as school counselor. "A zone defense I could handle," he said. "But what do you say to a sixteen-year-old who comes in announcing she's pregnant?"

I have no idea what happened to the unfortunate girl, but our basketball team won seven games and more importantly for me, toward the end of the season, I suddenly discovered that I could dunk! What a pastime! Over and over the thrill was the same. The new respect too, was great. I remember one day when Lefty Van Bergen, a star from a neighboring town, ran into me downtown and said "Hey, I hear you're averaging twenty three a game." I was too shy to answer and anyway, the truth was that I had one game with twenty three, not an average. The recognition was good, though. We were to face their team the next week, and, equally important, he had a little sister my age who was the classiest act around, so I just muttered something neutral about how the corn was growing as I waltzed off to buy some Topps.

We lost that game but won a few more including one in the sectional before bowing out to Newkirk to end the season with nine wins. Coach Potts told us we were a step above mediocre and that, with a lot of work, we could reach the "good" level. He was allowed to buy two new balls, and most importantly, he had a key to the hall. No more sneaking, begging, conniving, to access the court; just ask coach.

By then TV had come to town. Even though Bill Russell had been responsible for the demise of Iowa in the NCAA, I had to love the way he and Bob Cousy took the game to a new level. My favorite, though, was Jack Twyman, who seemed to have more heart and hustle than anyone. "The Big O" brought a multitude of talents to the Royals, but effectively eliminated the emotional Twyman factor with his deliberate style.

That summer, a new factor came into play. Bobby Schneider, an incoming high school student, had grown to well over six feet. Even as an eighth grader, he had a beautiful long range jump shot. It didn't take much to get him to buy into the compulsive fanaticism of a true basketball junky.

We shot around, did drills like George Mikan right hook-left hook, played h-o-r-s-e, chance, and shot free throws; but most of all we played one-on-one. I mean hours of it—him with the hooks and jumper and me with the fade or power move. Games to one hundred with hardly a word spoken except for the score. We still played baseball and were pretty good. I pitched and he caught. More than once we cranked out back to back homers. Some evenings we played pinochle or euchre, but our passion was hoops.

When the next season began, Coach Potts got us all a bargain on new low cut black "Chuck Taylors." We were really quite studly! With my older brother now six-four and a strong rebounder, me and Bobby at 6'3", and our other starters at 6'2" and 6' even we were formidable.

After a month we found ourselves 9-0, having even crushed one team 88-28. For the first time, our team appeared in the regional ratings as number ten. Next up was the Sioux City Diocesan tournament which included all the Catholic teams from northwest Iowa. St. Mary's had never won it in their seventy-five-year history. Our first two games were relatively easy but in the semi-finals we had to face the talented Ashton, St. Joe's squad.

Coach gave us a rousing, inspirational speech pointing out that rebounding would be crucial. After the traditional team prayer we were pumped to the max as we lined up for the opening tip. We scored and then, as they missed their first shot I felt an explosive surge of power as I rocketed skyward for the board. Instinctually, I had developed the habit of kicking out to the sides both feet at the peak of my jump. Later one of their players told me that the toe of my All Star just touched the tip of his nose on that rebound. Our whole team played well and when the final buzzer sounded we were headed to the finals. Needless to say the old school bell got quite a workout late that night.

For the big game, our entire parish proceeded in peregrination one hundred miles east to Fort Dodge. We players decked out in white shirts with ties accenting our brilliant blue letter jackets bracketed by buffed beige sleeves. The decorated autos proudly honked announcing our passage to each friendly farm town on the way. Mgsr. Tolan welcomed us and guided us through the throng of three thousand popcorn eating, pop drinking rowdies warming up with the consolation game. Everyone was there!

Except my father! He never attended our games. I can only speculate as to why. Did his father, who could have been arrogant and self-centered, go to his games? If not, it could have set a precedent. Or was it designed to send a message that academics were more important? My uncles included a doctor, dentist, lawyer, and judge after all. Maybe we kids were just so obnoxious during our abominable play years, always blaming the ball, the floor, the lights, the referees, anything but our own incompetence, that he just tuned it all off. Most likely it was his job as the only physician in town and for several surrounding towns in days when beepers and cell phones were non-existent. Over five thousand career deliveries imply a certain dedication to community severely compromising personal and family pursuits. As a sixteen year old heading into the biggest game of my life, I didn't have to ponder such machinations for more than a fleeting moment. The electricity of the situation dominated cerebral activity like an aura.

Up against us was the undefeated five from Fonda O.L.G.C. Neither team had ever played in such a big gym before so many howling partisans. Adding to the charged atmosphere was another first, live radio play by play coverage. We had two Schneiders, two Murphys, and four Mousels on our roster. They had another two Murphys, and a Snider on theirs. An announcer's nightmare it most certainly was. One imaginative listener compared it to reading "Finnegan's Wake" and "Naked Lunch" simultaneously while downing a sixer of Blatz.

As the teams huddle round their respective coaches reciting the ritualistic "Hail Mary," one can only imagine the consternation felt by

Our Lady, as both supplicant squads beseechingly implore her intervention for the "W" as the day's double duty patron.

As the game began it was easy to see that Fonda's strategy was to push the pace. They were good athletes and excellent shooters who loved to run and gun. We were bigger and, while we had lots of offensive weapons, rebounding was our strong point. Neither team got ahead by more than five points, and, with two late baskets, St. Mary's led at half time 41-40.

In the locker room Coach Potts congratulated us for the fine first half effort, "Way to go guys! Listen, we've got two with three fouls and I know the long floor is getting to you guys, so let's try a 2-1-2 zone and focus on every rebound. Your offense is fine. Work the high-low game and keep fighting!"

Another prayer and we were back out on the floor to the deafening roar of the crowd. To our dismay, Fonda hit their first five shots, several from long range. During a quick time out Coach explained, "Back to man to man, guys, and in their faces. Help on the backside on the drive. Try not to foul except on lay-ups. Let's go!"

Slowly, we worked our way back into the game. At one point, as I was defending an outside man, he tried to feed a wide open back cutter with a bounce pass to my right. I anticipated perfectly, catching the certain assist with my advancing instep. Pele couldn't have done better as every eye followed the ball's high arcing parabola peaking within inches of the ceiling before gravity asserted its confident dictate guiding the sphere downward toward our undefended goal. A chorus of collective oh's followed by light laughter brought a brief moment of levity to the intense unfolding drama, allowing brows to relax as leather clanged off iron before bouncing back toward the frozen ten. The next day's paper was to read, "St. Mary's scored in every way possible, even trying to boot the ball through the basket."

Early in the fourth quarter one of our starters fouled out. Within minutes two more followed, and Fonda didn't miss a free throw. We scored consistently down low and Bobby hit some outside J's. With one minute to go, I got a tip-in to put us up for the first time in the second half 84-83. As they came flying back up the court I thought, "It's like going against Marciano; he just keeps coming." Suddenly, their star Fulcher gets by his man and is slashing down the lane. Bobby comes to meet him and times his leap perfectly as his opponent adjusts in midair and goes to the finger roll. Uniforms converge to the sound of whistles in stereo. The ball climbs the rim, like a perfect putt, and drops as both players fall to the floor. Noise approached the level of that fateful day at Shiloh. All eyes anxiously observed one referee poised over Bobby, arm extended like a fixed bayonet, while the other touched his duck tail with the fingers of his left hand. The requisite conference terminated with an authoritative arms akimbo punctuated by a peck of the index finger.

Burning our last time out, coach set up strategy and we hustled back to the floor with eight seconds to go. The free throw was good giving them a two point lead. Then the shocker. A full court press, something they hadn't used all day. We were deep into our bench and just weren't ready. Yes, we got it in bounds but then the trap forced a desperation turn over and we were sunk. We had to foul and they calmly made both charity shots. Game over, 88-84, a definite barn burner. They had made thirty free throws and missed only three. We had four players who scored seventeen points and we got the biggest trophy our school had ever received. Of course we were disappointed but each of us knew we had given all we had and it was one heck of a basketball game.

We had little time to ponder as we were in mid-season and had new challenges almost immediately. Inspired by our success, we continued racking up victories.

Archer was a new team on our schedule, thus we were a bit antsy heading north the thirty five miles to the small farm town. Consternation grew as we entered the Cracker Jack gym, shabby being a charitable characterization, with lighting comparable to a full moon. Adding to the evening's mood was our captains' report that emanating from the officials was that special spiritual aroma well known to every cruet bearing acolyte. Any doubt that we had entered a different world was removed when, as we lined up for the opening tip, we saw that they had no leather ball! We were playing with rubber!

Rough doesn't begin to describe the nature of that game. We responded in kind especially on the offensive end, realizing that aggressive defense on our part would be disastrous. I had one of those nights where my muscles felt unusually primed. Time after time I was able to take it strong to the hole, finishing with either power moves or reverses facilitated by the superior grip of rubber on bank board. Despite combat level contact on nearly every take, I got only three free throws on my way to thirty one points. After the game, victory in hand, we quickly exited without even showering, never to return.

Through the darkest of winter, we continued to play well, losing only once in our regular season games. In the latter part of February, all the better than four hundred teams in Iowa began play in one huge tournament to find the special team who could best them all. Stringing together three straight victories, including one over Ashton, the proud St. Mary's Bluejax entered district play with the sectional crown in hand.

Our next opponent was Paullina, a very good team from a school with an enrollment of over two hundred. Despite a valiant effort on our part, we were simply outclassed and couldn't keep up in the fourth quarter. We had ended our season with twenty two wins, the most successful in school history. Coach Potts was named Diocesan Coach of the Year, and I was lucky enough to be named MVP by my teammates.

"I'm going away for a few days," my father announced as we all ate breakfast before school one morning. "Aunt Frances will take care of you." Sounded innocuous enough; besides, we were all too engrossed with our own lives to even begin to realize that a bombshell had just been dropped. Dr. Murphy never just went away for a few days. His dedication to work was like a snapping turtle to a stick. At any rate, we continued spooning up the Wheaties, Corn Flakes, Rice Krispies, and Shredded Wheat, failing to notice the momentary break in the rhythm of Frances' motion.

Twelve years my mother's senior, Frances Koelzer had known trauma excruciatingly well in her life. At age sixteen, she left home for two years of "normal school" and then became the marm at a series of country schools with duties ranging from chopping wood and building the fire to teaching all grades in both English and German. Married at twenty two, she proceeded to successfully

16

negotiate her first pregnancy and was near term in her second, when, within weeks of each other, her husband died of encephalitis, and her father succumbed to a stroke.

How little time for grieving as Frances, in rapid succession, moved back home, delivered her second child, and began work in a hardware store, in a valiant effort to keep both families functional. My mother, then an adolescent, besides going to school, was expected to handle much of the care for her two small nephews. Somehow they all not only survived but thrived and became quite close.

As her children grew up, Frances continued working, never remarrying, preferring to live at home caring for her aging mother. At age sixty one, thinking that she would retire and peacefully live out her life in her childhood home, she received the following fateful letter.

Dearest Frances,

As you know, I've been struggling with breast cancer for the last four years and have slowly exhausted all forms of treatment. I'm so weak now that it's all I can do to walk around the house. Con and I know the end is near. He is so busy with work and I can no longer adequately care for the children.

Of all people, I know that you can understand what I'm going through. The idea of imposing on you is so difficult to contemplate, but I see no other viable option. Can you come help? Mother could stay with Sophie.

The lilacs are beginning to blossom. It's my favorite time of the year. Hope all is well with you.

Your Loving Sister,
Ethel

Thus Frances, in lieu of quiet retirement, entered into the turbulent situation of five children from age six to thirteen trying to cope, and one adult male burying himself as deeply as he could in work. It turned out to be a new lease on life for her as she proved to be a tower of strength through those difficult times.

For six years, through thick and thin, she dedicated herself to raising her sister's children, just as Ethel had helped her so many years before. Physically, we were well provided for. Emotionally, on the other hand, things were left to work themselves out; not only for the kids but just as certainly for the adults. Ethel's death was not dealt with, a not so subtle form of psychological denial. Many therapists believe that, until one deals with unresolved grief, other forms of emotional expression will be hampered. All of us sibs most certainly exhibited signs of the burden we carried in one way or the other.

More at issue on this fateful day, however, was how Con and Frances had dealt with these delicately charged times. Where was he going and why? What was behind her curious start that morning?

Three days later, father returned to announce that next month he would be married to a nurse he had known thirty years earlier in Minneapolis. Flabbergasted, we kids listened as he explained that her husband had died and that she was bringing two children along to live with us.

What was going on in his mind? And what about Frances? Had something happened between them? A spurned initiative by one or the other? As a physician, dad was constantly dealing with young women in various stages of undress. Meanwhile, he is getting no closeness, no intimacy, no sex. And Frances, could she have been thinking, "Yes, I'm a little older, but wouldn't it be natural for Con and me to have a relationship and maybe even marry?" One can only speculate as neither ever intimated that anything was awry.

A Twin Cities wedding followed and, without skipping a beat, it was delete Frances and insert Margaret, and Mary, and Jimmy. The keyboard, however, contained no cope button for us kids. This was not a beloved aunt coming to help out, it was a new mother. To my two younger sisters the situation was intolerable and it showed. No one could replace their mother, move all kinds of stuff into their house, and change the way virtually everything was done, without an all out war. I mean these people weren't even Americans, coming from Moosejaw, somewhere near the North Pole. The humiliation, embarrassment, and rage couldn't have been more acute.

Being much more sophisticated, I felt that it was morally wrong for dad to marry someone for any reason other than true love. What was happening seemed to be a slap in the face to our mother. Realistically, at that age, we kids knew less about human nature than we did about the incubus theory of Immaculate Conception.

My father could have met with us and asked us what we thought, how we felt. We, in turn, could have listened to what his thinking was on this pivotal change in our lives. Counseling would have been a logical option during the period of adjustment. None of it was to be. For those who lived through WWII, emotions were spent. Nothing could approach that cumulative horror. People didn't want to dwell on difficult or negative perceptions. Exposing your innermost machinations, for many, is much too threatening. Thus we stumble along as best we can. For us principals, the times would be trying.

Crisis, traumatic confrontation, a temporary separation ensued. But, ever so slowly, adjustments were being made by all, and Margaret eventually became a loved and respected member of the family.

My time was filled with everything from checkers at the Conoco station and late night penny anti poker, to mowing lawns, baling hay, and a never ending whirlwind of sports.

In golf, I won the Jr. Club Championship and even carded an ace one day. In track, a new sport for us, I high jumped six feet even and won the blue ribbon at the diocesan meet as St. Mary's captured first place over all. We won seven straight tournament baseball games including a no-hitter I twirled for the district championship before losing to Laurens and the Ziegler brothers in the game that would have sent us to Des Moines.

But what was truly legendary, occurred one fall Saturday after a bunch of us finished a touch football game. Somehow we got started seeing if anyone could throw the football over the water tower. I waited until last as no one could even come close to doing it. Then with one prodigious heave I launched the ball skyward. We all watched incredulously as the perfect spiral propelled the missive to a position just above the tower top. It then arched nearly horizontal just enough to clear the landmark structure before falling victoriously to the ground amid the chorus of raucous cheering. No one, to my knowledge, has ever matched that feat.

Senior year basketball began with mixed feelings. We had lost half our team but still had some potent weapons left. I was 6'3" and 190lbs and Bobby was about the same. Both of us were formidable offensive threats.

For preseason conditioning, Coach Potts had us "run the section," meaning go around the four miles of country roads just outside of town as he timed us. I remember one exquisite halcyon afternoon when, as I ran along those perfect rows of golden Iowa bounty, a deer jumped out and for just a moment, seemed to be running with me. Feeling inspired I began running at close to full speed. Even though I had two miles to go I just didn't seem to tire and flew along effortlessly. On the final leg of the run I felt so exhilarated that instead of going through a final gate, I decided to take the short cut, meaning I'd have to negotiate a barbed wire fence. Here is where my judgment failed me. Instead of stopping and carefully climbing over, in my exalted state of mind, I thought I would just soar over in one glorious bound. My basketball life passed before my eyes as the top row of barbs ripped into my trailing thigh. Teammates found me lying on the other side of the fence, blood streaming from two deep gashes just above the knee. A quick trip to see the good Dr. Murphy, however, revealed no serious damage. The tetanus shot ended up bothering me more than the injury.

Early in the season, we had a road game where early in the contest I could tell that my game was plainly out of sync. Bobby and the others tried to carry the load but we fell short and lost. Coach didn't let it get to us and we went into the Diocesan tourney 9-1.

We breezed through the early rounds without a hitch. Funny how what seemed so fantastic just a year earlier, now seemed expected. Filled with confidence, we caravanned once again, one hundred miles east to the finals. Our opponent, once again, was Fonda. In our locker room, just before the game, Coach explained, "You guys know this is the last year of St. Mary's since next year we consolidate. They aren't near the team they were last year so let's go out there and have some fun and make history while we're doing it."

Immediately in the first quarter things were going our way as we built a substantial lead. Bobby was hitting 25 footers and I contributed an assortment of inside power moves while they struggled. At half time we led 37-24. "Great half, fellas! Keep cool," Coach told us. "You know they'll be coming at us with a press second half, so if it's a zone, keep your spacing like we practiced, and pass just before the trap gets to you. If it's man-to-man, Dan, you and Jimmy dribble through, and if they double, Bobby you spot up and you should have a good look. You don't have to rush, guys, we're up thirteen."

Sure enough, second half they came out in a full court man press but we were up to the task. For hours, it seemed, Coach had had us practicing bringing the ball up against pressure. He did it like a game, first going against one defender, then, if you made it to half court, two defenders, etc. I once made it against four and had developed a nice crossover dribble. Fonda never challenged and we even got to clear the bench winning going away 68-52. What a madhouse afterward! A huge trophy was awarded. Bobby and I were both named all-tournament, and even the bishop came into the locker room to congratulate us.

Headlines the next day were "St. Mary's Wins First Championship." Part of the story read, "Murphy, although hampered by thick glasses, had no trouble seeing the basket as he led the team with twenty seven points." History had been made.

Although we were kings of the small catholic schools in northwest Iowa, that was a far cry from being competitive in the all-inclusive state tournament set up. To our dismay, after redistricting was put into place, we drew Paullina in the first round of sectionals. They had lost no one from the year before, and everyone had grown several inches. Their center was 6'6". They were 18-0 and averaging 100 points a game. The Des Moines Register had them rated fourth in the state overall. This was David vs. the mother of Goliaths.

The leader of their team was 6'4" Dennis Pauling, who was destined to go on to be all Big Ten for Iowa. To complicate matters, knowing they were to face us, he began hustling one of our cheerleaders who, to our chagrin, fell for his treachery and started hanging with him. The sub plots were as thick as Iowa chops. If

21

Marv Albert had been there to announce, the scenario would have been perfect.

Coach Potts got together with the public school coach in Alton, the legendary Orv Madden. He had thirty years' experience and had pulled off the upset of the decade the year before by using a slow tempo, staying close, and then in the fourth quarter, bursting out of a zone defense four successive times into all out pressure in the half court set, to get turnovers and winning the game on a last second shot. Together they set our strategy.

For a week we held closed door practices. One of our offensive sets was a form of "box and one" where, if they played man, we hand the ball to me at the top of the key, and all four of the other guys go line up near the far sideline. First option is me one-on-one against Pauling. Other options included double picks for Bobby. And we practiced press breaks over and over.

The day before the game it snowed fourteen inches. That made a total of seventy five inches for the winter. I had seven sidewalks and two driveways to shovel, and yes, that would be by hand. Already the snow had been piled up so high that there was literally nowhere to throw the stuff. Game day morning found me so stiff I could barely get out of bed.

The contest was to take place at the Northwestern College gym, a beautiful floor with super square glass backboards. The place was packed well before game time. During warm ups, in spite of the muscle aches, I felt exceptionally strong and coordinated. My body seemed to be trying to get out of my uniform and finally I just gave in to it and left my tank top jersey hang free over my belt.

Just before the game began, Coach gathered us up and said, "As far as I know, these guys put their shoes on one at a time just like we do. Let's go out there and do something special." Adrenaline maxed out as we lined up for the opening tip. A quick glance at Pauling and at our cheerleaders put the finishing touch on my determined mind set.

To my amazement I got the tip easily but pushed it too hard and they had first possession. Quickly they scored easily down low and we had the ball. They were in a man defense so we went immediately to our "gimmick" offense. All four defenders followed our guys out toward the sideline leaving me and Pauling just like we

22

wanted. Boom! I fake left and go hard right, but this guy doesn't shake and instead of a lay-up, I'm left with the quick fade from the baseline. Swish, two all. "Nice shot, Murphy," he says with a big grin as we run back up the floor. I don't grin and I don't talk.

We can't really stop them as the game goes on but Bobby and I are on fire and our plays are confusing them enough so that at the end of the first quarter, we're up 15-14. As the second quarter begins, we notice the beginning of a new look on their faces, a slight wrinkling of the brow, a clenching of the jaw. Meanwhile, we keep our poise, and continue to execute. I score a left reverse with Pauling all over me at the buzzer to put us up 30-29 at half. That's right; St. Mary's 30 and the great Paullina 29. They had not been down at half all season, and only 29 points, and why can't you stop Murphy and Schneider? Must have been a very interesting half time for them. We, on the other hand, were barely touching the floor. Coach brought us back to reality severely, "Sit down and shut up! We haven't got anything yet. The second half is going to be much tougher. They're going to come out fit to kill. Our job is to keep our heads in the game at all times and stick to business. Let's go out and give it everything you got!"

The third period saw full court pressure on their part with Pauling, doing the Spandex thing to deny me the ball. A bad pass and two ten second calls and suddenly they're up five. Doubt was about to enter our minds but Coach, during a much needed time out, barked out the instructions, "Stay cool! Double picks for Dan coming to the ball then clear out!" I also wasn't ready to throw in the towel and vowed to crank it up a notch.

The plan worked and the next three possessions saw me with the ball, going like a water bug down court. After breaking the ten second line, it was, pass to Schneider for two, flip it to Mousel for two, and then a keeper terminating with an all-out collision with Pauling at the rim. The ball banks in and I'm at the line. He stares right at me. No grin, mouth shut. One of their more volatile guys claps his hands and says, "C'mon, do ya wanna lose to these mackerel snappers?" They hadn't been challenged all season and it showed.

Later, one of our most loyal fans, who was also the local bartender, told me that, in forty years of watching basketball, he'd never seen anyone break full court pressure dribbling the whole way without the ball ever coming out from behind the back. Hyperbole? Aggressive tailgating? Move over Mr. Bunyon!

Third quarter ends with no press and us down one. Looking over at their bench, a definite sense of urgency can be detected, maybe even fear; not a pretty sight.

As the final eight minutes opens, I knew I had to make a statement. Dribbling the ball nonchalantly to the left across the top of the key, I notice that Pauling is a little low, hands only about shoulder height. So I figure don't stop and pop, but do it so fast that he can't react, like stop-pop. Describing it in slo-mo: dribble rising, body stops dead then accompanies ball upward uninterrupted as it releases toward hoop, drop of sweat shakes off chin, end of nose, and extended middle finger tip as wisp of hair separates and returns to forehead, defender leaps late, all eyes follow leather to silk, deafening decibels accompany the slow frustrated head shake of the humiliated one.

See-saw 4th until 28 seconds to go down three. My head is swimming as if in a dream. Things are swirling. I see myself at about 25 feet and no opening, nowhere to go. Instinctively, against my better judgment, some primordial nucleus fires. The ball follows a Tommy Heinson trajectory before rattling four times off front and back of rim and drops. Down one!

Immediately they barrel a baseball bullet down court. Someone had missed an assignment and their center was all alone streaking for the dunk. Our hearts were rapidly sinking, but no, from out of nowhere, and I'm sure he'd never moved so fast except the time the bull charged him in the south feedlot, came Henry rising up to shingle that shot sure as a doubly vulcanized inner tube patch. No one even heard the whistle and it's a wonder the roof didn't fall in with the screaming.

Gaining control, the referee sent the poor, reluctant assault victim to the line. His knees were not only shaking but actually wobbling with each feeble attempt as two successive air balls bounced harmlessly toward the stage. Quickly we in bounded and advanced to mid-court to call our final time out.

As we huddled around, Coach Potts looked directly at me and laid it out, "Dan, you're the man. We got 21 seconds, no time outs.

Wait until six seconds and run Cincinnati. Gary, be sure you get the good pick. This is it, guys, let's go!" In Cincinnati, I'm "O" and I get a pick at the top of the key and go right to do what Oscar did, create and score. I envisioned a tomahawk slam at the buzzer for a nice finish.

Everyone is allotted one special moment in their life, when, transcending all, you levitate, enthralled in the union of time and space. The universal engagement peaked as we in bounded to Jimmy who dribbled the ball until the appointed time, then handing it to me before cutting through the lane and clearing out. Gary set a solid pick that stopped Pauling cold. I don't know what their coach said during that last time out but whatever it was, as I drove right, their 6'6" center came charging toward me like a rogue elephant. Having little choice I was forced out on the court toward the corner. With every ounce of power I could summon, I leaped up and back for the fade. He, too, maxed out every fast twitch fiber he possessed with a prodigious leap. As the ball barely cleared his outstretched fingertips sailing toward destiny, the clock hit 00:00. I hit the deck surrounded by frenzied partisans, still able to see the ball hit rim, bounce to glass, hit and balance momentarily on rim again...and fall off.

Bedlam ensued. I didn't move for what seemed like an eternity. How I got to the locker room I don't know. First thing I remember is seeing the unusual sight of their coach walking up to me in the corner of the room. "That's the best I've seen anyone play in a long time. Good luck." He said shaking my hand.

I had gone 15 for 18 from the field and totaled 33 points. I held Pauling to 12. Later, the Des Moines Register called to interview me for "Prep of the Week" for the state. Nice, but none of it really mattered 'cause our season was over.

Instead of going home that night, I found myself walking the streets of Alton. A cold, crystal clear, calm milieu befriended me as I wandered through the gloriously snow lined pathways, pondered the meaning of it all, ad infinitum. At one point I let myself fall into the softly sculpted wispy white shag, staring at the bears, warrior, snake, and twins. Each shared their wisdom but how many yet to be heard? Eventually, adrenals stabilized, I entered the silent house.

Being the tallest in my class, I was the last to receive my diploma at St. Mary's in its final year of existence. The St. Louis

Cardinals invited me to a camp but I knew that college was a must and declined. My sister Mary was at St. Catherine's while my brother Mick had chosen University of Dayton. Limited only by my own vision, I finally signed with St. Thomas College receiving a partial scholarship to play basketball.

For my final summer at home, I was "fortunate" enough to land a job at the cement works one block from our house. The pay was 95 cents an hour with bonus pay for anything over 40 hours a week. On my first day, one of my coworkers advised me, "Try to get your day off early in the week so it won't cut into your overtime." Later I found out that this same guy had once taken a truck load of drain tile six miles out of town before realizing that he hadn't been given any instructions on where to deliver them. He did teach me one good lesson though, when he talked me into trying a pinch of Copenhagen. The severe burning was enough to keep me from ever going that way again.

One evening at the swimming pool, one of the girls suggested we all go to a "haunted house" that night. About an hour later we were on our way into the countryside heading toward the old abandoned abode. I was easily talked into being the first brave soul to enter the pitch dark dwelling. The squeaky door and creaking floor boards only heightened the mood as I courageously ventured farther into the unknown. Just as I felt myself passing into a third room, the dead silence was shattered by what can only be described as a blood curdling, death defying, bone piercing scream, so close that I could feel the inhuman heat of the greeting. Overcome with panic, I fell uncontrollably to the floor, wailing like a held rabbit. Immediately, I was surrounded by my laughing colleagues, flashlights aglow, helping me to my feet. Judy, who had sneaked around through the back entrance to deliver the coup de grace, now spoke. "An evil spirit has entered your soul. Thus you must be exorcised. Only I can accomplish what must be done. Come with me."

Still trembling, I followed the group into the adjacent room where I was instructed to sit at a small table with Judy directly across from me. "Listen closely and do exactly as I say," she intoned as she lit a small candle that materialized from nowhere. "This candle, made from the wax of mutant wasps from Borneo, contains ingredients found nowhere else which have the power to free you." As she made up this wild story she worked a golden patin in and out of the flame. Finally, handing me the all-powerful object d'art, the self-appointed bruja lowered her voice, "Do exactly as I say or you will be forever cursed."

"Forever cursed." repeated the others obviously entranced.

"The demon lies within the brain and controls your five senses," continued Judy as the shadows flickered. 'With the index finger of your right hand, trace the sign of the cross three times on the underside of the sacred patin.' I carefully complied, not being totally sure that I might not be in way over my head. All the others bent closely uttering 'oh's' and 'ah's'. 'Now place three 'X's' on your forehead and rub your five senses; eyes, ears, nose, lips, and skin of the face.' The crowd was becoming more frenzied, my fear rising once again.

'Be gone Satan!' shouted the anointed one, the others echoing the command and following with a flurry of invectives. "Leave! Go! Out with you, o vicar of woe and malice!"

"Yes! Yes! I see him parting! Mercy me! Thank you, Lord!" she screamed, as all fell to the floor in glorious exhibitions of jubilation.

I still had goose bumps as everyone exited excitedly, congratulating each other on their stellar performances. The car was filled with laughter and joking as we wearily wound our way back to our little one horse town, Alton, Iowa.

I didn't realize the full extent of our "fun" until after being dropped off at home, I very quietly entered the house and flicked on the bathroom light. Glancing into the mirror, I was taken aback. My entire face was smudged with black soot and grime! Lucifer lived!

In the fall I matriculated at St. Thomas with trepidation, and rightly so. Just being in the Twin Cities was intimidating since where I came from didn't even have street signs. As an all-boys Jesuit school, there was no shortage of rules and regulations. No BR privileges between eight and ten, lights out at 10:05, mandatory ROTC, etc., etc. In opposition, filling those dorm rooms were seasoned kids from Chicago whose names were spelled with all those seldom used consonants, along with the filthy rich crowd from Gross Point, Mich., and the bucolic others brimming with naivete.

During my first week there, I got a good taste of how things could be, when the Chicago guys across the hall, in retribution for a perceived unjust punishment for a minor infraction, kidnapped Fr. Krause's terrier and dropped him off the nearby bridge into the Mississippi.

The same group of guys was dumbfounded when I actually got up on Sunday morning to attend mass. "Your parents ain't anywhere near here," commented Willie. "Why would ya go to church? It don't make no sense." My 'mortal sin' retort brought derisive laughter. By the third week, I was in the chapel confessional saying, "Bless me father, for I have sinned. I doubt the existence of God." Seemingly unfazed, the hidden voice responded with "one mass and communion, followed by one rosary", instead of the usual "three 'Our Fathers' and three 'Hail Marys'."

I learned cutthroat Polish pinochle, where any error brought unmerciful condemnation. There was drinking and carousing, new things to me. One night, after a particularly abrasive encounter, I was told, "When that happens, always be sure to keep your back to the wall." My grades suffered. With nineteen hours, including zoology, chemistry, and math analysis, there was little margin for error. Lending stability was basketball. The routine of daily playing with the team and then the official opening of practice gave me an anchor line to grab on to. This was something I knew and could rely on.

In week two, we scrimmaged the U of Minn. freshman squad including Clark, Yates, and Hudson, three future NBA standouts. Humility was the order of the day. Hudson made one dunk that made us all want to check his shoes for cork.

I made the first five on the freshman team as the season opener neared. The varsity went to Bradley to be decimated by Chet Walker, while we went to Macalester and won one.

The most impressive thing I accomplished was putting so much effort into a rebound that I split out the entire seat of my pants costing the team an emergency time out. As I sashayed to the sideline, Coach stared at me and said, "What in the hell is going on, Murphy?" In the huddle, I turned, bent forward, and grabbed the severed seat to demonstrate my vulnerable situation. "Stop! Stop it! I don't want to see it. Billy, grab a towel and assist this sorry bastard." Turning toward the locker room, I heard him mumbling something about 'a Christian institution' as the rest of the team instinctively exhibited a more primitive pagan reaction: a cacophony of ribald hooting, jocular jeering at the thigh slapping hilarity, and a most unkind finger pointing. Minutes later as I attempted an inconspicuous return to the floor, I was greeted by a standing 'O' from our entire bench. Quickly, they all moved down, leaving only the seat next to Coach, who gave me a quizzical glance and edged toward the scorer's table. Within seconds he said, "Murphy, get in there for Fields." At the time, none of us recognized these classic signs of ambiguous sexual identity.

Going into semester finals I had ten hours of 'D' for grades. No high school chemistry, a profoundly provincial background provoking near atrophy of the right brain, and an apparent adjustment reaction were the reasons. Lack of sleep may also have contributed. At any rate, only with a Herculean effort was I able to pull straight 'C's' with an 'A' in religion.

Second semester began with a very memorable road trip to face arch rival, St. Johns. The late afternoon bus trip several hours to the northwest was nothing short of splendid. Fresh snow decorated the pine and poplar filled terrain highlighted by spirals of smoke ascending from the scattered fishing shacks on ten thousand lakes in a kaleidoscope of peaceful reverie. As we wearily wound our way over the final portion of our journey to the hidden destination, the setting sun startled us by saving its final and most precious rays for a dazzling display of relief centered momentarily on the marble and glass facade of the new campus chapel.

Our soporific state was to be violently shattered as the bus pulled up to the door to the old gym. Entering as a team we were greeted by the entire student body screaming invective like Afghani women at a bread riot. This was one hour before the freshman game. I actually feared for my life as we were pelted with old towels, shuttlecocks, and wadded up essays on the schism of 721 AD. Our center, Dave Palacek, put his arm around me and said, "Don't worry, Murph, these animals are just posturing, all bark." I wasn't sure what he meant but felt somewhat reassured by his unconcerned attitude. Throughout warm ups they continued relentlessly, and during introductions I thought physical confrontation was imminent.

The game, inevitably, was to be extremely hard fought and close throughout. I could scarcely believe the exclaimed epithets, creative comments on our school, our uniforms, our names and physical attributes, and the pejorative references to absent mothers, sisters, and referee's wives. All done in an odd, tastefully orchestrated manner, of course. When the game went into double overtime, however, I thought the end was nigh. Purple faced nerds in the front rows were leaning two or three feet out onto the court screaming through foamed mouths. Theology majors were stripping off their T-shirts and hurling them to the floor invoking fallen archangels, while the debate team chanted, "They shall not prevail."

My apprehension climaxed when Jerry McGary's last second prayer was answered to give us the one point victory. Surely, the lions would now be released; the horse would be slapped signaling the terminal tightening of the noose. But instead, a dead silence ensued, as if the pressure cooker had exhausted the last drops of water. Without being told, none of us gave any sign of celebration as we purposefully exited the floor. My adrenals didn't recover for a full two days.

Overall, our team was average. We freshman lost the last game of the year to St. Johns at home and then watched the varsity also lose because of a forty point outburst by a Johnnie football quarterback, Craig Meyers, who put on a performance better than anything Rick Mount ever proffered. For me personally, while I had learned a lot and grown in many ways, it was clear that I was not to be a star at this level. Everyone seemed to be a somewhat accomplished player. My game was much too inconsistent; I was impulsive, too small for a forward and not coordinated enough for a guard. Being the undisputed go-to guy was much more suited to my psyche than the role of generic participant in a balanced team game.

Fortunately, as the school year progressed, my brain gained in proficiency, better grades coming on a regular basis. During finals, things were clicking and I could see a decent GPA on the horizon. My last test was particularly important, being in a five hour course, math analysis. Having done well on my last few quizzes, I was now near the 'B' range. In preparation, I pulled my first all-nighter, passionately devouring chapter after chapter, pouring over class notes, and simulating test questions with Ronnie down the hall. With barely one hour of sleep, I walked alone to this final challenge, hoping that my synapses could handle the massive overload now stored within, waiting to be disgorged.

A twinge of trepidation tried to crack my resolute determination as the professor marched into the dank class room carrying what appeared to be reams of copy. Could that be the test? Sighing and shifting abounded as one by one, each student received the sixteen page all inclusive final exam. Beads of perspiration formed instantly as we realized this would be, not only a test of knowledge, but also of speed, having only two hours to certify two thousand years of accumulated mathematical verities. Luckily, the first couple of pages covered relatively simple algebraic principles and went smoothly. The section on quadratic equations followed and, although challenging, was relatively straightforward. As I went along I sensed an uncanny focus developing in my thought processes. Just like when a streak shooter hits his first shots, I was heating up and rapidly entering the 'zone'. Even calculus couldn't faze me; derivatives, routine; integration, automatic. I was on a roll, combining formulae like droplets of mercury coalescing, pages turning as if blown by a fan. "Time's up! Turn in your papers", I heard as I scribbled in the last two or three answers.

In a daze I wandered out of the classroom hearing other students commenting dejectedly that their careers were ruined; how unfair the whole thing was, and did anyone finish that thing? I wasn't sure, but either I had become delusional during the test or something very special had happened. Later that evening, my apprehension jolted to the fore as I was called to the phone. It was Professor Barger asking me to come to his office. What was this, I wondered, as I headed across the beautiful spring campus to the math building. "Come in and sit down, Mr. Murphy." he stated noncommittally as he indicated a chair next to his desk. I saw my test sitting on top of a pile of papers between us. Sam Barger was a no nonsense instructor with a sharp mind, just the kind of teacher I responded best to. "I have some questions on your test." He began. "How did you come to this answer?" he asked. I dutifully explained my thought processes detailing how I had derived my conclusions. I told him, that, because of the time factor, I felt I had to skip as many steps as I could and go right to the answer. After probing my thinking on several more of the problems, he pushed his chair back from the desk and put his hands behind his head. "This is one of the best finals we've ever had." I heard him say as he stood up and reached out with his right hand. 'I'm giving you an 'A' for the course." In a state of disbelief, I shook his hand and left the room. The full impact of what he had said didn't hit me until I got outside the building and into the fresh air. He didn't say 'A' for the test, he said 'for the course'. Wow! Five credits of 'A'! My academic opportunities had taken a huge step forward. I felt like a budding Bodhisattva who had just encountered his Guru as I returned to my room, my mind filled with contemplation.

Without delay, I headed north for my newfound summer employment, counselor at Camp Foley on beautiful Whitefish Lake. This wasn't a subsidized get well temporary transplant place for the underprivileged ghetto youth but a swank, upscale, multi-activity hideout providing breathing room for parents of means. The rustic decor blended smoothly with the natural surroundings, a perfect showcase setting in which we greeted our charges, smiling as we spoke, "Nice to meet you, Senator McCarthy," and "Welcome, Mr. Busch. How are the Cardinals?"

Our first task, even before campers arrived, was setting up the waterfront, three days of twelve hour sessions of rude awakening. Donning only a scanty swim suit, we dipped into the recently ice decked flatness, toting ponderous segments of dock. Up and down the steps and into the breach we quickly bypassed blue numbness, and as we got to the deeper structures, entered the lavender zone of hibernation. The third day greeted us with near gale force winds and drizzle. Our final chore, in what had become over the years, a rite of passage: walk out the diving tower. Several among us cursed the day we were born or even conceived as we gazed at the two ton structure. "It gets lighter in the water," stated Mr. Schmid as we strained to negotiate the steep embankment leading to the beach. "Curse him too," I thought, "and all you other guys who aren't lifting your share." Ropes were used next to stand the monstrosity upright in preparation for the descent into Neptune's nightmarish playground. Legs had to be adjusted as we discovered the incline of the submerged topography, moving synchronously toward our destination, a depth of two fathoms. Disregarding the perpetual goosebumps and constant enamel-threatening tooth chattering, we mechanically obeyed, "OK, deep breath, dive to the bottom, lift, and five steps out. On three. One, two, three!" What fiendish mind devised work such as this? Martin Eden had never suffered such indignant depravity! Hours later, our slave master mercifully signaled his final approval of the albatross' position and wearily, as if we had just crossed the channel ungreased, we swam ashore and helped each other up the hill. Turning back to gaze at what we had accomplished, thoughts of the Iwa Jima monument and Sir Edmund Hillary flashed through my mind. I was so cold they would have had to warm me up for open heart surgery. Even hot chocolate was useless, but later, after twelve BLT's, I began to come around. Auger driven, I had consumed sandwich after sandwich, like a lumberjack on piece rate, never satiated but finally warmed, metabolizing to the max.

By the time all the campers arrived, the waterfront looked beautiful. Stretching for two hundred yards, were areas designated for swimming and diving, boating, canoeing, fishing, water-skiing, and sailing, all supplied with state of the art equipment. Along with the kids, I learned about a gainer, Lazy Ike, slalom, J-stroke, gunwales, coming about, Chinese jibe, and caught in irons; while my main area of responsibility was swimming and life-saving. Also available were activities ranging from nature hikes, portage-paddle canoe trips, and archery, to crafts, tennis, horseshoes, badminton, Ping-Pong, and basketball.

Staff varied from impetuous college students to seasoned seminarians, a good mix. Like campers, they came from diverse backgrounds all over the U.S. and even foreign countries. Each counselor lived in a eight to twelve bed cabin with boys in a similar age group. I started in cabin Mandan with twelve-year-olds. One day the calm was shattered by the hysterical screaming of Pedro running down the path toward the cabin. "Ja me voy! Ja me voy! Me quiso agarar un animal!" he wailed grabbing his suitcase. "Pedro, Pedro, calm down. What happened?" I said sitting him down on the bed. Gradually he stopped hyperventilating and was able to tell me the story in English. Jogging along the trail to the archery range which was a bit into the woods, he rounded a curve at the same time as what, from his description, had to have been a black bear, came to the same curve from the other direction. As he told it, they nearly collided, provoking Pedro's precipitous panic. With a lot of laughing and joking and the fine help of counselor Mendoza, not only did Pedro stay, instead of returning to Guadalajara, but he remained for the entire summer, choosing, however, to focus on the waterfront, especially skiing, at which he became the most proficient of all campers, mastering both slalom and barefooting.

Many good times were had in the staff lounge later in the evenings, after ghost stories were told and our cabins were quiet. We played guitars, chatted, listened to Bob Dylan and Percy Sledge, and generally wound down sipping on barley brew allowed in "moderation".

We did get days off, and, especially on weekends, we could check out camp equipment and sign out even until midnight if made imperative by social protocol as it generally was. Around the lake were scattered various resorts, nightclubs, cabins, and camps. Directly across from our docks was a large resort including a staff dorm filled with coeds at their summer employment. Invariably our boats and canoes seemed to automatically be drawn in that direction. Playing lead roles in these vignettes were the splendiferous and shapely Cindy the salad girl, the high goddess Candy Demeret, and of special interest to me, Suzy Q, whom I shared with Chuck. We scuba dived, louowed, danced, sailed, and partied as often as we could, adventuring as far as Manhattan Beach, Piquot Lakes, and even, on occasion, Breezy Point.

I learned so much that summer. Like Al showed me that, when you're taking a shower, you don't need soap. Just use the lather from the shampoo to wash the rest of your body. He also showed me how not to drive a car as he frightened us badly one night by hitting a mail box with his '58 T-bird. And I learned to teach, something I would do all my life. Much too soon, the summer came to an end. My last night at camp, I was sitting on the dock, gazing on the lake, totally content. A song came on my radio which seemed to capture the mood perfectly, "If This Must End" by The Impressions. The next day I was in Iowa, and within a week, back at St. Thomas.

Classes including calculus, physics, and quantitative analysis hit like a slap of after shave cologne. From the first day I knew that I could not get behind and survive. That, combined with not-so-subtle messages from the coaching staff, made the decision to pass on basketball, a foregone conclusion. Still, atavistic impulses beckoned quite regularly, reinforced by the squeak, the smell, and the whoosh. Pickup games, marathon Saturday morning sessions, and then intramurals kept sanity always within sight. The frustration of being asked test questions like, "Using what you have learned, estimate the mass of the universe. Show your work", was more than compensated for by the joy of winning the IM championship and going on to the conference finals before succumbing to Augsburg.

Towards the end of the year, my brother, who was at the University of Dayton, wrote that he was accepted into the new medical school at the University of Kentucky. I was a science major and my grades were good but pre-med was not what I had in mind. My father had worked, and still was working, basically non-stop. It seemed like every meal he was called. Nights, every Christmas, Saturday, Sunday, to the hospital, to the farm house, the office, front door, back door, "Yes Hattie", "OKAY Mr. Engledinger", "I'll be right over". How much time does it take to deliver 5,000 babies? No, not for me. Life's too short. Still.... lots of my college buddies are beginning to bone up for MCATS and I'm rather directionless. Almost by default I find myself in the process of transferring to the University of Iowa in the pre-med track.

At Iowa, I had an older sister, and a younger step brother, making the adjustment easier. Nevertheless, jumping from Jesuit to Jezebel was not without significant traumas. Classes were a breeze, even organic and genetics, the challenge being "Joe's", "Doc's", and "Lil' Bills". To say, "Don't let college interfere with your education," is not only trite, but, if taken to extremes, perilous, overrated, and crass. Options can vanish into the fog never to return. My star, however, continued to shine, even if hidden by passing clouds many a time. I soon found myself face to face with a cadaver as an M1.

"Welcome to Gross Anatomy." intoned the prim and polished professor with the long pointer. "During the next year, you will be expected to learn approximately 10,000 new terms, including the exact spelling, pronunciation, and meaning. Your Gray's is your bible. Patella, piriformis, and sphincter of Oddi will become household words. Take your task most seriously. You are being initiated into an elite professional corps whose charge is nothing less than the health of the world." As he paused to inspire, some 140 IQ miscreant near the rear, let fly a fusillade of flatus resembling an off key trombone score terminating like the last gasps of a John Deere on empty. A very brief silence ensued, but when the perp squeezed out one last irreverent toot, the place broke up. "Silence!" shouted our angry anatomist. "Observe how the skatols an indols involved in the formation of such an effluviant have little effect on the olfactory receptors in the face of the pervasive penetrating essence of formalin. Yes. An occasional moment of levity may be indicated but rest assured, all will be taxed severely in this room. You may now open your tanks."

I thought, "I think I'm going to like this."

Luckily, our "patient" was thin and, with minimal dissection, anatomical structures were apparent. Next tank over housed "Big Bertha", meaning endless hours spent negotiating avenues of adipose, boulevards of blubber, and freeways of fat, many times ending with the positive identification of nothing smaller than an organ such as the heart. Nary a surgeon from that bunch.

Eighty four steps running from the medical science building brought one to that threshold of salvation, the Mecca of Midwest basketball, the Iowa Fieldhouse. Forget formalin and cyclic AMP. Hematoxylin and eosin enter not. Abandon Odontology. And toss your Phi Beta Kappa key, 'cause now we got sweat, bumpin', pejorative posturing, and creative cursing. Most times we had only one hour between classes at noon, to be spent "reviewing notes over a salad in the cafeteria or possibly a sack lunch." Whom are you kidding? One can only take so much! So, get out of the way, we're coming through, heading the other direction. Twice, I saw innocent nursing students nearly trampled by our stampeding hoard. Last class seating position, the clothes you wear, even haircuts take on new significance, as any advantage might place you in the first ten to reach the court with at least shoes on. Not washing your jock and shorts lent a crescendo edge with each passing day as material stiffened more and more conforming to the shape of your body allowing the use of the fireman dressing technique saving critical seconds. Added benefit, distancing oversensitive defenders with an ever more powerful odeur du parfum.

Frequently, main court was open, making the games neater yet. We were the "Hawks" as in Connie Hawkins, or Don Nelson, or John Johnson, Freddie Brown. The games were hot and played near the edge like a patient with gram negative sepsis. To eleven by one, call your own and argue it out, losers sit. Will Synhorst dare attempt another outrageously long hook shot risking universal rath and ridicule for the remote chance of, not compliments and glory, but a kind of perverted satisfaction of having put people in an uncharted situation and watching them react? My game was predicated on "coming out of the toaster" better than anyone. Get up and create, right, left, double pump, fade, it doesn't matter. Bombs and banks, dipsy-do, power reverse and finger roll, did someone say defense? My Synhorst-like offering was a leap from about fifteen feet on the left side facing the hoop, directing my body at an absurd angle, near horizontal, to the right, out of the reach of the defender, and flipping the ball to glass with the spin of a slider, meaning the lower the release the better the advantage of using the downward rotation to guide the ball through the cylinder.

Fast and furious was the order of the day, with games right up to the last possible minute. This meant there was only time for a dip of a shower, I'd say 10 to 30 seconds max, and we learned quickly that ice cold cut sweat much better, so we yipped through it like young sled dogs running to the traces. Then trot back to class refreshed and either waltz in nonchalantly at the last minute, or do the slithering snake entry slipping silently into a back row seat if the great hand had eclipsed vertical.

Many of us joined professional fraternities for the convenient housing. With most fraternities being too rowdy, I had chosen the house with the studious, no nonsense reputation. Trouble was, most of the other reprobates in our class must have thought the same because we were all Phi Rho Smegma's(sic.). Almost immediately the character of the house was transformed. Not only did we party harder, but we marked our arrival on the scene by kicking the AK's butts in IM flag football while being innocently incidentally etiologically implicated in two of their devastated participants going to the hospital, sending shock waves through the medical community.

Academically, we held our own too. I had the extremely good fortune of having grown up two doors down the street from Daryl who was now two years ahead of me in med school. I would never have suspected it but he had become a meticulous, seriously academic note taker, reader, and outliner. I have never repaid him but allowing me to use his excellent work saved me endless hours and gave me the assurance that all I had to do was pour through his material the night before a test, and I couldn't help but do well. One night, while cramming, just for fun I memorized Daryl's "EKG diagnosis of pulmonary embolism" notes, hardly knowing what any of the words meant. I could barely contain myself the next day when I saw that the main question on the test was on pulmonary embolism. In a flurry of scribbling, I eloquently regurgitated the fourteen signs I had imprinted on my brain from the previous night. I got the highest score on the test which was fine but when the professor approached me after class and started to discuss the subtleties of the topic, I had to think fast to change the subject because first, I had already forgotten most of the material, and second, I had absolutely no comprehension of what little verbiage I still retained, leaving me with nothing relevant to say.

Intramural basketball was always intriguing. Creative refereeing could present more of a problem than the opposition. Knowing how to handle them was one of the keys to being able to play the game, making full use of your natural strategic advantages. A good example of how it worked was a game we had where the refs were two young undergrads who looked like they had just arrived from Corn Cob, Ia. Early in the first quarter, following a few admittedly minor errors in calls and/or non-calls, there occurred the miscue of sufficient magnitude to set up the pivotal interaction. Immediately after the call, Matte, from the streets of Chicago, walks right up to the face of referee Alfalfa, and delivers the Clint Eastwood, "Ref, after the game, it's you and me, right outside that door."

We all felt the floor tilt just a little as the game went on. The rotten calls continued but overwhelmingly our way. In the shower, after the victory, I noticed that Matte, whose ruddy complexion was particularly aglow, had his entire back covered with a series of fresh parallel linear excoriations. Exertional adrenaline highlighting histaminic effects. "Matte, did you sack with a bearcat last night?" I probed.

"I'll take the fifth," he quipped, "but it's all part of the mental preparation for our games. Don't underestimate my dedication to the cause."

Some of our most enjoyable basketball took place in back of "the house", where there was a rickety old hoop on the edge of a classic circular pounded, worn dirt surface. After "study breaks" at "Joe's" which invariably turned into marathon babble sessions over pitchers of brew, we would wind down with a game or two, using car lights to illuminate the scene. What made it fun was that not only did everyone feel good but it was an entirely different mix of participants, i.e. the study break types. Scores and rules varied from play to play not really being important. Creative color commentary was key along with innovative use of props such as trees or a nearby steep embankment. Pete always played in wing tips and was renowned for his uncanny ability to test the structural integrity of the backboard on nearly every shot. Pat once called time out and ran into the house to return minutes later in full military gear just to get an intimidation edge. Upper classmen, who were cut from a different mold, were baffled by our behavior and complained repeatedly. Noisome noise at night, failure to accept the overarching seriousness of our chosen profession, and, most of all, excessive use of fun. We would acquiesce in just enough to avoid violent confrontation, but keeping our sanity while enduring medical school was much too important not to take full advantage of situations pregnant with the potential to blow off steam whenever possible.

During those years, dark clouds were slowly accumulating on the horizon in the form of a small nation in Southeast Asia called Viet Nam. Cracks began to appear in my guiding motto: booze, bebop, and apathy. Military advisors, Gulf of Tonkin, half a million troops, light at the end of the tunnel, body bags, body bags, body bags, body bags. The Hippocratic Oath. Doctor, do no harm. Demonstrations, protests, marches, teach-ins, my first friend, Jerry McGarry dies. Now it wasn't political. Damn the domino theory, I'll take Jerry back. He was our Gail Goodrich with everything from the long jumper to the running kiss off glass. Even writing this brings tears to my eyes, not just that he's gone but that he was such a happy human being with a one of a kind sense of humor. His idea of fun can be seen in the following anecdote. We're going through the cafeteria line at St. Thomas, and Jerry says, "You guys sit by yourselves, and let me find my own place."

"What are you talking about, McGarry," I asked, "you getting claustrophobic?"

"Just watch." he retorted with a tell-tale twinkle in his eyes, a grin decorating his lips.

We knew we were going to be in for some fun. Curiosity mounted as we progressed along the line and observed the clown choose the strangest combination of dishes imaginable. Later we were told he was looking for color combinations and texture. He then proceeded to misbutton his top two and muss his hair before wandering over to a table where three or four guys none of us knew were eating. As he sat down with a perplexed look on his face, we took a nearby table and anxiously waited for the show to unfold. Slowly and deliberately, with his head bent down over his plate, he begins to mix his food with his spoon and even using his fingers a little. All the time he's making low pitched, primordial sounds with his breathing. The people at the table are noticing and giving him chagrined glances not knowing what to make of the situation. We, as if being tickled in church, are desperately trying to remain calm and not blow the cover. As Jerry begins putting the color coded concoction into his mouth, glances become stares. His freaky noises come to a crescendo, punctuated with choreography of twitches and spasms. Chairs begin to move as he allows the mixture to dribble ceremoniously back to the plate. We could no longer contain ourselves as we saw him complete the act with a perfectly executed maneuver somehow allowing streams of puree to release through his nose in a glorious finale. His table was empty as we picked ourselves off the floor, all of us in stitches with tears streaming down our faces, applauding the stellar performance.

We, as med students, had deferments from the draft, but, contrary to all official pronouncements, the war was not proceeding well, and many young physicians were being called.

With the exception of one small break, which I spent hitchhiking around Europe in a fascinating reprieve of culture, history, and interaction with broader face of humanity, medical school was a continuous exercise in data entry. Histology, physiology, and biochemistry, became pathology, pharmacology, and physical diagnosis. Suddenly, our white frocks say M3 and we are facing real patients with real diseases. Through it all, I continue to use up the black, low cut, Chuck Taylors, keeping me anchored.

Early in my junior year, I elected a six week rotation at Broadlawns in Des Moines. Being mostly indigent and understaffed, this hospital provided a hands-on, baptism of fire, in stark contrast to the ivory tower atmosphere of academia we breathed at the university. My first night on duty, helping in OB, I was asked by Nurse Kathy, to check the pleasant gravida fourteen in six, just admitted in early labor. I entered the room, filled with the confidence of ten thousand words and a thousand principals, and introduced myself to the laboring parturient, politely asking permission to do an examination. She, having much more experience in such matters, nodded in gracious assent. As I palpated her distended abdomen, I thought I felt the rounded, ballotable induration of cranial tables in the left upper quadrant. Suspicion mounted with auscultation, the fetascope definitely transmitting loudest above the umbilicus. Well, it could be that the presenting part hasn't dropped far enough yet to position the baby's heart lower, I surmised. Kathy gave me a silent look of urgency as she applied Betadine to my now gloved left hand, both of us observing a crescendo contraction in the patient accompanied by a distinct urge to bear down. Deliberately, and not without trepidation, I proceeded to perform the confirmatory internal exam, revealing what I was sure was the curve of baby's sacrum and a soft buttocks. Worse yet, the cervix was eight centimeters dilated and the presenting part near crowning. Delivery imminent and breech! I nodded in affirmation to Kathy, who, although young and beautiful, had extensive front line experience, complimented by calm and compassionate, yet efficiently businesslike professionalism. "I'll be right back." she explained, exiting the scene leaving me to tell the now consternated mom what we had found. By chance, a staff obstetrician was in the house, and

41

within minutes, he and Kathy returned just in time to witness a bursting bag of waters followed by the appearance of a meconium smeared anus on the perineum. Approximately one minute was consumed by the transfer of the patient to the big delivery room two doors down. Kathy broke open a delivery kit as the doctor and I quickly gowned and gloved. With the next contraction, chubby legs dropped down one by one to dangle in the air, followed almost immediately by the appearance of a still pulsating cord and the tips of the two scapulae. I held the legs extended applying gradual purchase as instructed while the obstetrician smoothly swept the fetal arms across the face and body using his index and middle fingers of his right hand hooking the baby's upper extremities at the anticubital fossae. He then positioned the same two fingers in a "v" around the posterior aspect of the face down fetal neck grasping both shoulders firmly as he slipped the left index finger into the baby's mouth thus flexing the half born child's head. The next contraction was beginning as we carefully extracted the aftercoming head using mother's pubis as a fulcrum for the emergence of chin, mouth, nose, eyes, and finally bregma to complete the textbook breech extraction.

Then, disaster struck!

Immediately after the delivery of the significantly unmolded head, there followed a torrent of sanguinous vermilion, the volume of which immediately captured the collective medical attention present. "It's arterial and it's big," stated the doctor already clamping and dividing the umbilical cord, leaving me somewhat aghast with a wriggling neonate decorated in vernix and heme poignantly appropriate for both his and our world. "Kathy, one amp Pit IV push, then ergotrate. Open up the LR and add twenty units of Pitocin to the bottle." he barked, his left hand now disappeared up to the elbow, fingers following cord to its origin. Stabilizing the globular uterus with his right hand on the now panicky patient's abdomen, he probed and teased, seeking a loose placental edge, and then peeling along the natural plane carefully preventing retained cotyledans. "Dr. Murphy," he said, glancing at my name tag, "put the baby in the incubator on its side, suction nose and mouth with the bulb syringe, and then start another IV, number fourteen, if you can get it." As he spoke, in a definitely R-rated scene, his crimson arm and hand came forth carefully clutching that which it sought. Rapidly cupping the afterbirth in his hands verifying integrity, he silently slid the miraculous organ of interface into the sterile basin spoiling its silvery sheen. Turning to see the hemorrhage unabated, he asked Kathy," Can you give me Trendelenburg, and we need four units of O negative or typed if it's been done. Have lab cross match for four more. Dr. Murphy, how is that IV?"

"Got it, number fourteen, running Ringers wide open, Doctor." Luckily her veins hadn't collapsed in shock and the huge needle had entered easily.

"I'm exploring the uterus," he continued, thoughtfully tutoring as he proceeded. "check the left side of the uterine cavity and cervix with your left." His red glove disappeared as he spoke. Beads of sweat covered mother's face now exhibiting a forlorn vacant stare. " Nothing here. Cavity empty and no sign of atony. Probably the right side." he surmised, switching examining hands and using the left on the abdomen. "Got it! Ten cm. tear into the uterine wall, probably involving branches of the uterine artery or the artery itself. Kathy, get anesthesia and the crew in and call whoever's on second OB. I'll tamponade and we'll do a hysterectomy over my hand. Dr. Murphy, frequent vitals and run the blood with cuffs as soon as you can get it."

What followed was a whirlwind of activity, all of it new and exciting to me. Two hours later, we transfused the eighteenth unit as we completed the dramatic surgical procedure. The room now resembled an abattoir. Blood, sweat, and tears for a healthy mother and child, and a dramatic detailed imprint etched on my brain permanently, in a way no lecture or book could even begin to match. With each of the hundreds of breeches I was to deliver, I remained acutely aware and attentive to that moment when greatest cranial diameter passes through maximally thinned cervix. Expeditious, yet gentle!

Later that year, while attending a Father Grappi anti-war lecture, I was introduced to a friend's younger sister, Janet. Long dark hair, an engaging smile, shapely with enticingly lithe limbs, and hands that were a pianist's dream, combined with a discerning mind to initiate chemistry. We seemed to have a lot in common, and began seeing more and more of each other, in and out of her cluttered classic '55 Chevy. Convinced that I was very unlikely to end up throttled in Middle America, she was able to overlook the multitude of idiosyncrasies and identify with what were to her my more endearing characteristics, a rather implacable sense of justice and a willingness to stand alone when necessary. A particularly clumsy breakup with a former tulip queen I had been seeing, paved the way for Janet and I to spend our last year in school sharing an apartment. At the same time, not coincidentally, my drinking decreased dramatically, more time spent reading, studying, planning and protesting, all things we could do together.

Then came Kent State. Peacefully demonstrating students gunned down by the National Guard. More at Jackson State. Why not Iowa? Or anywhere in the country? None of this was supposed to happen in the U.S. One thing for sure, opposition to the war wouldn't disappear. Senator McCarthy speaks out heroically, Bombs on campus at Madison, riots at the Chicago convention, mass arrests outside Joe's in Iowa City, RFK and Martin Luther King killed, all indicating a country being ripped apart. Angry and insecure, I graduated wearing a white arm band with a red peace symbol and hair to my shoulders.

Now draft eligible, I had matched with a hospital in New York City for a one year rotating internship.

Fortuitously, Janet and I found a rent control, boxcar apartment on the lower east side at Avenue B and 2nd street, $85.00/month. We proceeded to furnish the place, on the advice of newfound friends, availing ourselves of early morning perusal of Gramercy Park trash, and by patronizing a certain unmarked back alley outlet whose prices related inversely to the temperature of the items. A few posters and incense completed the decor.

A stroll around the neighborhood led us to Katz's on Houston featuring quarter draws and the best deli in town, then bocci ball-don't ever play for money with these old guys. Proceeding to Broadway and Bowery, we learned to step over the bodies, trade quips with the pan handlers, and recognize the bagged bottles of Muscatel and Thunderbird. First Ave. featured the smells and sights of the bustling outdoor food markets. I'll have the dark bread, thank you. Then back through little Russia, and past the Upstairs at the

Downstairs and the new vegetarian restaurant, and we're home. Further east we ventured least. There, gentrification wasn't even in the long range plan. C and D were like going to Brownsville or Bed-Sty.

Adjustments had to be made, just like anywhere else. Con-Ed. provided a daily dusting that, within hours, filled every nook and cranny, even accumulating under finger nails and in the corners of eyes. With no air conditioning and being on the third floor, our ungraded windows were open much of the time. Entering along with the carbon was non-stop cacophony of honks and whirs, accelerations and braking, dog barks, smashing glass, intermingled bits of conversation more Spanish than English, exacerbations leading to frequent screams, cries and altercation. This, however, was only background to the all too frequent explosion of sound emanating from the fire engines bursting from their blocks just below us with a full repertoire of close range tympanic torture, making sustained sleep possible only by entering a state approximating general anesthesia. After a while, we were awakened only in the wee hours of Sunday morning, by the uncharacteristic silence.

The ubiquitous cockroaches reminded me of Iowa hogs, big and gluttonous. Parathion had only a moderate temporary effect and was hardly worth all the worry about cholinesterase levels. Tolerance, like in so many other situations, was in order.

On one of the first weekends, I ventured up to Tompkins Square Park to play hoops. To begin with, I had to lie egregiously about my credentials just to get into a game, and next, barely into the encounter, two guys started fighting. I thought it was settled as we resumed play, but immediately, they're at it again and one has a bloody lip. "I'm going to kill you, mother f-----," yelled one of them.

"No, it's you who's going to be dead,' was the response. 'I'm going to get something right now," rapidly followed as the bloody one exited to courtside and lifted a bag from under a sweatshirt. People were strategically distancing themselves from the madman as he waltzed back onto the court, hand in bag. I was hardly relieved when he pulled out a sandwich and took a big bite. We proceeded to finish the game, and, through no fault of mine, we lost. Never was I

45

so accepting of defeat, even grateful. Quickly and quietly, I left, temporarily losing my taste for basketball.

On the positive side, what could be better than beginning a lazy Sunday morning with a cup of Cappuccino, sipped over the Times, discussing endlessly everything from articles to opinions, entertainment and letters, and even the ads? Or whiling away a few warm evening hours sitting out on the fire escape observing life on Ave. B as if it were a Monet. Puerto Ricans, blacks, black Puerto Ricans, interspersed with hippies and movement people. "Check out the fire up on 6th." "Hey, look at the reverse Henry Ford action on that Pugeot."

There was so much to do, plays and concerts, lectures and exhibits, movies, restaurants, clubs, parks, Madison Square Garden, Yankee Stadium, Coney Island. Always something new and interesting.

Janet's establishment job was in market research, midtown. Surprisingly, nearly everyone working in that field was gay. The work seemed frivolous but allowed us to save a few dollars.

I took the Second Ave. bus every day through the garment district, past Delancey, little Italy, China town, and down by the Fulton fish market, heading to Wall street and then approaching the World Trade Center, before going on to South Ferry. A nickel got me on, then either a bagel or coffee, something to read, Times, Post, Daily News, or Voice, or watch the people including the classic "shiners". There were always the impressive ever changing skyline, the Statue of Liberty, and the acrobatic gulls. Then the Castleton Ave. bus taking me to the Staten Island Hospital. A true commute!

My first rotation was ER, 24 on, 24 off. I don't think I even took time to go to the bathroom during my first shift. Room after room of knife and gunshot wounds, MVA's and CVA's, MI's, OD's, psychotics, botched back alley Ab's, and exotic illnesses, presenting in multiple languages, all obligating the intern to think fast and learn to make difficult decisions under duress. After one month of that, I felt ready to handle anything. But I wasn't. I knew very little, and still had to go through internal medicine, psych, OB, peds, and surgery. Even then I knew almost nothing.

Meanwhile, Viet Nam would not end! As Richard Nixon et.al. escalate and widen the war to include Laos and Cambodia, we street people try to do the same. Janet was now putting in as many hours or more at War Tax Resistance, as with her day job. I helped whenever I could. We drew added inspiration from the group in the adjoining office called War Resisters League, a truly disciplined, dedicated, class act. Protests grew and activities increased, some involving dumping blood or cleaning blood from heads as "hard hats" retaliated. Courting arrest was now a given. We all underwent training in non-violence and passive resistance no matter what the provocation.

All of this was tested severely as events continued to unfold. Arriving at the hospital one morning, I was pulled to the side by three of my activist friends. They told me in hushed tones how the night before, as they were returning to the house they lived in, which also served as an anti-war office, they encountered a Fire Dept. truck. One of the firemen informed them that smoke had been reported at that address and that no one was allowed to enter. After a few minutes the crew emerged announcing that everything was under control now and left. Inside, the place was destroyed, printing press smashed, files decimated, even closets trashed, and absolutely no trace of fire. Some of the suggestions made in the following discussion would have made Ghandi cringe.

A similar scenario, only worse, unfolded two weeks later, when plain clothed NYPD detectives, arrived at an apt. in the building next to ours, where more leftist friends slept. Unannounced, a la Freddie Hampton, the door was bashed open, and our startled neighbors faced sawed off shotguns before they could even get out of bed. Helplessly, they watched the entire place be ransacked in a "search for an alleged fugitive." A powerful atmosphere of fear and anger pervaded as the peace officers exited, laughing to each other.

Shortly thereafter, the dreaded letter arrived. Uncle Sam was offering me a commission in the Navy. I figured it was inevitable. I had done endless hours of soul searching and even counseling in draft resistance and by then had paid my dues on the front lines of the anti-war movement. Well aware of all my options, and knowing that accepting the offer was completely out of the question, I ignored the notice, and redoubled both my anti-war activity and my personal strategic planning.

The Staten Island ferry will always hold a special place in my heart because it was one of the few peaceful parts of my day, totally predictable, no stress. I looked forward to it as a time to just relax and let the mind wander. So, on this particular day, as I strolled down the chute, I was looking forward to some quiet introspection. Going against the grain, away from Wall St. in the early morning, I could always find a nice empty bench, where I could sit in a corner and even put my feet up. As I settled in and yawned once or twice, I decided to at least glance at the NY Times I had picked up strolling through South Ferry. On the front page was an unusually long article on Viet Nam. Just what I needed, as if I didn't get a steady diet of this kind of material all the time. After reading one paragraph, however, I could see, this was different, way different. As I read on, I found myself sitting bolt upright and even rechecking to be sure this was indeed the New York Times. What it said was essentially seditious, explaining in detail how much of the execution of the war was predicated on fraud, the Gulf of Tonkin incident being a fabrication, all meticulously documented. We, in the movement, of course had seen over and over, how almost any tactic was acceptable, so the facts were not so surprising, but to see it here. This was the most influential establishment newspaper in the world!   I couldn't put it down. Unbelievable! What are we to do now? Revolt against our government? I felt an ominous foreboding as I pondered the import of this momentous publication. Was this to be one of those pivotal turning points in history, where events loom so large that personal considerations are dwarfed by the tidal wave?

Soon after, I received a repeat offer, this time by certified mail. Changing my reaction, I decided to respond, politely declining their so graciously proffered naval commission. Meanwhile protest was spreading rapidly, now including large segments of middle America, movie stars, Republicans, vets, doctors.   Nationwide planning was underway for demonstrations in Washington the first of May. These were to be the biggest and most confrontational ever. Some of us even thought in terms of a contingency plan for when riot troops would be called out, we might possibly be able to convince them to come over to our side. Why not? Essentially, they were us. Then, D.C. and the government would be ours, we reasoned.

The first day in the capitol, we got Nixon's attention with a march of one million around the White House. Then came civil disobedience, blocking access to buildings, dragging things into streets, spray painting green lights red, changing clocks, tying up phones, flushing toilets as much as possible and stealing all remaining toilet paper, anything to disrupt. People like Josea Williams and Dr. Spock gave impassioned speeches. Janet made national TV to the chagrin of her parents. Medal of Honor recipients flung their decorations over the wall in protest as the momentum built. Then came the hour of reckoning, as the president called out riot troops and a large contingent of National Guard. In an all-out frontal assault with tear gas everywhere, sirens and screams, batons swung liberally by Pinkertons on horseback, chaos reigned.

Janet and I were among the ten thousand arrested that day. In the D.C. jail, I saw many long haired imitation protesters among the police. We had been routed, but in a way, the challenge was effective. We had been noticed and in no small way. Could the country stand much more of this? Yet it seemed that nothing changed.

As talk began of a possible invasion of North Viet Nam, I promised myself that, should it occur, I would go underground, sacrificing everything, giving my all to stop what I thought would be WWIII.

Meanwhile, I was making a valiant effort to finish my internship, and, at the same time prepare for a dramatic move to California, where a job awaited working for a brash Chicano organizer, Cesar Chavez, who had started a union for migrant farmworkers.

Just before we left NY, I received another registered notice telling me that I had now been drafted as a private in the Army, further instructions to follow. I sent no forwarding address.

Arriving in Delano, Ca, Janet and I went directly to union headquarters at "Los Cuarenta Acres" just west of town. No one had even heard of us, there was no health clinic, and it was 115 degrees. Following several phone calls, it was determined that someone did remember a clinic being discussed at a board meeting some time back and that some doctors might be coming. Welcome to the third world. My real education was about to begin.

Later that day, I met Jerry Cohen, the union lawyer. As we got talking, he stopped momentarily, sizing me up, and asked, "You a basketball player?"

I said, "Well, ya, I am."

"Good, we're playing tonight at seven. I'll pick you up."

The Community Center was on the "wrong" side of the tracks, white guys didn't go there, except Cohen, and now me. The basketball was fast and furious, blacks, Chicanos, Filipinos, and mestizos. Jerry was my in but it didn't take long to realize that if you didn't have two balls on his team, you might as well concentrate on defense. He brought new meaning to "gun". Still, I managed to bring attention to myself with a thundering tomahawk dunk. It felt so good to be playing again.

Three more young doctors arrived, all fresh from internships, two straight internal medicine, one straight surgery. Unlike me, they had been granted conscientious objector status by their respective draft boards and were serving two year alternative duty tours. These were highly intelligent academic track types, who had already been accepted into prestigious residencies, two years hence. Especially impressive were their extensive, consistently leftist credentials, highlighted by a recent victory in the U.S. Supreme Court establishing the right for them to do rotations in a V.A. Hospital without answering the onerous question, "Are you now, or have you ever been, a member of, or associated with, the communist party, or any other group or organization, having policies or goals contrary to the best interest of the United States of America?" Having once ridden my fully decorated bicycle in an "I Like Ike" parade regaled in my freshly pressed cub scout uniform, it would be nearly impossible for me to be fully accepted by this group.

Anxious to begin working, we all congregated that Monday morning at the hiring hall, waiting for what seemed like, and probably was, hours, for instructions or direction on how to proceed with our task. Presently, a dignified looking, thin gentleman with a neatly trimmed mustache, approached us, introducing himself as Gilbert Padilla. In hushed tones, he told us we were to be at a specific phone booth, in Visalia, the next morning at exactly 8:00 a.m., allow the phone to ring three times, then answer, and we would be given further instructions. He muttered "buena suerte" as he left the room. Amazing! We were all left flabbergasted. What had we gotten into? It seemed like a nice lead for a spy novel, or could it be some sort of cruel hoax?

Playing our roles as best we could, being sure we weren't being followed, we parked several blocks away and cut through an alley, arriving at the prescribed booth at one minute to eight the next day. Almost immediately the phone sang out on cue. We counted in unison. One, two, three! The only thing missing was the background music. Peter picked up the telephone, "Hello, this is Peter Rudd." We watched him scribbling furiously, punctuated with "OKAY's" and "all right's". Hanging up, he turned and said, "The die is cast. Let's go, guys." Walking at a brisk pace, we returned to the car and began driving following the directions exactly, finally reaching our destination.

Filled with apprehension, we approached the plain looking, small green house, in a quiet neighborhood on the outskirts of town. All the shades were drawn. Before we could even knock, the door opened and a slightly pudgy Chicano motioned us in as he introduced himself, "My name is Richard Chavez." Quickly closing the door, he continued, "C'mon down the basement, Cesar's waiting."

At the bottom of the steps, we entered a well-lit, windowless room where a large table with pencils and paper had been prepared for us. Coming around the table to meet us was a diminutive, simply attired, unimposing figure. His brown skinned face, expressionless, led one to feel the serious, penetrating effect of the look in his eyes. His light handshake left me with an almost ethereal feeling. "Nice to meet you, sit down, please." There was barely a hint of accent in his slightly nasal voice.

Richard spoke first. "We apologize for the funny arrangements, but recent threats on Cesar's life are making us extremely cautious. We welcome all of you as brothers. Bienvenido a todos. An enormous challenge awaits us but, with your help, we can begin to realize our dreams. Powerful forces are aligned against us. However, we have time, justice and our hearts on our side. We're very happy to have you here, working with us, through thick and thin, and all we ask is that you give it your best, and there's nothing we can't accomplish. Si se puede."

As he sat down, Cesar arose to speak. "Let me tell you about the farmworker movement. For as long as I can remember, life has been a constant migration, following the crops, looking for a job, never in one place long enough to get settled, always poor. Children, if they're lucky, get a few weeks of school here, and maybe a few more weeks there, discriminated against because of their skin, their speech, or their clothes, finally realizing that they were meant for the fields; there is no way out. My education has been life in the barrios, seeing the poverty and the despair daily, the rickety old cars, the farm labor camps, being cheated along the way by everyone from the growers to the gas station, harassed by authorities, hounded by la migra, with little or no recourse. The doors are always closed. Imagine what it's like to be reminded every day in so many ways, that you have no chance, work if they want you, under their conditions, for their wages, always by their rules. Suffering, deprivation, tragedy, become realities of day to day life.'

'The work is backbreaking. El cortito, the short hoe, sooner or later, makes everyone pay. Working in the row crops, bent over all day, let me tell you, you feel like you'll never walk straight again. Or try pruning in the grapes for eight hours, piece rate, always piece rate, and see how your shoulders feel. Check your hands after a day grafting roses. Then you can stoop over to cut and field pack lettuce, or squat to cut and tie bunches of asparagus. The injury rate is high. Maybe the worst work is girdling, very few can take it. Even picking wine grapes is difficult; you're running all day to keep up with the gondola, dump your tray, and run back to fill it again. Pesticides are always there, on the crops, in the air, in the water. Sickness and skin rash happen all the time. And all of it is seasonal, there may be months with no work. Where do you go? What do you do? Or you might travel from Calexico to Salinas only to find they gave the work to someone else, usually at a cheaper rate.

On top of that, we have babies born, children get sick, TB, injuries, diarrhea, we have old people, all the problems, and no health care, no health care," his voice trailed off momentarily. "Our health care is to rub down with Ben Gay, or use some home remedies, or just pray to the Virgin of Guadeloupe. But what if we need an operation? It's not enough. You see what I mean? Rodrigo Terronez was left to die outside the hospital right there in Delano because he was a farmworker and had no money.

"Even though we have all these problems, they haven't broken our spirit. Farmworkers are poor, yes, but they keep a positive outlook. There is always a birth, a baptism, a wedding, or something to celebrate with a little fiesta. People help each other; they have to, there is no other way to survive. Poor people share more than anyone. Asi es la vida.

"Still, the growers try to separate us. There are Chinese, poor whites from Oklahoma, Braceros, Filipinos, blacks, Latinos, and now even Arabs from Yemen. Organizing has always been difficult. Strikes have been broken. Desperate scabs are brought in. Violence. No legal protection. Pretty much ignored by the media and society. We have to fight for ourselves.

"But now there's a spark. We have the beginnings of a union. Fred Ross has helped us a lot. We're learning what to do. Larry Itliong and the Filipino brothers are with us. We're active everywhere in the state, and you can see we've got their attention; that's why we're meeting hidden in a basement. The growers are very worried, worried that they might not be able to continue calling all the shots like they always have. We are in a very big struggle, up against all the odds. It's a huge challenge, but I know we can do it. We will never stop fighting, never. We have justice on our side. Anything can be accomplished if you keep trying and have faith in what you're doing."

He hardly raised his voice as he spoke, yet he easily captivated our full attention. The seriousness of his commitment was obvious, and I for one, sensed a certain resoluteness in his dedication, a kind of persistence that would make him a most formidable opponent.

"Everywhere I go, people have always asked me about health care," he continued. 'Cesar, can we get our own doctors? Will we have our own clinics? Our children are sick. We can't afford the hospitals.' It's the first thing farmworkers want. It touches every one of their lives. It's a dream. And now we want to realize that dream."

The meeting went on until midnight, with only short breaks for arroz, tortillas, and frijoles. Cesar wanted to know everything. Every aspect of health care was covered. It was easy to see how important this planning was to him by his intense interest down to the smallest detail. When we were exhausted, he was just getting warmed up. The man was insatiable. One of his original ideas was to use us like the prototypical Chinese barefoot doctor, going from field to field tending to whatever problem we encountered. My colleagues, fresh from Stanford, where clinical medicine and even clinical research is looked down upon, only fundamental basic research having any validity, quickly squelched any such notions with a myriad of rationales that, in the end, convinced, even Cesar, that a modern approach would be much more beneficial.

In the end, our charge was quite simple: we four doctors just out of internships were to design and put into practice every aspect of a comprehensive health care system for an unspecified number of diverse farmworkers in an unspecified geographic area, with no resources, in as little time possible. And, oh yes, learn Spanish, and enough Arabic and Filipino to get by, and there are two really nice chicken coops in Delano to put together to make a clinic, do you know any carpentry?

Vertigo, double vertigo, a pox on all of you, we thought as we drove down Interstate 99 toward Delano. Early the next morning we began our task in earnest. Two hours a day were dedicated to construction, one hour to language proficiency, the rest to intense planning of everything from the design of the plan for workers under contract and for those still being organized, to making up a pharmaceutical formulary, dealing with patient flow through a clinic, lab and x-ray, cost analysis, referrals, chart design, medical library, preventative medicine, getting a staff together, literally a million things, none of which were we particularly prepared to do. Besides this, patients knew we were in town and wanted to be seen, and we were expected, and wanted to attend all the union functions, rallies, fiestas, speeches, strikes and boycotts. In a whirlwind of extremely intense activity, we accomplished more than we could ever have imagined and in October, the Rodrigo Terronez Memorial Clinic opened for full service!

That first day, forty patients came through. We had a beautiful opening ceremony with speeches by Cesar and many other dignitaries. We doctors even gave short addresses in halting Spanish.

It was a near perfect day. But as we passed through the food line, listening to the mariachis, I noticed a small group of people just across the property line. They had flags and were yelling things and kicking up dust. No one seemed to be paying attention to them, but, being curious, I asked Esther, our clinic administrator, who they were. "That's just Lola and her crew," she informed me. "They're paid by the growers to protest anything we do. She says we need a company union, not Cesar." She explained how powerful the crew boss was under the old way, controlling workers destinies like in a feudal system. The hiring hall alone, based on seniority, posed a major threat to the old power structure. And now a clinic for farmworkers! Too much!

This kind of benefit had major propaganda value as an organizing tool. Growers had to find a way to counter. Control of the richest agricultural enterprises in the country were at stake. We doctors had to realize that everything we did would be scrutinized by the opposition and exploited for their benefit whenever possible. Being young, energetic, dedicated, idealistic, and highly motivated was not enough; we had to be cagey, politically astute, socially aware, and delicately diplomatic. Sure, every patient had to get well, but beyond that, it behooved us to know where they worked, what was going on at that ranch, what was their position in the farmworker community, how influential were they.

The temperature in the San Joaquin Valley could get oppressively hot, but, in those days, we didn't notice because of the pervasive fire like intensity of the farmworker struggle. Several times we had to evacuate the clinic after bomb threats. These had to be taken seriously because one night a nearby garage was dynamited. Glass and nails were scattered under our cars. A bullet hole was found in an exam room window one morning. Tires were slashed. A fine work atmosphere! Even the union bull wasn't safe. Usually grazing contentedly in a small pasture area, one morning he was found belly up. Cesar wanted us to perform an autopsy, which we respectfully declined. We were, however, able to say that the bloated appearance was quite consistent with poisoning.

From the beginning we were very busy, seeing upwards of one hundred patients a day. Still, I frequently found time for basketball, and was soon accepted as a regular at the center. The exercise, for me was crucial, helping me get through another demanding day. The dynamics and the talk were also instructive and entertaining. One black guy might say to another, "You ain't got nothin', nigger!" Then a Chicano dude, after a particularly dramatic hoop, would yell out "arriba raza!". Soon the black guys would let fly with a "raza negra!" Filipinos would do an occasional "mabuhay". One time a player asked me, "Ain't you got nothin' to say?" I said, "Nope, I just let all those points rainin' down on you guys do the talkin'."

One night when we were done playing one of the guys asked, "Doc, you in the one on one?" I told him I didn't know anything about it. "Well," he went on, "some of the guys is sayin' you no good, but me an' Delon say y'all could win it." Before I knew it, the guys had me signed up. This was for bragging rights. Half court games to ten counting by one, call your own except in the championship game.

The next week, for three evenings, the preliminary rounds took place and I was able to progress through with little difficulty. Then came the final night with just eight of us left. My first match up was with Ramon, a quick young Chicano about six feet tall, who could both shoot and drive well. His defense, however, was suspect, and I was able to take advantage, mostly going to the hole, and prevailed, 10-6.

Next up for me, in the semi's, was Howard Bonner, arguably the most gifted player around. Strong and an excellent leaper, he reminded me of Elgin Baylor with his creative assortment of shots. We had matched up many times in games in the center so we knew each other's moves well. Luckily, I started off hot and got an early lead before he stepped it up on "D" and got back into it by simply jumping over me to score. Soon, we found ourselves at eight all, the whole place screaming on the sidelines. My ball top of the key. Noticing him overplaying me a little to the right, I ball faked left to get him to shift his weight, and then took it as strong as I possibly could down the right side of the lane. He recovered and was right with me as I rose up off my left foot with all the force I could

56

muster. In the air there was contact from our legs all the way up our bodies to the elbows, but as we met, just enough space was created to allow me to hook one over his hand high off the glass and in. "Do it, blood," someone yelled as Howard readied himself on top. Without hesitating, he drove right, trying to do to me what I had just done to him. But no, just as I'm loading up for the shot challenge, he put the most perfect spin move on me finishing with a left handed jam. The place was going bonkers. Now it's sudden death. "Da le duro," I heard as I held the ball firmly waist high. Knowing I would have to come up with something special, I slowly worked my way to the right, dribbling deliberately, keeping my body between him and the ball. Then a sudden quick dribble behind the back reversing direction, two quick steps, and a pull up "J" from seventeen, got it! Game over, I showed no emotion, knowing I had gotten lucky.

For the finals, it was the loquacious and extremely talented Spider Lockett. This guy not only could move, but he had a reach that wouldn't quit, making it impossible to block his shot and difficult to get anything off on him. Also rather disconcerting was his nonstop verbal diarrhea if you weren't used to it. He even talked while he was shooting. I started off hitting a left reverse, then a step through, then two bombs. Spider was content to fire from long range and couldn't find the basket. With a 4-0 score, he kind of lost enthusiasm, and I was able to gun away with almost anything, seeing if I could make enough to finish it. Mostly just going through the motions, he was able to get to 9-7, but I finished it off with a launch from somewhere near the county line that hit the mark. There was a lot of hootin' and hollerin' as we shook hands and I was awarded the trophy. "Not bad for a white boy," joked the spider. "I got you next time," he said turning to walk away. "Boy can shoot the ball, yes he can. I was tired, I think I got the flu, he mine next year..." the voice trailed off as he entered the crowd.

"They found you," announced Janet solemnly one evening, handing me a letter we had both anticipated and resented, now more than ever, since we were so fully engaged in the farmworker movement. I was to report for my induction physical in Sioux Falls, South Dakota, the next week. After hurried arrangements, I flew home prepared to "take my medicine", whatever that might entail.

On my arrival, I was both pleasantly surprised and moved emotionally when my father, after greeting me with a big hug, announced that he would accompany me. Knowing that I planned to resist, it must have been a most difficult decision for him to stand by me. A stalwart in a staunchly conservative community, he knew how unpopular what I was about to do, would be. Yet he stayed by my side. I know he was proud of the medical work I was doing in California, but no one from around there had been a resister, and several of his patients had already been killed in the war. I think he understood what I was going through and empathized with my feelings. I, in turn, was never more appreciative of his support.

The actual physical was pretty routine, although I resented both the rectal and the radiation from the mandatory chest x-ray. Apprehension arose as we inductees lined up at the end of the proceedings to face the C.O. Having rehearsed my plan several times in my head, however, I remained outwardly calm as he recited his canned ditty, finishing with, "I now command you all to take a step forward." As everyone else complied, I felt a momentary weakness in my knees but remained motionless. The officer walked to within about six inches and emphatically reiterated, "It is my mission to command you to take a step forward."

Looking him straight in the eye, I responded somewhat disrespectfully, "I'm refusing induction. Surely you've heard of that."

"Have this man arrested," he glared, motioning for two nearby M.P.'s. Later that day I was arraigned before the federal judge in the same city. I had done my homework and felt quite certain of his political persuasion, but, nonetheless, could not be sure of anything as he read the charges and asked for my plea. "Guilty, Your Honor," I stated.

"Do you have anything to say for yourself?" he asked.

"Yes I do, Your Honor." Now was my moment. This wasn't to be a rhetorical rally speech nor a torrential tirade against the establishment, but a simple truth telling coming directly from the heart. I began slowly, "Your Honor, I'm not an eighteen year old fresh out of high school. I've had nearly ten years of watching, listening, reading, and studying about Viet Nam. Along the way, I tried to digest not just the standard media pronouncements, but also books and reports of all persuasions, innumerable speeches and interviews, and the poignant personal witness of returning veterans. Your senator, George McGovern, has been particularly influential. From Dien Bien Phu to Me Lai, the Tet offensive, Kent State, Madison, the '68 democratic convention, Laos, Cambodia, and the Pentagon Papers have helped shape my opinion. Simply stated, I cannot participate in this war. Strictly speaking, I don't consider myself a conscientious objector although I have the highest respect for those who are. A situation like WWII would certainly evoke a different response in me. However, in Viet Nam, I firmly believe our prosecution of the war is wrong. Without a doubt, Your Honor, I am guilty of violating the Selective Service Act, but much more importantly, in doing so, I remain true to myself. Thank you, Your Honor."

As I sat down, I thought of more things I should have said. Still, I had made my point, and was relieved to have it finished. Feeling my undershirt completely soaked, I glanced back at my father. Showing no emotion that I could detect, he responded with a slight nod.

"Mr. Murphy, I understand you're a physician."

"Yes, Sir. I am."

"Where are you working, Dr. Murphy?"

"We've just opened a new clinic for migrant farmworkers in California, Your Honor."

"The court will take a short break. Please remain in your places." Judge Heege got up and went directly to his quarters. I barely had time to contemplate the $10,000 fine and five year federal prison sentence people were getting in some parts of the country, when he returned.

"All rise."

"Dr. Murphy, I have no doubt as to your sincerity, and I agree with much of what you have said. I also recognize the value of the work you are now doing. These are truly tumultuous times we live in. What you have done is a very serious matter. The court feels, however, that nothing is to be served through your incarceration. With this in mind, Dr. Murphy, you are hereby sentenced to two years federal probation, with the proviso that you continue in your present work for this time period. You will be receiving more detailed instructions by mail. Court dismissed!"

With a deep breath of relief, I walked over to a heartfelt embrace from my dad. All the way home we talked medicine, his experiences, and my plans for farmworker health care. "Son, you're doing your best, and I respect you for it." I couldn't ask for more. Now a felon, I was soon back in California, working harder than ever.

Our clinic, in those early months, had to address the problem of literally hundreds of elderly Filipino men suffering from a laundry list of chronically neglected medical conditions, osteoarthritis, gout, and hypertension occurring regularly. These are not particularly romantic diagnoses, but still presented challenges for us as inexperienced doctors committed to doing the best for each patient. A review of the pertinent medical literature proceeding to the development of a scientifically based, yet practical protocol for the diagnosis, treatment, and follow up, was in order for each condition. With great relish, we performed our task; these were real patients depending on us alone for their well-being. This is the essence of meaningful medical education.

Young Filipino workers had been lured initially, in the 1920's and 30's, to labor in the Hawaiian pineapples. History of their homeland, suffering first from hundreds of years of Spanish colonialism, followed by a hostile U.S. military takeover in 1898, had kept the populous disenfranchised and desperate. Heads filled with promises of financial reward and dreams of returning secure to their beloved islands, thousands left their families, migrating East, first to toil in the volcanic soil of the newest U.S. acquisition, then, unfulfilled, on to serve agribusiness' burgeoning concerns in California, the vast majority never again to see the Orient. With no legal right to own property, socially limited by anti-miscegenation laws, and squeezed by the inevitable exploitation of the labor contractor system, many, now 30 or 40 years later, found themselves still living permanently in rural farm labor camps. Their lives were filled with, not only work, but also rich and unique subcultural activities. Any special occasion called for adobo, pansit, barbecue, even balut. Betting was a big diversion, with games of cards and group trips to neighboring Nevada to experience blackjack, keno, and other "pleasures". In Delano, there was always the wide open "China town" section of town, also offering the full assortment of entertainment. Sundays, of course, were the big days, which can be explained by the following anecdote.

In the midst of the usual hectic work day at the clinic, I entered the next exam room to see a new Filipino patient, a sixty-five-year-old man named Calixto. Introducing myself, I asked what I could do for him. With a beguiling twinkle in his eye, he began in characteristic halting, staccato English, "I need, a prescription, for, some hormones, Doctor." Oh, I thought, he's sixty-five. None of these guys are married, but yes, they do frequent the services of the opposite sex, as evidenced by a significant number of STDs we were seeing, and so he must be experiencing that dreaded crisis: impotence. But how to approach this most delicate subject? "You're not married?" I probed. "No", he responded with a slight chuckle, "the medicine is for…my cock. I can, pay for it." Well, I thought, he's rather direct about it. What should I do? After, what I can later say was, some hilarious, round about dialogue, it became clear that Calixto had one of the top roosters in the area, and he was trying to get an edge for an upcoming fight. The medicine was for a chicken!

I agreed to write the prescription if he would take me to the big showdown. Later that week, I visited him at the camp and observed him meticulously crafting the razor blade and its tie to be wrapped exactly in position on the posterior portion of the banti's lower leg. The workout included repeated provocation of the colorful avian avatar, working the invaluable principal into an ever more intense frenzy, terminating, chicken exhausted, with calculated kind caresses and softly soothing Ilocano phrases falling on the garrulous gladiator who harkened with a series of eerie clucks. "The medicine is already working," announced Calixto.

The following Sunday, we traveled to an isolated rural area way off the beaten path. Hundreds of people were already gathered, mostly Filipino. Preliminaries were already underway as lesser chicks tried to build a rep. In one area, food was being prepared and sold, including barbecued chicken, of course. Small groups of men visited and laughed without even a hint of the shy, hesitant manner so apparent in my world. Everyone was friendly as I wandered around chatting with the various groups. Most were from the Ilocos Norte region of the Philippines, notorious for the much maligned Ferdinand Marcos. Others hailed from Leyte, Cebu, or Mindanao. I tried to learn phrases in all the dialects, including Pangasinon and Bisayan. Surprisingly, almost no one spoke Tagalog, the national language. Lookouts were in position, a necessary precaution Calixto explained, because of occasional raids.

It didn't take long to see that action was the attraction. Before each encounter, as trainers displayed their wares, odds were shouted out and greenbacks flowed to remain between the designated bet taker's fingers until settlement following the knockout, which, in this setting was a bleed out; clear endpoint being when Yankee Doodle went down for the count.

When it came to the main event, everyone gathered round excitedly. As Calixto showed his cock, erect and puffed up in a proud, knowing posture, the scene resembled peak hour at Wall Street. Fifties and hundreds saved for this moment now flowed in abundance. In opposition was a much bigger beautiful bird apparently oblivious to the pervasive hype. Then the ritual began, with both trainers, cradling cocks, circling each other exclaiming ever more powerful epithets as they repeatedly thrust their prized champs forward in menacing maneuvers designed to provoke peak frenzy. The sun's rays reflected off the artificial spurs carefully secured, as, on signal, each released his feathered knight, now crazed with excitement, to charge headlong like bighorns, colliding mid circle. Dust and feathers flew, amidst the deafening roar, and as suddenly as it began, Calixto's chicken was down, blood flowing from one wing. Rapidly revived, he successfully repelled the successive flying attack, succeeding, even in severing a tendon in the large foe's leg, leaving him limping noticeably. Then the final flurry when, goaded on by the crafty Calixto, the smaller contestant, ignoring his compromised upper extremity, reached deep to fly high, avoiding the weakened defense, and delivering the coup de gras, a slashed neck for big bird.

In addition to the blatant brutality, the cultural lessons learned that day were important. Filipinos, a significant portion of the farmworker population, were a group that, many times felt ignored or taken for granted in union decisions. They were always given special attention and treated with respect at the clinic. Many of us volunteered in the construction of Agbayani Village, a retirement complex for elderly Filipino workers. I personally tended to Larry Itliong, vice president and cofounder of the union, including many home visits, as he succumbed to amyotrophic lateral sclerosis. Two others were soon elected members of the board.

Gradually, as a union doctor, I was becoming more accepted by the Filipino community. In addition, my BB prowess gave me Rec Center status, where most were at least seasonal ag. workers. Nevertheless, it was not without surprise, that I was approached by Doug, a half Filipino, half white, BB regular, to see if I wanted to be a member of his league and tournament team. Pleasantly surprised, I graciously accepted, and soon we were playing anywhere from Bakersfield to Lemoore, having fun and winning most of the time.

At the close of our first season, we had to travel to face Tulare for the championship. Not a little intimidating, this big, all black team burst from the locker room, fully decked out in matching warm-ups, boom box blaring "Sweet Georgia Brown", circling the floor for a full five minutes, terminating in a series of dunks by all players. Quite impressive! I told the guys about Calixto's cock in our pre game huddle and laughing, we went out to engage our powerful opponents. They got off to an early lead with superior athleticism, rebounding, and a good number of resounding jams. We hung around with Doug's bombs, Danny's dancing penetration moves, Wes' leaping putbacks, Joe's "J's", and a few lucky lofts and launches by yours truly. Down five at half, we wouldn't disappear, and found ourselves down two with twenty seconds to go in the game. Taking advantage of a pick, I drove hard to the right, pulling up near the free throw line for a jumper. About to release the shot, I saw, entering into my field of vision, help "D" in the form of one of their pogo sticks, springing across to snuff anything I served up. Instinctively, while airborne, I hovered and reloaded as he floated harmlessly past, then deftly soft touched it into the cylinder, taking care to curl my legs to avoid the walk. Their star responded with a coast to coast, finishing with a circus finger roll from at least the dotted line. We called a quick time out, down two, six seconds left. "Any bright ideas?" asked Danny as we grouped on the sidelines. "Joe, you pick for Doc," said Doug, coming to me taking it out, then let him go the length and create. "Take the best shot you can get!" he said, directing his eyes at me. Good strategy, and it seemed to go as scripted as I got the rock and advanced full speed up court against the press. However as I got to within about ten feet of the basket, I found myself surrounded by shadows with nowhere to go. Then, out of the corner of my eye I saw Wes cutting down the lane. Wes had been a 6'11" high jumper in college, and as I no looked it to him he used it all to soar toward the hole. Smacked on the release, falling to the floor, he heard successively, whistle, horn, and our screaming as the ball dropped into the net. Picking himself up, Wes calmly went to the line, alone on the court, and sank the throw. It all had happened so fast that they didn't really comprehend that the game was over. No overtime, they had lost. Us jubilant, them stunned, we quickly exited, later to celebrate the dramatic victory at a bar back in Delano.

Daily work at the clinic never seemed routine, resembling more, a full court press late in a close game. I might begin at 4 a.m. with an hour or two on a picket line at a particularly critical "huelga", then to the hospital for rounds or surgery, and on to la clinica. Consultation began in the parking lot, continuing into the waiting room. Rapid fire, no nonsense, chart review, read EKG's and x-rays, check lab results, see patients, teaching session for nurses, med students, and paraprofessionals, phone calls from various universities, see patients, delegate, a quick delivery, welcome visitors, see patients, ... where did the day go?

For young, energetic doctors, it was quite a rush. There was plenty of "routine" medicine to go around, but, ironically, we also encountered the bizarre and unusual, the fascinomas, on a daily basis. It was as if a sample of all the medical problems of the world, converged on one small facility, packed into a brief interval of time. Sending a patient to a specialist proved virtually impossible, both financially and logistically, not to mention politically, leaving it up to us to assure the best expected outcome. Early on, a decision was made to expend the needed resources on a relatively extensive medical library. Books, journals, and the telephone guided us through the vast array of conditions presented.

Gull's, Grave's, Addison's and Cushing's; scabies to tabes, VSD, ASD, PDA, tetrology, Eisenmenger's. Complete congenital heart block! Tonsillar lymphoma, retinoblastoma, seminoma, amoeboma, a month's gone by. Hymenolepsis nana, disseminated coccidioidomycosis, miliary tuberculosis, recurrent Serratia marcescens sepses (chronic granulomatous disease) - take a breath - red cell aplasia of pregnancy, inverted uterus, complete placenta praevia, and dementia precox. Pesticides? We got rashes with luster, Potter's in cluster, endemic ALL. Brucella abortus, Shistosoma mansoni, Chlamydia trachomatis, P. vivax, and M. leprae, step right up! Testicular feminization, Blackfan-Diamond, omphalocoele.....

One night I was called out urgently. I arrived to find a six-year-old-girl convulsing. As the nurse handed me the syringe of Valium, I noticed a tennis sized bulge on the child's forehead. Slowly, the seizure came under control, and I asked the mother if the swelling was from a fall. She explained that the child was born this way, but being from a small village in Mexico, they had no access to health care. A cousin, working in Delano had told them about our clinic so they had just arrived, after an arduous journey, including a perilous border crossing. The diagnosis was encephalocele with herniation of cerebral tissue leading to seizure disorder, all complicated by pronounced hypertelorism. In other words, she was missing part of her skull, and her brain was poking out just beneath the skin, forcing her eyes too far apart. Her only hope was corrective surgery. I didn't know if it was possible.

The next day, I began making phone calls. Only two surgeons in the world were even attempting this type of procedure, and by chance, one of them, a Frenchman, would soon be visiting Stanford University. Through the cooperation of many people, arrangements were worked out and our little patient underwent twenty one hours of surgery by a team of six top specialists. A part of her brain had to be cut away, and her entire skull reshaped along with her upper face, filling in the defect with a Teflon plate. The operation was a success and the smile on both the girl and her family's faces, on their return to Delano, was special to all of us.

Delivering babies was one of the major functions performed by us union doctors. Early on, my own personal guiding principle became, "there is no such thing as a normal delivery." In other words, be prepared and anticipate any complication at any time. Having almost no O.B. experience, the other physicians looked to me as the local expert. The good thing about delivering babies is that, almost always, you know what the problem is and it will be resolved in the near future, one way or another. Assuring the desired outcome of a healthy mother and a healthy baby, is a nerve wracking, demanding proposition. Exacerbating our anxiety was the reality of not having C-section as an easy alternative. My transitional object was Williams Obstetrics, each successive edition worn down from compulsive use, most times with slightly damp finger tips. I had difficulty sleeping after a delivery because of the adrenaline rush of the situation, and if I did happen to be lucky enough to enter the REM stage, I had a recurrent nightmare of being surrounded by women with grotesquely huge bare bellies repeatedly buffeting me like "the wave" in a stadium, allowing no escape, my absolute worst fear being that all bags of water, spontaneously and simultaneously, rupture, inundating me in an inexorable tide of meconium stained amniotic broth.

I liked O.B.; in it I became alive, fulfilled. I delivered in the clinic, at homes, in the hospital, even several in cars. One of my happiest memories is visiting the postpartum ward and seeing a group of cheerful mothers, each with their newborn, chatting and laughing. "Ai, que chulito este bebe, y mira aquel, con tanto cabello." Nearly always, the repartee was simply wonderful. Sharing a trying experience and enduring creates a powerful bond; being in a whole room full of it, left me floating on air. As one young mother so aptly explained, "Sabe doctor, para nosotros, los pobres, que no tenemos nada, la familia es nuestra riquesa."

When it came time for our own first child to be born, Janet and I decided to have me do the delivery at the clinic. By then, I had a good amount of experience and, quite truthfully, we didn't trust anyone else. Our son, Liam, was born uneventfully at what was more like a party than a medical event. Our joy was tempered on day three, however, when, an ever more noticeable jaundice being apparent, a lab result revealed a bilirubin of 19 (20 being the critical level for kernicterus and possible brain damage). Visions of dangerous exchange transfusions and other dire consequences passed through as arrangements were made to place him under the bili light. Janet's blood was type O, and Liam's was B, a minor incompatibility. That, accompanied by the occasionally seen rise in levels with breast feeding, turned out to be the cause. Fortunately, after several days of anxious preoccupation, levels dropped into the safe zone, crisis averted.

As that year's grape harvest approached, union activity was increasing faster than the sugar content of the Thompson seedless. Setting the tone for the ensuing campaign, was a state wide peregrination, converging on Modesto, where there lived two brothers, Ernest and Julio, whose decisions drove the entire grape industry. In a scene not easily forgotten, ten thousand perpetually disenfranchised stepped up to assert. "Huelgista, seguro, al Gallo da le duro."

Intransigent growers vs. the upstart, indomitable United Farm Workers donde quera. Spirited picket lines vs. Pinkertons and scabs. Redneck, company bought Teamster goons vs. Dorothy Day and Joan Baez. American officialdom in the form of judges and all authorities, consistently placing "property rights" above the right of those who feed the nation, to organize for an even minimally dignified existence. Each evening, meetings, planning, strategy. Each morning, streams of vintage vehicles, crimson flags flying as many implacable Aztec eagles, crisscrossing the land to encounter destiny in a thousand forms. "Be creative in whatever situation you encounter. Prompt, coax, cajole, laugh, cry, pray, but never, ever, even consider violence." Directive, El Jefe,, C.C..

The huelga was so big, with so many people involved, in so many places, and the intensity so acute, that it may have been inevitable. Nagi Daifullah, Yemeni union member, skull crushed by a hired thug. Caleb and Peter, two clinic doctors, rushed to the scene, only to witness the agonal respiratory efforts of the then decerebrate martyr. Even as preparations were being made for his memorial ceremony, as if a fuse had been lit, long time loyalist Juan Dela Cruz, was gunned down on the line, by a scab.

For Cesar Chavez, it was as if two family members had been lost. It was personal, he was responsible. Now it was up to him to react. One measure of greatness is how one responds in the time of crises. It calls for vision, assertiveness, tact, and boldness. We were not to be disappointed.

Delano resembled a war zone. City, county, state police, National Guard, everywhere. Military choppers hovering overhead, activating the sea of flags, now black, held high by the thousands thronging to join the dirge. Slowly, Garces highway, like a wick touched to kerosene, was saturated with humanity in a seemingly endless flow over the three miles leading to "los cuarenta acres". Watching from the verandah of the clinic, where our full staff was on duty in preparedness for anything, I saw the poignant procession approach. At the front, bearing the casket, were thousands of Yemenis, chanting Islamic platitudes in Arabic. One bore a large placard of Gammal Abdel Nasser. Then came Cesar and union staff along with selected dignitaries. Following directly were all the Filipino brothers, flags and banners in hand. There were Mexicans, media, supporters, trailing behind as far as I could see filling both lanes from town to the huge gathering area adjacent to our clinic and the hiring hall. Finally, with everyone assembled around the hastily constructed platform, Cesar deliberately ascended the steps and approached the podium. "Hermanos y hermanas, brothers and sisters, la huelga se acabo, la huelga se acabo, the strike is over!"

My mind was racing. What was he saying? He was quitting? Because of the deaths, he was giving up? Hardly. Within the hour it became clear. Because of the violence, the strike activity in the fields was ending, but a new phase, a new strategy, even more difficult, was beginning that very day. An international grape boycott was being launched. Immediately, farm worker families, staff, and organizers were being assigned to a city that could be anywhere in the world to execute the plan. A family with eight children, speaking no English, might be sent to Toronto. Others went as far as Scandinavia. Wherever grapes were sold, we needed a presence. Amazingly, everyone accepted their assignment, and began preparations to leave as soon as possible. It had been one of the most dramatic days I had ever witnessed.

Our medical work continued unabated. One night, just after getting Liam to sleep by reading the book "Hociquito, el Zorro" to him for the eighth time, the phone rang. I jumped to get it, hoping not to have to read another eight refrains. "Dan, this is Kate. Delores Huerta called and it sounds like she's in labor. I told her to come in. thought you'd want to know." Instantly I went into my high alert mode. "I'll be right out," I politely responded, hiding my apprehension as best I could. Delores was in her eighth pregnancy at thirty nine weeks gestation. Her last baby weighed over nine pounds. All of this was significant, of course, but paled in the light of what I found the week previous, when called into the room to verify fetal position. BREECH!! Curses and woe is me!

And, oh, did I mention that this was the Delores Huerta, vice president of the union, the most visible, high profile personality in the struggle next to Cesar. My, oh my, why was I ever born? Delores was a beautiful, gregarious, extremely intelligent Chicana. On a picket line she was, without a doubt, the best. Her charisma echoed through her wonderful, lilting Spanish, combined with her uncanny ability to think on her feet and react to her advantage, no matter what the situation, made her invaluable as an organizer. I had seen her call out a scab and melt a Teamster at the same time with a mesmerizing, hypnotic discourse lasting but a brief five minutes. Why was she doing this to me? Dios mio!

As I was driving out Garces Highway in my Corolla, possible scenarios raced through my mind, each more horrific than the other. I couldn't shake the thought of the seventeenth century English physician called to attend the queen who was about to deliver her first child, the heir apparent to the crown. After waiting anxiously for twenty four hours with no word, attendants entered the royal bedroom to find the queen undelivered and quite dead, and physician likewise. In a desperate attempt to calm myself, I replayed the episode still fresh in my mind that had occurred several months earlier. Responding to an urgent call, two of us doctors arrived at the small home of Lenny, a farmworker now working in our clinic laboratory, who was presently extremely pregnant. "Blood everywhere, Lenny passed out, come quick," had been the message. Indeed, glancing up as we entered the bedroom, I noticed fresh blood stains even on the ceiling. Placenta previa, quickly to the hospital, rapid transfusions and emergency section with help of the good Dr. Keagy. Mother and child none worse for the wear, young doctors aging rapidly.

For one hour our precious parturient dallied, putting Kate and me in an absolute twit. I read and reread Williams on breech extraction as Kate placed the instruments in the minor surgical area. Pacing, pacing... Finally, in waltzed La Sra. Huerta, laughing and joking. She actually enjoyed the whole situation, including our consternation, having full confidence that all would be well. Naivete. Barely undressed, her first contraction told me that we were in trouble; this was advanced labor, there would be no time for anything. Rapidly gloving, my focus intensified as Delores casually informed, "Dan, I've got to push." My anything but vigorous exam was greeted by a rush of clear fluid and the distinct feeling of umbilical cord on my fingers.

"Don't push for a minute," I urged as I assured myself that the pulse in the umbilical artery was good and that the presenting part was baby's butt. Affirmative on both counts, no worry about baby's head pinching off fetal circulation by squeezing too tightly into mom's pelvis compressing the prolapsed cord. "OKAY Delores, please don't force it, just pant like a nice little puppy during this next contraction." No matter, legs, body and arms all delivered in smooth succession, just on the force of her uterine muscle. Now the aftercoming head was deep in the pelvis and we had only minutes to complete the delivery or face fetal demise. Keeping clearly in mind my early Broadlawns initiation, I took a cleansing breath and directed, "We're doing fine. For this contraction, we need more little breaths, and Katie, I want ever so gentle suprapubic pressure just enough to deliver the head slowly." Positioning our hands, we all watched the unimpeded progress of the dark haired cranium emerging to join us with a lusty cry. Whew! And no blood! Si, se puede!

"Dan, what can I ever do to thank you?" queried Delores as we finished up.

"Well, why don't you just set me up as a Brown delegate to the convention," I joked. Jerry Brown, governor of California and passionate advocate of the farmworker cause, was in the midst of a dramatic run for the Democratic nomination for the presidency. Much of the credit for his success was due to the nationwide, grassroots collaborative effort put forth by our then, most powerful organization. The very next day, I stood shocked, phone in hand, as I listened to the call from the Brown campaign office informing me that I was to be a member of his California contingency at Madison Square Garden, all expenses paid.

As it turned out, the Olympic Games were taking place just prior to the convention in Montreal, where Peter Rudd, our former colleague at the clinic, was now training at McGill. We were invited to stop over. Taking advantage of a much needed break, Janet, Liam, and I were soon on our way east.

Stopping for a day in Iowa, we found my father, who was just recovering from a small heart attack, in the hospital. Mysteriously, he had developed pleurisy. Looking over his med sheet, I noticed the likely culprit, Pronestyl, which had been given to him because of a few extra heart beats. Diplomatically, I suggested to the attending that a test for Lupus might be instructive. Later, dad called to say that the test was positive, the medicine stopped, and he was fine. Never can be too careful with all those fancy medicines. My father was philosophically opposed to taking anything other than the essential. He was later to undergo abdominal aortic aneurysm surgery and recover without any pain medicine. Not surprisingly, I'm the same way, maybe worse. After a brief, but greatly appreciated visit with Grandma Margaret, we were on our way.

While in the air to Montreal, Liam became increasingly inconsolable, probably ears plugging. Out of desperation, Janet gave him a cherry tomato from her tray. It seemed to work temporarily, but then the unspeakable happened. The innocent youth, in his vigorous excitement with his new plaything, squeezed too hard, sending the contents of the ripened fruit arching into the air like a mortar. Sitting in front of us at the time, was a young black male with the most beautiful, flamboyant "fro" imaginable. Splash! Direct hit! Apologizing profusely, we offered to help get it out, how, I don't know, which he politely declined. He was an athlete heading to the games. Two days later we saw him running futilely with the rest of the pack chasing a Cuban named Juantorena. No one was a match for the effortless gallop of "el caballo."

Visiting New York again was great, but Brown's momentum had been crushed in the two weeks leading up to the convention by decisive primary defeats, especially on "Super Tuesday." Wearily, yet at the same time refreshed, I returned to Delano, anxious to renew my work.

By that time, the boycott was going strong, with amazing reports coming in daily. My medical work continued to be fascinating, clinical research, teaching, new challenges daily. Playing BB was more fun than ever because my skills were at their best. I could move athletically, jump, shoot the lights out, and even defend. Despite all this, my passion, the highlight of each day, was spending time with our son, Liam.

First of all, and this is based on objective clinical criteria, he was, simply put, the most attractive looking child imaginable. With natural Hollywood blond hair, an ever alert twinkle in his eyes, and a perfectly proportionate smile exhibited frequently yet always appropriately, he was irresistible. Naturally, at union functions, where we were well known, people would all come up to him, want to hold him or at least touch him and talk to him. But what never ceased to amaze, was the number of perfect strangers on the street or in a store, who would stop, transfixed, and feel compelled to say something like, "What a wonderful child". Yemenis called him "walad," chicanos "huerito." Nearly always happy, he loved playing, music, exploring, climbing. At an early age it was plain to see, that his imagination was very active, books and stories being one of his favorite activities. Verbally, he was without peer, never using baby talk, equally comfortable in English or Spanish, pronunciation perfect. This, coupled with his appearance and demeanor, gave him a magnetic presence, and made him special.

Whether it was playing with a ball, going for a walk, visiting someone, telling stories up in a tree, or reading, I didn't want to miss a day of doing something together. Twice, I got speeding tickets trying to get home before Liam's bed time. These encounters with the authorities, because of the charged atmosphere of the times, put me in a politically precarious position. Explaining that I wanted to see my son, while putting a human spin on the situation, didn't influence the officer either time, to cut me some slack. It all came to a head one evening when I got a call from the clinic that a patient had just arrived in labor and that she was already eight cm. dilated.

Hopping into my Toyota, I proceeded cautiously yet expeditiously to the edge of town where Garces Highway has a four way stop. I could see that no other cars were anywhere near the corner, so, in a sudden gesture of complete and total dedication to my work, I rammed it into fourth and sailed through the crimson octagon at a speed somewhere in the vicinity of MACH 1. Motating like the road runner, right brain orchestrating either Al Green falsetto or "Huelga en General," left brain negotiating the historic byway and anticipating the rapidly approaching task at hand, I was abruptly sensitized by the whirling red and penetrating advisement of Smokey's siren closing fast. Duty calls, I concluded, pressing my advantage with the heavy right foot, soon swerving solicitously onto union property. My erstwhile nemesis, was forced to pause at the entrance, caution and bewilderment taking their toll, allowing me to enter, evaluate, and sweep the immanent parturient into my protective arms, place her in my still purring transport, and pull out accelerating past my brave opponent just now arriving, pistol drawn. Having risked all, and not about to be inveigled, he spun around and before I could say "arriba, arriba, adelante cabrones", the beleaguered bear was once again narrowing the gap. Determined, I pressed directly for the hospital, barely arriving ahead of my tormentor. Slyly, he maneuvered around my gassed and tired automobile, cutting us off from the hospital entrance. In a clever twist, I swerved off at a tangent, delivering my charge to the convenient service entrance at the rear, which opened directly adjacent to the delivery suite. The door was swinging shut just as he was jumping out of his car. Of course, he didn't know the release code. Already seething, this must have brought foam to his mouth.

Having been forewarned by my nurse, all was in readiness. Always known as a fast changer, this time I literally leapt from lays to scrubs and, condensing a five minute cleansing ritual into a perfunctory dip augmented by my most focused imagery seeing shed microbes swirling helplessly down the drain, I side kicked the DR door into motion and backed my way calmly into the professional sanctuary, arms held high and free.

"Just a rim, Dr. Murphy", advised the unwitting accomplice. While I gowned, gloved, draped, and evaluated, in rapid succession, the offended officer, intent on the collar, bulled his way past the front desk, around the hallways, and back to labor and delivery, accompanied by an ever enlarging coterie of hospital employees bent on averting the ominous scene of ugly mayhem now imminent.

My Hippocratic mind, at the moment, was busily engaged, "She's complete. Why isn't she crowning? Might be this little bit of asynclitism I'm feeling. Hope I don't have to use Kielland's." At the same time, my ears can't help but hear the ruckus developing a mere ten feet away through the swinging door.

"Jerry, you can't go into the delivery room, and put that gun away! Have you gone crazy," I heard the nursing supervisor saying.

"The son of a bitch ran a stop sign doin' eighty! Twice! Then he damn near side swiped me on Garces!"

"He's a young, dedicated doctor, Jerry. He didn't have time! Did you want to assist with the delivery out in the ditch somewhere? Get a grip! I'm telling you it's not personal."

I was seeing blood running, mine. "Contraction starting, Doctor."

"Empuje, Amelia, con toda la fuerza que tengas." Slowly, I watched the head turn and descend, all in one mighty push, as nature recapitulated its prime directive. The beautiful newborn offered a lusty cry immediately. We were home free. In a most deliberate fashion, I finished the necessary procedures, even helping the nurse transfer the patient to the Gurney, all the while listening intently for any indication of what my destiny might be on exiting the room. Resigned to my fate, I pushed the door open, only to be greeted by no one, nothing, empty.

After changing and writing on the chart, I went down the hall to find the nurse supervisor. "Janie, what happened?"

"I took care of it," she explained. "He was hot, though. I think you're all right, but it might be prudent to avoid any further provocation for a while." Thanking her profusely, I went out to my car and drove SLOWLY home, finding Liam fast asleep. "Oh well, tomorrow's another day," I thought, and soon, I too was asleep, dreaming of fantastic clones of smart antibodies flowing from my fingers, fixing everything in sight as it should be.

Golden State was the team that year. Rick Barry, always an offensive machine, had finally come to the realization that keeping everyone involved greatly enhanced the probability of getting jewelry. My Mill Valley brother in law, Bob, had gotten us tickets for the Sixer game. Arriving early, we hung around the sideline appreciating the humungous presence of the pro's especially Daryl Dawkins. But the main attraction was, without a doubt, Dr. J. As the game progressed he pulled off one amazing play after another. Once he drove and I swear he was so far behind the basket I thought, no way can he score, but, not only did he score, he dunked. From where he was, it was clearly impossible, yet he did it. That was Julius.

74

Forever stretching the laws of gravity. Tied late, the game came down to a pass from Barry to Attles for the last attempt. As the ball caromed harmlessly off the rim, we all thought OT, but Clifford Ray was there to clean up at the buzzer. It was that kind of year for the Warriors, who went on to flatten the Bullets in four for the rings.

My own game continued to develop, or maybe evolve is the better word. The dunk was fading, outside shots definitely becoming more frequent. What I was adding to my repertoire, though, was a signature move. This is something you get to be known for. Everyone has seen it but it can't be stopped. Oh, sure, if you spend all day thinking about it, you could cut it off, but, in the heat of battle, it rarely fails. The first time I remember using it, the guy guarding me said he thought I had disappeared off the court, quite a compliment. It starts with me dribbling, nonchalantly, along the perimeter, heading towards the right baseline. Slowing to a snail's pace, or even coming to a complete halt, I maintain my dribble with the right hand. My body faces approximately, the right corner. The defender is prepped and waiting for the incision, lulled half to sleep. Now, here is the key part. Keeping everything else the same, including my dribble and my body, I turn my head only, as far back to my right as I can for, and this is crucial, a count of one thousand one. This sets it up perfectly. Now the smoke. As quickly and explosively as possible, I step to my left, rapidly pivoting and curling toward the hoop with the strong dribble. Invariably, the defender, thinking I'm likely to go the other way or doing nothing, is fooled, most times, badly. The key is the deliberate head turn, and not moving it back until well into the power action. Of course, it's a blind play for me, so I have to be sure no one is between us and the basket as I initiate the move or I'm the fool. The first step is with the left, then it's usually one step with right and finish with the left handed finger roll at the rim or looped over help "D" if necessary. Tough shot, but easily mastered with a couple hundred repetitions. Actually, the closer to the baseline, the better; more unexpected. You are always taught to never get beat baseline, cut the guy off at the out of bounds line. People think within six inches of the line means you've got the man cut off. But, with my move, I can pivot around the defender, placing my left foot just inside the line, while the ball and all the rest of my body swings over the out of bounds territory, never touching, bringing the next dribble (the last) back in bounds, stepping back further in bounds with the right foot, to then avoid being too far under, setting up the beautiful left handed roll into the net. There's something about using that centrifugal force to my advantage that ranks right up with delivering a baby. So many have been burnt – even quick guys – because it's not about speed or quickness; it's deception.

At work, it had become customary for me to hold a brief teaching session every week. Present were the permanent clinical staff, and the current contingent of med. students, paramedics, and volunteers of various stripes, who came and went according to the vagaries of their particular situations. Always well intended, these people were, for the most part, helpful, but could also be a burden, mostly because of the time taken to lead them through our always demanding type of work. The more formal teaching served to upgrade my own skills as well as to help the others be able to function more efficiently. I usually focused on a recent interesting or classic case we had seen, giving a practical approach to the main concerns in diagnosis and treatment. In addition, we kept a list of particularly difficult, interesting, or representative patients, and, when enough accumulated in any specialty area, we would arrange a day of "grand rounds." Amazingly, on contacting an appropriate expert, usually from an ivory tower institution in or near California, acquiescence was universal, the allure being, politics aside, an interesting array of clinical cases away from the often smothering confines of academia. On the designated day, together, we would analyze, probe, and discuss in detail, the exigencies of each clinical situation. Combined with the always authentic ethnic gastronomic spread we provided, these days were both valuable for all and festive. We had Daley for cardiac surgery, Einstein for pulmonary, Diamond for peds hematology, Peters for G.I., Linde for congenital heart defects, Ling on O.B., etc. We learned, patients were extended the best care possible, and the specialists went away fulfilled. Definitely a win-win situation.

A special concern arose as we became aware of the possibility of the diagnosis of schistosomiasis in the Yemeni population, many of whom we were seeing with a myriad of suggestive symptoms.

Virtually unknown in the U.S., except for "swimmer's itch", a temporarily symptomatic benign condition caused by a related species, bilharzia, as it is also known, is endemic in many parts of the world, including Yemen. Protean in its manifestations, and potentially carrying significant morbidity and mortality, this parasitic infestation loomed ominously before us. Placing a call to Dr. Kenneth Warren, arguably the most knowledgeable authority anywhere on this problem, constituted our opening salvo. Literally salivating at the possibilities our situation presented for clinical research and effecting permanent cure, the helminthic guru agreed to fly in, accompanied by his hand-picked team including Dr. Mahmoud from Egypt, for an extended attack on our abdominal adversaries. Before long, we were embracing malachite green as our favorite hue, embarked on a comprehensive stool screen for everyone responding to the greeting, "Keif hallak" from Bakersfield to Fresno. We became the only place in the country, with FDA approval to use out-patient niridazol, thus vanquishing vast numbers of these unwanted eosinophile stimulating interlopers. Two papers flowed from our work, thus placing us at the vanguard of domestic clinical research in this unique medical niche. Most unforgettable was the bash Dr. Warren threw for us at a local Chinatown restaurant the night before his departure. Addressing "schisto" for us, was now as routine as avoiding Modesto wine.

Occasionally, despite the demanding nature of my work, I was able to break away a day or two here and there. Any drive East from the San Joaquin Valley is a dramatic departure. The rapid transition to foothills ascending immediately to the Sierra Nevada's is in itself rejuvenating. Whether skiing, mountain climbing, hiking, or just wandering, the brief respite never failed to work its catalytic magic. One weekend was even spent in Death Valley, a grim, yet beautiful reminder of the forever more imaginative expression of nature's artistry. Day trips West, to Paso Robles, San Luis Obispo, and beyond, worked like a cloudburst in Mojave, providing caustic relief for life's aggravating abrasions. And what better psychotherapy than a culinary interlude of enchiladas or chile rellenos with margaritas in the peaceful atmosphere of Santa Maria?

To the North, Sacramento usually meant picketing or lobbying; nice camaraderie, but at the price of experiencing first-hand the political muck that unglues many of our lives, and not even escaping the oppressive Valley heat. Salinas, on the other hand, where we had a new clinic, was definitely refreshing, with lots of Union activity, although Steinbeck's classic depiction, remained fundamentally apropos. Palo Alto and Stanford were like a sojourn to another planet, being in such contrast to the pronounced squalor of the barrio shacks and farm labor camps we were so accustomed to. Nevertheless, we had staff affiliation at the medical center and received invaluable assistance on numerous occasions. Continuing up the coast, I could imagine the ruminations of Clint Eastwood, Patty Hearst, and George Jackson, before being forced to focus on the hills and hubbub of Marin County. San Francisco, while beautiful and interesting in many ways, seemed too predictably progressive and even provincial, in a trendy sort of way. Still, treading in the paths of a pair of Jacks, proved inspirational; London with his biting social commentary best exemplified in his classic characterization of "the scab," and Keroac whose search high and low, and ultimately, within, was, and continues being instructional to so many.

From Delano, going "over the hill" to L.A. was just a brief jaunt, but brought a totally different reality. There was "East Los" with its Pachucos and sweat shops, Watts, L.A. County Hospital, and the downtown Catholic Worker Clinic, side by side with Hollywood, UCLA, Santa Monica Beach, and Disneyland. Careening down cemented paths, choking on sulfurous emissions, always on the lookout for Manson wannabes, I never ceased to be amazed at the heroic struggles of the too many good people packed into Southern California like almost ripened table grapes in a lug. We saw the Dodgers, the Lakers, and an Iowa-USC game, and visited our friends Tomás, Maria, and their children, Xochi and Jaime. Several times our travels reached to Calexico, where we also had a clinic, barely a step from Mexicali, a true third world city. Once, Janet and I spent a week going by train to Guadalajara and Mexico City, enjoying a bit of Matzatlan on the way.

No matter what, I always kept the greater part of my focus on my job as a farm worker doctor. Trying not to perseverate, it seemed that the birthing process was permanently etched in my awareness. It was not only the heightened drama of this aspect of my mission, but also the shear frequency of deliveries to be attended. In one humbling and chaotic month, in addition to seeing 100 plus patients per day and participating in all the union functions, I, by then the only union doctor left, managed to catch 46 newborns. A virtual marathon of sleepless nights, rupturing bags of water, running here, running there, sitting gowned urging "empuje!" constantly arranging and rearranging instruments on the tray to keep occupied while awaiting nature's rhythm. It was like being at a malfunctioning street semaphore, either stuck on red, or switching erratically to either amber or green without any warning. An ongoing tiredness that coffee doesn't even begin to address. Being young, energetic, type A for sure, and politically motivated, while helping extend the limits somewhat, couldn't blind me to the realization that such a pace would exact an intolerable toll before long. Dr Norman Bethune, quite admirably, through a soaring superhuman spearhead of medical miracles, made the dramatic transformation of China possible, paying the ultimate price in the process. For any number of reasons, I considered too closely emulating that great physician both inopportune and improvident.

The Union was on a roll, with a new farm labor law in place, winning elections and signing contracts like an underdog team mounting a charge with full court press. However, as so often happens, the changing dynamics, to be fully exploited, called for equally dramatic adjustment in executive union function, which never occurred. Instead, an ever more vulnerable Achilles' heel was exposed. Using the climate provided by the Brown administration to sweep across the nation in a comprehensive agricultural worker organizing drive while consolidating gains already won through delegation and specialization into areas of concern including true grass roots enfranchisement and solid contract enforcement never took place. Instead, management by crisis, and top heavy decision making persisted. Competent dedicated people, sensing a growing alienation, began looking for another cause. Paranoia became a buzzword. Even our clinic, which I felt was so strong that it could never be threatened by any outside power, began to lose its luster as the onslaught of seemingly arbitrary directives began to curtail our effectiveness and function. My own level of frustration gradually became intolerable. In a last ditch attempt to change the course of events, I asked Cesar if the two of us could sit down privately to discuss what I felt were important matters. I had delivered five of his grandchildren and had been through everything from fasts to disabling back problems with him. Graciously, despite a very hectic schedule, he consented to meet. Early the next week we were alone in the back room of the clinic.

"Cesar, thanks for coming. How are you doing?" I asked as we both took a chair.

"Well, you know, Dr. Murphy, we always have lots of problems, and it's no different now. What's on your mind?"

"Cesar, let me say first, that working here at this clinic has been extremely rewarding for me personally, and I think I can speak for all the others too. We are very busy doing meaningful work, and I feel that we have accomplished things that haven't been done anywhere else. What bothers me though is that, over the last few months, I've seen attitudes slipping. We've lost several good people already, and more are close to leaving. It's beginning to affect our work. It's gotten to the point that if things don't change, I don't know how long we'll be able to function. That's why I wanted to talk to you."

For a brief moment, he seemed to be thinking, but then looked up and said, "What do you see as the problem, Dan?"

Here was my chance, and it had to be good, or it would all be for naught. "As I see it, Cesar, the Union has changed. It's grown. Now it has to mature. Our clinic has done a tremendous amount of work. We've had to evolve as we went along according to whatever circumstances we found ourselves in. Many of us have been here from the beginning. We know about delivering health care to farm workers like no one else. No one could come here to challenge us on that because we have paid our dues a thousand times and not only survived, but thrived. We're the prototype. Personally, I'm very proud of our work." I paused for a second to collect my thoughts and then began on another tack. "You know, Cesar, people come in here and, after a few days or even a few weeks, in good faith many times, try to make suggestions or tell us how to do things. Every time, I find myself biting my tongue, and even feeling resentment, because we have already thought about those things, under duress, under fire, knowing that even little things had to be carefully dealt with, for the clinic to be able to function the best that it could. Do you see what I mean? These were outsiders, they had no power over us. Now, however, we're beginning to see decisions being made from within the Union, that we don't understand, and worse, that have begun to limit our ability to work and do our jobs effectively, and we have no recourse. Very frustrating."

"Dr. Murphy, on top we face the same kind of problems on a daily basis. Not for public consumption, but do you know that we're infiltrated by the FBI, maybe even the CIA? It's a fact. They know they can't stop us from the outside, so they're trying to destroy us from within. Do you know what it's like to have worked so hard, come so far, and sacrificed so much, only to now face such a threat? It isn't easy at all. Who can you trust? Who can make decisions?"

Thinking hard, I tried to react, "I can see where it must be very difficult, but at the same time, I feel that, from our point of view, things can't go on as they are. If I may, I'd like to throw out a suggestion."

"Sure, go ahead."

"I have a friend, a strong Union supporter and someone who has been very helpful to us here in the clinic. He's a psychiatrist in L.A.. He deals a lot with the rich and famous, and the powerful, helping them sort out the issues in not only their personal lives but also in their professional positions. My thinking is that he might be able to take a fresh look at things, broaden the perspective, add his insight to a lot of the things we've been discussing.' Knowing it was crucial, I continued, "I've already taken the liberty of discussing this with him, and he's willing to meet with you any time, any place. Cesar, as a doctor, a Union man, and a friend, I think you should take him up on his offer." There, I'd said my piece. Now it was up to him.

Silence.

Then, finally, "I'll think about it." And as he was getting up, "Thanks." We shook hands and as he was leaving the room, "I'll let you know." Meeting adjourned.

I've relived that encounter many times in my mind, wondering if I could have done something differently, said it in another way, perhaps another forum. Hindsight can be just as exacting as the actual experience. I never heard back from him on what we had talked about. Things continued to deteriorate, and within several months it became clear that I must resign. I gave them more than adequate time to find a replacement, but it was never addressed. Six years had gone by, an immense amount of work, the best time of my life. Not only was I now a doctor, but I was ready to take on the world.

A month before we were to depart, in as perfect a scene as we could ever have imagined, our second son, Conor, came into the world. Doing the candle light home delivery myself, surrounded by friends, and having Liam there to participate, was about as good as it gets.

The timing, however, may not have been perfect. Tying up loose ends, knowing that things were precarious, and receiving the overwhelming displays of gratitude coming so naturally from the hearts of farm workers, all while trying to deal with a newborn, left us emotionally drained.

Farm workers themselves, organized a going away fiesta for us. It included great ethnic food, emotional speeches, and a dance where each aspiring partner, following an old tradition, pinned money on my clothes while asking for the dance. I ended up covered from head to foot with bills, some even twenties. I received many gifts, including an entire box of jars containing homemade chili. Finally, I was presented with a gold plated plaque inscribed with the following:

AL DR. DANIEL MURPHY M.D. Y FAMILIA
LA COMUNIDAD HISPANA DE DELANO,
MCFARLAND, RICHGROVE, EARLIMART,
WASCO Y PUEBLOS VECINOS CALIFORNIA,
EE.UU. HONDAMENTE AGRADECE Y
PUBLICAMENTE ATESTIGUA SU
RECONOCIMIENTO.

All in all, it was a very moving experience. To top it off, Peter Cummings, one of the doctors I had worked the most with, hugged me and made the following comment: "Dan, I just wanted to let you know, that, in my experience so far, you're the best primary care physician I've seen." Coming from him, that was a great compliment.

My wife reacted to all of this by coming down with the worst flare up of colitis she had ever experienced. Thus, in mid-December, Janet with temps up to 105, along with me and the two children, filled with mixed emotions, got into our Corolla, with a few humble possessions, and no heater, heading for Iowa where the temperature was approaching twenty below.

Traveling East, during those rare interludes where neither son demanded attention, Janet and I contemplated our future. Now, deeply enmeshed in leftist thought, we discussed every progressive option we could dream up. Che, the most dramatic example of revolutionary physician, received a thorough airing. Country by country, we reviewed the world. Movement by movement, we analyzed. "Well, I don't like their Maoist tendencies," she might say. Or, "I like the way they seem to combine democratic centralism with a holistic approach to medical care," might pop up. On the second day, as we inched our way along the odd numbered channels ascending the map, we began to feel the sting of winter on the prairie. Kansas to Nebraska, we're putting on more clothes, stuffing towels into the radically rent rubber housing of the median floor stick, saying very little. Nebraska to Iowa, running on empty, I mean us, teeth chattering, worried about swaddled children, Janet sick, destination ever closer. Somewhere near Sioux City, gas station thermometer -19 degrees Fahrenheit. We're almost there, frostbite a real possibility, hard to even turn the wheel. As we pulled into frigid and frozen Alton, Janet tuned her head toward me and softly uttered a single word, "Mozambique."

Welcomed with open arms, within minutes, Janet was in bed sipping grandma's chicken soup, Conor was getting a warm bath, Liam was listening to "Bozo at the Farm," and I was sitting down with dad, each a seven-seven in hand.

"Great to be here, dad. How's the house coming?"

"We're still doing some painting, but the electrical work is done and, actually it's quite nice."

"And the clinic is ready for me?"

"Sure are. You start Monday and can work as long as you like."

My father, now retired, along with another recently retired colleague, Alex, had been renovating an old farmhouse on the edge of Orange City, three miles away. It had been hit by a tornado several years earlier, but was still solid enough for what we all knew would be, our temporary use. The four Orange City physicians all worked together in a single office near the thirty bed local hospital. Since dad no longer practiced, they were seeing lots of new patients, mostly Catholics venturing across the huge cultural gap for the first time. Knowing and respecting my father, they figured if I was anything like him they couldn't go too far wrong, so they accepted me graciously, expecting me to attend to the Luxemburgers and whatever other overflow there might be.

"Dad, Janet's pretty sick right now. Do you think I can go to work so soon?"

"Of course, I'm a doctor, Margaret's a nurse, we're both parents, and there's nothing we'd love to do more than help you right now, so don't worry. It's a chance to get to know the kids and Janet can rest and recuperate. You can work. Believe me, I know how you feel. I had the same disease. If I was off for more than two or three days, I just didn't feel right. I guess the worries are somehow addicting. Even now, I feel best when one of my old patients stops over to ask for advice. Besides, from the way you've been telling it, work here will be a breeze compared to what you've just come through. Take it easy, enjoy yourself for a while."

"Thanks, dad. We really appreciate it."

We went on talking for the longest time. Funny how now we related so closely. A lot of it was medical, and a lot of that was OB. Dad had done five thousand deliveries in his forty odd years of practice, an accomplishment I now appreciated more than ever. He told me about his two maternal mortalities. One was a farm house delivery before antibiotics. Everything seemed routine but the next day the mother spiked a temperature of 103. Aspirin and cool compresses were no help and by the second day she was at 106, and within another twelve hours she was dead. The other case sounded like an amniotic fluid embolism, with uncontrollable seizures. We could have talked for hours on breeches alone. One of his first deliveries in Alton was a young farm wife experiencing her first delivery, breech. "Just seeing the size of the feet coming out struck fear in my heart. As you can guess, I had trouble with the head. Maybe it was my relative inexperience but I don't think so. In the next terrible ten minutes, try as I might, I could not finish the delivery, finally losing the baby's pulse and resorting to a feto-destructive procedure just to be able to finish. Later I weighed the baby at just over 13 lb. It was horrible for everyone there, but the positive side is that she went on to have eight normal births." Many other topics entered in, from politics to family, even religion. When it got to subjects like "capitalism" though, dad seemed to lose interest.

Margaret joined us and filled me in on a recent murder in town, an unspeakable scandal. The gun had been discovered in an old well in the park just across from our house as she watched out the window hardly believing what she saw. One of my friends, now County Attorney, had just completed the successful prosecution of the accused. Quite a deal for such a quaint and quiet community. Later that evening I slipped into the other room and gave John a call. "Hey John, this is you're old buddy, Murph. My folks are telling me all about your big case. Quite a local hero."

"Murph, welcome back to town. You got it all wrong. I'm not made for this stuff. Someone hates me now. I'm number one on his list. Life's too short. So what're you up to, Murph? Rumor has it you're workin' here for a while, right?"

"Ya, john, but what I really got to know is: are you guys still playin' ball?"

"You bet. Need it more than ever. Tomorrow night at seven, elementary school, west door."

"Great, I'll be there."

That quick, the old routine was reestablished, the athletic supporter, shorts, sweat socks, Chuck's, faded T-shirt or jersey. Then the drive, the anticipation, enter to check out who's there, already planning match ups and strategies. Chitchat while loosening up with a few shots, then the game. Just like the old Catholic mass when it was still in Latin, the same everywhere, a soothing ritual bringing to life a certain reassuring rhythm. "Et introibo ad altare Dei. Ad Deum qui laetificat juventutem meum."

Good friendly games, everyone being on their best behavior because this was middle class America and I was new to the mix. Still, the game has a way of showing new shades of participant's personalities. Situations arise, intensity builds, and reaction is called

85

for. Always, winning has a degree of importance. That first night, superficially at least, the prevailing mood was Midwest, Christian cordiality. I was matched against a certain Terry Meekema. I wasn't particularly trying to show him up, but my outside J was going good, and, even though he was perfectly polite and proper, the subtleties indicated a potentially volatile dynamic. A forced smile here, clenched fist there. I saw Crusades, maybe even Inquisition.

Terry was an interesting character. You can see from his name he was Friesian, acceptable but not perfect. Worse, he wasn't originally from Orange City, only arriving for college, to study and play football, or, I should say, play football and study. Keep in mind that almost nowhere is the population so homogeneous, not even Holland. Meekie had become an insurance salesman, a position where being an insider is important and sucking up is a way of life. For a guy whose most basic gut characteristic is bulldog competitiveness, even abrasiveness, this meant significant frustration building like water behind a dam during a cloudburst. I was from Alton, Irish, a (former) Catholic, a draft dodger, all juicy "did you hear..." gossip goodies being whispered about at the "coffee klatschs" around town. But none of that was the real icer, as I was to discover later that night as we stopped at the one local establishment for refreshment.

John and I had been talking for a while when Terry joined us. After a couple of minutes of right talk, he proceeded directly to the point.

"So, Doc, you've been working for that radical farm worker labor union in California, and now, I hear you're heading for Mozambique," he began.

"Ya, we're thinking about it."

Obviously, having done his research, he continued, "Well does that mean that you're a c..., c..., c....' At first perplexed, I quickly surmised what he was getting at. Actually, a gutsy move. McCarthyism of the '50's still in full force, but he was going to plunge right in. On the one hand, curiosity and bravado were at work, yet when it got right down to saying it to me, a deeply ingrained uncertainty, even fear, surfaced. Demonization is a tough barrier to waltz through. Could I have had some sort of secret weapon in my athletic supporter just for such occasions? The look on his face, momentarily frozen in anguish, relaxed to a 'what the fuck' look and he spit it out: '...communist?"

A little flabbergasted, I quickly regained my composure, "Terry,' I said, lightly patting him on the shoulder, 'if you mean, good health care and a decent standard of living for everyone, ya, I guess I am." Typical ambivalent answer, I'm sure he thought. Oh well, more grist for the gossip mill.

John and I had a good time. Despite being the Republican County Attorney, Harvard graduate, he was as apolitical as they come. His attitude was eternally adolescent, enjoy life and minimize conflict. Better yet, his basketball game was an exclusive focus on defense and rebounding, the perfect complement to a hopelessly addicted gunner.

The next time I faced Meekema, it was in your face aggressive play. He was about my size, but had no outside game, relying on brute strength to get to, at least paint, if not the rack, and he could leap well and finish consistently. Several times the contact approached football level. We both fought to control ourselves, but I could see his blood beginning to boil more than once, just beneath the surface. Still, it was a words only game and afterwards we both congratulated each other on a spirited, good workout. As competitive as anyone, I rarely lost control, but with Meekie, we took it to the edge more often than I was really comfortable with. He did lose it several times, but with other players. I've always wondered if the secret weapon factor protected me from his wrath.

Working in Orange City went well, for the most part. Instead of "cansado," it was "benouwd", and for "sofocando" it was just "suf". There was no political context and I knew many of the patients, making for a more relaxed atmosphere. Still, being compared frequently to your own father brought certain expectations, and disease has a way of demanding respect no matter what.

One day I saw a nurse's child, a one year old with fever. No unusual findings, probably teething or a virus. Watch closely, symptomatic treatment, call if any change. That same night, a call, child worse, more fever, still alert. Options discussed. A few hours later, more concern, change in level of consciousness, meet me at hospital. At the hospital, it was readily apparent that this was serious.

The mottled look of the skin and the definite lack of appropriate responsiveness made the decision easy, for both of us, to ship the child to the regional hospital pediatrics department in Sioux City, an hour away. In a nightmarish end to the story, there was a respiratory arrest on the way, and full resuscitation had to be instituted, all with mom present. The child died. Autopsy showed overwhelming Hemophilus sepsis. I can't imagine a more horrible way to be taught a lesson about that condition.

Slowly, Janet was regaining her strength, and the children were adjusting to the new surroundings. It was a great opportunity for all of us to bond more meaningfully. Showing Liam all my childhood hiding places and reading the old books together were frequent activities. On one of our exploratory walks, having now moved to our own bucolic abode, we ran into a woman at the farm across the road. She had just strolled out to get the mail. Very friendly, looking as if she had stepped out of "American Gothic," our neighbor showed us all around the place, taking care to introduce Liam to all the animals and to explain how chores were done. She couldn't have been more down to earth and amiable. "Come and visit any time," she called as we headed out the long driveway. Only later did I discover that she was a sister to Robert Schuller, also an Alton native. I couldn't imagine anything farther from the "Crystal Cathedral" than the beautifully simple farm scene we saw that first day.

Our existence, there, was tentative if anything. We had taken the plunge and written to the Ministerio da Saude in Mozambique asking for work, thinking we would hear at any time. Little did we know that it would take better than a year for final arrangements to be made.

"Hey, Murph, you guys want to go skiing next weekend?" It was John on the phone.

"John, this is Iowa, if I'm not mistaken. Remember that glacier that came through? No hills, or are we going to pull each other behind the tractor?"

"Good one, Murph,' he responded laughing, 'I'm talking Breckenridge, as in Denver. The Sioux City Ski Club is sponsoring the trip; all we have to do is show up Friday, they take it from there."

We had done a little skiing in California, and had excellent baby sitters in grandma and grandpa, so I impulsively answered, "Por que, no."

"I don't speak French, but I take it that means you'll go. I've done it before; really a blast. Consider the arrangements made. I'll call you back with details."

Janet agreed, but not without some reluctance, having already learned that, with John, you never knew what to expect. "Hey, we could use a break, and, really, it's just a short drive to Sioux City," I reassured.

"Yes, but, if I remember my geography, Sioux City and Denver aren't even in the same time zone,' she cautioned, 'and you say we'll be back for you to work Monday? I've never experienced time travel before."

The next Friday after work, at 5 P.M., we piled into John's car, pulling into Sioux City just in time to load into a rickety old school bus, filled with smarmy office type people ready to chill for the weekend. We hadn't even exited the parking lot, before I began hearing pop tops, and registered the unmistakable waft of reefer. Guitars, song and merriment all the way through Nebraska. I don't even remember Colorado, but I vaguely recall a mawkishly maudlin decompensated version of "Mr. Tambourine Man" as the bus delivered us to Breckenridge just as the Saturday morning lifts were breaking their traces free.

"Murph, I'll get you these 210's so we can make more black runs today," intoned John as we geared up for the action. I was feeling no pain at the time and didn't fully catch the implication of what he was saying. Within minutes we were ascending the splendid slopes, high and higher. The thermometer at the summit read -28, but with little wind. The crisp air and marvelous panorama alone, made the trip worthwhile.

"I'll follow you," I yelled as we took off down the mountain in six inches of new powder. Pell-mell, my oblivious accomplice, roared between the ebony diamonds, me trailing, not wanting to appear adverse to adventure. Fun but foolish, as I quickly discovered that I had bitten off significantly more than I could chew. Covered with snow, after innumerable cataclysmic spills, failing even to negotiate a respectable traverse on the black, I limped into the presence of my erstwhile friend, who disregarded all semblance of subtlety in his animated display of amusement over my catastrophic dysfunction.

"You got to point the tips downhill more, Murph," he laughed.

"Objection, he's leading the witness."

"Overruled, Doctor. You said, last night, you'd carve up these hills like a cadaver."

"Extenuating circumstances, John. I do now know however, that my skiing technique, while in no way, shape or form, approaching the ugliness of your jump shot, may still be in need of polish."

"Touché, Murph. Let's go find Janet and do some bunnies."
The day was spent on a variety of trails, all beautiful. My skills increased considerably, but even with my "210's" shushin' to the max, I was always looking at John's butt. Light snow was falling as we finished the last run before dark. "I don't know about you guys, but I'm feeling something that's somewhere beyond total body pain, and that includes a near fatal dose of sheer exhaustion," offered Janet as we walked in stilt like fashion to the bus.

"I'll pretend I didn't hear that sorry remark," countered John. "I know this fantastic restaurant, just down the road from the hotel. I'll pick you up at your room in ten."

"Make that twenty, you glutton. We need hot showers to better enjoy this next phase of reckless abandon." My compromise was accepted but it seemed that almost no time had passed before John barged into our room with three 'purple snowshoes' in hand.

"Hey, Kids, thaw out with these."

"What is it John? I'm allergic to pomegranates."

"I don't know, exactly, but it's what the doctor ordered for occasions like this."

"Spare me the color commentary, you guys. I'm still not sure I'll live," commented Janet as we both helped prize her out of maturing recumbence.

After the second 'purple passion' or whatever, things became considerably less complicated and we had our last supper and crossed the Styx into the world of oblivion and even approached the place where the universe turns back on itself. All that remained the next morning were blurred images of dancing, drinking, discoursing…was there a disrobing in there? John said, at one point he distinguished himself by saving Janet from an avalanche.

The miracle of it all was that our Harvard wonder managed to arrange for the three of us to be at the lift line for Sunday morning's first run. It was like we were compelled to pack an entire season or even lifetime of bourgeois recess into one dramatic experience of excess. After the last run we literally crawled back to the bus, having now known the "ski weekend." But no, some of those decerebrate sons of hog farmers, had the audacity to reinitiate the goings on of the westward segment of our outing. To be completely honest, try as I might, I was unable to fully participate in that, somewhat anticlimactic, portion of our haute haj. Greeting the rising sun, we rambled into staid Orange, setting our minds back to the other dimension. The transformation was completed for me as, not a minute after entering the old farm house, I answered the clanging phone. "Dr. Murphy, we've got a gravida three para two patient of yours here who's eight centimeters dilated …."

"I'll be right over."

Mozambique was the poorest country on earth. A former Portuguese colony, recently added to the burgeoning list of sub-Saharan states gaining independence one way or another, it had an estimated 12 million inhabitants and twenty physicians. Our patient waiting had finally been rewarded when, one day, a beautifully stamped envelope arrived announcing that we were accepted and our tickets would be arriving soon. We located a Brazilian exchange student and began studying the new language. "Boa tarde, como vai?"

Meanwhile, life continued with work, lots of time with kids and grandparents, and a sizable dose of B-ball. John and I had entered a small tournament with a few of our local buds and we had been able to do enough things right to get to the final game. Our opponents were to be "The Kraayenbrinks," a team made up of five brothers and their father for a sub, all about 6'4" and very good. For me it was a flashback of sorts, because they hailed from Paullina.

The game was clean but hard fought. They were excellent shooters and seemed to draw fouls at will, getting to the line way more than their share. I was having one of those nights, nailing a sizzling percentage of shots I had no business taking. John kept feeding me as the battle came down to the wire. With 10 seconds to play, their youngest "special K," Randy, then just a 9th grader, hit a bomb to put them up two. We inbounded, and quickly advanced across the line before signaling for a time out.

In the huddle, John took charge. "OKAY guys, five seconds left, who do we go to?"

"Murph."

"Murph."

"Doc."

"Murph."

"Doc."

It was unanimous. "Listen up, then," I began to suggest. "Davey, you take it out. It'll be right here near half court. I'll be at the free throw line. You other guys start low, under the hoop. I don't think they want me to get the ball, so they'll be right on my butt. I'll break to mid court, then you guys sprint to the corners, as I pull the quickest about face I can muster. Davey, hit me at the free throw line, headin' toward the hole. Let's see if we can part the waters."

As we lined up, I noticed they had two guys on me. Great, I thought, they'll overplay for sure. As Davey slapped the ball (go slomo), I took off, as if out of blocks, for half court, both defenders doing their damnedest to deny me the rock. Then the power stop and reversal, yes, I got a half a step. Stride, stride, the ball crossing the now cleft Red Sea, perfect, entering my grasp with the inevitability of a total eclipse, a family of waning faces turning back to see the dagger play unfold, unable to react, or prevent their synchronous tide of anguished looks from punctuating the, as well as, delivered script. Lay-up completed, surviving a harmless half court heave, we went to O.T.

To our chagrin, we proceeded to dig ourselves a deep hole in the extra stanza, and only with desperation full court pressure, were we able to even maintain a feeble pulse. Down three with eight seconds left, we had all but given up. Just as my mind said, "If I get the ball, I've got to draw a foul," theirs must have emphasized, "no

---

foul." John winged it to me and I, determinedly, advanced it up the floor against properly token opposition. Just inside the free throw line I verged right carefully noticing the position of young Randy just off to the left. Sure enough, with just a tic or two left, he was drifting slightly towards my position. Instantly, I left my feet, jumping back towards the surprised neophyte, loading up and firing a prayer as our bodies met. Ball banked in at buzzer, but, unbelievably, no whistle. I waited, rubbed my ears, nothing.

"Ref, that's a call even in football," I begged.

"Incidental," he quipped.

"That could have been my moment," I continued. "And you're takin' it."

"I don't get paid enough, Doc. You'll have to live with it."

So it goes—the rhythms of a gym rat and life. Always push ahead, forging forward, keeping options open, no matter what. I clung to an old anonymous imperative directed at me during a game in the distant past, using it as an empowering alliterative metaphor, "Don't double dribble, Danny."

One nondescript day, four year old Liam pulled the tail off our pet gerbil. We tried to be non judgmental but did explain things in a way that could have been construed as being negative. During the night, she had babies (there was no mate), and in the morning mail, plane tickets for Maputo arrived. Do you know what that does to a child with an imaginative mind?

"I didn't really mean to pull that hard."

"It's okay, Liam."

"All night I dreamed about lions trying to get me."

"Umm."

"Where did the babies come from, Daddy?"

"Not from pulling the tail off, Son."

"Are there gerbils in Africa, Daddy?"

"Come on, Liam. Let's go outside and play."

I had signed a two-year contract to go half way around the world, with my wife and two toddlers, to a destiny unknown; the operative question being: how does one pack? We were told, anything you might need or want, bring, because you probably won't find it there. That's a tall order. We meticulously packed three trunks and shipped them by sea (dumb, really dumb), while the minimal bare essentials, we put into suitcases to fly with us.

Grandma and Grandpa were indispensable, helping with everything, especially the kids. The day before we were to leave, I gazed out the window and saw my dad playing nurf pepper with Liam and Conor. I wish I could have canned up the scene. It was a perfect summer day and the three of them were joking, laughing, and improvising in a totally carefree interaction. As I watched, I was thinking, "Look at Conor. He almost caught that one. Man, Liam is like a cat. And, dad, wow! At 72, reminds me of Pee Wee Reese. Must be genetics, we're just meant to play ball." Quickly, I caught myself and concluded, "No, this is about enjoying each other and getting the most out of every moment." Tears in my eyes, I turned back to help Janet and Margaret finish packing the last piece of luggage.

In the morning, all of us were in the car for the one hour trip to the Sioux City airport. Many things were left unsaid, but tugged at all of us, as we hugged each other for the last time, before walking to the tarmac and ascending the steps, turning to wave over and over, finally fatefully entering the plane for our flight pointing east.

First to Chicago, no problem, then on to JFK, where Janet and I both wanted to visit the city, but with only a six hour layover, we didn't think there was enough time. Liam was disappointed. First of all, the hero of his first and favorite movie, *King Kong*, had lived here. So, the Empire State building should definitely be seen. Secondly, thanks to my innovative story telling in situations where I had exhausted every tale from the troll under the bridge to variations of the wicked witch, our inquisitive four year old had become somewhat of an expert on Son of Sam, and was convinced we might be able to get a glimpse of him. Instead, we slowly wandered through the terminal, working our way to our next connection. Still, six hours is a long time, and it's difficult to keep your guard up at all times. As we were reading and talking, the boys played in the then, near empty portion of the huge airport. Suddenly, near disaster struck. Shattering the relative silence, a piercing scream came to us from behind. "Conor!" Turning quickly, we saw Liam running toward Conor who had somehow climbed onto the luggage conveyor belt and was being carried toward the flap covered opening like a bowling ball being returned for the second shot. No time to lose, both of us jumped over the seats, scurrying toward our endangered baby, heading toward who knows where. He could have ended up in a baggage compartment on a flight to Afghanistan, Cusco, or Reykjavik. Images of power takeoff incidents flashed through my mind, while Janet saw only Willy Wonka's chocolate factory. We got there just as Liam was about to lose his fragile grip on the only part of his brother remaining in the continental U.S.—his foot. Pulling him out, we all breathed a sigh of relief. Conor, on the other hand, thought it all a big joke, and was laughing. Unlike a near death experience, he says he can't describe what he saw on "the other side."

Then on to Rome and a one day wait, which we tried to take advantage of to experience the new culture. First, we were hardly able to get out of our hotel because of a huge throng of marchers/rioters hoping to overthrow the government. Next, Liam got us asked to please leave the area, as he vomited three times in the Sistine Chapel. Finally, fearful and frustrated at the airport, encountering considerable communication difficulty, we were told that our luggage was too heavy and wouldn't be allowed on the plane. Desperation mounting, I played the dedicated expatriate doctor card, and, more importantly, agreed to pay "divisas." Wearily, we walked onto the Mozambican Airline flight to Maputo.

Far into the night, sailing over Mediterranean, skirting the land of the wise sphinxes, and blowing past the dune draped Sahara, I could not sleep. East, the Horn of Africa, approaching Earth's greatest latitudinal circumference, I couldn't help wondering how Columbus felt as his ships passed the point where supplies no longer allowed the return option. Dosing, dreaming, the mother of sunrises, catapulted from the site of Lord Jim's catastrophe, stopped momentarily, highlighting Hemingway's snowcapped tombstone, then slowly lifted the veil from the vast Serengeti, where life and death timelessly coalesce.

"Da licenca, da licenca." I awakened to see La, tall and elegant queen. Immediately the line, "To your knees, jackal," came to mind, but seeing no Lord Greystoke, I was forced to pause momentarily, as I attempted to correctly construe the raft of novel sensory cues overloading my semi alert central nervous system circuitry. "Matabichu," explained the smiling stewardess, handing us our breakfast trays. No insects being found, we dug into the offering, finishing just in time to hear, "Estamos, quasi a chegar a Mocambique." Madagascar to our left, we followed the Straight of Mozambique, gradually descending over the Tropic of Capricorn, traversing the Limpopo, finally approaching Mavalane, and touching down 12,000 miles from Iowa.

Getting off the plane, we easily accomplished, but there ended any semblance of control we had hoped to have over our destiny. Surprised at the moderate temperature, in custody of two rambunctious, inquisitive charges, pathetically inadequate at interpreting the signs, much less what people said, we were literally lost within minutes. Not that the airport was that large. Of the two doors, we had entered the wrong one, and found ourselves in the "diplomatic area." A friendly Mozambican gentleman noticed our confused, helpless appearance, and guided us to the larger section of the terminal. Everyone seemed to know exactly what they were doing but we hadn't a clue. No one met us, no waving sign, "Dr. Murphy," nothing. Looking outside the building, I saw no taxi, no bus, only a single road heading off through countryside, no city in sight. "OK Janet, this is no big deal. We both have college education. We can deal with this. Now what do we do?"

"Well Dr. Doolittle, how about I watch the kids, and you find somebody who speaks English or Spanish, use your brain, improvise, beg, cry, and call 911. We've got at least five days without water, more with no food, go!"

"Thanks for the encouragement. Isn't Africa wonderful, kids?"

Wandering off, I could have just as well been on the moon. The place was now nearly empty, but I did find a woman who was patient enough to give me what hints she could with our limited language abilities. Changing dollars into escudos and finding a phone, I taxed my brain to properly follow the right procedure for placing a call. We had a phone number for a friend we had worked with several years earlier in Delano, who had just recently signed on as an obstetrician in Maputo's Hospital Central. "Hey, it's actually ringing," I said to myself on about the fourth try. When George himself answered, I nearly swooned.

"George, old friend, old buddy, we're here at the airport, kids fading fast. What do we do?"

"Just stay put, Dan. I'll try to hustle up a vehicle and come rescue you. Great to have you here."

Music to my ears. Nearly two hours later, George arrived. We were learning rapidly the underdeveloped world meaning of the Portuguese phrase, "ha de ver", or, translated, "in just a little while." Nevertheless, we were advancing, anxiously observing and registering all we could.

George's flat was on the eighth floor of a fairly modern high rise overlooking the Indian Ocean. After a meal of fish and rice, we got the children settled down, then proceeding to pump our host for every bit of info we could think of. The discussion rambled far into the night, an expatriate tradition, before George pulled out his guitar and treated us to his version of "Guadalajara" followed by "La Cucaracha." A few sips of wine, and we too were singing, "Mocambique oie, oie, oie," and "Nos somos amigos de Frelimo."

Early the next morning, George had to go to work, leaving me detailed instructions on what to do, none of which seemed to work. I managed, however, to make it to the Ministry of Health, and eventually ended up in the office of the minister himself, Dr. Helder Martins. His English was worse than my Portuguese, but after an animated discussion, I came away with the phrase "tu vais a Gurue."

Arriving back at the apartment, I helped get everyone ready for a venture out into the city. The day was gorgeous as we walked the wide boulevards richly swathed in verdure and floral decoration. To our amazement, monkeys cavorted in the trees, delighting the boys. As we observed the people and the shops, everyone seemed busy and yet friendly. Traffic, although not heavy, stayed to the left, steering wheels on the right, mostly Land Rovers, Land Cruisers, Nivas and Ladas, along with an occasional bus and even a few Mercedes, all with diplomatic plates. By chance, we ended up in a large well-kept park bordered by a maze of terraced pathways winding downward, through beds of tropical shrubs and flowers, to the sea. Distributed along the way were statues, some classical, others modern, including one of a dragon that particularly caught Liam's fancy. Waves breaking at our feet, gulls flying immobile, warm never ending breeze beckoning, we traced the promenade, basking in the carefree feeling of the moment, now festinating, now pausing, lead on by the spontaneous whims of uncluttered playfulness.

Later, back at the flat, George arrived, bringing along three of the total of six Americans known to be in the entire country at that time.

Following introductions, he asked, "Well Dan, what did you find out?"

"I'm not sure,' I answered, 'but I think I'm assigned to a place called Gurue."

"You're kidding." It was Joe speaking. He had been in the country the longest, and had traveled quite extensively. The serious look on his face had me concerned, but then a wide grin began to form as he continued speaking, "I've been there, and it's probably the most beautiful place in Mozambique."

"Damn, guess we're lucky."

"Hard to get to, though. Almost in Malawi. You'll be on your own. Good luck!"

Two days later, our plane tickets were handed to us. I had been to the hospital with George, and we had been exploring farther out into the city. A visit to the local Museum of Natural History revealed much about what the colonial mentality had been, as we encountered scene after scene of ferocious animals preying on each other. Language skills were coming, but not nearly fast enough. Exhilarated by the freshness and shear proportions of the challenge, but certainly not without anxiety, we said our good-byes to our host, before boarding the domestic flight for Quelimane. Our trunks hadn't yet arrived, but George assured us that he would have them forwarded to us as soon as they came in.

Soaring north for one thousand miles, we chatted with whomever we could, even attempting to engage the children in our new mode of communication, not knowing that as we jetted past the maw of the legendary Zambezi river and touched down at our destination, it was as if we had entered another world. One step out the door of the plane, our faces were slapped by coastal tropics. Hot and humid is a woefully inadequate cliche. Sultry, sauna like, steamy, get closer to the feel of it. Languor, lassitude, total cellular ennui, yes. Maybe a metaphor conveys the ambiance. Picture yourself in a vast swamp. There's drizzle in the air yet the sun is bearing down mightily. You've been secured to an insect ridden mangrove all extremities tangled by slimy vines. Just in front of you is an open door to hell where legions of condemned souls, naked all, perform Jane Fonda aerobics in slow motion. Trudging to the tiny terminal, we looked in vain for the promised functionary, who, of course, wasn't there, and maybe didn't even exist. Standard procedure, I thought, as I proceeded directly to the phone, and performed the magic, hearing the now familiar refrain, "ha de ver, ha de ver."

"Well," I said to Janet. "Here we are. It has to get better."

She looked at me, beads of sweat—or were they tears—running down her face, flicking a roach off baby Conor's leg, and said, "What have we gotten ourselves into?"

"They're coming, " I reassured halfheartedly. "Remember, this isn't Gurue. They said it was beautiful. It's lonely and trying when you're at the vanguard. This is our initiation, we're being tested. Now we cope, and continue our commitment. Can't look back from here."

"Nice speech, Che. Could you put the revolution on hold for a minute and help me change this kid's diaper?" Just as we finished performing the pedestrian chore, we saw an official looking black man coming towards us.

"Doctor Dani? " he inquired, reaching out his hand. "O meu nome é Bilal. Boas vindas a Quelimane."

Yes! Hope springs eternal. There was a structure here, I thought as we jumped into his Land Rover and took off through the wetlands. Bilal explained many things to us as we wound our way toward the provincial capital, most of which went wasted or, at best, misinterpreted. Realizing our difficulty, he attempted English in a futile effort to communicate, but was equally unsuccessful. Nevertheless, we newcomers were fascinated just viewing all the strange and wondrous sights. Now a water buffalo pulling a cart, rice paddies, rice paddies, bamboo stand, thatched roof waddle dwellings, papaya and mango abound, banana and cane, passing through a huge coconut grove, more and more cement buildings, and people, people everywhere. Men on bicycles, women wearing capulanas, some topless, all toting children, firewood, packages, on their strong backs, twenty liters of water atop their heads, human, vital, purposeful, engaged in life.

Pulling in to the rambling complex of provincial medical buildings, my mind was exploding with ideas and questions. So much to learn, so much to do! I couldn't wait to get started. Soon we were in the office of Dr. Ching, diminutive, youthful, Chinese ethnic, but Mozambican to the core, now responsible for the health of the most populous province in the world's poorest country.

"Welcome, very glad to meet you," she began, businesslike and confident, yet friendly. "Dona Janeta, Bilal will take you and the children to your flat, and Dr. Dani, I'll show you around our hospital."

Our first stop was the Emergency Room, where I was startled to encounter four small children receiving blood transfusions. Had there been some sort of horrendous accident with blood loss? Seeing my consternation, my host explained that these were routine cases of children found to have hemoglobin levels under four (normal in our country being 11-14), who are given blood to prevent congestive heart failure, while treatment is being started for Ancylostoma, falcip., and iron deficiency, invariably present in all these cases. "Oh," I said, which pretty accurately reflected how prepared I felt, at that moment, to deal with such things. On and on we went, TB ward, leprosy section, a huge area devoted solely to malnutrition, kwashiorkor and marasmus along with everything in between, obstetrics with high incidence of ecclampsia and ruptured uterus, surgery and orthopedics, with hernia, hydrocoele, vesico-vaginal fistula, burns, and fractured femur being most frequent. Moving between buildings, twice we saw rats scurrying about. "That's a big problem," Dr. Ching told me. "They're all over town and we can't control them. People have no good way to store food and garbage is collected irregularly at best." We ended at the Preventative Medicine dept. Never have I felt so overwhelmed and ill prepared.

Later as I walked through the downpour, a near everyday occurrence, engrossed in serious contemplation, a small child ran up to me, offering a protective banana leaf to deflect the worst of the onslaught. "Obrigado, menino" I carefully articulated, accepting the gift. He smiled, revealing perfect ivory white incisors, before scampering off barefooted, wearing only a pair of ragged shorts, apparently impervious to the cloudburst. That one act symbolized the spirit I was to encounter over and over.

Soon I was telling Janet all about my experiences, and she hers. She had one pressing concern, however. "I hate to bring this up, but we have no food."

"Nothing?"

"Unless you count those little crackers we saved from the plane. I talked to the Swedes down the hall and they said they'd get their servant to arrange a servant for us. Then he can scour the town to get something. Apparently there isn't much out there. You have to know someone, and even then, it's a matter of luck. The stores have been basically empty for the last month. Lots of flooding, roads impassable, I guess. They didn't seem too excited about it, like it's normal."

"When do we get this helper?" I asked, already knowing the answer, which we both exclaimed in unison. "Há de ver."

That night we went to sleep hungry, a new experience for all of us. Funny how your priorities change when you venture deep into the third world. Basic survival instinct comes into play, adjustments in ways of thinking, certain things always just below the surface in your mind like food, potable water, shelter, contingency planning in case of who knows what. Suddenly all senses are on alert. You must see all, know all, language, culture, customs, current conditions—even rumors take on added significance. Insecurity can be a powerful motivational force, especially when you have small children. What I came to understand more as I observed others, was the relativity of perspective. It all depends on what you're used to, your experience. If things are as they've always been, you don't expect more. One can't even dream of things outside of their repository of information. For us, that night, such philosophical musings were not only irrelevant and superfluous, but actually offensive, doing nothing but exacerbate the pangs.

Our scariest thought, though, was that we had taken a quantum leap from the U.S. to Maputo, and another even greater vault to our present situation, yet still, we were nowhere near our destination.

We stayed in Quelimane for ten days. The man did show up and was able to find rice, shrimp, and tangerines. My time was spent in the hospital voraciously registering all I could, diseases, protocols, available resources, and language, language, language. Early on, assisting in the E.R. on a case of a young girl who appeared disheveled and disoriented, I learned about "feitisaria," the local version of witchcraft, and "macangueiros," the practitioners of the age old tradition. Janet became like a frontier woman, learning to do all the basics from scratch. Here, nothing was for sure. It was survival by wit, hook and crook being viable options. We did manage to take the children on some long excursions exploring the nearly five hundred year old dilapidated former Portuguese outpost and port. Vasco da Gama had first visited in the year 1500, Arab traders even before that, interacting with the local dominant Chuabo culture. A new hotel had been built in the center of town providing sharp contrast to the prevailing architectural style, early "canisu." On the bank of the Licungo river on its way to the nearby sea, we visited the abandoned white chapel where, for two centuries, slaves were "blessed" before being shipped out. One evening we attended the local theater and saw a Hong Kong version of "King Kong" titled "O Coloso Pekin," with Portuguese subtitles. Liam was fascinated. There were several parks in town where, while not well kept, still flowers proliferated in abundance, thriving in the tropical climate.

Just as the intensity of our situation was beginning to ameliorate, Bilal informed us that our ride was in town. We would be leaving early the next day for the journey up country to Gurue.

"What are we going to do? We still don't have our trunks?" Janet was hurriedly putting things into our suitcases.

"We don't have any options," I said. "They'll send them when they get them. There's definitely a different rhythm here."

"Dan, nothing happens unless you personally make it go yourself. We'll never see any of it. All Liam's home schooling stuff is in there, books, toys, clothes, medicines, toothpaste, even your stupid deflated basketball and nets!"

"Hmm, I'm beginning to see your point. I'll remind Bilal. All we can do is keep on it, but we have to go. Rides don't come very often."

It was like heading to another planet Passing a restless night, at the first crimson sign of day, filled with apprehension and excitement, we four green but determined American expats piled into the back of a no frills jeep transport driven by Agostino, the young Italian physician whom I was to replace, not so sadly abandoning our squalid surroundings, hoping to reach the Namuli highlands by dusk.

Winding our way out of town, we watched the women already building morning fires, scraping coconuts, pounding corn into meal, beginning the nonstop quotidian grind of work that is the life of virtually every third world female old enough to have language skills. Following the two lane blacktop, being careful to avoid the increasing numbers of school children, all in blue shirts, some on bicycle, most walking, on their way to learn, for the first time, anything but the colonial perspective. Many greeted us by waving and shouting "buleia." Liam waved and returned the call, "buleia," thinking it was a form of "bom dia." Laughing, our driver explained that they were all asking for rides, an experience few had ever enjoyed.

The road straightened, our velocity increasing, whizzing past the ever more scarce "palhotas," surrounded now by "machambas," fields of rice, manioc, corn, and beans. Peasants paused saluting the passing vehicle, before resuming their short hoed labor. As the new sun relentlessly dispersed the morning haze, we approached Namacurra, a mere bump in the road by our standards, but here, an important district capital. Slowing down, we passed a few stores, a diesel powered mill, a small outdoor market, and a train station, serving the one short span of tracks existing in the province.

Continuing northwest out of town, we noticed a large sisal plantation, hardly producing because of lack of demand. Sailing along, just as the heat was usurping its predestined share of our consciousness, relief appeared just off the road. Pulling over, we all jumped out, stretched momentarily, and approached the small entrepreneur proudly displaying fresh cut pineapples, perfectly aligned according to size.

"Cuanto?" I queried in perfect Portuguese.

"Doze quinientos o pequeno, e viente e cinco escudo o grande," recited the unknowing capitalist.

A quick calculation into dollars, an exercise that I soon realized to be totally futile since their currency had no value elsewhere and almost no value even within the country, and I was ready to purchase. The driver suggested that I could negotiate down but the price was so insignificant that I just couldn't see it.

The fruit was dramatically better than anything found in a supermarket. Chomping on what has to be one of nature's most perfect mixes of fructose and ascorbic acid, we ambled back to the jeep. I had learned an essential lesson for survival in the bush; always be on the lookout for any opportunity to acquire anything you might need. I could soon further elucidate the principle; be prepared to barter. Soap, matches, cooking oil, all proved much more efficacious than any currency, especially in remote regions.

"Pode guiar," offered Agostino, making a circular motion with his outstretched hands. Before I could respond he threw me the keys and hopped into the left door leaving me no option.

"Damn," I thought as I clumsily sat down on the right, finding the ignition, clutch, brake, and accelerator unchanged, but having to shift with the left. Fortunately there was little traffic and by repeating "stay left, stay left," over and over, I was able to avoid head on collision. Before long we were approaching Mocuba, second largest city in Zambesia.

On the outskirts of this apparent slightly overgrown ragtag village, was a partly constructed large complex of modern buildings, looking very out of place. "Pull in here, Dan. This is an Italian project, a cotton mill. We could use a break, and I told my compatriots we'd stop."

The Italians were very friendly and insisted that we stay for a meal. While Janet and I kept busy with Liam and Conor, we both, also, observed this new anomalous scenario. Servants abounded, obsequiously following frivolously given orders. There were cigarettes, meat, butter, and even wine. This was a slice of Italy! We enjoyed the privilege, yes, but, feeling excluded by more than language incompatibility, both of us were automatically troubled by the thinly veiled patronizing attitude. They, themselves, may have been well intentioned, their actions being merely standard operating procedure, but, on the other hand, there was no tinge of Gramci here. Exhibiting a different mindset, these were capitalist consultants, mercenaries of a sort, here with what seemed like unlimited foreign currency, willing and able to tap into unfathomable resources. Definitely a different sort of commitment, and one that we would come to know all too well.

After this renaissance repast, Agostino and I went to town to pick up supplies at the regional hospital serving upper Zambesia. While he collected medicines, I toured the grounds with the local physician, also Italian, named Reno. Coming from Naples, his family being lifelong communists, this man showed me a poignantly contrasting ethic. Soft spoken, intelligent, respectful, and obviously dedicated, he carefully explained to me, all the problems his position presented, and what his plans were. He introduced me to the new surgical technician from Zambia, now to be responsible for covering major operations for this half of the province, more than one million people. As we departed, shaking hands with Reno, he promised to visit Gurue soon, as it was one of the most important districts included under his jurisdiction. Inspired, I now felt I had a colleague, someone with whom I could share concerns, a true internationalist with an agenda basically congruent with my own.

Returning for Janet and the kids, we stopped to fill the jerry can, before beginning the final and most difficult leg of our 400 km. inland thrust. Gradually, we were gaining altitude. People were now Macua, not Chuabo, and cashew trees became ever more prevalent. The air was becoming noticeably more tolerable. Twice, in what the boys thought were exciting diversions, we had to leave the road to carefully drive through rivers at natural fords, bridges either nonfunctional or not yet built. "During the rainy season, you can't pass," explained Agostino, leaving unanswered the obvious concern of what to do if you absolutely had to get to the other side. Now men were seen carrying spears and bows and arrows. Shoes had long since disappeared. Continuing up the veldt, we entered Namarroi district, passing an occasional roadside store, colored with a smattering of whitewash, run by either a mestizo, or a Muslim Gujarati, invariably carrying a Karachi passport, all Hindus having been expelled by Portugal in the aftermath of Goan repatriation. Mostly it was open countryside dotted with ever increasing clusters of mud brick huts occupied by groups of matrilineal tied inhabitants, surrounded by fields that now included sorghum and ground nuts.

Then came Ile, most densely populated and geographically largest district, yet the most primitive and isolated. Running out of pavement, we tested the heavy duty shocks, bumping over the corrugated, then profoundly pocked track, observing cattle, goats, chickens, dogs, alternating with guinea fowl, monkeys, and an occasional antelope.

"Gurue has a direct connection with Malawi, and is much better off," stated our guide. "Here they have excellent agricultural conditions, but they're stranded, isolated by location. The Portuguese left little infrastructure, so getting here is difficult."

Now we began visibly ascending, gradually coursing our way into more forested surroundings and finally stopping at a sizable river crossed by a small but solid looking bridge. "Pull over here. This is the Rio Lua, doesn't look like much now but a monster during the rains. The other side is Gurue district, your responsibility. To the right, up in those hills, is Socone, three tea plantations, very beautiful. But let's walk up to that little store; I want you to meet someone."

Still far from fluent, but realizing that from here on in, everything would be more crucial and relevant to my work and our lives, I struggled to enter all the data I could as we approached the small apparently generic roadside shop. Inside, although I didn't really notice any different products, there did seem to be more abundance. The Portuguese proprietor, a Mr. Junqueiro, greeted us with unmitigated exuberance, as if we were long lost family, insisting that we stay for a snack. Winding through the trees, we first came upon a clearing which he had developed as a garden. Rows of vegetables, neatly outlined by spaced trees, papaya, mango, and citrus, all highlighted by rectangular beds of tropical flowers, made us feel like Alice in Wonderland. His house came right out of what I imagined to be, rural Portugal, a generation past. As his servants worked, one even taking the children out to play, he told us his story. Having little education and seeing no opportunity as a youth, he and his brothers, decided to make the adventurous leap to Ultramar. Finally arriving in this area, they started with nothing and built up everything to its glorious pre-independence colonial state. Gurue had been Vila Junqueiro then. Much of the tea was that of their family. He, however, never enjoyed the bustle of the city life and settled here in the bush, and loved it. His wife had died recently, and, while he thought frequently of returning to Portugal, this, too had become home, and maybe he would die here. Later, I was to hear a far different interpretation of these events. After an excellent meal and the mandatory tea, we departed, promising to stop again, whenever we could.

This close to the equator, you get 12 hours of day light year round, and already shadows were stretching out further towards the East as we bumped along. "Still two or three hours to go," informed Agostino. "It's not dangerous at night, just more difficult." Higher and higher, we climbed, finally passing the mission at Invinha before entering the wondrously manicured plantation area surrounding the city of Gurue, nestled at the base of Mt. Namuli. Snaking from one tea production unit to the next, all recently nationalized, we saw the sun grow and turn a brilliant orange before dazzling us with a dramatic dip beneath the undulating true western horizon, retracting its long strands of light from the panorama of strange and wondrous sights. The mood of Nat King Cole's "Twilight Time" seemed apropos as we entered the town triumphantly. We had completed an incredible journey over two continents, half way around the globe, from the most to the least developed, capitalist to communist, traversing oceans and rivers, crossing numerous social, cultural and language barriers, penetrating deep into the darkness. As we stepped out of the jeep for the last time, immersing in the perfect still of night, the intricate intermittent rhythm of tom-toms, echoing from somewhere in the surrounding hills, reverberated an apparent greeting.

This was Africa, site of the most personal of Darwinian manifestations, where adaptive development of melanin and apocrine function boosted Homo sapiens to a dominant position under direct attack of ultraviolet rays. Inexorably, waves of Bantu peoples filled the continent, culminating in the great societies of Zimbabwe, intricate trade hubs like Timbuktu, keen Kalahari Bushmen, fierce Zulus, and a vast array of groups from the Masai to rain forest pygmies. In this millennium, the seeds of commerce were planted by Arab traders skirting the Sahara by sea to exploit both the human and material resources of the eastern coastal areas. Western Europeans, capitalizing on ever more sophisticated weaponry and sea faring capability, began to partake in the feed. White man's burden, mostly typhus, smallpox, syphilis and measles, along with the devastating assault of slave trade, dealt the continent a crippling blow. Quarreling over the spoils, in 1925 the dominant western monarchs and despots finally met to arbitrarily carve up the sub-Sahara, according to their ignorant self-serving whims, leaving the region with boundaries very close to what is presently extant. Disastrously ethnic borders had been left without consideration.

Early on, the area that was to become Mozambique, despite many fierce attacks by other competing sea powers, came to be dominated by Portugal, then a force to be reckoned with. Known along with other colonies as Ultramar, and settled in coastal areas only, by the under classes of what was becoming one of modern Europe's least developed countries, this colony and it's diverse hodgepodge of ethnic groupings, was given a 500 year lesson in the workings of western culture and capitalism. A major area for slave trade, brutal forays deep into the bush, always accompanied by Christian missionary presence, motivated by an equal greed for ivory to be unmercifully gleaned and toted to the coast, left a trail of death and grief, finally culminating in vast tracts of geography devoid of human or pachydermic presence. Always in revolt, indigenous people were press-ganged into service, "taxed" into cotton production, squeezed into sugar and coconut work, and induced out of desperation into distant mines, but without citizenship in their own land, having no suffrage, denied any education beyond elementary, and provided with no infrastructure where it didn't directly benefit the Portuguese colonialist.

Talking to Africans in Gurue, I heard how the Portuguese arrived in the late 20's, and built the tea factories and plantations intimidating local chieftains and utilizing liberally gun and whip to assure progress. One infamous incident, following an insurrection, included a retaliatory raid on Namorroi, leaving many dead, securing temporary peaceful production, but also an undying hate and resentment. Africans had no legal recourse and had to defer to whites at every juncture. Everywhere I went people stopped and bowed, even at a distance, showing how ingrained their subjugation had become. Everyone could relate tales of indiscriminate prejudicial recrimination resulting in everything from material loses to physical abuse, including sexual incidents and even occasional fatalities.

As African independence movements, influenced by the cold war, gained momentum, indigenous struggles within the Portuguese colonies asserted their demands. In one example of classic misguided response, in the northern Mozambican locality known as Mueda, after calling for a town meeting to resolve growing demands for human rights, Africans found themselves surrounded by Portuguese troops, who promptly opened fire with automatic weapons in a particularly appalling display of arrogance and brutality.

As confrontation escalated Frelimo's first leader, Eduardo Mundlane, friend of the Kennedy's, succumbed to an exploding package. Samora Machel took the reins, and, as General Salazar, Portugal's answer to Spain's Franco, reeling from the effects of multiple colonial struggles, was toppled in a coup d'etat, guided the East African nation to independence.

The U.S., in varying degrees, backed its European allies in the colonial struggles, more so in the case of Portugal, due to our huge military presence in the Azores which was critical in supporting our growing debacle in Viet Nam. Lip service by the State Dept. and various Administration spokespersons couldn't hide the overwhelming posture of support for white colonialism pervading CIA and military thinking. Leaders in Frelimo, including Machel who had spent considerable time in Algeria, recently winning independence from France in an epic struggle, and having visited USSR, drawing on their long and bitter experience with western ideas, chose a single party socialist system of government, and soon declared themselves a Marxist-Leninist state.

Their agenda included an end to racism, sexism, and tribalism. Guided by a true internationalism, they supported democratic grass root movements whenever possible. Universal education and health care, along with state development of infrastructure and large agricultural and industrial projects along with thriving small scale private family ventures, were to be the backbone of development. True enfranchisement, based on local autonomy, under the guiding wing of democratic centralism structured within a vanguard party, was the order of the day. Despite the flight of the vast majority of Portuguese nationals, basically all the skilled functionaries present within the country, who also systematically destroyed all they couldn't carry out with them, hope abounded throughout the fledgling country as we came onto the scene.

In health, only about twenty Portuguese doctors remained, most in Maputo, for a population of twelve million. I was District Medical Officer for a 5000 sq. km. area of rugged mountainous terrain, with no paved road, inhabited by 200,000 people. Well-thought-out plans existed for dealing with all the major diseases and conditions. Implementation was like dribbling alone, through an endless full court press with one hand tied behind your back, not knowing where the dead spots were on the floor, opponents, each with their unique garb, sometimes trapping, then fouling, screaming and crying in a cacophony of barely intelligible invective, and nary a time out available. I couldn't wait to take the ball out of bounds.

My first day was spent on an extensive tour of the entire district, a daunting undertaking in itself. Ricardo was my official driver, and proved to be invaluable, knowing not only roads, paths, and shortcuts, but language, customs, and, most importantly, people. Even in the most remote corners, he seemed to not only know someone, but even to have a distant relative of some sort. "Ricardo," I asked, after one particularly friendly stop to visit what he had said was his family, "I thought you said your family was in Noela?"

"That's my other family," he smiled.

With each encounter, I tried to learn names, meet local leaders, talk with any health providers, official or other, make connections, always planning in my mind, thinking of health, health....what could be done here...hmmm... how can we do this...let's see...I wonder if.... The names of the places alone were challenging: Nicorropali, Tetete, Maxixe, Vehiua, Nintulo. As we traveled on, Portuguese was useless, so I began learning "Lumwe," an unwritten Bantu dialect. "Moni, moni, mocala pama?" Hello, how are you?

At one point we seemed to be off road, heading randomly through the bush. Ricardo reassured me that this was the best way. "You wanted to see the whole district, didn't you?"

"Yes, but..."

"It's just ahead."

Over an hour later, we entered a beautiful valley, and pulled up to a small group of huts, near a stream falling from the adjacent mountain, and gurgling past our end of the world location. This is where I'll come, I thought, in case of nuclear holocaust, or if I ever have to go seriously "underground." While we waited for the mandatory meal, I got the grand tour by the enthusiastic head honcho host. They wore bark, cut from special trees, soaked in water and beat with a stick until soft. Could last months, he explained, but be careful not to get too near the fire. We saw fruit trees that Ricardo said had no name in Portuguese, cleverly irrigated small plots with a variety of grains and vegetables, and a special area where just the right clay was found for making pottery. I saw almost no metal here, people living probably much as they had a thousand years ago. The meal was quite tasty, piri piri held back a degree in my honor. "Halacani," I repeated, in a sincere attempt to relate in their language, shaking everyone's hand as we got up to depart.

"By the way, Ricardo," I inquired as we motored away. "What was that meat we had?"

"Rato, senhor doutor," he smiled, giving me a quick glance.

Well, there's a first, I thought, suddenly feeling a touch of ptomaine. About three kilometers later, without warning, our Land Cruiser died. Two attempts with the ignition. Nothing. Great, we're only a week's forced march from the nearest garage, and I can't remember how Tarzan kept off the hyenas.

"Nao ha problema," reassured Ricardo routinely, sensing my consternation, as he swung open the door and jumped to the ground, nonchalantly heading to the gas cap.

"Oh, we're out of gas?"

"No, no. It's nothing. I'll show you!"

I could hardly believe myself as I watched him take a deep breath and carefully place his mouth in an air tight fit, inside the uncovered fuel aperture. I knew that I was being reality tested nearly every minute lately, but this must have been something in the rat meat or some secret herb they gave me, hallucinogenic fungi. He proceeded to blow as hard as he could, puffing up his cheeks like a bull frog, holding it until his face turned approximately lavender. Then, not only did he jump back into the driver's seat, he shut the door, like the fool imagined that he actually did something, fixed it. His expression, however, didn't even show a trace of doubt. That was worrisome. When the motor purred with the first flick of the key, I nearly fell out the window, post graduate degree and all. Meandering along, now through forest, I recovered enough to ask exactly what had happened. He told me that lots of times the fuel we got wasn't clean and had a tendency to form sludge in the fuel line or pump, and with a little air pressure it would clear. Two weeks later, the same thing happened to me when I was out alone. Confidently, I blew into the tank just as I had seen Ricardo do, holding it as long as

I could. Running out of air, I abruptly let up and loosened my tightly pursed lips, only to be greeted by a tremendous backwash of dirty diesel filling my mouth and instantly spreading by surface action to my deepest alveoli. I thought I'd die right there in the bush, dyspneic and coughing worse than a malnourished village child with advanced pertussis. After about ten minutes, to my chagrin, I realized that I was going to survive and forced myself back into the jeep. It started, of course, and drove back to Gurue. Barely able to speak, I went directly to Ricardo.

"Oh," he laughed. "I forgot to explain that, depending on how full the tank is, you have to let up slowly. The same thing happened to me twenty years ago." How would I ever make it here! Shaking my head, I went home to sit and sip some hot tea, thinking a million thoughts at once.

As District Medical Officer, I was given the house of one of the former colonial physicians. Strategically positioned, it's verandah afforded an awe inspiring view of Namuli, dressed to the waist in Jacaranda hemmed plaits of tea, and from whose mouth, at an altitude of 900 meters, fell faintly whispering, the Rio Licungo, announcing her origin, in a never ending calendar cataract. Our yard was more like the grounds of an estate, including papaya, quince, guava, mango, orange, peach, passion fruit, and avocado trees. A garden area included perennial strawberries and flowers highlighted dramatically by porcelain rose. Down one path was a chicken coop, rabbit hutch, and a sand box, with nearby rubber trees. Enclosed by inlaid stone hedge, the set up provided an adventurous contained play environs for the children. Tastefully tucked under the residence itself, were the servants quarters, along with adjacent open air space for laundry and charcoal cooking. We occupied the main living portion, consisting of six high ceiling, parquet floored rooms, and two verandahs, one protected from the rain dancing down from said elevations, the other more like a granite deck, tastefully positioned to welcome any visitors. On the tiled roof was the customary collection tank, assuring availability of our share of the 75 inches of rain regularly blessing the locale each year. At first glance, it seemed our greatest adjustment would be mastering the subtle ritual of the bidet. Practical reality, however, slapped us early and hard.

Infrastructure, designed purely for the support of the Portuguese elite, collapsed and vanished at independence. Priorities now included all Mozambicans. Having the potential to produce an export crop gave us a slight edge, but being so far removed from Maputo, and depending on functional roads, transport, docks, shipping, etc., along with technical necessity of spare parts, fuel and machinery, all of which had to be imported, proved to be a near impossible challenge for the infant nation. Thus electricity, and all that depended on it, like running water, appeared sporadically for any of a number of reasons, mostly lack of diesel fuel for the city generator or mechanical difficulty. Food, even staples, the same. Basic products like matches, soap, and cooking oil could disappear for months. Many times, stores had nothing, and the market place displayed only garlic and tobacco. Having one of the few telephones proved to be mostly ornamental, even local calls to the hospital frequently not available. Mail, tortoise like at best, was about a 50-50 proposition for ever getting through at all. Combined with the fact that no one else in the district spoke even rudimentary English, our isolation was severe. Life style, even survival, was by connections and arrangements, of which, initially, we had none. Soon Janet met Toni Encarnacao, nee Junquiero, of the Lua Junquiero's we had already encountered, and I, through work, began connecting throughout the district. Gradually, options became known, adjustments fell into patterns, and we were able to relax ever so slightly.

"Daddy," it was Liam running up to me. "I can't understand what they're saying." Neighborhood kids had come into the yard to meet the new strangers and to play.

"It's all right," I reassured. "Just use your imagination and have fun." Skipping off happily in the perfect weather, he soon had a game of soccer going, using a ball of wrapped up vines. He had been fairly fluent in Spanish in California, and I hoped that would help him. Conor, on the other hand, was just beginning to develop language skills, clueless to the artificial distinctions between the basically, three tongues he was being exposed to simultaneously. Fascinated, Janet and I followed the amazingly quick transformation as both became functionally fluent in Portuguese and Lumwe within a matter of weeks. We, of course, were still struggling mightily, our brains cemented in thirty years of monoculture. Later, when visitors came, our kids provided interpreting as effortlessly as rolling a bike tire rim with a stick.

Running the household, was itself, a full time proposition. Wash by hand, including diapers, was a never ending chore. Janet soon discovered that the bathtub was much less harsh on the clothes than the outdoor cement scrub board. Soap had to be carefully doled out, and ironing was done by the hot coal method. All food preparation was from scratch, most cooking with wood or charcoal, only rarely with the use of the electric stove. A constant ear had to be kept to the wind to take advantage of even the flimsiest rumor of anything useful becoming available. Then a decision had to be made if only a servant should be sent, especially if it might involve a long wait in line, or if a personal note would be more appropriate to be sent with the employee, or, possibly she herself would have the best chance of obtaining the desired product. Each situation was different, and only through experience did one become proficient at the game. What quantity to purchase depended in how it could be stored, insects and mold being a concern, and when it might likely again be available. The kids helped make cheese and butter, and became familiar with such activities as hand pounding grains to flour, butchering animals, shredding coconut, and the skillful use of teeth to rip off the bark off cane to get to a chaw of sweetness.

At the hospital, I encountered disorganization, ineptitude, and lack of initiative. Supplies depleted, equipment in disrepair, patients languishing, programs not implemented, virtually nothing the way it should be, and I'm a ball of fire. In my mind, I'm already visualizing how I will fix everything, not just here but throughout the district. I will not allow children to die, that's ridiculous. Yes, this is Africa, but we're in the 20th century, modern technology exists, it's a matter of organization, education, motivation. Thrown into the original mix was the fact that six young, brash, and more than a little arrogant, Maputo medical students, all Portuguese except for one mixed race fellow who was able to gain enough education to somehow qualify for medical school, had just arrived to spend two weeks learning rural medicine. Never had I felt such a need for better language skills! I wanted to learn it all instantly, but was overwhelmed with what seemed like equally, or even more urgent concerns. Fortunately, they had with them, a pediatrician and some medical supplies. After a spirited meeting, during which we laid out a rough plan of action, everyone dug in for a frontal assault on disease, ignorance, and complacency.

It didn't take long for the first of innumerable lessons in humility to be experienced in the form of a relatively innocuous virus known as measles. Shouldn't be a problem, just good supportive care, and in most cases, in a few days everything is better. Slap! Harder slap! Kick in the groin! One, two, five cases....we have an epidemic. First the fine rash leads to peeling skin. Then, runny nose, cough, conjunctivitis, and a little diarrhea. Wait a minute. Cough getting worse, trouble breathing, antibiotics, steroids. No help! Throat swelling shut. Tracheotomy impossible, no respirator, child weakening. Helplessly, we watch life ebb from the small innocent messenger. This was the first of what were to be many mortalities from what continues to be a major third world scourge, especially in Africa, making up 10% of all childhood deaths. It came in many forms. Most common was the respiratory condition described above, but vomiting and diarrhea leading to dehydration also took many victims. Measles encephalitis and pneumonia also occurred regularly. Two of the worst complications made me feel like even death might have been more kind. The first was xerophthalmia, where, in a matter of hours, malnutrition, specifically lack of vitamin A, with the added insult of measles, resulted in irreversible blindness. The first sign would be a slight clouding of the cornea, progressing rapidly to dense opacity, even perforation and herniation of the iris. Even when I was fortunate enough to have injectable Vit, A, it was too late. Inevitably, even if the child was able to survive, it was only by paying the price of obviously scarred eyes, with all the social and cultural implications, and total blindness, an overwhelming burden in such an underdeveloped situation. And, B, the most hideous of all complications and seen too frequently, is noma, or, chancrum oris. Weakened immunologically, the patient contracts a mixed infection beginning most often in the gums, and progressing rapidly to become a full thickness necrotic process of the face. The worst case I saw spread from the chin, around the cheeks, and over the bridge of the nose, all of which fell off in a matter of a few days leaving exposed, basically, the underlying osseous structure of the facial bones and teeth, no skin or mucous membrane. Once again, antibiotics little or no help. Add a third horror to Marlowe's last pronouncement, "the horror, the horror." Before this particular district wide pandemic burnt itself out, there would be in excess of one thousand deaths, all my responsibility. If I never see another case of measles, it'll be too soon.

A few of the other clinical conditions frequently encountered were tuberculosis, leprosy, shistosomiasis, malaria, worms, whooping cough, filariasis, neonatal tetanus, and scabies. Exacerbating all of this was malnutrition, mostly kwashiorkor. I'll describe the typical scenario, which I saw probably every day. Up came the mother, infant on the back, carrying a second child aged two or under, exhibiting the classic signs: swollen legs, thin, spindly arms, and a miserable disposition. Add scraggly reddish hair, pot belly, cracked, dry skin, and profound weakness and you have a full blown case. If mom isn't carrying a baby, it's not because she left it at home, it has recently died, you needn't bother asking. It became that, at a glance, I knew what it was. A breast fed baby did quite well. However, traditionally, with the next pregnancy, the unlucky already born child, would be abruptly weaned, and placed on "papas," a gruel of hand milled grain flour, quite course, cooked in water from a stream, over an open fire. All too often, grain not being available, which was, at best, only partially digestible, cassava was substituted, having a woefully inadequate 0.5% protein content. The tummy is filled so the crying stops. There may even be enough calories present, but a rapidly growing child can't build muscle and bone from carbohydrates. So, from a diet clean and rich in fats and complete proteins, we get one frequently contaminated, marginally digestible, and missing the crucial ingredients needed for even a modest shot at growth and survival. As it turns out, it's not just a matter of providing the proper nutrition, cultural patterns must be changed, a much more daunting challenge. As Paulo Friere so aptly elucidated, the great white savior has little chance of success, dropping in to tell local people what they must do. A process involving the development of trust, communication, and shared identification of problems followed by a coordinated search for solutions, is the only way to arrive at significant change by way of self-empowerment. Tedious as it may seem, I was to learn that cutting corners, simply had little or no lasting effect.

In addition, I had to face the standard ills we all know: cancer, arthritis, headaches and depression, along with liberal portions of trauma, burns, pneumonia, and hernia, not to mention the more exotic diagnoses like rabies, crocodile bites, ainum (a condition of unknown etiology where a digit mysteriously chokes itself to death and falls completely off), tropical ulcer, and accidental cyanide poisoning from improperly prepared cassava, all of which was not without considerable challenge. But also, never to be disregarded was the ever present anxiety provoking attention grabber, obstetrics. Statistically, Gurue district experienced approximately 20 births a day, by itself a staggering load to be responsible for.

What to do? A huge area, much of it impenetrable, little transport, few supplies, primitive conditions, an illiterate populous separated from me by an enormous cultural and linguistic barrier, with no reasonable expectation of outside assistance other than an occasional high minded directive from the Ministry in Maputo that happened to find its way clear to Gurue, and me, a good doctor, yes, dedicated, yes, but woefully inadequate and ill equipped to address such an entrenched, multi-factorial health quagmire.

Early on I concluded that to spend prolonged periods of time on single, acutely ill cases, was unfair to the district and an inappropriate use of my time. This was a hard rule to follow, especially when I thought that, with a great effort, I might be able to turn around a particular case, but I knew that I had to stick to my plan, almost no matter what. Teaching, also, would have to be a major part of anything I did, since I couldn't be everywhere at once and I wouldn't be there forever. I dreamed of health care presence throughout the district, beginning as small posts and growing as more resources became available. Nutrition, hygiene, good water supply, vaccination, family planning, insect and rodent control, and even such peripheral issues as type of abode, village planning, and finding foot ware all seemed relevant.

I began by making the best map of the district that I could, including roads, paths, all localities, circles, and even the smaller divisions called cells. Rivers and streams were placed in position, as were tea plantations, mountains, landmarks and all existent health facilities, no matter how insignificant. Early each day, many times 4 a.m., I would arrive at the hospital to make rounds on what was usually twenty to thirty patients, carefully leaving instructions with the one of four nurses on staff, always explaining why I wanted things done a certain way and asking their opinion too. Then a visit to maternity, which was a separate building with two delivery rooms and twelve beds in a ward. As the sun came up, I tried to be off into the district, visiting every corner, talking to all kinds of people, listening, learning, taking notes, paying due respect to each local leader and, of course, all the "macangueiros" or "healers," since they were to be my colleagues. Traveling between places was time for learning language, always pumping Ricardo for the word for every animal, tree, plant, activity seen, or whatever came to mind, first in Portuguese, then Lumwe. We hit a hole in the road, that's "buraco" and then "ligi," got it! People, places, words, planning, all the while doing medicine, reading, studying, go, go, go. Back to the hospital. It's dark. Where has the day gone?

After nearly a month of this type of intense activity, I reluctantly admitted to myself that I couldn't maintain the pace I was on. First, I didn't see Janet and the kids nearly enough, and second, lack of sleep was taking its toll. By then, language was coming much better, and I felt I had a good grip on the geography, people, and resources of the district. I decided that a plan I could realistically sustain would include only three long forays into the bush a week, meaning that I would get to every location once a month. The other days would be spent teaching, planning, seeing patients locally, and visiting reasonably close spots.

By the end of one year, our district had in place, a functioning health representative at each and every state production unit, mostly tea and agricultural, at least a small health post at most of the significant population areas, a much improved system of care for in-patients, an active preventative medicine plan, and a newly constructed guest house for term pregnancies coming from a distance awaiting labor.

One of the most appreciated compliments came from an American surgeon, by then working in Mozambique, who had extensive experience around the world, after visiting us for a week and seeing the whole set up. "Dan, what you've got going here is the best Third World health network I've seen."

"Oh come on, Coke, what about Ibadan?"

"No. First, they receive a massive amount of money and resources from the UK, and second, I've been there and it's not spread out and comprehensive like here. I can see what you've done locally at the hospital, and yesterday I questioned health workers at even the most remote posts, and they had the necessary supplies and could explain how to use them properly. I was extremely impressed."

"Well, thanks Coke. That's nice to hear. Of course, there's still so much to do." We went on talking well into the night, trading ideas and discussing possibilities.

After about six months, lo and behold, our trunks arrived in Quelimane, and we were able to persuade a local store owner to bring them up on his next trip down for supplies. What a celebration when we got them. Especially exciting were the kids' toys and books. We had gradually been accumulating things we could use, and were surviving, but this was a huge jump forward.

The very next day, I dug out the basketball, needle, and the nets, and soon I was gleefully on my way to an old abandoned outdoor court at the secondary school. With some innovative improvisation and fixing up of the goals, I was soon playing with a group of local kids. They really had no idea how to play but were quick on their feet and eager to learn. After about an hour, being wary of the sun, and having had a good workout, if not a greatly competitive game, I excused myself and started home, happily promising to return soon to play some more.

That night, while making late rounds at the hospital, I was forced to spend extra time at the bed of a small toddler who had come in several days earlier with gastroenteritis. Nothing unusual, he was moderately dehydrated, but with an NG tube delivering our mix of electrolyte solution, he improved nicely. Still, diarrhea remained, and intermittent fevers. Chloroquine had been given, so I concluded that it was probably a lingering virus, and that with decent nutrition, he'd recover fully. At the time the hospital supply of food was worse than usual, and somehow the idea popped into my head that I could just take this child home for a day or two and have Janet and Chico

119

prepare a better balanced diet for him and he'd recover and be able to go on his merry way. Little did I suspect that I was about to be taught a severe lesson.

Two days at our house with the best food available, which he took only sparingly, and not only was he no better, but Conor and I both, were getting similar symptoms, loose stools, weakness, and low grade fevers. Reluctantly, I sent the boy back to the hospital and tried to seriously focus on my own family's health. The very next day, despite all we could do, the poor child expired, a bitter outcome in itself, but taking on an unspoken ominous significance, since we had the same thing. Now, despite the fact that I wasn't feeling well at all, I poured through every book I had, wracking my brain for any clue as to what exactly we suffered from, and more importantly, what could be done. With basically no lab to help me, my best bet was that this was Salmonella, quite possibly typhoid.

"OK, so now it has a name. What can we do?" Janet had been hovering over Conor, who didn't seem to be getting worse, and was doing an excellent job of suppressing some of the feelings she might have been having towards me, like, "Now you've really done it," or 'What were you thinking?" Obviously, my intentions were good and she realized that I felt lousy, and that now was a time to pull together and keep our wits the best we could.

"I've never seen a case, I'll have to admit. Somewhere, in my studies, I remember an infected water pump in London, and 'Bloody Mary' in New York, but to me, up until now, it's been just an anachronism. According to my books, the fatality rate isn't that high, and we should concentrate on good supportive care and frequent hand washing. Antibiotics don't really seem to make any difference. Problem is that it might not go away so quickly. Sometimes it can last weeks."

"You go get some rest. I'll watch Conor and call you if he gets worse."

I couldn't rest. Frequent trips to the bathroom, and rereading the books seemed much more important. Finally, late into the night, I managed to get a few hours of much needed sleep.

The next day, both Conor and I felt somewhat better, but as might well have been expected, Janet, and then, later in the day, Liam, began feeling sick. This brought on a whole new set of concerns. Janet, with her history of colitis, and Liam, with absolutely no extra body fat, could get it worse than Conor and me. For two days, I watched the disease evolve. Janet was bad enough, although I never felt she was in jeopardy, just miserable. Liam, however, soon had me seriously questioning why I had ever come to Africa. The second night he had near constant diarrhea, and, at one point spiked a temperature over 105. Chico and I attended him constantly. Janet did what she could but was still weak herself, and needed to rest frequently. We gave aspirin for fever and sips of different kinds of fluids, whatever he said sounded good, trying to avert dehydration. I watched closely for signs of peritonitis or any other complication. What I would have done, I don't know since the nearest decent hospital was in Malawi, at best, an eight hour trip, hardly a viable option. Concern mounted when Liam could no longer get up to get to the bathroom, and we put him back in diapers. Fighting back emotion, I mechanically sponged his body, trying to break the roaring fever in his now frail little body. I had seen too much of this, and knew perfectly well how things can progress and escalate, terminating, quite suddenly at times, in irreversible shock. Our son was now delirious, mumbling incomprehensible phrases. Checking his pulse, I found it to be just over 200. Discreetly taking Chico to the side, I instructed him to go to the hospital to get IV's and injectable antibiotics. Trying to console Janet, who sensed how serious this was, and keep a close watch on Liam, I had tears rolling down my cheeks as I waited anxiously for Chico's return. Even now, writing about it, I can distinctly remember the exact smell that permeated the scene accompanying the frequent uncontrollable stools. Finally, he arrived with the supplies, and helped me carefully arrange things on the small bedside table in preparation for initiating the IV treatment. I was just to begin the search for a good venous site when, to our amazement, this very ill child woke up, looked straight into my eyes, and said, "Daddy, can I have more of the chocolate?" Touching his chest with the back of my fingers, I knew immediately his fever had broken. Giving him a hug, I turned to Janet and announced, "The temperature's down. I think everything's going to be all right."

It took nearly a week for both of them to fully recover but there were never any more problems like what we had already gone through. The whole episode made me realize how tenuous is the grip on life under these conditions. No child, living as the vast majority of the population here did, would have survived such an episode. Once again, an even more poignant lesson of respect for a disease was permanently etched into my memory bank. And, more than ever, I realized how crucial it was to improve infrastructure, to have any hope of overcoming even basic medical problems plaguing Third World societies. Trying to look at what we had been through positively, I told Janet that our immunity had probably taken a quantum leap forward because of the assault provided by those nasty little bacilli. "Small consolation," she responded. "I think I'll still do some serious hoarding of toilet paper, just in case."

Commitment renewed, I plunged forward with my ever expanding plans, not only doing medical work but adding things like the distribution of rabbits and pigeons, planting citrus, mango, papaya, and avocado trees, and getting wells and latrines started everywhere I went throughout the district. I even began to visit several areas out of my district, like Ile and a small hospital in Mutuali, just over the border, placing it in another province, Niassa, both areas having no doctor.

More and more expatriates began to arrive, Brits and Indians along with several others, spoke English. Our social life was ever more varied and resources were becoming more available. Liam had, besides completing his initial set of home Calvert lessons, ended his first year in Mozambican school by being awarded the socialist emulation certificate, quite an honor. In general, things for the entire country were going well. People everywhere were filled with hope.

Because of the work I was doing, I had been invited to attend the first ever, national "Jornadas," a scientific meeting of physicians from all over the country, who were to present their clinical research or summary of any significant aspect of what they were encountering in their work. I was to make a small educational update on the diagnosis of tuberculosis, with an emphasis on its multiple manifestations, and a major report on my innovative, district wide approach to obstetrics. The meeting was to take place in Chonguene, a beautiful resort 150 km. north of Maputo on the Indian Ocean. My tickets had arrived. After driving to Quelimane, I would fly to the capital city and then ride to the meeting with George. Janet encouraged me to go, knowing how important it was to me and even for the country. By then we were better prepared for any contingency and so, not without considerable trepidation, I had sent in my acceptance and, on a perfect Gurue day took off with Ricardo in the Land Cruiser, on the first leg of the arduous journey south.

Now knowing both language and "the ropes," I was easily able to negotiate any potential glitches in the trip, and arrived in Maputo on schedule, even having time to spend most of a day with George in the Central Hospital. Driving north the next day he told me that everyone was anxious to hear about my OB experience, and that even the minister himself, now Pascual Mocumbi, had asked about it.

Chonguene was very adequate, even glitzy, but knowing that it was a legacy of colonialism, detracted somewhat from the atmosphere. What was truly inspirational was the powerful spirit of internationalism exhibited by physicians from literally, all over the world. Following the opening evening meal, there was a social function for people to get to know each other. Making the rounds, I met doctors from, not only the communist bloc countries like USSR, China, North Korea, Cuba, and Eastern Europe, but also medical people from the various Western European nations, Canada, Mexico, South America. Then there were those hailing from various regions of Africa, even several white South Africans. As intriguing as the roots and personal histories of each participant were, the dominant focus was on sharing experiences from working within this dynamic new independent African nation. For most, political motivation was high, although certain Easterners were advancing their home country careers and, hence, benefits, by spending time in Mozambique, and some of the Italians, because of a glut of physicians there, were doing this as a job under their country's foreign aid appropriation. But, imagine, if you will, doctors from all parts of the planet, diligently uniting, communicating in Portuguese, in a most serious attempt to address the health problems of the poorest and most underdeveloped of all nations. To me, this was exactly how things should be. Highest priority to the most needy. Yes, there was hope for the world!

My talk on TB went well. Drawing on my experience in Delano and Gurue, I presented a series of clinical vignettes, trying to make each a diagnostic dilemma. Of course, the answer was always a form of TB. Like, a 24 year old male with a six month history of purulent drainage from the right ear, failed on three different antibiotics and various topical drops. Diagnosis? Tuberculous otitis. Three months of INH, thiacetasone, and streptomycin and he became asymptomatic. Included was the entire spectrum from TB meningitis, cavitary TB, and tuberculous pleural effusion, to the more exotic peritonitis, orchitis, and the dermatologic manifestations. In my line of work, William Stead's all inclusive publication, "Tuberculosis", had become indispensable, and my copy was one of the most worn books I had.

Attending as many of the other presentations as I could, I also took time to be well prepared for my OB talk which was scheduled to be one of the last on the agenda. Introducing the topic, I explained how, immediately on arriving in my district and surveying the health situation, I was struck by the high incidence of both newborn and, worse, maternal mortality. Everywhere I visited, I made a point of asking, in detail, about recent cases, gradually giving me a good grasp of local customs and traditions surrounding childbirth. Women might deliver by themselves away from the village, almost out of shame, it seemed, or in their mud hut assisted by an older female relative, who observed, more than anything, rarely taking an active role. Premature marriage, as soon as breast development appeared or with menarche, often led to a pregnancy before full pelvic growth and development occurred, ending in a horrible situation of a fetus too large to pass through the outlet, three or four days of tortuous ineffective labor, visits by the local "macangueiro" accompanied by incantations and various herbal remedies, and, finally, fetal demise, ruptured uterus, and maternal death. Everything about it was deplorable. Picture a young innocent, inexperienced, budding adolescent, without her consent, being sold into marriage for a blanket, an antelope, or, in the worst case I heard of, four rats killed during a recent bush fire used each year to clear land in preparation for planting crops. Soon she's pregnant, and, with no prenatal care, the only possible positive being her anticipation of the fulfillment of her female role in society, she rapidly advances to the above nightmarish and terminal scenario. Other times, women might be urged to bear down before complete dilatation of the cervix, leading to maternal exhaustion. Newborns weren't to be touched until the placenta delivered spontaneously, an event that might not happen for hours, even days. I saw women with retained placentas for up to a week post-partum, a dreadful clinical dilemma. Babies were born onto a dirt floor, wrapped in an, anything but clean, cloth, cord cut with a piece of glass or a sharp sliver of bamboo or cane. Exsanguination might take place for lack of uterine massage. Tragically, a frequent sequela of a maternal death, was the accompanying demise of any other of her children under age five or so, because of inadequate attention, they being ill prepared to survive on their own in such a harsh environment. Seeing all of this, and having had extensive experience in OB, early on, I knew that this had to be a major focus as the one responsible for the health of the entire district. Within months, I began implementing my plan of training, supplying, and integrating lay midwives into each population area throughout the district. Before long, I received a visit from the provincial director, Dr. Ching. "Dr. Murphy, I've heard you're starting a program using lay midwives. Is it true?"

"Yes it is, Dr. Ching. We have so many OB problems here."

"You know, Dr. Murphy, that this is not a part of the national health plan. We are striving for high quality care, given by appropriately trained personnel. This kind of program cannot be allowed."

"I appreciate your concern, but what you're saying is a throwback to the methods of Portuguese colonialism, focusing exclusively on formality and process, at the expense of practicality and positive outcome. Ethically, I can't ignore these pressing problems when so much could be done with relatively simple measures."

"We are training well educated midwives in Maputo. Plans are being made. Progress will come."

"That's all well and good, Dr. Ching, but for us, here, Maputo could just as well be in a different world. Those people don't even want to come to Quelimane, much less Gurue, and out in the bush, where the greatest need is, never. What are there, 100 in training? We need thousands. Our district alone could use 60 or more. Besides, they don't know the language or the culture, and no matter how dedicated, would be miserable. It's just not a good solution at all. We're talking about a local problem. The real solution for now is local empowerment, people themselves doing what they can about their own perceived difficulties. I'm just facilitating."

"They can't be put on the payroll, you know."

"Each village is taking care of that themselves – donations, help with the crops or other chores. I expect nothing from the province. But now that you mention it, a few extra supplies like bulb syringes, hemostats, and fetascopes would be greatly appreciated."

"Aarghh, you Americans are dedicated and industrious, but so hard to work with!" She realized that I wasn't about to stop what I was doing, and decided to let it ride, for the time being. Later, she herself sent a message that people at the national level were interested in hearing about my work.

My system began with a meeting of the citizenry at a particular village. Health problems were discussed and eventually, childbirth came up along with the invariable litany of difficulties. Solutions included building a small maternity house, with a waiting structure for women residing at a distance when near term, and, most crucially, choosing a hardworking, intelligent woman, whom they all trusted, to be trained and then return to work as a midwife. Some of these choices had to be redone at later dates for various reasons, but as we went along, we eliminated many of the methodological problems and things proceeded smoothly. The chosen one would return to our central maternity to be trained with a combination of lessons and hands on practical experience, until deemed competent according to a check list of skills and knowledge I had designed. These women were illiterate, speaking only Lomwe, but quite intelligent, and usually completed the content within two months, returning to their village with what minimal equipment I could arrange, to begin work. The first trainee, after starting her work, completed thirty deliveries the first month without a maternal or newborn fatality. Next to the village leader, she had already become next most prominent in social status. I visited each location at monthly intervals, whenever possible, to encourage, supply, and upgrade as much as I could. By the time of my presentation, over twenty midwives had been trained.

After my talk, I received nothing but compliments. Dr. Mocumbi had many questions, but concluded that he thought something similar should be done on a national level. George suggested that I write up a more formal version of my work and send it to "Tropical Doctor" which I did, resulting in publication for worldwide distribution, and allowing me the feeling of satisfaction that I was contributing, in a small way, to the betterment of health among the poor, in general.

Back in Maputo, before flying up country, a small incident occurred, which, although I didn't know it at the time, was to be an omen of soon to come, cataclysmic events. While shopping at the marketplace, a paper bag of mine, including a few small items I had purchased, was stolen from our car as we browsed through the maze of outdoor stands. It was a new experience for me as I had heard of virtually no crime in Gurue, people, unlike in the rest of Africa, didn't have to bribe their way along, and I felt safe, day or night, anywhere in my district, and even throughout Zambesia province. My passport had been in the bag, and that was important. Without documents, travel, even within the country, becomes impossible. Swallowing my admittedly fastidious political paranoia, I decided that I had to go to the U.S. Embassy, for the first time, to get a temporary replacement. The next morning, feeling very uncomfortable, I walked briskly between the two armed Marines and entered the solid red brick structure. "I lost my passport and would like to apply for a new one," I told the receptionist.
"Second door on the left."
Walking towards the partially open door, I heard muffled short wave messages coming from the room, but couldn't catch the words.
Entering the room and going up to the counter, I observed a young, square shouldered, short haired, neatly dressed American get up from the radio and walk over to me. "We have your passport, Dr. Murphy. Someone turned it in."
I hadn't even introduced myself, hadn't told anyone my name, nothing. Without even looking around for hidden mike's or cameras, I just reached out for the booklet, muttering a perfunctory thank you.

Before releasing his grip on the passport, he looked at me with a wry smile and said, "Dr. Murphy, if you notice anything 'unusual' up in the tea country, we'd appreciate it if you'd let us know."

I couldn't get out of there fast enough. In fact I just wanted to get back to Gurue to family and work. Sharing my experience with George, on the way to the airport, he told me that rumors were beginning to crop up with increasing frequency that a foreign sponsored coup, paramilitary attack, or any of a number of geopolitical shenanigans was imminent.

This time, on my flight, I wasn't thinking of the King of the Apes or Cheetah, but kept mulling over things like the reported CIA sponsored assassination of Patrice Lumumba and the horrific blood bath rained down on Angola, a former Portuguese colony just like Mozambique, the U.S. arming both sides. How foolish to think Mozambique would be allowed to develop independently with a black president and a multiracial government, making significant gains in eliminating tribalism, racism, sexism, sickness, illiteracy and ignorance, championing a Marxist-Leninist structure, right next door to rich and powerful Rhodesia and South Africa, last bastions of sub-Saharan colonial apartheid.

Touching the tarmac at Quelimane, I was elated to find a truck departing immediately for Gurue, and six hours later was knocking on the door of our house under a full moon. Janet greeted me with open arms, not expecting me until the next day. I had to go in to at least look at the kids as they slept. Reassured that my family was fine, and also hearing that nothing special had happened at the hospital, I sat down to fill her in on all the details of my adventure. She gave special notice to the passport fiasco. "You know, we've seen it in New York, Washington D.C., and California, but this is half way around the world. It really is global strategy. Nothing goes unnoticed or uninfluenced. They either buy it, or take it violently. Things seem to be going so well here."

"Yep, and the better they go the more jeopardy for Mozambique. What chance is there for the poorest nation on earth against the CIA, State Dept., AID, not to mention IMF, and the World Bank, all actively conspiring with Botha and Ian Smith. George said Banda has allowed the Mossad to set up in Malawi. That's only 50 miles from here. Anything could happen."

Before long I was back into the routine of medical work in the district, but I got into the habit of, late at night, listening to my six band short wave radio, sampling BBC, Radio Moscow, Amsterdam, Canada, and Mozambique. I got Wolf Man Jack on a Jo'burg station, and one night, to my total enjoyment, I flipped to American Armed Services Radio and heard Iowa basketball in the NCAA final four. Ronnie Lester injured his knee and Jacksonville got the narrow victory, but what fun to have the pure diversion of my favorite sport again.

Days were spent teaching, organizing, seeing patients, improving services however I could. A typical day in the bush would include meeting with local leaders, then with health personnel, followed by an educational talk with the local population, vaccinations, prenatal visits, and general consults. When available, Lippe's Loop insertion was offered. I usually had to gauge the sun and knock a hole in a wall or roof so the natural light could be used for the procedure. One particularly nice afternoon in Nintulo, 26 women received IUD's. We had to extend the hole twice. Many times we were offered a meal, then on to another place. Usually we visited two or three destinations in a day, and, invariably we would return with the ambulance transporting an assortment of critically ill patients back to the hospital for more complicated treatment. Included might be severely anemic children needing transfusion, advanced kwashiorkor, dehydration, pneumonia, fractured femur, strangulated hernia, or any of a number of other conditions.

One day, in a distant village, I encountered a beautiful innocent looking young woman in the prenatal lineup. After careful examination, I informed her that she was carrying twins, and that the first one was coming feet first. "I'd like you to come to Gurue for delivery," I told her.

"Where is Gurue? I've never heard of it," she answered in Lomwe, trying to hide a frightened look.

"It's only two hours away by ambulance," I explained. 'We can help you have the babies, get you started right, then bring you back."

"I've never been away from my village."

129

I had little doubt that this was nothing less than a life and death crisis. What was the chance of this 15 year old in her first pregnancy, being able to get through the delivery alone? Almost none. Furthermore, twins don't survive in these conditions. For a single baby to survive was challenging, 30% failing to reach age five. Already, I had delivered numerous sets of twins at the hospital, but there were none at Liam's school. One evening , walking to maternity, I heard some whimpering in the weeds. Investigating, I discovered one of a pair of twins I had helped into the world that day, abandoned by the mother. Carrying the baby back into the building I was able to convince the woman to accept the child. A week later I heard that the child died, leaving the other baby to thrive. The explanation is that women know instinctively or historically, that two at a time is just too much. Once, far into the bush, I saw identical toddlers playing nearby. This was so unusual that I got out to find the mother, knowing that there must be a special explanation for this rare occurrence. Laughing, she told how her sister had miscarried at just the same time and was able to help her breast feed the new babies.

Determined to have this case turn out well, I tried to summon up my most caring, compassionate look, took her hand in both of mine, and slowly formed the words, "Please, trust me."

Hesitating for a moment, she seemed to be gazing deep into my eyes. She had probably never seen a white man before. Here was a complete stranger from a place she had never heard of asking her go away in this funny looking vehicle. Her lips parted and, as a smile broke, revealing perfect white teeth, she blurted out, "haia." Four days later, we were delivering her twins in Gurue, the first one breech with a difficult aftercoming head. Then, with the midwife aligning the second baby in the vertical plane, I ruptured the second bag of water and guided the remaining child through the already dilated birth canal head first. Both children were a little premature, but extremely vigorous. She named the male, Daniel, and the female, Janet. Our young mother was the model patient, following all our instructions meticulously. We told her to use one breast always for one child and never trade off or the stronger baby will steal more than it's share. She learned all about diet so that her milk supply would be adequate. We gave each child an injection of iron, and four days later she was back home. Never missing one of our visits, the three of them were a joy to see, always healthy, well clothed, and well nourished.

Liam and I took frequent exploratory walks near dusk or on weekends, finding monkeys, flowers, secret trails, or plants that prickled or closed up. Once, venturing up the mountain, we rounded a curve in a path to come upon a long green snake stretching from one side of the trail to the other. Instantly freezing, we gave wide berth even after the slinky fellow had long since disappeared. Liam couldn't wait to get home to tell Conor about "uma cobra grande, assim", stretching his hands out as far as he could. Conor, in turn laughed with excitement. A month later, he was to find himself face to face, just outside the yard, with a spitting cobra. Not realizing that he could be blinded with one squirt of venom, he at least hesitated long enough for one of the neighborhood men to sneak up behind the intruder and whack it with a stick, leaving Conor seeing and wiser. Now he had something really momentous to share with Liam, "aquela que cuspe," he carefully explained wide eyed, unable to contain excited spasms of laughter. Both of them laughed and laughed, running out to tell it over and over to Chico and all the neighborhood kids. So goes the life of small children in rural Africa.

By now, we had developed quite a social life. People were constantly arriving from all over the world to work on various new projects. Gurue being so picturesque also assured that we would have visitors nearly every weekend. If they spoke English, had anything, even remotely, to do with health, or for whatever other flimsy reason, people stayed at "a casa do doutor." Many times four or five languages would be spoken at the same time. Visiting and eating, especially if it was something special, were major pastimes. Before long we had friends from nearly every country on earth. Frequently, one of Janet's main difficulties was keeping a sufficient supply of food on hand, although she was vastly more resourceful than when we first arrived.

One day, after a particularly grueling day out in the district, I arrived home a little late, hoping we wouldn't have "guests" so I could relax. As soon as I walked through the door, Janet greeted me with a message from maternity, asking that I stop by.

I took a minute to clean up and then headed directly to OB, where the midwife presented me with a case. The pregnant woman had walked all the way from Nintulo, over the mountains, quite a feat in itself, because she felt increasing abdominal pains different from her other labors. She did have a low grade fever and, on exam, seemed to have a very sensitive vagina with a lot of discharge, but actually, her cervix wasn't dilated at all. Fetal heart tones were normal and I couldn't palpate her spleen so I ordered what rudimentary tests we could accomplish and told the midwife to call me with results. Two hours later, I got the call, tests inconclusive, but there must have been a glitch in communication because the patient had vanished. They had checked everywhere and she was not to be found and no one had seen her. Worried, but with nothing else I could do, I settled down on the verandah with Liam, to read him the exciting conclusion to our latest book, "Treasure Island."

The next day, returning from a day out in the district, I was called to see the same woman. "She just got here," informed the midwife, 'yesterday she says she was scared and went to see a macangueiro. Now she seems worse." Examining her, she was definitely in labor, and within half an hour, delivered a good sized, apparently healthy, baby boy. Her condition, on the other hand, was not good, with temperature spikes above 39 degrees centigrade. Despite antibiotics and IV fluids, she was slowly going into shock. Six hours later, despite attempting everything we could think of, we lost her. Now we were left with a motherless baby, another desperate situation. It hadn't taken me long to realize how cruel and self-serving were the campaigns by formula companies like Nestle's to market their product as a viable choice for third world infants. Contaminated water, improper mixing to stretch the supply, lack of refrigeration, and primitive hygienic conditions, all weighed against successful outcome. I had seen enough deaths to make me go out of my way to approach a mother any time I saw a bottle being used, and even offer hospitalization to reintroduce nursing, if needed. Without breast feeding, Lucas, as his mom had named him before expiring, would have almost no chance. All of us began asking around for anyone who might help. The father lived so far away, and realized that he could do nothing.

"What do you think?" I asked Janet that night. "We don't have much time, and no one is stepping up. A couple post partum women in maternity are giving a little of their milk, but that is so temporary. Do you think we could handle him?"

"I'm leaving for the weekend tomorrow with Liam and Conor. Can we decide when we get back?"

"Sure."

While my family was spending a few days at Socone with friends, Lucas was deteriorating. Losing weight steadily, and becoming more irritable, now pus was beginning to come from one ear. Unable to wait longer, out of any other options, I made the decision, and brought Lucas home, along with a few amps of ampicillin. Our servant Chico and I stayed up the whole night with the baby, giving him tiny sips of boiled sugar water by spoon and injecting antibiotics every six hours. We kept him warm with hot water filled whiskey bottles wrapped in towels placed at his sides in the little basket we had arranged. By the time Janet arrived the next day, Lucas was already looking better. Our decision had been made.

"You got him!" cried Janet, entering the house, finding us tired and huddled over the basket. Both kids ran over to see what Lucas looked like. Everyone wanted to hold him.

"Wait! He's been really sick, and he's just getting his strength, so let's be very careful with him. He needs to rest and eat."

"What are we going to feed him?" asked Janet, reaching over to touch Lucas' drawn face.

"I've got two cans of powdered milk. He was so weak and dehydrated last night that Chico and I started him on sugar water by spoon, but he's perked up enough to try milk. We were just going to fix it. All the ingredients are in the kitchen."

"Ingredients? What are you giving him? Gourmet milk?"

"Sort of. What we have isn't formula. It's just cow's milk without the water. Even reconstituted, it's too thick and it doesn't have the right amount of fat. But don't worry, nurse Chico and I have it all figured out and have everything ready to mix, boiled water, powder, and cooking oil. I looked at three books to get the proportions right. Sounds delicious, doesn't it."

Janet came to the kitchen to see how to put the drink together. I apologized to her for springing such a surprise, but explained that I knew Lucas probably wouldn't have lasted the day, and I just felt compelled to act. Together, we mixed the concoction, allowed it to cool, and then went back to try it with a small spoon and cup. With the first sip, we could tell, Lucas loved it. Great! We had a fighting chance. Leaving careful instructions, I took off for work, confident that everything was under control. By the time I returned that evening, Lucas was drinking up to three ounces at a time from a bottle, no less, and looked like a different baby.

Finishing up the antibiotic, Lucas' ear was fine and things seemed to have settled into somewhat of a routine. The word was out and everyone stopped over to see the baby and even offer things to help. Most, especially the remaining Portuguese, although not saying it, were amazed that we would even consider such a thing. This baby, through our action, had been immediately catapulted from being another inconsequential black African native child, to becoming a member of the doctor's family, meriting the highest social regard. But then, for two nights in a row, for some unknown reason, the normally contented infant, became increasingly more irritable. He still ate well but it got to the point that, the second night, he hardly slept at all. Concerned, tired, and frustrated, I went over everything in my head, reviewed the milk preparation, and examined him meticulously. Nothing. Well, he did have a slight rash, like little red spots scattered around his body. One of the spots even looked like it was growing and possibly getting ready to break open.

"Well, Doctor, what's he got?" asked Janet, clearly near the end of her rope.

"Everything checks out," I answered. "I'm stumped."

Chico had been standing humbly in the background, like a good colonial servant, but he was becoming used to our more equitable approach to things, and had been very involved in the care of Lucas. At any rate, sensing our consternation, he felt confident enough to step forward and announce hesitantly, "The baby has mafwenya."

Sure, like the reason it's raining is so the crops can have water to drink. I know how that logic works. Thinking he was referring to some sort of old superstition, or evil eye type of explanation, because of Lucas' circumstances, I gave Chico an admittedly somewhat disrespectful look, highlighted by a doubtful wrinkle. "Hmm, mafwenya. I don't think so. Chico, what is mafwenya?"

"Little animals. Their babies come out of the skin."

"What do you mean?" I asked, still thinking he was probably nuts, but never knowing when another gas tank incident would appear.

"This is the nest," he explained walking up and indicating one of the little spots. "And this one," pointing to the biggest lesion, "is ready to open up so the bichu can come out."

I had never heard of such a thing but after Chico told me he'd seen it many times, I started to believe he could be on to something. Lucas had become inconsolable, so, however reluctantly, once again I felt I had to throw discretion out the window, and go with Dr. Chico's diagnosis. Cleaning the area with alcohol, and using a needle, I carefully unroofed the biggest spot, immediately revealing two black dots, side by side. "What's that?" I asked.

"Those are his eyes," informed Chico matter-of-factly, anxious to see what I might do next. As poor Lucas continued to cry harder than ever, I took a tweezers and grabbed on to what I felt was most likely to be foreign material, assuming Chico was right. To my total amazement, as I slowly retracted the instrument, out popped a squiggling white worm, about twice the size of a grain of cooked Basmati rice. Janet nearly fainted. Liam and Conor both had open mouths and backed away instinctively. Chico, fighting to keep from looking proud, reached out to take the bichu and throw him outside. Quickly, I proceeded to repeat the procedure over every spot, until, 13 minor operations later, all the nasty little critters were out. Lucas was left with small drill holes scattered over his body, but after we cleaned them up the best we could, he almost instantly fell asleep for six hours straight. Later, as I gradually learned more through a combination of reading and experience, I found out that this was miiasis, or African maggots. In maternity, Lucas had been wrapped in sheets that had been hung out to dry and not ironed, on which flies had laid eggs. Unlike American maggots that thrive only on necrotic tissue, these aggressive types can invade normal skin, and have been known to facilitate bacterial superinfection which can be fatal. So, once again, we and Lucas had dodged the bullet.

Late one afternoon, just as I was finishing seeing, what I thought was my last patient, I looked up to see a young oriental appearing man standing expectantly in the doorway. "Come in. Sit down," I offered, "I'm Dr. Murphy."

"My name is Park. I am very sick, Dr. Murphy. Please help me."

Immediately, I was on full alert. This guy looked ill, and worse, his eyes showed that significant fear, which, many times, is associated with an ominous situation. From his accent and clothes, he was obviously not Mozambican, meaning that I would have to deal, not only with a serious medical problem, but also language, cultural, and, as it turned out, political factors. Doing my best to put him at ease, I pushed my chair back and encouraged him to tell me his story. Using more Spanish than Portuguese, which he had studied in college just outside of Pyongyang, Park explained how, along with five other technicians, he had been chosen to come here to work on a construction project. The trip had been arduous, and each day, his stomach had gotten worse and worse, to the point that now, he could barely eat anything. My first thoughts, as I listened to his tale unfold, were so knee jerk in nature, that I felt compelled to reach over and gently touch this man, Park, on the arm, in an attempt to cut through all the overtones that I presumed were going both ways, and make this a straightforward doctor patient interaction.

Many a time, as a small child, I had run down to the highway to cheer for the military convoys passed through Alton, as part of the raging Korean conflict. Associated with this, were the scenes at the cemetery, trumpets, off in the distance, wailing into the wind, followed by the synchronous explosion of M1's, echoing over my playmate's older brothers as they sank into the rich Iowa loam. Yes, the same demonization that worked so well against Japan, had indelibly imprinted the spin masters' stereotype on our naive cerebral hemispheres. Rare indeed were any comments in our media, on North Korea, and all of those invariably negative. In counter balance to this, I had stored somewhere in my memory bank, Izzy Stone's account of the same war, explaining how the key factors were General McCarthur's ego, gravely smitten with the recent loss of one-fourth of the earth's population to the "Reds," and equally important, manipulation of the world rice market. Only through intensive unscrupulous intervention, had the U.S. been able to create the Rhee republic, and then by repeatedly provoking Kim Il Sung across the DMZ, finally get the desired conflict going, bullying the U.N. into the fracas.

Sweeping all that baggage off the table, after listening to and examining Park, I concluded that he suffered from severe peptic ulcer disease. The stress for him was immense, crossing yawning geographic and cultural divides, he had arrived in this completely foreign hinterland, scared, tired, and homesick. On top of it, he now had to face an American doctor, symbol of as traditional an enemy as there ever was. Slowly and carefully, I explained to him what I thought and, after discussing options, we decided on a trial of rest, medications, and diet, within the means available to us. The next day, I went to visit him, their house being very near the hospital. He greeted me at the door with a smile. Feeling much better, he and his compatriots were enjoying a hot game of Ping-Pong. Insisting that I play, graciously, they allowed me to win, although later, as we became friends, we were to have some very competitive battles. Then it was cookies and pictures of their homeland and families, putting a human face on my previously painted preconceived perceptions.

Several months later, delivered to our house was a beautifully hand printed, formal invitation for me and my family to attend a movie that the Koreans had just received from Pyongyang, scheduled to be shown the following Saturday at the local cinema. Arriving just before show time, we were proudly escorted into the somewhat dilapidated Portuguese theater. The film was a stirring action adventure romance set during the "American War." The hero, a Korean Audie Murphy, fighting against immense odds, vanquished scores of GI's, played by local talent wearing white powdered makeup, even jumping into a fighter at one point, and downing seemingly hundreds of U.S. planes, pulling off innumerable loop-de-loops in the process. The climax was a nothing less than epic battle involving tunnels, city hand to hand guerrilla combat, mass casted field encounters, and flashy aerial dog fights, ending with the dramatic rescue of the beautiful damsel, in the last set, embracing our hero, surrounded by dead Americans as far as the eye could see.

Teary eyed, I exited into the brilliant African sun, looking about for Park. "Great movie," I said sarcastically. "Every American dead and not one Korean even injured. What do you think?"

Giving me a proud look and then breaking into a smile, he answered, "Those were bad Americans. You're a good American."

Walking home I did my best to think that, somehow, there was still a glimmer of hope for the world. For the next three days, the kids played war games outside, them being the Koreans against the Americanos. If ever one of our goals was to expose our children to diverse perspectives, we were succeeding. Directly connected to the heartland, USA, we were now stretching to the leftist limits, somewhere between "Sendero Luminoso" and anarchy. Liam began each school day singing the words, "a luta contra o imperialismo, FRELIMO ganhara."

To celebrate Independence Day that year we had been invited to Tetete, a relatively new "aldeia comunal" filled with "antigos combatentes" and their families. The village was located at the far northern edge of our district, and was extremely isolated and difficult to get to. Nevertheless, it was a wonderful place to visit because here was represented every ethnic group in Mozambique, each with their own particular dress, housing style, language, and culture. All had participated in the armed independence struggle, and had many stories to tell. This day was to be filled with traditional dance, music, food, and celebration. Accompanying us on this special occasion were Steve, a Canadian doctor working in Milange, a neighboring district bordering Malawi, his wife and two young daughters. I doubt if anyone could have had a better time than we did on that day. I was well known there because of being "O Medico Chefe Distrital" but all of us were treated well. The dances were so different than anything we had ever seen, mostly choreographed to conga riffs, harmonious voice, and at times, marimba. The exhibition of grace, athleticism, and stamina also served as a stage for the colorful creative dress, innovative accessories like the dried bean pod ankle rattles, along with the artistic body painting, all of which was upstaged by the magical masks, key ingredients in African symbolism and mythology for millennia. Several times all of us were invited to join in, my years of perfecting the jitterbug finally paying dividends.

138

Eating and drinking at each ethnic sector of the hamlet, we soon realized that, if possible, we would be best served staying the night and leaving the next day. Our hosts graciously arranged a place for us in the modest guest house. Sleeping silently, under the Southern Cross, we dreamed of caves, clubs and loin cloths, simplicity, cooperation and beauty, atavistic instincts and anamnestic amino acid sequences, clouds, earth....

"Doctor, Doctor," someone was shaking my shoulder. "Please, they need you at the hospital." Realizing where I was I quietly arose, dressed, and accompanied the nurse's aide to the small local medical facility. Greeting me at the door was Ninito, the head nurse. "Dr. Dani, I'm so glad to see you. They just brought my cousin in. He was out hunting and, with the accident, he had to be carried all the way back. He's lost a lot of blood. Can you help us?"

"Sure, let's have a look," I responded in my most reassuring manner. The brisk nocturnal walk through the cool atmosphere of the high African plateau had me almost awake. Entering the adjacent room, I approached the concerned looking adolescent, lying on the military cot, and, holding the kerosene lamp up to his neck, carefully exposed the wound. Three inches of what appeared to be a broom handle sized stick protruded from an area half way between his clavicle and the angle of the jaw just medial to the sternocleidomastoid muscle.

Instinctively checking the radial pulse, I asked the poor victim what had happened. Barely able to speak, he uttered the single word, "assagaia." Seeing the difficulty he was having, I didn't push for any more. The brief flash of his perfectly filed incisors, told me that he was Makonde, most likely from an isolated region in the far northwest of Mozambique, since that style of decorative marking had been largely abandoned from early on in the independence movement. His use of Kiswahili, meant that he had fled with his family, as a small child, across the Ravuma river, spending significant time in Tanzania, while older relatives pursued the revolutionary cause. Many such words, although originally from the upper coastal reaches of East Africa, had become a normal part of the universal trade route language used all around the perimeter of the sub-Sahara. His friend told me of how they had been hunting far from the village and had encountered a wild boar. During the ensuing chase, he had tripped and somehow fallen on his recently sharpened spear. After cutting off the long shaft with his knife, he then carried his bleeding buddy for most of the night through the bush to get home.

Transporting to another facility was not even a consideration. This one was going to be me, make or break. As I prepped the area with Cetavlon disinfectant, I asked for a description of the spear head. "Rounded metal tip, all the edges sharp, with barbs on the sides angling back towards the shaft so it won't come out of the animal."

How wonderful I thought as I began thinking anatomically. Carotid artery, jugular vein, trachea, larynx, thyroid, parathyroid, yes, but what about recurrent laryngeal nerve, thoracic duct, vertebral artery, and probably just as many important structures that I couldn't remember at the moment. It took us a week to dissect out this part of the neck in gross. I thought it was all a big joke at the time. Now I wished that I'd done an ENT residency. "Ninito, can you give me some local anesthesia," I asked, finishing the careful scrub. No one moved. Looking directly at him, I repeated, "Ninito."

"Nao ha," he reported, trying as hard as he could to sound helpful but avoiding my eyes completely. Great, now I was to pull off a delicate procedure that even Mayo Clinic would have had a 50/50 chance on, using a dim kerosene lamp, with no anesthesia. Trying to gather strength and composure I took a minute to rummage through some old boxes of medications on a nearby shelf. Wiping the dirt off one of the last vials, I held it to the light and barely made out the word "ketamine." Sometimes things just happen, I thought, as I tried to recall a distant lecture heard many years before. It seemed like this was a medicine that put one into a kind of trance. Not really believing in fate or destiny, I knew that to attempt this with nothing was extremely undesirable. Loading up a syringe and finding a suitable vein, I slowly injected the entire amount. His pulse and respirations remained steady. For instruments, I had an already used scalpel, two medium sized curved hemostats, and a bandage scissors.

Carefully extending the wound, I was relieved to see that the patient didn't move at all. Working my way along the shaft, I meticulously avoided cutting whatever remotely resembled anything other than connective tissue. Twice I had to tie off smaller bleeding vessels with catgut, but each time was able to clear the field enough to proceed deeper into the hole. By now I had reached metal, but had to get to the barbs, free them, and then extract the spear. As I worked, even though I thought it was higher in the neck, my mind called up an old freshman med school poem: "Around the curve, came lingual nerve, over the hyoglossus. Well, I'll be fucked, said Wharton's duct. The son of a bitch has crossed us." Good, I'll watch out for that, I thought, as suddenly the first barb appeared. Gingerly dissecting out first one, then the other, and seeing them completely clear, I was now ready to remove the spear. Damn! It wouldn't budge. Was it somehow embedded in the vertebral body of the cervical spine? I was afraid to just yank on it with full force. I could just see blood squirting to the thatched roof. Looking at the situation, Ninito turned and said something in Makonde to the other lad. Turning to me, he reported, "This one has two levels of barbs, so there's no way an animal could rub it off."

"Are you sure?" I asked.

"Yes, I remember, because I helped make this one myself."

"Okay, we'll dig deeper." Most of what I now did was blind since the light was so poor, hemostasis lousy, and exposure woefully inadequate. Somehow, nearly half an hour later, drenched in sweat, I felt the last strand of flesh give way as the razor sharp weapon loosened and was able to be withdrawn, centimeter by centimeter from the stunned hunter's still intact cervical anatomy. Bleeding controlled, I left the wound unclosed, to heal by secondary intent, and applied a loose dressing. Stepping outside into the immeasurable, sequined African dome, I pondered the amazing capacity of such incidents, so insignificant in the light of the presence I now felt, to monopolize every iota of your consciousness.

"Doctor." It was Ninito. "He wants to thank you."

Walking back to the cot, I bent over in the dim light so he would know he had my attention. "Obrigado, senhor doutor."

Ninito insisted that I come to his house for tea. Soon we were chatting about everything from his exploits as a long term participant in the anti-colonial struggle, to the nuances of hunting for game in the bush. One thing led to another and before I knew it I was invited to go out on a quick visit to an isolated water hole just to see what interesting creatures might show up. Knowing I wouldn't be able to sleep anyway and seeing that the moon was now up, it seemed like a nice opportunity. After asking if Liam could come along, I finished my tea, before quietly waking Janet to explain our plans. Reluctantly she agreed, but made me promise to be extra careful. Soon I had Liam up and dressed and we were on our way across the veldt.

Our guide, who was a much decorated independence militant, widely known for a bravery bordering on lunacy, told us story after story in a brilliant exhibition of stream of consciousness, as we traversed the bush. Makonde's, in general, were a proud and intransigently independent people whose territory straddled the border between Mozambique and Tanzania. Masterful art work, especially abstract ebony carvings, had recently brought them considerable worldwide recognition. Colonial powers rarely take such factors into consideration, and Portugal was certainly no exception. Mueda was bad enough in and of itself, but Mueda was Makonde, making it, in addition to a monstrous, brutal, barbaric atrocity, what many would say, the critical strategic error in the war. Not only did it become the rallying cry for freedom fighters all over the country, but it took a group, brimming with the best fighters, who basically paid loyalty to no one, and made them implacable, vanguard, FRELIMO activists. Ninito jumped from hunting stories to war stories with the greatest of ease. Now he was telling about one of the times he was captured and held by three people. Seeing his chance, he burst free, grabbed an AK 47, and blasted everyone in sight, stopping only when no one moved anymore. At this point I noticed Liam actually skipping along as if in one of those "it doesn't get any better than this" commercials. Looking up into the sky, I saw Saturn, Venus, and even Mercury moving together in a pathway through the stars. That's us, I thought. There are bears and scorpions, but they can't get us.

Ninito had brought a spear, knife, and bow and arrows. He let Liam carry the bow part of the way, a big thrill. After what seemed a long time on trails, we cut cross country over a plain towards a bluff. Our host explained that from there we could see the water hole, and that we should be perfectly quiet as we got close. He pointed out some nearby trees that could be climbed in case of emergency. This would protect us from everything except leopards which weren't aggressive, and rogue elephants which were very rare and got you no matter what if they put their mind to it so don't even bother trying to get away. By now I think we were into Niassa, an area known for lions. I knew it was a long shot but I hopped, for Liam's sake, we could get a glimpse of one. Creeping up to the ledge, we silently imitated Ninito.

Light was accumulating in the east as we began to be able to distinguish the water hole two or three football fields away. Just as we were getting comfortable, our nurse/warrior tapped us on the shoulder and pointed off to one side of the clearing. I know his vision had to have been at least 20/10, because I could barely make out anything around the hole. Breathing as quietly as we could, we watched intently, and as the light improved, sure enough, we were able to see a male lion gorging on what appeared to be leftover buffalo from an earlier kill. As we observed, something else was moving ever so slowly, coming out from the water. I had heard about crocodiles as long as seven meters, over twenty feet, in nearby rivers. That had to be what this was. Nonchalantly, the reptile began to tug at the corpse, slowly dragging it towards the water for storage in his larder. The Lion seemed unperturbed, too busy being a glutton to bother with this stupid cold blooded amphibian. Unbeknownst to any of us, the pea brained participant actually had a plan, a brilliant hidden agenda. While appearing to be pulling away rather ineffectually at the carcass, he was really positioning himself for a move toward his real objective. Keeping his dangerous jaws on the beef at all times as a diversion, the monster had gradually inched his earth hugging tail into perfect position.

Wham! The lightening quick rump of the crock swept the legs out from under the unsuspecting feline and almost before the toppled king hit ground, massive rows of dental bayonets entered lion flank, holding like a vice grip as powerful legs drove pell-mell toward wetness in one dramatic flurry of motion. Astounded, none of us breathed as we heard a sound emit from the victim that would surely drive the sun back beneath the horizon. Then only a short interval of thrashing water, and it was over, all quiet, as if nothing had occurred. Ninito jumped up and was laughing hilariously, Liam and I laughed a little but we were too scared and overwhelmed to react much at all. If you've never seen it, it's impossible to understand how swift and deadly these forces of nature can be. We were in awe.

Heading back to Tetete, we checked various traps that had been set earlier and discovered a freshly caught antelope in a spear filled hole that had been camouflaged with long grass. This served as our breakfast and by noon we were on our way back to Gurue, filled with wondrous tales and adventures.

Not that my regular routine wasn't physically demanding, because it included lots of walking and carrying, but I wanted, needed, more. Running around the house, usually dribbling the basketball wherever I could, was a frequent occurrence. Jogging up into the mountains was another. This day, for some reason, Chico came along. I'm not built for running, but I could string together five or six seven minute miles as part of my "Prevent the Murphy Heart Attack" program, without too much difficulty. Chico didn't run that I knew of, unless he secretly sneaked out at night to rip off a quick five or ten K, so I presumed that he wouldn't be able to keep up. Wrong! Not only did he keep up but he wasn't even breathing heavy, or sweating as we headed up toward the presidential retreat house high up on Namuli. Stopping briefly there to check out the house and grounds and to view Gurue from above, I turned to our own Henry Rono and asked, "How are you feeling?"

"Muito bem, senhor doutor. Nao sei por ai?" he said, feigning perfect polite subservience.

"I'll make it. Let's head back. I don't want to push you too much." Smiling, I took off at a lively pace.

The downhill portion was beautiful twisting turning pursuit with innumerable exquisite overviews, but always, I had a shadow that, try as I would, could not be shaken. At the lowest point, we still had about half a K of significant upgrade to get back home. Compulsive and competitive as always, I turned to Chico issuing the challenge, "Let's race from here, Gurue championship on the line." Taking off, I left the poor neophyte in the dust. Continuing to stride out to assure maximal aerobic benefit, I became aware of something just off my right shoulder. Somehow he had made up all that distance and was now breezing past loping like a gazelle. Damn, I thought, I got nothing left, but I can't let a guy who's completely out of shape beat me. Reaching deep, pushing the wall away using all the mental leverage I could summon, I rounded the final curve, 100 meters to go. Miraculously, he was coming back to me. I was reeling him in. Anoxic and near syncope, I went into the desperate do or die all out sprint. We entered our yard, stride for stride, in a dead heat. Sucking for wind and bending to hold both my knees, I heard applause from the verandah. Glancing up I saw Janet and the boys giving us a hand, but a quick look at Chico revealed no trace of air hunger. Realizing what he had done, as I walked past him on my way to the house, I patted him on the shoulder and gave him a sincere 'obrigado.'

Prematurity didn't seem to be more of a problem there than in other places, but I did have one case where I was called urgently to maternity because a baby had just been born 'with two heads.' Now there's an interesting twist, I thought as I walked briskly towards the hospital. First, how was the baby born, and second, what on earth can I do with it? As it turned out, I didn't have to worry because entering the building I saw the staff huddled over what had to be, Siamese twins, looking to be about twenty weeks gestation, with only intermittent ineffectual respiratory efforts. Sharing a thorax, they had been small enough to be born spontaneously but were nowhere near viability. What next, I thought returning home after leaving instructions for supportive care only, making it clear that nothing meaningful could be done in this case.

About a week later, we did have a child born, that was to provide us with all the challenge we could ever want. Weighing in at 1100 grams, this baby may have been small for dates, but was also definitely premature. Outwardly appearing vigorous enough, I knew that the effort of breast feeding would burn more calories than it would obtain for the infant, assuring an inevitably downhill course. We had been over this quite a few times before, but never with anything this small. The midwife had already filled our two whiskey bottles, as was our custom, the child covered close to mom to create the best environment possible. Carefully, I measured the length of soft rubber tubing, cutting it to reach from baby's nose to just below the xiphoid. Setting up a simple flow chart, I issued the following challenge. "Let's go on a mission for this baby. Express the breast milk as clean as you can. There's no gag reflex so you can let her swallow the tube orally and remove it after each feeding. Every three hours religiously, around the clock. Start with three cc's and increase by one ml. if there's no residual by the time of the next feeding. Remember, let it run in by gravity, use the little funnel, never a syringe." For two days we had no respiratory difficulty and the child's intestines were intact and functional. Weight, however had dipped to 980 grams, and, secretly, I felt we had almost no chance. Still, hydration was good, and I knew we couldn't increase the feedings too rapidly. Mom had good milk was very cooperative. Her family helped with the other kids and the nurses and midwives were superb. Each feeding was critical, but this special child lost no more weight, and, unbelievably, over the next several days, began slowly to gain. Fourteen days later, at 1350 grams, we attempted breast feeding, and all cheered with amazement as the miracle infant took hold and efficiently fed to satisfaction. Another two weeks, a shot of iron dextran, and our two stars went home, healthy as could be. Totally gratified, I congratulated the entire staff on a job well done. Things didn't always turn out this well.

One day, a young man was brought to the hospital in extremis with dyspnea. A quick exam, closest x-ray being 200 kilometers, left me with the conclusion that, most likely, he suffered from a tension pneumothorax secondary to TB, judging from his somewhat cachectic look. Desperately scrounging for anything that could be used for a chest tube, all I could come up with at the time was and old oversized Foley catheter. While I was attempting to insert it beneath the right clavicle, the poor patient used what little breath he had to inform me that I was killing him. As it turned out, he was right, because just as I thought I had everything in place, he got noticeably worse, and within a short time expired.

On the other hand, in a similar case, this one, however, being a post traumatic flail chest, I was able to dredge up the idea of splinting the injured hemithorax with a half filled gunny sack of sand, and it worked, the man walking out of the hospital two weeks later, no worse for the ware.

Never was there a shortage of interesting challenges, and with each passing day I became more proficient at what I did. My greatest fear, however, was about to be realized, as the storm clouds, always looming on the horizon, began shifting our way.

146

The first drops of rain came as word of an attack on the Maputo suburb of Matola arrived. Pulled off by South African military commandos, several getting killed in the process, the raid was an attempt to eliminate ANC refugees allegedly sheltered in the house. Most disturbing was the evidence found implicating the U.S. embassy in the diabolical affair. Notwithstanding the lip service being issued at the time in favor of democracy, freedom and self-determination for people in both South Africa and Rhodesia, not to mention Mozambique, apparently the powers that be had decided Mozambique could not be allowed to succeed, and that the status quo in the apartheid states was to be maintained at all costs.

More incursions followed, with a front organization called Renamo, being created and championed as the true moral saviors of all that's good in this newly independent land. Over and over, playing significant roles in all of this nefarious treachery, were the CIA, the religious right, Afrikaaner Boers, Ian Smith's henchmen, both Israel and Saudi Arabia, and countries as diverse as U.K., The Comoros, and West Germany. Even Malawi and Kenya plotted actively against the fledgling republic. Ordinary Mozambicans began to suffer as infiltration, bombings, and direct assaults escalated. The enemy had sophisticated submarine and helicopter supply support, the latest telecommunication equipment, and all the money and military hardware they wanted, backed, as they were by the world's richest.

At first, most of the trouble was in the south, but then problems began to show up near the Malawi border, and before long, inevitably, I, personally, was sucked into the cesspool. The three young women entered my office walking gingerly, as if on sharp pebbles. "Moni, moni, mocala pama," I greeted them. What I first thought were stoic looks on their faces, was, I was soon to discover, closer to spent terror. Each of them, not without considerable embarrassment, revealed to me first their backs, which were covered with welts, then, lowering their capulanas, their buttocks, or what was left of them. Taken aback initially, I proceeded to carefully examine the damage. Deep and repeated flays had been inflicted on these poor women's behinds, leaving hanging ribbons of skin and flesh mixed with areas of full thickness early eschar. Some areas appeared already infected. I knew we were looking at long, painful sessions of debridement, and the likelihood of multiple skin grafts. One of the victims I had met before on a visit to a village near the border with Milange district. She was the wife of the local political leader and had just had her first baby.

Hesitatingly, as I began cleaning her wounds, she related what had happened. "The three of us were down at the stream doing wash when a group of men jumped out of the woods carrying guns. They wanted to know where our husbands were. We told them that were out hunting, but they didn't believe us. They tied us up and started hitting us, first with sticks, then with some canes they found. It went on and on. We answered everything they asked but they were never satisfied, calling us liars and communists. They said Frelimo was dead and they were taking over. Our children were crying so much and we couldn't say any more so they finally left us there saying they would come back later to kill us. Some village people found us and helped us."

"What language did they speak?"

"They spoke Lomwe to us but Nyanga to each other." This meant that Malawi was implicated. Both the U.S. and Israel had extensive intelligence and military advisory presence there. Frustrated, I filled out a detailed report for the provincial authorities. To think that some white male think tank in Washington, playing geopolitical monopoly, had made a decision causing these innocent, hardworking black Mozambican women to suffer such horrific tortures, left me with a simmering anger. Shouldn't they be here to attend to these wounds, see the anguish, and touch the skin? It was to get worse, much worse.

Two weeks later, from deep in the hinterland, a woman arrived with a similar story. Except to teach her a lesson, the brave, western sponsored counterrevolutionaries had sliced off her ear with a machete. In shock initially, she came around with fluids and blood transfusions. Not being trained surgically, the medieval mercenaries had whacked off the pinna and a portion of the lateral neck, severing the external jugular vein in the process.

Reports were coming in from other parts of the country of attacks on any government vehicle, fatalities mounting. Gruesome incidents of misogynist machination demonstrated in the hideous tactic of amputation of a lactating breast were especially disturbing, threatening the baby and marking the mother, if she was fortunate enough to survive, in a way guaranteeing outcast status for life.

Many black Rhodesians, at that time, were inside Mozambique, either as refugees or, in some cases, as participants in their own independence struggle. In fact, Robert Mugabe spent considerable time in Quelimane during the early revolutionary period. Mozambique's open policy was that, just as Tanzania had played a critical role in harboring Frelimo, so too would independent Mozambique give safe haven to its neighbor's politically displaced people. Intense negotiations were being pursued at Lancaster House, as the only viable solution to the Rhodesian dilemma. Great Britain knew that the apartheid conditions in her African colony were unacceptable, but still wanted to find a way to assuage white people. War was taking its toll both inside Rhodesia, and more so, within Mozambique. International pressure for a settlement escalated while South Africa desperately did all it could to sidetrack any agreement, not wanting to become isolated as the only remaining pariah. Partly, the price for continuing the conflict had become intolerable, but mostly, through brilliant and dogged negotiation coordinated by Mozambican president, Samora Machel, a satisfactory document was signed, creating the new, independent state of Zimbabwe. Janet and I were proud to have been, in a peripheral way, a part of the struggle. We hoped that this would end the now widespread suffering affecting nearly every part of Mozambique. Almost immediately it became clear that Pretoria had assumed the leadership of Renamo, and planned to punish Mozambique like never before.

Violence, much of it gratuitous, escalated as not just transportation and communication infrastructure was targeted, but any economic or even remotely political entity came under attack, and finally even schools and health facilities were included as "despicable communistic infringements" on the freedom of the people. All had to be brutally destroyed. Renamo began "recruiting" combatants by press ganging ever younger villagers, mostly by horror tactics like forcing them to shoot, bayonet, or incinerate family members, thus alienating them forever from the only society they knew, and leaving them with Renamo, where only brutality was rewarded.

Gurue was an important economic district because of tea production, and therefore had been allocated a sizable military contingent for protection. Still raids were becoming more brazen. I continued to see victims with an assortment of injuries. A truck load of tea workers was attacked and rolled over resulting in three dead and sixteen admissions to our small hospital for fractured limbs, concussions, various cuts and bruises, along with two men who had been shot. Rumors abounded, making decisions much more difficult. I felt I had to continue my work, but wasn't ready to risk my life.

One weekend, we had visitors from Quelimane, two Brits, a Portuguese teacher, and a Brazilian doctor. Saturday, after a nice dinner, we talked well into the night, even sharing a bottle of wine they had brought and singing some songs. Tension was building all over the province and indeed, the nation, as Renamo pushed their puppet campaign. Some expatriates were forced to abandon their positions for safety's sake. About two a.m. we went to bed. Usually an inveterate light sleeper, on this occasion I faded quickly and dreamed of the bucolic African village life I had come to know so well. Although the fleeting images floated through my subconscious state in a completely non-threatening stream, from somewhere in the shadows a lurking ominous presence was sending out negative vibrations. Who was she? Wearing only a capulana around her waist, young and silent, she's coming closer. I can feel the heat, see the smooth skin. "O que? O que e que quiere?" The words come muffled from my mouth. My eyes are opening wider, neurons and synapses are engaging. Shetan, Shetan, SHETAN!!! Janet! Janet, someone's in here. Jumping up, running. "Ladrao, ladrao," her scream reverberated around the corners of the rooms. I grabbed the mace. Our friend was swinging a baseball bat.

"Are the kids okay?" Everyone is up, now. We have flashlights to run outside with. Nothing. Nobody. Darkness. Silence again.

Somehow, our dog, Abeli, had been dumb. They had climbed up an outside wall, slit the screen over Liam's bed, reached in and unlatched the window, and entered. Money, shoes, sheets, and food were missing. It didn't matter. But another layer of security, in that instant, had been usurped. Political and economic uncertainty breeds desperation. Now we had to sleep with one eye open. Tin cans hanging at the end of twine, wedged in each night as we closed every window and door, served as our warning device. Once one fell spontaneously provoking near apoplexy.

Then the recently arrived Mozambican veterinarian was murdered up on the mountain. Communal villages were being sacked and burned out in the district. A Portuguese tea maker and two local workers blown to pieces indifferently by a land mine marked a new escalation, a definite threat to me as I continued to visit remote areas of responsibility. How could these "civilized," white, democratic, western societies produce and send such heinous tools of hell to be used, in my district, by these ignorant peasants kidnapped into service with Renamo, their front group having no agenda other than chaos and destruction. I could just hear them saying, "It's nothing personal. Chill. You know there's gold in South Africa, diamonds in Rhodesia, oil in Angola. You hear! Oil! What about business? What about votes in the U.N.? We've got to keep the big picture in mind. Don't want dominos."

My time was spent on injuries and listening to reports, trying to plan safe trips to deliver medicine and services to the bush. Suffering multiplied. Fear and frustration dominated.

One perfect evening, all of us collected on the verandah to finish the last chapters of "The Lunatic Express." Janet and I alternated reading aloud as the kids listened, fascinated by the tale of exotic Mombassa, coolies, the Masai, ferocious lions, and wonderful Lake Victoria. Themes of imperialism, colonialism and arrogance, significant in their absence, went unexamined as we chatted and watched a rainbow over Namuli gracefully directing a small rain cloud towards us. We had a brief downpour, lasting only minutes, cleansing once again, the ageless African landscape, leaving the air fresh, a peaceful stillness accompanying the sudden transition from day to night. Setting the alarms, the children in bed, Janet and I too, fell into a deep slumber. One high window, over our bed was left open, allowing the cool dark air to enter and make our sleep perfect.

At the deepest, most quiet moment of the night, the two of us were blasted from our bed by a noise having the physical force of a bomb, an earthquake, or a tornado. It was automatic weapon fire coming from directly outside our window. Feeling we were doomed, both of us hit the floor and lay still, barely breathing. Another horrible burst of staccato exploded, as if we needed another dose to seal the inevitability of our imminent demise. Cringing powerless, I saw Janet slowly sneak over to the bedside stand to grasp the small canister of mace. Minutes passed with no attack on the house. A few scattered voices from a distance, but mostly silence. Finally, I dared to peek out the window, seeing nothing. Checking the kids, and finding them still asleep, we begin planning where to hide, up in the cupboards, flee to the bush, don't panic. All seemed absurd and futile. Nothing more happened, except that neither of us slept the rest of the night. In the morning we found out that it had been a drunken Frelimo soldier, nothing more. No attack, no danger, nothing. Still very disconcerting to say the least.

This thing was sneaking up on us. Be rational! When does the safety of the children, if not our own, become paramount? Why do I still think of duty to the district and my job? Shouldn't I trash it all and bolt? I had no experience to draw on, no one to help me, only instinct and common sense, fairly worthless commodities.

Bridges had been destroyed, Namarroi was reportedly controlled by the enemy, and the side of our district towards Malawi was under constant attack, making many of the health posts inaccessible. People in Gurue, and Mozambicans in general were paying a heavy toll. I worked under constant pressure, doing mostly things I should never have had to deal with. We had renewed our contract for a third year, but now questioned whether we were contributing significantly enough to justify the risk. I had invested so much that to walk away would have been difficult.

One of my favorite places to visit was Muagiua. My first time there, the people had just killed a wild boar and everyone was in a festive mood. Now, two years later, we had accompanied and assisted them in the process of forming a communal village, complete with a school, a small store, and one of our nicest health posts. When I had first gone there, I had seen many cases of advanced malnutrition and preventable diseases. Most of it had slowly been eliminated by education, vaccination, introduction of appropriate crops, latrines, a new well, and improved social structure. It had been a team approach, many of us pulling together helping the local population however we could. Even though security was precarious, I wanted to realize our scheduled monthly visit to this special destination.

Early on the previously designated Tuesday morning, we loaded up the Land Cruiser ambulance and headed northeast over the treacherous track winding thirty kilometers into the bush taking us to Muagiua. All the citizens were gathered awaiting our arrival. Following a quick greeting, foreshortened by the dire circumstances of the times, we waded almost immediately into our routine of sanitary education, vaccination, prenatal visits, and medical consultation. Once again I marveled at how well the children appeared, nary a hint of kwashiorkor seen. Despite the unspoken urgency of our situation, Claudio, the newly elected village president, insisted that we stay for a meal his wife was preparing. We too, being victims of custom and protocol, were unable to refuse, despite my reservations on staying any longer than absolutely necessary. During the repast, Claudio told us of the constant fear felt in their community, more so because they had advanced so much according to the Frelimo model over the last two years. There had been so many raids close by that he and the members of the executive council had taken to sleeping in the bush lately. Speaking with us, his demeanor seemed to have an almost fatalistic overtone, as if martyrdom was inevitable. Just as we were finishing up the meal, a young man approached and asked permission to speak to Claudio. I watched a cloud come over our friends face as the messenger whispered the news into his ear and quickly departed.

"They've sighted two groups of armed strangers off to the west. Your best bet is to take the old road south. I'll send a shovel with you so you can fill in the gullies. I'm pretty sure the river is low enough that you can drive through slowly." Definitely worried, we quickly said our good-byes, and departed over the nearly invisible southern path.

"We have a lot of work to do," informed Pedro. "This way hasn't been used for years."

Three times in the first several kilometers, we had to disembark to fill in eroded areas with stones, sand and dirt to be able to advance. Once we thought we saw some people off in the distance and even considered abandoning the vehicle and walking back, but, after talking it over, decided to press on.

Soon we entered a more wooded area and as we rounded a bend in the path, we came upon a sizable log in the track, preventing our passage. Getting out to move the tree trunk, we immediately senses something was amiss as there were fresh tracks showing that the barrier was man made.

Instantly we found ourselves surrounded by about twenty armed men. Most were mere boys and they appeared ragtag and disheveled, except for the two older men who wore Frelimo military garb.

"We are a Frelimo patrol investigating reported enemy movement in this area. You'll have to come with us."

Knowing this part of the province better than anyone, hearing their accent, and judging by their appearance, Pedro immediately saw through their rather pedestrian ruse.

"We know exactly who you are and have seen your pitiful work," blurted out our driver, barely controlling his volatile temper. "So send these children to their homes and get out of the way so we can continue with our duties." Boldly striding forward, catching them somewhat off guard, he grabbed one of the leaders' rifle, and was about to rip it from his hands when the other uniformed goon dealt him a crushing blow to the skull, dropping him cold. My instinct was to fight but stronger yet was my medical role so I went to check Pedro's injury. Luckily it was only a concussion with a brief loss of consciousness. Almost immediately he stirred. Commanding his arms be tied, the vicious one spoke, "Yes, we are Renamo. Soon we will have the entire country and things will be right. All symbols of Frelimo must be eliminated." Giving a signal, he smiled as several of his men removed whatever they thought valuable from the ambulance, and then, as we watched in horror, they piled wood around the transport, siphoned gas out and poured it over the wood, and torched the whole shebang. After watching the conflagration for several minutes, we were informed that we would be going back to Muagiua. My three companions were tied in tandem while I was left untouched as we accompanied the bandits back to the village at gun point. Deferential treatment even now, I thought. What a joke. Meanwhile I tried to plan a strategy, think up contingencies for whatever might arise. So far, they hadn't even spoken to me. How much privilege did my skin give me? Maybe I could just walk off and the long years of colonial racism would protect me. I wasn't ready to take the chance.

Arriving at the village, we found another contingent of similar enemy troops and a sizable group of captured local inhabitants, Claudio among them. We were all tied to trees with our hands behind us reaching around the trunks. This time I wasn't excluded but noticed immediately that my rope wasn't pulled tight; there was some play in the knot. They wanted me to escape, probably so they could shoot me. No, my common sense insisted, it's the lack of epidermal pigment, plain and simple. Faulkner was right; there is, and never will be, another issue.

Deep in my twisted gray matter, I concluded that if I stayed within my role, dignified and aloof, I might be able to save myself, but to act heroically would surely precipitate Armageddon.

They were sacking every structure in the village. Intermittently, feminine cries of anguish penetrated through the tangled bush, violating the theatrical nature of this grim encounter. Despite the coolness left by the rapidly evaporating light, rivulets carved into my face like the torrents erasing the southward track. An emaciated looking ebony combatant had just emerged from the clean calcimine coated clinic. Shoeless, trudging past with a load of spoils, he paused, closer than necessary to me. For less than a second our eyes met. Quickly moving on, his desultory action had loosened a small vial in the stuffed pocket of his ragged shorts, causing it to fall to the ground. It came to rest propped against a root of my tree emerging from the African soil. Penicillin, it read. Looking closely, and feeling the texture of the bark, I realized that this was the same species of tree that was used for clothing.

Everyone was now gathered in the clearing before us. A small fire sent shadows out to meet the rapidly diffusing darkness gathering momentum around us. Their uniformed leader explained how this entire village was cursed, and that now, it was to be liberated. With a swift gesture of his hand, flaming bolls were touched to each structure, houses, school, store, and clinic. Soon all was alit in a spectacular extravaganza, symbolizing the futility of all human endeavor.

I felt a light tap on my shoulder. It was the vial marauder. "Manaquela mahi?" He offered a small water filled gourd. Instinctively I shook my head. "Hah-oh." Immediately I knew that I had made a horrible mistake; I must accept the drink. It was too late, he was gone.

As the silence of night quieted the satiated conflagration, the emcee spoke again. "To complete our task, we must destroy the spring from which the poisoned water flows. Sever the head of the serpent." Claudio was brought forward, tightly bound, hand and foot. Dread mounting, I knew that my moment had arrived. Instead, frozen, I watched as the smallest participant who was a teenager at best, step forward to receive the leader's weapon, bayonet in place. Claudio, motionless, gazed into distant blackness. A smart, deft thrust sent the M16's blade in, beneath the ribs and upward into the chest like a doctor relieving a pericardial tamponade.

As Claudio fell, bedlam ensued. People scrambling, shots fired. Ripping my hands loose, in a panic I ran, into the forest, falling, crashing, panting. Heading away from the noise, I gradually regained my poise and slowed down to a more deliberate walk. Soon I came upon a path heading in the direction of what I thought would be Namorroi. I decided to take it for a distance before cutting off towards Gurue again. The plan didn't last as almost immediately I heard shouting from up ahead. Hiding off the trail, I watched another group of enemy pass by toward the now distant imbroglio. Frustrated, I cut through bush, hoping to put more distance between me and the enemy.

The terrain was difficult especially not able to see more than vague outlines. Numerous times I slipped, and cursed myself for not being able to maintain better silence. Reaching an area that seemed to be a steady downward slope, I rested momentarily before beginning my descent. Finding it steeper than I had expected, I tried to go slow to keep better footing. Nevertheless, one fatal misstep and I felt myself tumbling and sliding out of control. After a fifteen to twenty feet skidoo, I came to a halt in an open area. As I sat up to be sure I was intact, a bright light suddenly flashed into my eyes from not more than ten feet away, blinding me. After an appropriately pause to evaluate the situation, the torch bearer spoke. "What's a bloke like you doin' out here? Speak English, do ya?"

156

As he lowered the beam, I could make out the luger in his other hand and the South African military insignia on his jacket. Not more than thirty feet behind him stood a large cargo helicopter.

"I'm American," I blurted out having no idea what to expect.

"Don't pay to ask questions in my business," he said, lowering the pistol. "Whole thing ain't worth spilling any white blood. Get in!" Climbing into the chopper, I took a seat in the rear. "No, up front," he motioned. "It'll work better."

Soon his charges began to straggle in and before long we were airborne. Nothing was questioned. I could hear the raiders chatting and laughing in back, but with the noise of the motor, I could make out very little. The captain explained how this was just a job, well paying, and that when he saved up enough, he was planning to move to South America. Within 30 minutes we arrived outside of Namorroi and dropped off the troops, before heading out for Malawi. Just over the border, he hovered long enough to let me slither down a rope to the ground before vanishing into the hazy eastern light beginning to accumulate over the horizon.

Exhausted, I quickly found a sheltered glen and propped my weary body against a tree and, for just a fleeting moment, contemplating Georgia O'Keefe's irises, and then sleeping like a hibernating bear, every neurotransmitter holding in stasis. Two monkeys chatting playfully in a nearby banyon, fast forwarded me back to the reality of my present situation. Family foremost in my mind, I set out immediately into the sun, knowing full well that a thousand dangers still lurked. After less than an hour of a relatively effortless stroll through beautiful pristine bush country, I saw smoke curling skyward not far ahead, signaling a cooking fire. Approaching cautiously, I observed from a distance before revealing myself. There were three daub and waddle houses in the clearing with two adults and four children that I could see. They spoke Chichewa, but the man wore a bought shirt, making me think that we might have a way of communicating. From experience I knew that women alone or small children would flee instantly at a sight such as me, but with this man present, it would be all right.

Clearing my throat, I emerged as non-threateningly as possible, "Moni, moni, hello," I blurted out, hoping to initiate a dialogue. The children edged instinctively towards their mother as I continued slowly forward extending my right hand.

"Hello," answered the father, stepping forward politely to shake hands. The ice being broken, as was my habit, I proceeded to shake hands with everyone present, as a gesture of friendliness and respect. One of the older children ran into the house and returned quickly with a chair for the guest.

"You speak English," I began, sitting down. "I can't speak Chichewa."

"I speak a little. I have worked in Blantyre."

"I live in Mozambique. Can you tell me where the border is?"

"We are very close, only two kilometers. But you must eat with us."

Going on a sense of trust that I felt with this family, I accepted graciously, and soon was given mealie meal, bananas, and even papaya. My host told me how the entire region was being inundated by desperate refugees from Mozambique. Crime and violence was everywhere. Military actions had become common place. He felt safer out here in the bush, the closest village being ten kilometers away. Sympathizing with him, I explained how things were decompensating within Mozambique too, and that I had to be very careful to avoid the wrong people on my way back to my family. Understanding fully, he pointed out a way for me to go, first keeping Mt. Milange to my right as I crossed the open border, then advancing to the Jehovah Witness village where he knew some Malawian refugees. He gave me the name of his friend who he said would help me from there to the Italian mission. Thanking them profusely, I took off in the direction indicated, my faith in human nature renewed.

Before long I was into Mozambique, and only once did I have to skirt an encampment of what I was sure were Renamo bandits. Twice I had to throw caution to the wind and ask directions, each time from what I thought were "safe" teenage boys. Constantly keeping on the move, off the beaten path, by evening I approached the anomalous settlement of religious anarchists. I had met and worked with the medical people here, but, not knowing the present political situation, decided to seek out my more recent contact. The first person I met took me directly to the house where, after explaining my story, I was offered a place for the night. I, however, refused, not feeling safe in one place, and wanting, above all else, to get home. Accepting a quick snack, I was set to continue, when the man called in his son, telling him to show me the way to the trail leading to the mission. I tried to refuse the imposition but he insisted, saying that it would be too easy to get lost taking the back way, especially at night, and it was the only safe route going in that direction. We had just entered the bush when rain began to fall, not a cloudburst, but one of those slow constant patterns. Great, I thought, people will stay put, and I need the fresh cleansing. Sloshing along silently, the feeling of a horse returning to the barn took hold of my spirit. To get to the mission took three hours, but from a distance, no light was visible. This being a totally isolated unprotected area, I decided to forge ahead. A brief whispered argument over the torch ensued. Winning the tiff, the young guide accepted my sincere gratitude and vanished, leaving me, flashlight in hand, within a lion's roar of Gurue district.

Initially, staying just off the sandy track, less than a kilometer out, I came upon a burnt out, overturned Land Rover along with two badly decomposed bodies. Land mines, what an ingenious invention. From then on, I stuck to bush, checking the road only occasionally for direction. Stopping once for rest, as dawn broke, land marks became more familiar. Soon I caught sight of a slightly more frequented route, leading to Belo Horizonte, a small agricultural project. Still thirty kilometers from home, spotting a small cluster of bananeiras, I appropriated from the most yellow amongst the low hanging bunches, marveling at the natural bounty of this now besmirched land.

From off in the distance, came the familiar sound of a motorized vehicle, probably a pickup, shifting gears and revving up according to the ever changing terrain. Keeping out of sight, as the government truck came into view, I immediately recognized both it and its driver. Running out to intercept this serendipitous relief, I hopped into the shotgun position before the wheels even stopped.

"Buenos dias, Sr. Aldo. Puedo yo pedir buleia?" Doing all I could to appear nonchalant, he, on the other hand, had the look of someone who had just seen a specter. Offering him the last banana, I continued, "What are you doing this far out? It's not safe!" In a way it was a rhetorical question. Aldo was Chilean, having experienced innumerable horrors during, and in the aftermath of the CIA instigated coup murdering the democratically elected physician, Allende, and installing the military dictator, Pinochet. Much of it still went unspoken even though he and his wife Ruth, had become some of our closest friends. Finding political exile in Sweden, and becoming true internationalists, they were now expatriates working in agriculture in Alta Zambesia. With them, we could mix both Iberian peninsula tongues and not worry about miscommunication. Our children played together, our politics was very compatible and we were all "Americans." Aldo, like me, continued to do his job, despite less than ideal security.

"Now let me see," he began, regaining his composure. "You were given up for dead two days ago at Muagiua, sixty kilometers from here, and now, ragged as a rat, half way to nowhere, you materialize. I've already pinched myself, so there must be a story here. Or was it just to bring me this really nice piece of fruit?"

"Let's keep moving. I'll tell you all about it. But first, how are Janet and the kids? Is Gurue OKAY?"

"Things are tense, and everyone is very worried about you. Eight people were killed at Muagiua, but Gurue and your family is fine. There haven't been any other incidents. More troops are supposed to be coming from Mocuba. Trouble is attacks are more frequent all over. I worry about the safety of the children."

As we headed back toward the town, trying to stick to all the wrong parts of the road, also avoiding adjacent walking trails, I filled my friend in on the details of my recent sojourn. He had many questions for me, wanting to understand the motivations for every faction involved. "You, of all people should understand. Money, power, and privilege are the keys. Anything seen as a challenge or threat must be stopped. Tactics are to persuade, cajole, intimidate, and, if that fails, buy it out. And as a last resort, have the spin doctors demonize it, and, either directly or indirectly, destroy it militarily."

"Exactly, in Chile we were foolish enough to think we could change things. Once we became effective, we had to be crushed.

Their intelligence tentacles are everywhere. It's very discouraging. Even Sweden sells arms for profit."

"Well, with the world population exploding, maybe another Gandhi or Martin Luther King will arise from the vast genetic pool."

"Or a Fidel."

"Umm-hm."

We had arrived in Gurue and pulled up to the house. Conor was out in the yard and came running up to jump into my arms, blurting out, "Os inimigos nao te mataron?"

"No, Conor. I'm not even wounded."

Soon everyone appeared: Janet, Liam, Chico, and Lucas, who didn't understand but sensed the excitement. After a lot of hugging and tears, the incessant questions began. To the kids, this beat the Korean film by far. Trying to temper their perception I became very serious, "I was scared. Everything was destroyed, and people were killed. None of this should happen."

Janet said that the local commandant came to tell her that a search of the area found not a trace of me. No one knew anything. One rumor was that I was a spy and had joined the enemy. Hardly! Chico was convinced that I knew some sort of "feiticaria," and how could I have been clear to Malawi in such a short time?

Soon the military arrived to debrief me. Then I excused myself to go to the hospital. Several wounded had been admitted but the nurses had treated the injuries well. One of the casualties was 15 year old pre- adolescent from rural Milange, who had been recruited by Renamo with promises of riches and glory along with threats of death and destruction for any who opposed. Trained in Malawi, this had been only his second raid. During the chaotic scramble at Muagiua, he had fallen and broken his ankle. Captured, he would have been killed if our nurse, Castro, hadn't intervened, calmly explaining that this small boy knew nothing and was just being used by the enemy leaders.

Visiting maternity, I encountered one of our best lay midwives there. She explained how her village had been attacked and everyone fled to the bush. She was here helping until she hears that things are safe again. Life had become difficult for nearly everyone. And as is the norm, the more acute the crises, the more desperation and self-interest predominate. Rare indeed is the individual who can keep his bearings and focus on what has to be done to ameliorate the broader picture for the good of all.

Janet and I had to consider leaving. The logic was safety for the kids, our work was being destroyed, and we could continue doing supportive actions from the U.S. As much as I wanted to stay for my dreams and to help a revolutionary country with its aspirations, too many other factors mitigated against such a course of action.

"What about Lucas?" He had become an integral part of our family, and would soon be two years old.

"Yes, what about him? To answer that, you have to first answer the question: what about racism in the U.S.? What would it mean for him and for our family? Here, he can rise to whatever level he's capable of. He's Mozambican."

"It's true. His brain and health are as good as they could be. Could you imagine the battle we'd have to wage to get him out? You know how the Portuguese took out young kids to be servants. It would mean multiple trips to Maputo or staying there for a protracted length of time with no guarantee of success."

"We could sneak him across into Malawi, then swing back through Blantyre and pick him up."

"You're dreaming. If we were caught, it would be disastrous. Maybe Silva would take him. We could send support to help raise him."

"See what you can find out. Let's think about it for a few days."

Reluctantly, we announced the decision that we would not be renewing our contract. What followed was a month of many farewell parties, both in Gurue and where ever I went. I still managed to get out to the district some. Vehiua threw me an all-night dance with skits, food, and cachaso (barely fermented), all punctuated with the best tom-tom talent I have ever seen. The hospital had a sizable celebration during which I was all but deified. We were invited to so many suppers around town we couldn't accept them all.

A courageous young woman from New Zealand arrived to be the next physician. I did my best to show her everything and make the transition smooth. Silva accepted Lucas to join his family as soon as we left.

Finally, on the designated morning, as the mist was just beginning to clear, we said our last good-byes, tearfully handing Lucas over, and jumped into the Land Cruiser to begin the journey south to Quelimane.

A thousand bumps to the sultry coast, prawns and coconut rice on the beach, interior flight to Maputo, safari in Kruger, diversion at Harare and, ohhhh, Victoria Falls, Maputo revisited, farewell Mocumbi et. al., non-stop out of Africa, out of Africa, out... Paris, wine, the Louvre, wine, Versailles, transatlantic, Chi town, heartland, USA, exhausted, arriving Cedar Rapids, Iowa.

"Grandpa, Grandma, how are you?" Lots of hugs and handshakes all around as we grabbed our bags and walked out into the typical August heat.

Getting into the car, Conor was amazed when Dick turned the ignition and suddenly cool air appeared. "What is this? First it's hot, and then it's cold. Ha ha ha ha." The poor primitive soul had never seen air conditioning. Like the time out in the bush, when I tried to tell a man that some people had taken a special airplane up to the moon, landed, walked around for a while, and then came back to earth. He gave me the strangest look. I knew I had gone much too far.

"That's nothing, watch this," said Grandpa Dick. Reaching over, he pulled on Liam's ear, and somehow the overhead light came on. Geez, this was going to be a magical land. Later we visited a supermarket and had to go down every aisle to see the unimaginable abundance.

All of us had major adjustments to go through. Within a week, we were in Cedar Falls, an hour north, where I had signed on with an old med school friend in Family Practice. He had rented us a house and furnished it minimally. Soon, as Janet set up household, the kids began American school, and I got back to middle class western medicine. Slowly, we melded into our new society, even succumbing to the cornerstone of the "civilized" world, television.

To ease the transition, after getting our precious local library cards, Liam and I began checking out and reading together, each of Edgar Rice Burroughs' Tarzan series. Every night at bedtime, we would pass through another vicarious adventure, a battle to the death, an impossible situation, always reminiscing of the real Africa.

For the first time ever, Liam was totally immersed among racial peers. Acceptance demanded that the slang be learned, the look imitated, the then fashionable frivolities included in the seemingly complex life style. Portuguese, Lomwe, and, what I missed most, all the beautiful, lilting African inflections and changing cadences, vanished like the early morning mist over a watering hole. Try as we might, Janet and I were unable to stimulate the preservation of these hard come skills. All that remained, and that, purely for shock value, were two words, chi-chi and coco, having to do with bodily functions.

We all enjoyed being out of doors, so visiting parks and exploring became a frequent pass time activity. Robinson Crusoe Island became a favorite. Located in the Cedar River, accessible only by footbridge, this sizable hideaway featured winding wooded walkways, perilous paths, hidden treasures, secluded sandy beaches, a shipwreck, plenty of climbing areas, and a primitive fort with a lookout tower. The kids never failed to run to get there. Actually, the metro area included Waterloo, a city of 80,000, providing us with numerous parks, ponds, creeks, school yards, and preserves, all of which we investigated assiduously. The University of Northern Iowa, enrollment 12,000, situated on the western edge of town, alluring as it was with the many sidewalks, open areas, and passageways, during the fall of the year, became irresistible as the maples rained on raptured retinae, a splendiferous kaleidoscopic array of color.

On this particular day, wondering around the campus, we came upon a building labeled PEC. Finding the doors unlocked, we ventured inside. My first breath told me that we were within diffusing range of gym air. Poles for vaulting on the floor to the right, locker room to the left, and somewhere, not too distant, the irregular pat, pat pat, that could only mean one thing, basketball in progress. Cues abounding, dopamine crossing primordial cerebral synapses, I was drawn inextricably through the next set of swinging doors and up a wide stairway to a landing where I paused, now able to pick up the squeak of sneakers in perfect synchrony with the muffled expletives and exhortations. Crescendo- decrescendo, like the pounding hooves of a herd of wildebeests, this was full court engagement. Bounding up the remaining steps, racing the kids to the top, we came upon large, wide open doorways revealing an expanse of eight adjacent courts, all in use. The sight, the sound, the vibration, the feel of adrenaline, all combined to complete my epiphany. Boinggg, ball off rim, rebound!!, let's go, run, run, squeak, get him!, loft, swoosh. Ball through net. What a hypnotic habit former.

As we watched, I noticed that the players on court one were particularly adept, most of them being over six feet, and several looking like six-eight or nine. One youthful appearing participant seemed strangely familiar. Yes, this was the boy I had played against in Orange City once. Their game was just ending, so, as he was picking up his sweats, I approached him. "Kraayenbrink, right?"

"Yup, you look familiar but I can't place you."

"My name is Murphy. I'm a doctor here in town, but I'm from Alton and I played against you in a town tournament, a couple years back."

"Oh ya, now I remember, aren't you the guy who schooled Pauling once?"

"Uh huh, this is really a nice facility. You here on scholarship?"

Nodding in affirmation he replied, "I'm a freshman, and most of these guys are on the team. You still play?"

"I haven't for a while, but I'd like to get back into it. Can anyone come here?"

"I've never seen 'em check ID's, and lots of times older guys like faculty and even some of the coaches play over on court five."

"Great, nice to see you again. Good luck this year."

"Thanks. Are these your boys?" he asked, flipping a soft bounce pass to Liam. "You guys ball players?' he questioned, catching the return and sending it delicately Conor's way. Too shy to answer, both seemed excited to be involved in the proceedings. Waving goodbye, we wandered around the courts before heading out the back way. I knew we'd be spending more time here in the future.

The next day, after discussing it with Janet, I got season tickets for the family to attend UNI basketball games. Janet liked the game but had never been given the opportunity to play, making it difficult to have the same level of passion that I had. Both of us agreed that we should make diligent efforts to expose our children to a variety of ideas and activities, hoping that they would then be able to choose which direction they wanted to go in their lives as they matured. We got tickets for the Waterloo Children's Theater, took lots of small weekend trips, and went to a diverse mixture of events around town. Still, with the Iowa Hawkeyes being televised for every game, UNI, and the NBA on TV, we three boys inched toward fanaticism. Liam liked the Lakers with Magic. Conor picked Patrick and the Knicks. I had been a Celt for years, and with Bird there, why change? While other kids collected baseball cards, ours did basketball. There were some courts around town with low hoops and, quite often we'd go just to play around and shoot.

My first time back in action came on a Sunday afternoon. I went up to the PEC with the intention of just shooting around. I'd been jogging a few times but knew that my skills would most likely be dreadfully inadequate after playing so little in Africa. And it was true, my touch had vanished, footwork faded, timing off, and, in general, out of sync. After about twenty minutes, I noticed what I thought was at least a minimal atavistic response and was beginning to get a feel for the ball and the moves again. Then, unexpectedly, the call came from the adjacent court. "Hey, we need one. You in?"

These guys were streaming sweat and I had noticed that they were going at it hard. No way was I ready for it. "Sure, I'll go," I said putting my ball down as nonchalantly as possible but thinking, "Fool, they'll eat you up alive. How are you going to participate and save any face at all? At least try and stay in good position, give up the outside shot but not the layup. Just pass, pick and rebound. Hero, you're not today."

"You got Rider, over there. Stay on him. He can shoot." Great, I thought, first time back and I got Jerry West. This should be interesting. They take it at the top of the key to begin the game and immediately the ball comes to Rider. They said he could shoot but that's just to get me to play "D", so I stay off a little and "whoosh", he scores from twenty. Hmm. As the game goes on, he makes two or three more, despite me trying to tighten up a little. I guess they mean he can shoot, as in lights out. At least I'm not dyin' out here. I attempt a jumper. Brick! Rider gets the ball. This time I challenge the heck out of him and he actually misses one. I'm starting to feel a little better. Finally it comes down to game point. They set a pick for Rider. I fight through, but not soon enough to keep him from getting the ball. Still, he's deep in the corner and I'm right on him. Somehow he quick releases so fast that, even though I'm ready, he gets it off. Big deal. No worry. A person can't hurry a shot that much and have any control. Swish!! I had almost forgotten how much fun the game could be. Not!

Walking over to get my ball, I see the guy who torched me heading my way. "Hi, I'm Paul Rider. I teach chemistry here at the university."

"Dan Murphy. I'm a new doctor in town. Nice shooting."

"Thanks. Do you play much?"

"Well, I like the game, but I'm not in very good shape. I need to play more."

"Good. That's what I wanted to talk to you about. A bunch of us play here noons. We always need more players. You can sign up for suit service that gives you a locker and clean stuff every day. All you need is your own shoes."

"Sounds interesting. Thanks for telling me." It seemed like a good opportunity. I did have time off at lunch, and it was convenient. I thought I'd keep it in mind and find out more details.

My job was primary health care, interesting, but nothing like what I'd been doing. I was also working several shifts per month in E.R. and was gradually being introduced to the subtleties of third party payer, fee for service medicine. Always be aware of what insurance a patient has, doctor. Use words like pain and bleeding as much as possible, and include references to multiple systems in as many cases as you can. It's essential for coding, as in up-coding. Always order tests to protect yourself. And be on the alert for any potential procedures, they're reimbursed so much better. Africa, where are you? Still, I was meeting lots of good people, and Janet and I were frequently asked to speak or give slide shows around town.

We joined a group called Citizens for Peace which was becoming quite active over the Nicaraguan situation. Another one of our government's puppets had fallen, and our leadership was bound and determined to fix it in a reign of terror heaped on that country's citizenry. To top it off, rather than having their supply planes come back empty, enlightened business oriented leadership utilized the cargo space to bring back cocaine for distribution throughout the U.S. As things heated up, Janet and I, leaving the kids with grandparents, accompanied an Iowa group, by charter bus, on a trip to a D.C. weekend rally. Marching, waving placards, hearing speeches and lobbying congress, we felt, once again engaged, even though, most of it fell on deaf ears.

What did come of it, however, was, through contacts made with Sandinistas, an invitation to attend a colloquium on health care in Managua. Due to my work on midwifery in Africa, I was asked to make a presentation on how my program had developed in Mozambique. The conference wasn't to be for several months giving me lots of time to prepare. I decided to do both the English and Spanish presentations myself and asked Janet to help with the formal language appropriate for such a gathering.

Meanwhile the kids were in school, Janet had begun doing volunteer work, and I had joined suit service, playing ball nearly every day instead of eating lunch.

Mozambique was rapidly deteriorating. Gurue had been overrun and occupied by Renamo with many reported casualties. Silva and his family, including Lucas, had fled to the bush. We hadn't heard any more.

Finally the day arrived to depart for Central America. Flying first to Miami, I then crossed over the Gulf of Mexico, before pausing briefly in Tegucigalpa, just long enough to see the pervasive military presence and observe the evident poverty of that desperately underdeveloped nation. Managua, on the other hand was positive and upbeat. I sensed the same kind of hope that I had experienced early on in Mozambique. Fresh from shaking the shackles of Somoza, here was a country on a mission of empowerment. The enemies were hunger, illiteracy, ill health, and disenfranchisement. Changing the distribution and control of food production resources was a top priority. Even relatively prosperous Costa Rica was buying Nicaraguan crops. Poetry readings and workshops abounded, cultural awareness added glitter to the multitude of new activities taking place throughout the country. There were cooperatives, clean up, construction of new infrastructure, autonomy for the East, protection of rain forests, and an emphasis on women's rights. All with no cult of personality in sight among the leadership. Amnesty had been granted to the majority of counterrevolutionaries, and the death penalty abolished.

In the field of health, nationwide vaccination campaigns had, for the first time ever, eliminated completely, the scourge of poliomyelitis, and drastically reduced the incidence of measles. Improved water supplies and ongoing educational efforts coupled with widespread distribution of rehydration mixtures were making serious inroads into diarrhea mortality. Although private practice still prevailed, every physician contributed time to national health efforts and access to at least the most essential health care was in the process of being provided throughout the country. Dedicated expatriates poured in from around the world to assist in the realization of this improbable dream. Cuba, as they had done consistently in the past in other similar situations, provided generous delegations of enthusiastic technicians in all the most needed fields, along with significant amounts of materiel aid.

Spending two weeks, traveling around the country and visiting a wide variety of sites and projects, and being able to communicate in Spanish, I was truly impressed. Why, then, wasn't I surprised that the United States was doing everything it could to destroy what was happening here? Because, first hand, I had lived through the hell that was Mozambique. The scenario varies little throughout the world. Any perceived threat, no matter how insignificant, to the U.S. led multinational corporate power structure, must be addressed aggressively. It's very impersonal, having more to do with long range geopolitical strategy and bottom line numbers, than anything.

In the town of Estelí, after an inspiring visit to a new maternity center run by a Chilean nurse midwife using all the progressive and proper methods in her teaching, I spotted a basketball game on a small outdoor court just off the town square. Approaching the action, I saw that these were just young teenagers, mostly shooting around and showing off rather than playing a regular game.

Totally unable to help myself, I blurted out, "Puedo yo jugar?"

"Simon," responded the bright eyed youth with the ball, using his best Pachuco jive, and flipping me a behind the back bounce pass, which I immediately sent through the netless rim with an effortless five meter right hook shot.

"Bien hecho, hombre. De donde vienes tu?" I explained that I was an American with a medical delegation visiting their country. As we chatted about various topics, I tried to keep the mood going by displaying, with as little arrogance as possible, my humble repertoire of shots and tricks. One of the guys told how he was a member of "La Mano Negra" as the others snickered. I was momentarily caught off guard when an innocent looking street urchin type asked, "Conoces tu a Doctor Jota?" Now how did this kid know any of the people in our delegation, and there wasn't anyone, that I knew of with a name resembling Jota. Then it clicked.

"You mean Julius Erving, plays for the '76ers'. Ya, he's amazing, but there's another guy, named 'Magico' who might be better and then there's 'Pajaro'...." Here we were, in an isolated area of a war torn, underdeveloped nation, discussing NBA stars. A good lesson in the power of modern, major media.

My portion of the conference went well, with many questions and positive comments afterwards. This was a country where the practice of obstetrics was extremely traditional, with active intervention, ranging from near universal episiotomy, to high rates of operative delivery for the minority able to access the system, coupled with neglect for the impoverished majority. Septic AB's, illegally performed under less than ideal conditions, drained scarce hospital resources in Managua with a daily double digit epidemic of morbidity and mortality. Nurses, and especially local midwives, wanted to know every detail of what had worked so well in Mozambique.

On a negative note, however, at a round table discussion, on that very topic, I was unmercifully excoriated by a vocal group of self-professed, lesbian, California, lay midwives, accusing me of being insensitive to making each delivery the most meaningful, beautiful experience possible. None of them had ever done work in the third world. Consequently, an overwhelming concern for reducing the outrageous toll of neonatal and maternal mortality was not even on their agenda. More disturbing was their seemingly inflexible stance, not listening, displaying little interest in dialogue, preferring diatribe at every turn. As a heterosexual, male, chauvinist physician, I had no chance.

That evening I skipped the proposed "house visits" with ordinary citizens, choosing instead to sit quietly in a nearby small bar sipping a local brew or two. Doing my best to unwind and with soft rhythmic music providing additional mood, I pondered the mess the world was in, but also the large number of motivated individuals I had met who were doing their best to improve things. Relaxed and mellow, I looked up to see a young, dark haired woman standing at my table.

"Can I join you, Dr. Murphy?" she asked, displaying an easy smile.

"Be my guest," I said, gesturing toward the opposite chair. "But it's Dan, if you don't mind."

"Sure, Dan. My name is Tempest. I'm a labor and delivery nurse at Mass General. I've attended all your sessions, and I have to tell you, I'm extremely impressed. I'd give anything to have done the things you've done."

"Thanks, I've had some good opportunities for meaningful work. Tell me about your life."

Ordering a beer, she began, "I got my RN five years ago and started right off in OB. I really like Boston, but I'm also a single mother. My husband was killed a year ago – a freaky street stickup that went bad. So now it's just me and Will, my three-year-old."

"Sorry to hear that. How are you guys doing with it?"

"It's getting better, but I'm still sad a lot of the time. I've gotten quite involved in groups like MADRE and TecNica. This is my second trip down here. Keeps me busy."

"What do you do with Will?"

"My mom. She lives in Worcester. They have a big yard, and Will loves it there, so it works out fine."

"Must be tough financially. I understand Boston's expensive."

"Very, and I do struggle, but I picked up a second job, and now, at least I'm keeping my head above water."

"What do you do?" I asked curiously.

Looking down for a moment in hesitation, she then lifted up her head and fixed her eyes directly on mine as if to measure my reaction as she responded, "I'm an exotic dancer."

Apparently I passed the test, because almost immediately she continued, "I have to apologize. Tempest is my stage name. I guess being here in the bar got me confused in my roles." Smiling she reached over the table, hand extended, "Let me introduce myself. Dan, I'm Maria. It certainly is a pleasure being here and talking with you." The temperature of her hand seemed to be exactly the same as that of the warm, inviting Nicaraguan evening. Certain questions popped into my head about her alter existence but instead, signaling an additional two, I stuck with discretion, "Maria, you could pass for Latina."

"Spanish. My grandmother came from Barcelona."

"Entonces hablas Espanol?"

"Tristamente, solamente poquito. Mi abuela se murio cuando yo tenia cinco anos, so I never kept up with it. I'm trying to learn more now. You sure seem to do well, even the technical stuff."

"I got help with those parts. Actually, I've never had formal classes in Spanish. All I know is simple campesino talk."

"How humble! I've heard all about your work with Cesar Chavez. Needless to say, you're my idol. Let's dance." Not even waiting for a response, she took my hand and led us to the adjacent room where a few couples were on the small floor, following the melodic, mood altering music, wafting from the vintage juke.

On the way to the dimly lit open area, seldom used recesses of my brain sent out urgent N.B.'s. Like, you, flat out aren't a good dancer. Remember your traumatic toilet training, on top of much too early introduction of beikost, not to mention the devastating loss of transitional Teddy's left eye, you're not prepared for this! Not true, I countered. I did a decent jitterbug, and a respectable twist, and the disgusting frat parties, and the countless soul nights at Li'l Bill's, the Mexican bodas, and the African dumdums, can't forget that. She's a pro, so just pull a transcendental switcheroo into a Baryshnikov, or no, a Travolta in "Saturday Night Fever," the mood fits better. It was true, tight medical or political situations, yes, speeches, yes, last second shots with game on the line, bring it on, but in navigating this genre of uncharted social encounter, I felt like a nervous novice. And from deeper yet, Danny boy, you're out of control. Think! Where is this leading? Does family ring a bell??

172

On the other hand she knew nothing of this, and I was her idol. Iowa could have been on the moon for this occasion. Her look was happy, confident, non-judgmental, natural, inviting. What a time for right brain assertion. Taking my other hand, the table was swept clean of clutter. Assuming the role of debonair master, I became Fred, she Cyd, majestically complimenting the romantic Latin sound. Now I relaxed, freely responding to each sensory cue, drifting deep, and irreversibly, into the zone. Our hands never separated for that entire first foray. Ever so subtly, her energy guided us as one with the sonorous phrases enveloping all like a passing shadow.

As the music ended, hands separating, I took advantage of the momentary silence, "Maria, I've been working on developing the practice of mindfulness. You just took me two or three lessons forward."

"I was a little mesmerized myself. Let's see if we can take it to the next level."

She was about 5'9"with shoulder length hair that seemed to wave in unison with her dancing movements. This record was faster, and even though I continued moving, this was her time, and more than anything, stepping back slightly, I let my eyes follow her choreographic spontaneity. In her own element, and feeling so very alive, she allowed her form more freedom. A halter, tied high at the waist, accented the defined shoulders and the tastefully displayed, smooth, tanned midriff. Her loose fitting shorts failed to preempt the image of a fine Arabian colt prancing proudly in a victory lap. Watching in admiration, I couldn't help thinking that this was indeed a rarity, highly developed stage presence, and yet, a respectful sincerity, asking nothing, expecting nothing.

Several songs later, taking appropriate measures to stave off any chance of tropical dehydration, I decided that a bit of boldness was in order. Striding over to unplug the box, I turned to the eight or ten people remaining in the room. "Atencion! Hombres y mujeres, hijos todos de Sandino, miembros de la revolucion, neste momento, orgullosamente, yo queria presentarle a Uds., la una y unica bailadora, la famosa, Tempest."

Reinserting the juice, I punched in the piece "Malagena", and turned to see how my new found comadre was reacting. Unfazed, she stepped to the center of the room awaiting the unknown cue.

At the first sounds of the classical guitar, Tempest took the pose of a graceful Flamenco. As she began to move, everyone present became riveted to her performance. Appearing effortless, she put on a show that, if spontaneous, was simply amazing, perfectly matched with the demanding scores. Soon, however, it became apparent that this wasn't to be the highbrow interpretation like one would see at the Lincoln Center. First the knot came undone, and as the drama unfolded, buttons exited apertures, and finally, in a dazzling display of whirling grace, the halter flew to nearby wall to an encore of whistles and high pitched Latin ahh-haa's and falsetto oowee's. Building momentum, she defiantly advanced, using a combination of deft footwork and intricate overlapping motions featuring lithe arms and obviously practiced hand action. Somehow, the shorts had become unzipped, the midline "V" drawing every eye to a sizzling series of thrusts, spins, and near touches, which even the NEA would have classified as prurient art. She ended synchronously with the piece, in a perfectly executed, deep, curtsy, arising to a cavalcade of applause, hoots, and smiles.

Grabbing her blouse and slipping it back over her bikini bra, she zipped up and came over to me, still breathing heavily. "How'd I do, Doc? Wasn't too raunchy, was it?"

"I'm speechless. No, extremely tasteful. Should provide a big lift to the revolution."

"Want to go for a walk? I'm hot."

As we exited through the open door to the verandah, I remembered. "Just a minute, I put on one more record." Standing just out of the light, we heard the music start, "Volver." Taking her in my arms, we began the last dance, outside, alone, and close. The athletic feel of her heavy breathing held me in a supportive, and at the same time, aroused state of mind. "Tempest, how did you come up with such a great show?"

"It's Maria now, and I do that exact piece as part of my routine. You liked it, huh?" she answered releasing my hand and wrapping both her arms around my back.

"Ya, very sexy and professional. But how do you keep the shorts from falling?" I asked, now definitely enjoying the feel of her hair, cheek, chest, and pelvis.

"Buns of steel. I work out a lot."

Slipping my hand down, I reported, "Umm, I see what you mean."

"Dan, I consider that an aggressive, provocative move."

"And your Tempest act, what was that?"

"That was visual. Tactile crosses the line in the sand. Now I can activate the Contras."

"Then I apologize, Colonel North, but most of our bodies are touching at this very moment. A pair of schistosoma couldn't get much closer."

Slowly moving her face to a position directly in front of mine, "We haven't even begun to get close. Don't try to throw us off with those erotic medical metaphors." With each word, her nose and lips approached mine, not gaining momentum, but softly exploring like two weightless objects in space. As the music stopped, our feet returned imperceptibly to the liberated Nicaraguan soil.

"Maria, I have to tell you, I'm..."

"Don't, Dan," she said, putting her fingers over my mouth. "Remember what you said about mindfulness? I've never had a time like this. Either it's predestined, or we're extremely lucky. It doesn't really matter, but I know we should experience this for all it's worth."

"Maybe you're right. Somehow, I feel like I'm in choppy waters."

"Great, I sail all the time. Take my word for it, now's not the time to come about."

"You got the words right, but it's the order I'm thinking of."

Pausing for a minute, she looked at me and broke out laughing. "You wry fellow, you! C'mon, let's walk."

Strolling through the streets, enjoying the many unfamiliar scenes, we chatted, wide ranging and carefree. I was surprised at how knowledgeable and sensitive Maria seemed to be.

Deep into the night we found ourselves on the shores of Lake Managua. The waxing moon was about to dip into the perfect mirror spread before us. Looking out over the water, I began, "How ironic. Here we are enjoying this great time, and it really is beautiful, but this is said to be the most polluted body of water anywhere, and we're in an embattled country with violent attacks and suffering everywhere, most of it paid for by our own tax dollars. It's like the horror of it all was enough to bring us both here, making these moments possible."

Running a finger over my body, she replied, "That's why we should live this and fix that. It's two sides of the same reality." This time an inextricable force did pull us together and the moon had vanished before we began the uphill walk to the hotel.

As we entered the lobby and stepped into the elevator, I said, "I'm on third floor."

"Me too," she replied.

Getting out we walked together down the hallway. The rooms were arranged in pairs, with doubly locked doors between adjacent numbers. My puritan self was still painfully ambivalent about what could come next. Arriving at 314, the second last door, I pulled out my key and said, "This is my room." Maria was still at my side, leaving me wondering what she was thinking.

Reaching into her pocket, she produced her key, holding it up for me to see. Three-sixteen. Taking my key and holding it next to hers, she said, "Like a pair of schistosoma."

Looking at her, unable to procrastinate further, I feebly joked, "Serendipity!"

"No, fate!" Handing me my key, she stepped to her door and turned, "Matthew 7:7" She was gone.

Matthew 7:7, Matthew 7:7, I thought as I entered my room, what is that? Not being particularly religious, and having previously been only a Catholic, I had to reach deep. Along with that, I remained hung up on notions such as morality, faithfulness, confidence. True, Janet and I were communicating less as of late, but would I be betraying my two sons whom I loved so dearly? After what seemed like an agonizingly long interval, suddenly my thoughts crystallized. Arising up off the bed, I walked calmly to the adjoining door, unlocked my side, and knocked ever so lightly. For a moment, nothing. Then I heard the turning bolt and the door opened.

The absolutely stunning scene captured my every fiber. It wasn't the negligee, her revealed form, or her distinct beauty, but the expression, magnified by and inseparable from the tears. Big Boy detonated, freeing and engaging every emotion at once, captivating my very essence. "Maria, I didn't know you were..."

"Dan," she interrupted. "The script is sacred, no deviation. Please sit there on the bed." Taking a position between me and the window she calmly announced, "In appreciation of the special and wonderful time we had tonight in Managua, Nicaragua, I dedicate to you, Dan, this very personal artistic performance. Imagine Linda Ronstad's version of 'Baby, Baby' in accompaniment."

What followed, silhouetted against the first dawn's awakening, was the most sensuous, exciting gift, surpassing even the most vivid visitation of succubi. The pace of her movements varied little but momentum steadily increased, weaving the web near, then back, a touch, a revealing look, graceful and exquisite, all. Concluding with a raw display of emotion and prowess, Maria executed her final deliberate pirouette and ended, head bowed, touching my feet with hands and hair. "Namaste, Sahib."

Arising, she then laid me down and took my side on the bed. "Maria, that was so far beyond anything I've ever experienced. I'm in a state of rapture. No more curare for a minute, I might stop breathing."

"OKAY, turn over and I'll give you a back rub while you tell me your dreams. And relax, I know CPR."

Slowly, glass ball repositioned, the artificial snowflakes began to settle around the country house, each finding it's unique resting place, until finally, the last particle alit, delicately balanced on the roof, before falling wisely to the ground.

Bzzz, Bzzz, Bzzz. "Doctor Murphy, son las siete horas."

"Dan, don't go."

"I have to. It's the closing ceremony and I'm going to be recognized. Tallez and even Daniel Ortega are going to be there."

"But there are things we haven't done."

"Always, the journey, right?"

"Right."

By three o'clock that afternoon, I was flying north, worried about a patient I had left in Iowa. Salome was a seventeen-year-old undocumented worker from Vietxuato, Michoacan, in central Mexico. Two weeks before I had left she walked into my office with a temperature of 105, BP 60/0, and a pulse of 210 beats per minute, complaining of weakness. Because I spoke Spanish, I had begun to attract this growing segment of the population almost immediately. Quickly putting her in a wheel chair, we advanced directly to ICU at the hospital. Hoping to avoid electrocardioversion, I had ordered cultures, IV fluids, and antibiotics in one arm, reserving the other for the aggressive protocol addressing the supraventricular tachycardia showing on the monitor. On the way in, she had told me of previous abbreviated episodes of rapid palpitations, prompting me to think of PAT. Just as I was beginning to lose hope, a double dose of verapamil took effect as her heart slowed, BP normalizing. Her 12-lead EKG now clearly showed Wolf-Parkinson-White Syndrome, a congenital abnormality involving anomalous aberrant impulse conduction fibers in the heart. Infection treated, she was now at the University, having electrophysiologic mapping in hopes of being able to effect a permanent cure by ablating the indicated pathways with probe cautery. Knowing that she had never been away from her family before, I had wanted to accompany the entire process to add what I could to the chances of success. At least in the larger hospital, there were adequate translators, and good social services. The whole process was delicate, but the attending specialist had assured me that no questions would be asked regarding immigration status. Still, experience had taught me to exercise all cautions in situations like this. I would call as soon as I got home.

Passing through Miami International, while others were harassed, some having items confiscated, and even missing connections, I advanced through unmolested. Finally touching down in Waterloo, despite the late hour, I was glad to see both Liam and Conor along with Janet welcoming me at the airport. Hugs then gifts for all, including a dramatic woven wall hanging depicting a bust of Sandino and a dove melded together in a powerful image of peace and freedom. Catching up on everything local, I answered questions as best I could about my exciting trip. At home, I found out that Salome's procedure had been unsuccessful despite eight hours in the cath lab. She was now being treated with medication, with another attempt at cure scheduled for a later date. Her appointment to see me was in several days. A man with a stroke had also been hospitalized during my absence, and there were a mother and newborn to visit. One advantage of being a doctor is that, although you're busy a lot of the time when you don't necessarily want to be, you can also be busy almost any time you do want to be.

Going to play BB the next noon, I was sure I'd be rusty because of the layoff, but I did surprisingly well. One of those games where the opposition keeps putting other guys on you to try to stop the scoring. It felt so nice that I decided to join the hospital team which played in the most competitive city league. Our first game was coming up soon. I made sure I got to play a few more times in preparation for the opening night so I would be in decent shape. As it turned out, it didn't matter. We just weren't that good, and lost by ten to a group of John Deere employees. Especially lacking was any semblance of defense. It was the guns of Navarrone firing mostly blanks. Quixote clones in a pitiful show of chemical inertia.

Next up for us was Donut Land, perennial powerhouse. We had a week to forget our initial ugliness, but I had a strong feeling that no amount of time could fix our problem. Still, it was a way to mix with my cohorts and get some exercise. The night before the contest, I had just gone to bed when the phone rang, "Dr. Murphy, this is Betty in ER. We've got an eight year old patient of yours here. Mom says he's been really thirsty lately and goes to the bathroom almost every hour. Tonight he can't keep anything down so she brought him in. He's very lethargic and pulse is 180."

"Get a blood sugar, lytes, and ABG's. You can run 20 ml. per kg normal saline IV wide open. I'll be right down." Thinking diabetes all the way, I replaced the telephone receiver and got up to get dressed.

"Sorry," said Janet as I pulled my pants up right over my pajama bottoms, a habit I'd developed to save time. Sorry, I didn't need sorry. Sure, I'd rather sleep, but this was my job. I'd chosen it. Maybe it was more the half asleep sing song tone that got me. Saying nothing, I walked out and hopped into the silver Ford for the five minute drive. Let's see, ketoacidosis. Avoid shock, watch potassium and renal function, slowly raise pH, and bring sugar down without hypoglycemia. I think I'll use IV drip insulin, better control. As I pulled into the hospital lot, I recalled a man I'd met briefly in Central America. Greenberg, I'm pretty sure his name was. Anyway, himself diabetic, he'd founded an organization called "Insulin for Life," dedicated exclusively to making insulin available to those in need in Nicaragua and, I think he said, El Salvador. I've got his card somewhere. Must send him a donation. In the ER, my fears were realized. Blood sugar 486, pH 7.18.

"How's he doing?"

"A little better with the fluids. Do you want insulin?"

"Give five units of regular push and set up a drip. I see his temp is up a little. Have lab do cultures with the next draw. I'll go see him a minute, then write admission orders." Walking into the room, I knew that this was a child and family that I'd have to know well. Getting diabetes is like having a baby. It pretty much takes over your existence for a long time. Carefully choosing my words, I explained what we'd found. The mother had suspected it, but had no idea of all the implications involved. As we stabilize, we'll search for, and treat any precipitating factors, teaching as we go along, hoping to achieve good control and as much independence as possible, I told them as I examined the now more alert child. Things went smoothly as I set up flow charts and sliding scales, wrote orders, dictated the H and P, read up, and checked more lab returns. It was 4:30 when I got home for two hours of restless sleep before getting up to begin a full day at the office.

By game time that evening, I was pretty much a zombie. It didn't even occur to me not to show. That's how compulsion works. I'd probably suggest one more game as the Titanic was going down. Should skip the after game beer, though. Expecting the worst, I volunteered to sit, letting others bask in the glory of the close part of the game, probably the first minute or two. Sure enough, half way through the first quarter, we were down ten, when one of the guys motioned me in. Feeling more numb than loose, I astonished even myself by hitting my first two, the second being from deep enough to, at least raise eyebrows. From there on it just seemed to flow on its own, and even more amazingly, my teammates were looking for me. What a pleasant surprise. At the half we led by five. The rest of the way, more of the same. The other guys picked their games up too, and we won going away by ten or so.

The next day at the gym, I overheard one of the refs talking to his buddy in the shower. "I heard Sartori (our hospital) knocked off Donut Land last night. How'd that happen?"

"Some new guy, Murphy. If he had one, he had forty, and that was just the first half!"

"Inside, or outside?"

"Inside, outside, don't make no difference to him. All he needs is the rock, and it's a done deal. The dude can play!"

Needless to say, all humility aside, I got a lot of mileage out that little exchange.

Between basketball, family, work, and speaking engagements, I had a full life, but I missed being involved in a "cause" like UFW or Mozambique, so it was not without excitement, that I responded to a phone call from Prexy. "Dan, we need you in New York City. As you know, things in Mozambique couldn't be much worse. President Machel is coming to address the United Nations General Assembly. I'm contacting all friends of Mozambique to be there, first to welcome the delegation, and also to lobby, help organize, and deal with the press. Your experience out in the district, lends legitimacy to the struggle, since that's the true Mozambique, peasants living by subsistence agriculture. What do you say?"

Prexy Nesbitt, son of a black minister in Chicago, had been strongly influenced in his youth, by Eduardo Mondlane, who attended Northwestern University. So much so, in fact, that as a nineteen-year-old, he left his home to join the FRELIMO independence organization in Tanzania, an amazing move in itself. His work as a partisan continued through the years in various capacities both here in the U.S. and in Africa. Articulate, knowledgeable, and dedicated, now working with Mayor Washington, as well as running the Chicago based Mozambique Support Network, he was an inspiration to us all.

"Prexy, I'll do anything I can to help."

"Excellent, Dan. I'll be in touch."

Many phone calls later, along with the typical last minute changes, everything was set, and I was in the air to La Guardia. Visiting N.Y. was always fun and exciting for me, but this was to be even more special because of the circumstances. Staying with Coke and his wife Susan, there was never a dull moment. Meetings with returned expatriates, then supporters, then various reporters and journalists, we were constantly on the go. A select few of us were chosen to present our concerns to people at the U.S. Ambassador to the UN's office. Sadly, for many of the people we dealt with, it seemed like their attitude was pretty much ho-hum, business as usual. Even President Machel's UN speech, which I thought was very moving, didn't generate the interest and response we had hoped for. Just one more fledgling basket case country with the usual laundry list of insoluble problems. How horribly unfair! This was a country that was developing and addressing its problems, and only through massive outside interference, was it now bleeding to death.

The private reception that evening was the high point of the trip. Fascinated, I observed the skillful way the African leader worked the receiving line. Dealing with a wide variety of people from all over the world, using many languages, Machel seemed at ease and in his element. Spontaneously chatting and interacting with everyone, it was easy to see how he had been able to work his magic during the Zimbabwean independence talks. As my turn approached, I decided to have some fun with him. Shaking hands, I began, "Moni, moni, mocala pama." Laughing he turned to his coterie momentarily. No one responded. "E a língua do Gurue,' I continued. 'Eu trabalhe ai como medico chefe distrital por tres anos."

"Aah, Gurue, muito bem. Depois havemos de falar."

Moving on, I thought nothing more of it, but about an hour later, along with vice president Chissano and Pascual Mocumbi then in line to be Foreign Minister, came Samora Machel. "So, Dr. Murphy, tell me about your experience in Gurue." One of the frequent criticisms of having a vanguard party using the principal of democratic centralism is that the leadership is out of touch with the problems of the common citizen, and only receives biased information passed on by those pressing their own personal agenda, making appropriate decision making much more difficult. Machel, however, much to the chagrin of his security corps, combated that by making frequent forays amongst the masses, at work sites, on the street, in villages, coaxing out the details of their day to day lives, including the difficulties along with the joys. Now I was able to tell all about my work in his country. He was very attentive, especially when I gave him a summary of the events at Muagiua. I had put together a collage from pictures I had taken before the tragic attack, mostly of Claudio, along with a short eulogy which I had intended to send back to his widow and children if I could find a way. Taking them out I presented them to president Machel, asking him, if it were possible, to get the material to the martyr's family. In all sincerity, he promised to do his best.

Later that night, a few of us medical people sat up until the wee hours with Dr. Mocumbi, reminiscing and discussing not just medical matters, but all aspects of Mozambique's situation, and life in general. In parting, I was told, "Dr. Dani, if you ever want to return to work in Mozambique, any time, just call me personally. We need you."

Events such as this, plus keeping in touch with Lucas' situation, and visiting friends we'd made while overseas, kept Africa in mind at all times. South Africa resembled an active volcano, frequently exploding in passionate billowing upheavals, mixing blood, courage, greed, and the quest for power. Mozambique was subjected to a new standard for horror, deprivation, and destruction.

Seemingly unrelated occurrences, for me, spelled out diabolical scheming and execution. Instructive would be Angola. Finally peaceful after a bloody independence struggle and subsequent "civil war" in which the U.S. armed both sides, a single dark cloud appeared on the horizon as the senate, in a murky low profile maneuver, repealed the Clark Amendment. Gulf Oil, which had an excellent working relationship in the Cabinda Enclave of that country, was bought out by Chevron, which just happened to have on its board of directors, a former senior state department official from the time of the Allende coup. The convenient revolving door of multinational corporate leadership, high government position, and "retiring" military personnel, worked it's magic and, bingo, a Jonas Savimbi was pressed back into service, buoyed up by unlimited support from apartheid South Africa, the most notorious of African dictator, Zaire's Mobutu, and the United States of America. Result? Another obscure African country was torched with incalculable suffering for millions of innocent black peasants similar to those with whom I had worked in Gurue. Cuba, with the majority of its citizenry having roots in west Africa, then committed, in a major contribution, and the would be, dagger to the heart, thrust led by South Africans, was thwarted, averting total defeat.

If any small recess of my mind remained free of cynicism, it was eliminated one morning when Janet picked up the morning paper, "What! Under mysterious circumstances, the presidential plane of Mozambique went down in a remote area of South Africa. Among the dead was Samora Machel, leader of that country since independence."

My immediate reaction, "Those bastards stop at nothing." Later investigation showed that, returning home from a hard-nosed meeting in Malawi where President Machel in no uncertain terms warned President Banda that any more incursions into Mozambique originating from within Malawi would not be tolerated. The plane began a routine decent still over South African territory heading for Maputo. It didn't crash, but "landed" way short, in an isolated area of jungle. South African military personnel arrived on the scene, but strangely, no rescue or medical assistance was called for until many hours later. Joaquim Chissano was now acting President in a smooth transition, side stepping the crises that many thought would follow.

My day to day work as a physician, always provided medical challenges, but it wasn't that often that politics entered into the equation. I realized that I probably had a sizable dossier in some government basement but thought that, considering the turbulence of the era, it wouldn't be so unusual. Still, it wasn't without some surprise when I was handed a letter indicting me for fraudulently billing Medicaid. Since coming to Cedar Falls, I had been performing, on occasion, an office procedure called a menstrual extraction, which involves curetting the uterus of a woman up to two weeks late on her period, using a small 6mm. cannula. Some of these women avoided pregnancy testing, not wanting to know the result, preferring to leave the question open. Others knew that they were definitely in early pregnancy. The state of Iowa had recently passed a law denying the use of any government funding for abortion. It boiled down to another attack on choice, discriminating, once again, on those of less means. After many exchanges, by both phone and mail, and with some heated moments within our own office, I was left with no other option than appearing in administrative court. Defending myself, I was finally given the chance to speak. "Your honor, thank you for allowing me this opportunity to explain my position. First, let me state that unequivocally, I support every woman's right to choose. In my present position, I work as a salaried employee in a medical office. I see patients without being told their insurance status, not knowing if they are rich or poor, having absolutely nothing to do with billing procedure or collection of funds. I believe that the best medical care is given when extraneous factors are not allowed into the doctor-patient equation. Your honor,

I have spent the last ten years working for virtually nothing among the world's poorest people. Is it likely that I would now turn to conspiring to defraud the government's medical assistance program for those most in need? I submit that the charges are false and that I am innocent."

Two weeks later the verdict arrived; I was acquitted of all charges. However, with the attendant publicity, patients were lost and a certain smoldering bitterness ensued.

At home, besides the frequent outdoor excursions, reading remained a consistent source of entertainment. Janet and I loved sharing the newspaper, especially on leisurely Sundays. The occasional splurge for the big *New York Times* always measurably quickened the pulse. Liam had become close friends with Jaime, a boy his age next door, but nevertheless was practically insatiable when it came to books. Jack London's *White Fang* and *The Call of the Wild* kept us both spellbound. Having read little as a child, I enjoyed this activity as much as the kids. Conor's literary discretion was becoming ever more sophisticated. Not wanting to follow directly in his older brother's footsteps, he accepted my suggestion that we see if Burroughs had any non-Tarzan offerings. Before we were done, not only had we become experts on the planet Barsoom, but also had a good feel for Apache Indians, especially Geronimo. Not infrequently, as Conor and I read, I would notice Liam, on the floor, peaking around the corner, powerless to not be a part of such engaging action.

Liam and I had begun to develop a second literary activity, the fast break vignette. Beginning with a coin flip, or the scissors-rock-paper duel to determine who would be first, and, readying ourselves with paper positioned and pencil poised, we waited anxiously for the chosen one to set our minds in action. For his turn, Liam might say, "Okay, you're in the jungle with only a small knife and suddenly, you find yourself surrounded by lions, *and*, there's about to be an eclipse of the sun. What do you do? Go!" Both of us then have to finish the story. You can't dilly-dally though, because whenever one person is finished, the other must stop too, allowed only to finish the current sentence. The real fun came next, as we read our masterpieces aloud and then obliged ourselves to analyze and criticize until we arrived at a consensus on which offering had enough literary merit to be awarded the Pulitzer. Not surprisingly, Liam frequently edged me out for the win, but not without a determined endorsement and/or rebuttal by both of us. Then I would have the chance to challenge with something like, "You're a ten-year-old boy playing happily in the park. Two girls, your age, are approaching looking directly at you. One is wearing blue jeans and a faded T-shirt and has a nasty scar on her arm. The other is dressed fancy and shows just a hint of lipstick. She's carrying an envelope, using both hands as if it were precious. What happens next? Go!" Nearly always, these turned out to be win-win situations, with a lot of laughter and personal interaction.

January 18, 1985.

With Janet working at The World's Window, a non-profit gift shop featuring items from third world, mostly women's cooperatives, and the boys being in school, I had no impediment to taking nearly every noon hour for my group therapy treatment, PEC basketball. The mix of students, professors, and community members from all walks of life, rarely failed to provide a fascinating milieu for both the sport and the invariable personality clashes. When combined with the excellent aerobic exercise involved, it was becoming an ingrained habitual activity.

On the blustery winter day, after a particularly frustrating morning at work where nothing seemed to turn out right, I hurried anxiously to the gym, knowing that I was a little late and might miss the first game. Sliding into the parking space, running into the locker area, barely slowing down to grab my bag of fresh gear, shirt already unbuttoned, I did my best fireman act, or I could say, doctor to delivery room act, to traverse and compulsively advance to the area of encounter. Little did I know that this was to be what I call, "The Day."

In any sport, an individual's level of performance varies from moment to moment, day to day, or even more. We would all like to play at the highest level possible, and do it consistently. So many factors are involved. Starting with your physical attributes, you figure in height, weight, strength, quickness, coordination, jumping ability.

Then there's practice, conditioning, and experience. And not to be forgotten are the mental aspects: desire, competitiveness, confidence, determination, judgment, reliability, and composure under pressure. Completing the picture are the intangibles: luck, predestination, astrological setting, and divine intervention. Players go to great lengths to get an edge, compulsive rituals, superstition, a favorite jock strap, the fingernails, a special meal, timing the pre-game bowel movement. Crucial, each and every one.

Cutting to the quick, what I'm getting to, here, is shooting the basketball. How did Elvin Hayes do what he did that night in the Astrodome against Lew Alcindor?

If you think about it, mechanically, anybody has the muscles, the eyes, and the nerve fibers; all the tools necessary to send a ball through a hoop. Why is it so difficult? Good question. My own shooting has been characterized as, and I'm the first to admit it, erratic. Anything from abysmally abominable to streaky, singey, uncanny hot. Kind of like Mariah Carey's vocal range. Well, this day's exhibition left peak performance in the dust, shattered the glass goblet, and soared through a wormhole past "zone" into some ethereal existence in another dimension, reaching that unique spot, off the records, beyond comparison, where even dreams can't go. World B. could go on a mind boggling tear, sure, and Vinnie J. did as a microwave, but this was in a new category, unplowed ground, unexplored territory. I mean people were rubbing their eyes and pinching themselves, like being at The Resurrection. Seriously, at one point, during a dead ball, I walked over toward two guys, and they backed off instinctively, fearful for their lives. The look on their faces, the dilated pupils and the open mouth, you just don't see it that often. It was like the final take on the critical set in an "X Files" episode. What do you do when all previous experience doesn't help you, the laws of physics don't apply, and a quick assay for LSD in the drinking water isn't practical?

The nine guys waiting on the floor didn't include any D1's or ex-D1's, but nearly all of them had played H.S. ball, and some had small college experience. Coming up tenth is perfect 'cause you can start immediately. "Murphy, you're yellow. John, take him. Yellow ball on top. Let's go!" John Larson was about 6'1" and had been a local H.S. star. He was an above average defender who took the game seriously and didn't like to get beat.

"Ball in!" I heard as I was finishing tying my shoes and was just standing up. No warm up, no practice shots, no stretches, no nothing as the second pass came to me standing out about 21 feet. People knew that I was an obligate gunner, limited only by the possibility of having people actually refuse to play with me for not giving it up sufficiently. There's a fine line there somewhere, depending on who's on your team, their personalities, team chemistry, and the match-ups. Winning, of course, is the bottom line, at least for most people it is, so if you are the best chance for scoring, it's your sacred duty to put up at least enough shots to assure the "W." Keeping everybody happy and getting each player involved are legitimate considerations, but if a guy's hot... Early in the game, first touch, fairly far out, John relaxed a little and my first salvo coursed over his fingertips and settled into net, 1-0. Nothing unusual, that first shot is nearly always there, and even if you miss, people think you can always make up the difference as the game progresses. Anyway, first and last shots were my specialty, my take being that, more often than not, they went in.

Basically, I'm a low self-esteem type of guy, always having to prove myself, but ironically, or paradoxically, there seems, also, to be a significant allocation of ego present in my psyche, forever rearing its ugly head. Silent pride is one thing, but haughty arrogance is both imperious and reprehensible. Still, it only makes sense that if you make your first, then try again. That part is fine, but why do I feel that, not only should I shoot again, but it should be from farther out than the previous attempt? Swisharoo! "Oh-oh, he's on a roll," someone said. From there, things rapidly decompensated; all previously personal experience, null and void; TV and movies, absolutely no help; dazzling dreams and psychotic delusions, you're not close. All parameters and imaginable guidelines were shattered, irrelevant and insulting in the face of what transpired. That second shot was from 23-24 feet, then 27, 30, 35, all, all "in." Comments were, on the religious side, "Jesus Christ," "God Damn," and "Oh, my God." From my guys, it was, "feed him," "get him the rock," "down town," "money," "ride it," and "let's see where he can take us." The defense screamed, "get him," "make him drive," and "let's double," quickly followed by "no way," "that is pure slop," and "there's nothing you can do about that." It's always nice when you can get the guy guarding you to look down at the spot and then glance back at the basket before running to the other end, but when all the players do it in unison, it's special. Now the shots were raining down from outer space, places on the floor that don't even have smudge marks. Each attempt was at least outrageous, most beyond. Middle of the floor, one step over the half court line, launch, bzzzzzzzzoouu, a new sound was created. It was like the net was getting a total body massage. No misses, none! Pull up J's, fake right fake left quick release facials, swish, whoosh, nothing but the bottom. One attempt from somewhere near the twilight zone tried to miss, landing on the front of the rim, but, as was inevitable, it bounced around the iron ever so softly, teasing, before falling through the aroused cylinder. Do you know how difficult it is just physically, to get enough on a jump shot just to get it there from center court? Try it from the corners at the mid court, and since it's good, how about running left away from the hoop to the deep mid court corner, and letting fly with a fade? People couldn't watch it with one breath; it took two. One guy even needed three. I just had to heave it to get it started in the general direction. You can't aim a shot like that. Then, I was the ball, or radar took over and it, too, found silk. An eerie silence had long since taken hold. It had all been said. No words, now, were even remotely relevant. Little by little, fear, a sense of foreboding, had captured the totality of consciousness for everyone present, save me. After two games, twenty some odd shots, each more phantasmagoric than the other, no misses, I had to walk off. One more shot would have left some poor soul flailing delirious, or others would have quit, not being able to withstand the geometrically progressive reality check crashing down like an avalanche.

For days afterward, people I barely knew would come up to me and say, "I hear you were really hot the other day." This, about games that were usually completely forgotten even before the next began. Years later, I still get an occasional reference to it by one of those who were there. I'd compare it to three straight holes in one, or ten consecutive pitches knocked over the center field wall. I mean, what would you think if you were watching and a guy and he threw the basketball the full length of the floor and made it? Pretty good, huh. Then he hurls another and it, too, falls. Luck, but still quite awesome. When the third falls, you begin to be tested. Something is awry. This isn't supposed to be happening. And each successive make from there on is like being hit on the head with a Nerf bat, over and over. No time to think, no answer, anchors rapidly being cut away. It's just too much. Ah well, we each are allotted one special moment in life, when the usual rules are suspended, and everything comes together for that magical occasion, that brief interlude, standing out, shining like a beacon, never to be extinguished.

"Dr. Murphy, I need your help. I have nowhere else to turn." As I listened to the young man sitting in the exam room, I studied his face, trying to get a read on what type of person he was, was he sincere, could there be a hidden agenda? His eyes were on the move constantly, never focusing for more than a few seconds, and as he spoke, each sentence ended with what seemed to be a decided whining quality.

"I'll try to do my best. What is it you need?"

"Well, it's like this; I live in Phoenix, but I'm originally from a small town near here, and my mom needs me to come back to help with the family farm. My problem is that I'm on this medicine, methadone, and I need a physician to prescribe it for me. "

"I've heard of it. It's for heroin addiction, isn't it?"

"Right, I've been on it for almost ten years, now, and I can't do without it. I've tried and every time I screw up and go back to dope. I'm fine as long as I'm on it. To be honest with you, I don't think I'll ever be able to kick it. Can you help me?"

"If I remember right, aren't there a lot of special rules involved?"

"Ya, but I'll make you a deal. If you agree to prescribe the stuff, I'll get all the paper work going. All you'll have to do is sign."

"Sounds easy enough," I answered, pausing to think for a moment. "I suppose I can do it."

"Great! I'm heading back to Arizona, but I'll get everything going, and when it's all set up, I'll be back. By the way, as long as I got you here, could I get you to write me some Valium. My mom's been sick, and my nerves have been just killin' me."

So began the next saga of my life. How innocently it was. Before long, this was to become an all-consuming passion, a haunting nightmare, a rason d'existence. At the time, although I had dealt with heroin addiction quite extensively in both New York and California, mostly dramatically exorcizing the terminal blues from those overenthusiastic with a stat spike of Narcan, I had no experience with this form of substitute therapy.

I thought little more of it as the endless stream of medical tasks continued. Push! Push! Give it everything you got! Now pant like a puppy! Easy, easy. Got it. Ky on latex fit index, through the verge, on the look for asymmetry, then guiac. "He was insensitive. You'll only have to be there for a few days and then back to college. Try to turn this into a positive." Pupils are equal and react to light and accommodation...

We attended the UNI home BB games as a family and it was always fun, with plenty of action keeping the kids interest. Their heroes became guys like Chicken Jackson, Herbert "the great intimidator" King, and, of course, Randy "Special K" Kraayenbrink, author of the most beautiful rainbows. He and his wife had become my patients and I had recently delivered their first baby. Just before halftime of one especially hard fought game, Randy took an elbow to the face, immediately drawing enough blood that everyone in the place could see. Leading him off, towel to face, the trainer signalled to me and I followed them past the locker room, through the open area filled with whirlpools and training tables, and finally into the small adjacent doctor's room. "Randy, haven't you ever heard of the word duck?" I asked as we helped him lay down on the table.

"You know quickness isn't my strong point, Doc."

Slowly removing the towel, I quickly noted the 3 centimeter gash over the inferior orbital rim, but my mind was thinking length of halftime, importance of game, and covering all medical possibilities. Quickly, pressure with 4x4, no hyphema, no diplopia or disconjugate movement on upward gaze, xylocaine with epinephrine through a #25 needle for hemostasis, sterile gloves, betadine prep, and drape, ready to sew. I chose 4-0 silk for strength of repair in case of another blow, knowing I could revise later. Finishing the last suture, I told Randy he could go full blast, no excuses. Turning as he sat up, he gave me a quizzical look and said, "I just have one question. Which was worse, this or my wife's episiotomy?" Before I could think of any response, he ran off, getting to the floor just in time to start the second half. The game went an amazing five overtimes, with UNI finally winning, due, in large part to Kraayenbrink's efforts. I cringed with every play involving any potential contact, worrying about the stitches. Slipping into the dressing room on our way out to check the wound, I saw that it looked perfect and decided to leave it as is. "Very nice game, Randy. Oh, and by the way, hers was much worse." Leaving it to him to explain to the rest of the team what that meant, I exited, barely able to keep a straight face.

Winters can be very long in Iowa, but this year, Janet and I shortened it considerably by finalizing our plans for a dream trip to the Indian subcontinent. Almost all of our Indian expatriot friends from Mozambique, were now back in their native land. By letter and, when possible, by phone, we had kept track of people and were now ready to embark on this ambitious journey. We adults had done significant preparation by way of history, geography, and literature, but for me what was most fun was reading, with Liam and Conor, the Kipling classics "Riki Tiki Tavi" and *Kim*.

As the school year ended, we packed our bags and flew west from Minneapolis to Seattle. During a brief layover there we were visited, in the terminal, by Steve Gloyd, who had returned from Africa to become head of The School of Public Health at the University of Washington. Reminiscing about our overseas experiences, the time passed quickly. Soon we were in the air arching towards the Orient in peaceful solar pursuit, then gliding back to humanity at Kowloon. Noticeably disoriented with the lag, and having but six hours, we passed on hotel and seeing Hong Kong, occupying ourselves in observation and roaming the airport until the 5 a.m. departure. A touch in Singapore, before breeching the Bay of Bengal en route to our final destination, the seething snake pit, the teeming anthill, the fascinating pulsating jewel that was Calcutta.

Every language strange, every sight new, you can imagine the surprise and relief we felt as almost immediately, walking up to greet us was Rajinder, dear friend who had lived one block from us for two years in Gurue. Without delay, we were led through the throngs, directly to his waiting car. Laughing and joking we advanced into the thickened nocturnal air, naturally cleansed by alternately heavy, then torrential downpours. "We've had significant flooding lately. They're in the midst of putting in a new subway system, so the streets are a mess, but we shouldn't have trouble getting through." Soon we were driving in two or maybe even three feet of water.

"Do you have outriggers, Rajinder? This seems a bit much," I said as we saw poor people carrying those better off across swollen streets.

"Have no fear. Here in India, the monsoon is our friend and savior. The boys do know how to swim, don't they?"

"That is not funny," interjected Janet, never having become adept in water.

As if on cue, we entered a particularly menacing accumulation of moisture. The motor sputtered and stopped dead, smothered by the inimical libation from Vishnu. Hopping out and with a practiced signal, our host procured instant generic assistance, pushing the disabled vehicle out of harm's way to a slightly higher point. Watching curiously, we saw bonnet up, plugs out, lighter to dry, and within minutes, we reentered the ever changing weave of bovine, human, bicycle, rickshaw, and honking motorized thread. Completing this initial foray, we turned onto a relatively quiet street where Rajinder pulled into his garage, carefully locked the door and led us up to their second story flat.

Poonam, the other half of the couple, met us with open arms, happily hugging everyone. The first time I met her in Africa, she shattered to bits whatever stereotypical image I had of Indian women. Wearing blue jeans and a simple blouse, she was not only conversant on almost any topic, but did so with a certain confidence bordering on brashness. "What a lovely sari," Janet said. "It's silk, isn't it?"

"Yes, I'm wearing it to honor our U.S. friends. Now come on and I'll show you around, then we have tea."

After completing the shoe removal ritual, soon the kids were watching *Jaws* on the VCR and we were looking at photos, discussing common acquaintances, and beginning to plan our stay. "Absolutely anything you want to do, short visit Indira, can be arranged. Have some more wine and we'll make a list."

Rajinder's state of Punjab would be difficult to visit, with the crisis at the Golden Temple in Amritsar. "The truth is that our prime minister is exploiting this situation for political purposes and now it's getting out of control. Sikhs everywhere are offended, which plays into the hand of the few radicals who initiated the crisis,' he explained. 'We have no true national leadership. Local and sectarian concerns dominate every agenda. I'm sure Nehru is turning over in his grave." Listening attentively, we heard how both our hosts' families had passed through "partition" with great sacrifice, in what seemed to be the antithesis of all that Gandhi had stood for. The Northeastern state of Assam, where we also had friends, was also under curfew due to violent rebel activity and border problems with Bangladesh. We continued planning, discussing many parts of India, and all sorts of issues. At the end of the second bottle, the exhaustive list came to a halt for lack of more paper. By then we were even attempting to learn the basics of Bengali. Finally Poonam stretched her arms and said, "Temus que dormir, amanha ha muito que fazer. See, I still remember Portuguese."

Sleeping soundly, not having to keep my hand over a telephone, I awoke to the early cries of the ever present itinerant street vendors. Slipping out of bed and moving out onto the verandah, I took into consideration, the less oppressive temperature, lack of rainfall, and clear streets, and decided that conditions were right for a delightful dawn-time constitutional jog. Within minutes I was executing my first Calcutta 10 K. Immediately I was impressed by seeing people sleeping in virtually every doorway, not to mention those poor souls who were huddled under make shift lean-tos or just next to a tree or a wall. I had planned twenty-five minutes out and then the same route back trying not to get lost, but it proved to be impossible. The streets didn't seem to follow any pattern and try as I might to keep it simple, over and over, I was forced to make quick decisions on turns and ended up going through all sorts of interesting neighborhoods. Another rather pressing dilemma was that while only a few humans were up milling around, canines abounded by the lakh. As I dodged and fahrtliched, all I could think of were the long series of continuous cases of rabies reported in the medical literature originating in India. The raucous barking was disconcerting but by pretending to not be afraid like I learned from my daddy visiting

Iowa farms, I didn't get bit. However, I did, through all the distraction, step more than once, on things I shouldn't have, thus learning, first hand, or should I say first foot, why people take off their shoes as they enter a house in India. At twenty-five minutes, I knew I was hopelessly lost, so, using the now visible rising sun as my only guide, I turned back in the direction I considered most appropriate. By this time people were up and moving, cooking fires started, streets becoming ever more congested. Just as I thought I would have to make my first attempt at using the last night's Bengali lesson, I came upon the original street and calmly found my way to the flat, arriving as if nothing significant had happened.

"Dan, still jogging, I see." It was Rajinder greeting me from the verandah.

"Good morning, I think I've just met nearly every dog and most of the people of Calcutta."

"There are many more; we'll see them today. The others are getting dressed. Come sit and have some tea."

Finalizing our agenda while familiarizing the children with items such as ghee, chapatis, and chutney, we piled into the auto to begin the adventure just like Tintin, about whom Liam had been reading so assiduously. Just observing as we rode was fascinating especially as we had two excellent guides patiently answering our endless questions. "Look, those cattle are loose!" exclaimed Conor.

"No, they're free to roam," explained Poonam. "Everyone defers to them."

"Why?" chimed in Liam. "Won't someone take them for food?"

Rajinder told us how most Hindu people are vegetarian out of respect for life, and how, traditionally, milk and milk products were, and still are, in many places, essential for health and survival. Thus the cow became both literally and symbolically, of great importance in this society.

Just then, we saw a man dressed only in a dhoti, scoop up a freshly deposited cow pie with his hands and carefully stick it like a patty on a nearby wall next to others, forming a pattern like a Chinese checkers board.

"Strange behavior," commented Janet.

"Not really, " answered Rajinder. "That's tomorrow's fuel."

"Dang," I remarked. "This morning I saw a dog gobble up human offal. Now this. You guys take recycling very seriously."

"Waste not, want not," interjected Rajinder.

"It's not a perfect system," I said. "I ran into some unclaimed dog detritus this morning."

"We try to do our best," he laughed.

"Can you imagine, Liam," I continued, "a new Tintin episode, 'The Case of the Disappearing Dung.'"

"Please, could we change the subject?"

"But we haven't explained to the kids yet, about the right hand, left hand bidet ritual."

"Enough! That can be done in private."

Crossing in front of us was a single line procession led by individuals with colorful flags. Many wore decorative necklaces. "They're on a religious pilgrimage, to Benaras, or to the Ganges."

While I visited several hospitals, they saw parks, and monuments before picking me up again. Suddenly, as we were driving along, Poonam indicated a store she wanted to show Janet. As the women exited the car, words were exchanged in what could have been Punjabi or Bengali, and we drove on, finally pulling over near a modern office building. "This is where I work. I've got some things I must do today, so the plan is for you to go back and pick up Janet and Poonam, then go visit the main market. By then I'll be done." Handing me the keys, he got out and started to walk away.

It hadn't dawned on me, but now I realized that he intended for me to drive. Instantly panicking, I jumped out and yelled, "Wait! Sahib, you don't expect me to negotiate this strange auto under these trying circumstances. I don't know my way."

"It's just where we came from. Nao ha problema!" Then he ran off a string of instructions including street names I couldn't even pronounce, much less remember.

All I could think of was me trying to proceed through the near gridlock conditions, horn use apparently being critical, ending up somewhere in Bihar with wet spark plugs. "But everything is reversed here," I said, referring to the right sided steering wheel and driving on the left.

"Just like in Mozambique, Dan. I saw you driving the ambulance all over back then."

"But there was no traffic there. Please, there's more in one block here than what I encountered in my whole three years there. What if there's and accident or something?"

Walking away he turned with a smile, "Do as we do, abscond."

Getting in and starting the car, I felt my head spinning. "What's 'abscond?'" asked Conor.

"I think it means if we hit a cow by mistake, abandon ship, run for your life. Remember kids, 'I'm an American citizen, take me to the embassy.' We'll all meet there."

Both were nervously laughing as I put it in first and slowly pulled out into the nightmarish mayhem of human, mechanical, and animal jostle. Soon, through immense bravado and creative imitation, we were swerving and honking with the best of them, even taking to the sidewalk when necessary to advance. With all three of us doing our damnedest to retrace our path, a miracle occurred and, within 15 minutes or so, we found the store, where the two women were waiting just inside the door. Soon, under Poonam's direction, we were at the vast market place, strolling both indoors and out, through aisle after aisle of fruit and vegetable stalls mixed with areas marketing nearly every product imaginable. What a vast infrastructure it must have taken to allow this place to function, I thought. No matter what else you can say about the British, at least they left a decent communication and transportation system. Nothing even remotely resembling this existed in all of Mozambique, nor would it be possible for many years.

"The prices are higher early in the day when things are fresh, but get lower as the heat builds, until by evening, people can survive on as little as one or two rupees for rice and the products that won't last the night. That, plus the green revolution, and improved public health, is why we have at least a 750 million population, probably a billion, if the truth were known. Birth control is improving, but so much was lost by the coercive tactics of the past."

"At the hospital today, I was told that women are limiting pregnancies voluntarily. Number of children is now 5-6, instead of 10-12 like it was 20 years ago. Still the growth rate is phenomenal, because of much less infant and childhood mortality."

The kids were kept happy with pop, ice cream, and little wooden toys having a stick with a top ball attached to a string, the trick being to swing it up into place with one sweeping motion. Gradually, they were learning handy new words like "bakshish."

After a rickshaw ride we went back to the flat and dropped the boys off before heading to a club to meet Rajinder. During colonial times, this had been an exclusive hangout for Brits. It still retained much of its original splendor, most patrons wearing white, but very few foreigners were present. We were introduced to many interesting people from diverse walks of life. After a few drinks and snacks, we all agreed that it had been a long day, and, following our friends to the car, we drove home in the dwindling daylight.

Liam met us at the apartment door. "Conor's sick. He threw up twice, and he has a fever."

Janet and I went right into the bedroom to see what was wrong. He didn't seem too bad, not dehydrated, and only 38.5 temperature. Probably stomach flu, I thought, although I'll have to admit that several other possibilities entered my mind.

"Don't worry. I have an auntie who can cure these ailments. We'll take him after dinner."

Janet and I gave each other anxious looks. "Okay, Poonam, but I've got to go along. I'm back into my Western medicine mode now."

"That's fine, but you're in India. These germs respond better to ayurvedic remedies."

As we enjoyed dinner, I couldn't help thinking of Conor and also being respectful of our hosts. I decided that if what was happening didn't seem dangerous, it would be alright. Two hours later we were at relatives home where auntie had been waiting our arrival. Actually, it was a bit of a party for us, with quite a few people present. We accompanied Conor to a dimly lit back room where he was placed on a small cot. The ritual began with incantations and went on to the application of secret unguents to his abdominal area. So far so good. What I was more worried about was ingestion of unknown substances. Finally, after several more ritualistic hand movements with accompanying verbiage, the patient was encouraged to spit into a small fire that had been prepared expressly for this purpose. Conor obliged, and was then left to rest after the ordeal, while we all returned to visit with the family and friends gathered for the occasion. The next morning, lo and behold, the patient was asymptomatic.

Our visit took us all over Calcutta. There were temples, mosques, churches, restaurants, museums, stores. One day, on a bus ride, we must have travelled 50 miles mostly in one direction, still in Calcutta, an unbelievable mass of humanity, mostly surviving as street vendors or small shop keepers. I spent one morning with a union executive. West Bengal was the most consistently communist state in India. Strikes and work stoppages were used frequently, but sexism and cronyism had yet to be dealt with. What was impressive was how local industry had become capable of producing nearly every conceivable item, large and small. India had become self-sufficient, importing technology, not products. Jet airplanes, computers, medications, cars, pop, movies, and condoms, all made in India.

"Next up, as you requested, is a visit to the 'House of Dying'", said Poonam. We were welcomed by sisters, Mother Teresa being abroad, and given an extensive tour of the quite large facility. There were cots in nearly every room, occupied with the poor in various stages of decline. Some were receiving IV's. One elderly gentleman expired while we were there, and seemed well attended.

"Some recover, but our main mission is for terminal patients," explained our guide. There were volunteers from other countries, nearly all western, as efficiency and cleanliness showed clearly in all the work being done. Lepers were all taken to another facility, we were told. Just before our visit ended, it was meal time, and one of the sisters led everyone in prayer before the food was served. I noticed Poonam dropping a donation into the box as we exited the building, once again into the hot, boisterous street.

In the car, it was she who broke the pensive silence. "The compassion is commendable. All of us should do more, but the aggressive proselytizing is quite offensive for any Hindu."

"Definitely no shortage of Christian symbolism," said Janet. "Every room had pictures, candles, and crosses."

"And can you imagine using such a vulnerable time to ask someone to renege on a lifetime of beliefs, an entire culture really." Poonam was tactfully exercising restraint.

"I see what you mean. We'll feed and tend to you, but in return, you must, at least witness our religious practices, if not join in with us." I had visited a Catholic Worker soup kitchen in L.A. where the philosophy was quite straight forward. People are hungry, we feed them, I was told. Quite simple ministry. Or the example of Maryknolls, working, for instance, in Muslim countries, basically living as the local people, helping in their day to day problems, saying nothing, only being of service, a much different presence.

"For anyone, the time of death is very important, so personal. How can you take that away from a person? Let me just say that it leaves a bad taste in my mouth."

"But Poonam, why did you leave a donation?"

"That's another of our traditions, sacred, I would say. Always give something to those who ask, even if it's a rupee or less." I had seen her do this as we went throughout the city, never seeming upset. This was in stark contrast to the dynamics observed, for example in the streets of New York, where panhandlers are considered a pest by many. In Hindu philosophy, living a simple life of meditation and presenting a cup for daily rice or alms, was an advanced state of being. I was pleased to have Liam and Conor seeing the different ways life can be lived.

The next day, Rajinder took us to the airport, and gave us careful instructions on how to proceed on arrival in Madras, where he had arranged for us to stay at a company villa in a quiet section of town. Using our Air India passes, we enjoyed an uneventful flight south to what seemed almost like another country. For one thing, we now learned the true meaning of "hot" cuisine, curry apparently not being in short supply. In many ways the life was less hectic. Partition hadn't affected this region nearly as drastically, and the division between Hindu and Muslim seemed less pronounced. We visited ancient sites like the seaside temple at Mahabalipuram, 10,000 years old, and read about the political ambitions of N.K. Rama Rao. These impressions were tempered somewhat when, the day after we flew on to Bangalore, the Madras airport was rocked by an explosion with twenty people killed, a reflection of the bitter struggle between Tamils and Sinhalese in Sri Lanka.

Reinvigorated by the cooler air and more European flavor of Bangalore, we advanced by bus to Mysore, reading about great tiger hunts on the way. After experiencing the historic Maharaja's Palace, we flew on to Trivandrum, where we were met by another friend, Sri

Devi. "So happy to see you. Look at these boys, how big they've grown!" Always formal, always restrained, she still came across as very genuine. Highly educated, she was, at the same time, traditional in a natural way. Kerala is matriarchal and, not only the most literate Indian state, but also one of the most developed, due to spice trade and remittances from family members working in the Middle East. "I had planned to take you around our capital city but there are stoppages everywhere. Our communist government never fails to keep the water muddied. Still, we can visit Ajay in boarding school, and then catch the Bombay Express for Cochin.

Liam had picked up a newspaper, and pointing to the print which resembled a series of squares and chairs, he asked, "What's this?"

"That's our language, Malayalam. Here, especially in the villages, neither Hindi or English is known. Quite provincial, actually. But most people are kind and friendly. Ainda fala Portuguese?"

Liam gave her a quizzical look, not responding. "They only remember a few words," answered Janet. "Tell us all about your son." "I'll get a taxi and we'll go see him."

Soon we were streaming through traffic, Sri Devi pointing out the important sights, including several manifestations. At the school, Ajay gave us a grand tour. He was hoping to qualify for dental school and was working very hard. "It's extremely competitive here; so many trying for the few openings," he explained. "I'm doing okay, but I miss the slow pace of Africa." Haridas, his father, was still working tea in Mozambique.

Finishing a light lunch, we hurried to the train station where Sri Devi bought us first class tickets just in time to board the already waiting locomotive. While all the lower fare cars were jammed, we had plenty of space in our compartment, quite comfortable, actually. Much of the way the kids entertained each other in the quiet, unobtrusive way that seemed to be their nature, as we adults talked on and on about everything from soup to sati. I even struck up a conversation with an elderly gentleman in an adjacent compartment who practiced his more than adequate English skills by giving me his life story as a railroad employee, including anecdotes on the seamier side of Indian life. In what seemed like no time we had arrived in Cochin.

"I'll call my cousin to pick us up," explained Sri Devi. "We should have time to visit the sea on the way to her house."

The sun was skimming over Africa as we parked the car to touch a part of the Indian Ocean that, for us Caucasians, had been only an abstract stroke of awareness, done in oil, now drying. Brave, deeply bronzed fishermen, helped to shore by the tide, unloaded their sustaining catch. Out of all of us, Sri Devi was the one who misstepped. In less than an hour it would have been gone. Scraping, cleaning, even scouring, will all be woefully ineffective; the sandal had to go.

Inexplicably, the first European explorers, five centuries ago, found pockets of Christianity here. Another stroke of the brush.

The next morning, while the others went to the market, I visited the nearby district hospital. The physician on duty seemed very sincere. "No, we don't get many cases of advanced malnutrition here," in response to my inquiry. "Rice, fish, and fruits are plentiful." He did have many other problems to deal with, and at the end of the tour, I promised to send him IV materials and reusable cord clamps for newborns. Later that day, we started the three hour trip inland to Sri Devi's village.

On the way, our host, already gracious, became perfect and so informative in her new foot ware. "See that brightly colored house over there; that's Muslim. We all get along well here. Those trees, as you know, are mangoes, and bananas are everywhere. Now we're passing a family planning center, the pill and IUD's are used by many women. On this side you see cardamom, just beyond those rice paddies. You can see we still utilize water buffalo. There, those kids in uniform are school children..."

Leaving the paved road we curved along. It seemed that every inch of land was in use. Finally we came down a gentle slope and pulled in next to an ancient appearing pathway lined by shoulder high stone walls. "Welcome to our traditional home," said Sri Devi getting out of the car and helping the servants with the luggage. "We are beginning to build a modern structure there through the coconut grove, but it's not yet completed." Already people from the surrounding village were arriving bearing gifts for us, mostly fruits, vegetables, and other food items. "They want to see you up close. We don't get many such visitors here." Later, we came to realize that

Sri Devi and her mother were like royalty here. It wasn't just gifts. They were consulted regularly on many issues and routinely helped villagers with their problems any way they could.

The house, although made of bamboo and thatch, was very substantial, having three stories and many rooms. The kitchen was at the back and had nothing above it so smoke could escape, everything done by open fire. Our guest room was top floor with spacious windows permanently open to the outside. There were no beds as such, but each of us had a thin but adequate straw mat. As we were finishing the initial tour and came back to the ground floor, Liam came up to me with a plaintiff look beckoning me to bend over to hear him. "Dad," he said, almost whispering. "Conor and I have to go to the bathroom. Where is it?" Discreetly, to protect the children's innocence, I asked Sri Devi. Taking them around the house, she indicated a path for them to follow, and both took off adventurously. We continued around the house, discussing the various flowers and fruit trees that abounded. There was even a small stable for the family cow.

Suddenly, the blissful south Indian village peacefulness was shattered by shrieks and screams as the two explorers came running back to us, eyes opened wide as the third story windows. "There's a big cobra back there," exclaimed Liam. The use of that word got our attention since we were in India. In Africa, where we had lived, the word just meant "snake."

"Ya, a long green one," added Conor half laughing, with safety now more certain.

"Oh, those aren't poisonous," assured Sri Devi, as if that were the only conceivable consideration.

Somehow baring your bottom for the use of these primitive facilities, with unknown slithery ground fellows lurking, didn't seem conducive to regularity. "Come along, I'll show you what to do. You can carry a stick if you like, but at night you need one hand for a torch or candle." Both kids were listening quite attentively, as were several adults. "Now here's the latrine. I'll let your father show you the rest." Turning, she and Janet walked back up the path leaving us to cope with nature's inevitable necessities.

The door had a wooden latch, but there was more than adequate room at the bottom for ventilation or for our green friend.

Inside was an earthen ware jug of water, a small piece of soap, and a covered hole in the ground. The lid had a handle and could be swung open, and there was a conveniently located back rest to lean against while performing the ritual. And, oh, yes, there was a roll of paper, the one concession to modern technology. Standing outside, I listened as Liam joked, "Conor, I think I saw the snake down in the hole." Conor just laughed and I couldn't help smiling as there was no end to the giggling coming from within where the two assisted each other in their intimate eliminations.

As preparations began for dinner, I decided to go for a jog. Running on dirt roads and pathways, I filled my eyes with the lush greenery, numerous rice paddies, well-kept houses, and most interesting, the people. Here, I noted a skin color as dark as many Africans. Without fail, everyone stopped to watch me run by. Children would accompany me for short intervals, excitedly chattering in Malayalam. I was surprised to see some of the women working topless – not what I would have expected in India. Funny how preconceptions sneak up on one! Many were busy making adjustments on irrigation schemes for the multi-leveled paddies, plugging here, opening there. Buffalo abounded, as did goats and burros. Crossing a small stream I watched several young boys seining for fish. Waving at them, I glanced at my watch and couldn't believe 25 minutes had passed. Time to turn back. This was so much more enjoyable than in Calcutta, the few dogs I encountered taking scant interest. Perplexed at several cross paths, I merely had to say, "Sri Devi?" and I would be rewarded with a finger indicating the correct way, one of the benefits of being in a close knit rural community. Soon I was back to familiar territory. As I approached the house, I was met by the rich aroma of wonderfully spiced cuisine emanating from the kitchen area.

"Dan, how was your run?"

"Very good. I saw a lot of the countryside and people were friendly. I do have a question, though. Why did the kids use the word 'phirangi' so much?"

"That means 'foreigner.' We get very few around here. Come, I'll show you the bath." Leading me to the far end of the house and handing me a towel she pointed to the door before leaving me, once again, to my own wits to proceed. Inside the room, the furrowed dirt floor was reddish brown and firm from years of use. A large stone jug was filled with cold water while next to it was a half-filled smaller metal container steaming with hot. I had learned from experience at Rajinder's and other places that 'shower' means dumping water over one's self, lathering up, then rinsing off. Using the handy ladle, I was able to mix the right amount of hot and cold and proceeded with the much needed process, even humming a few bars of what I imagined might be an Indian hit. The water ran down the carefully slanted floor and out through a groove under the far wall. Different but quite adequate.

The meal was absolutely delicious. Unlike the north where wheat is the staple, here rice, cooked in many varieties of preparations, is the heart of every meal. With all the fruit and vegetable dishes, along with soup, eggs, cheese, and sweets, what more could one want? Even the children did well.

"Tell your mother that everything is marvelous. I could live on dhal alone." Sri Devi's mother was nearly 80 years old, less than five feet tall and well under one hundred pounds, yet she was still very active and kept busy running the household in the traditional matriarchal manner. Through translation I was informed that spices were cut drastically for our benefit. Still I noticed that all of us phirangis kept our water glasses close at hand.

After the meal, as evening approached, we went outside to enjoy the slight breeze. My thoughts automatically turned to protozoans and viruses. "What about mosquitoes?" I asked.

"We don't have them, at least very few."

"You'd think with the warm temperatures and the wet conditions, you'd have lots of them."

"Wait a few minutes, and you'll see how they're controlled."

Looking up, I soon understood what she was referring to. Bats. Lots of them. I was wondering if Janet and the kids were thinking of those wide open sleeping quarters when, suddenly Liam exclaimed, "Look! What's that?" A huge flying creature that at first I thought must be a hawk or an owl was swooping silently over the house and around the trees.

"Those are fruit bats," informed Sri Devi. "Completely harmless."

Later that night, the kids having been put to bed, we sat at the table, illuminated by kerosene lamp, and reminisced about Gurue while planning our week's agenda in Kerala. Both Janet and I expressed our gratefulness for all the hospitality shown by both Sri Devi and her mother. For some reason I couldn't sleep well that night. Long after everyone else was quiet, I was still thinking, wondering about the endless array of people, cultures, religions, and life styles and what it all meant. Several times I heard what I knew were mice snooping around the room. I decided not to share that discovery until we had moved on to the next destination.

Now, after being so long absent, the cock's crow awakened me at dawn. On special trips like this, it's difficult not to try to experience everything and every minute, so I quietly dressed and went down to feel the new day's air. Just off the main room, a candle was flickering and as I approached, my ears were rewarded with the undisturbed soft monotone, punctuated regularly by inspiration of that which I sought. Once again I was in my youth, at early chapel, reassured by the Franciscan "pooja". Moments later, just outside the door, the lightest touch on my shoulder connected me with our diminutive matron, whose forehead was now adorned with what looked like the charred remains of palm fronds. Having no mutually intelligible language, we communicated richly and soon were enjoying the sunrise together, fresh tea in hand.

Here, our days were spent at a leisurely pace, visiting villages, small temples, schools, a traditional doctor, a tire factory, markets, and countryside. Most rewarding was having ample opportunity to be a part of people in their daily lives. Surprisingly, by the time we left, our children had established relationships with local kids, and played with them as if they had known them forever.

On our last day, we visited a logging site where the heavy work was done by elephants. Tusks below, trunk above, a bole to them is a mere toothpick. Seeing that their domestication was complete, none of us hesitated to touch and feel the prehensile snouts. During that night's sleep, I was the mahout, strapped high in the brightly decorated howdah, proudly pursuing my true identity.

Less than a day later, we had flown over Bombay, continued north, and unbuckled on the ground at Delhi. Meeting us as we exited was Vikram Malhoutra. His father, now dead, and I had become quite close in Africa as we battled against his advancing leukemia. "Welcome to our capital. Uma can't wait to see you. Let's grab your luggage. My car is just outside."

Soon we were sailing down a modern Delhi highway resembling more a European city than India, especially the part we had just visited. Uma lived in a nice flat in a middle class enclave with her beautiful daughter, Gayathri. Liam and Conor were noticeably indifferent as we sat down to tea and began the by then familiar litany of updates and interrogatives. Janet and I, however, waxed insatiable, every "achcha" followed by another pressing inquiry. Indians are inveterate talkers and never lacking in opinions, thus the conversation remained lively. Out of consideration for our two, their two volunteered to take in a movie with them. I claimed an overpowering need for a jog and was soon out the door leaving the two women engaged in an animated exchange on the impact of east-west politics on India.

Running mostly amongst embassies and fenced in residencies, I still encountered an occasional cow wandering freely in the sultry streets, laughing at the numerous Mercedes, intently advancing, enclosed in tint, to yet another critical formality. Our time in Kerala had been so special, allowing us to live, if only for a brief moment, as traditional Indian villagers, poignantly casting our present environs in bold. Ending my 45 in a weak imitation of an all-out sprint, I dallied to look, feel, and sweat, questioning if I shouldn't be engaged in a third world endeavor.

That evening, we all attended dinner at a nearby classy restaurant. I never tired of the delicious variety of flavors, already realizing that, for me, rice and spice would always be nice (did I really type that?). Later that night, with the others retired, Vikram and I shared wine and discussed youth culture in modern Delhi. Interestingly, heroin addiction was on the rise, becoming quite a problem. "What is it, Vikram? Alienation? Unemployment?" I asked.

"Much simpler, I think. In a word, availability. Our reality changed drastically during the Nixon administration. With JFK, we got along extremely well, but the dynamics between Tricky Dick, if you please, and our Indira, led to a precipitous decline in any cooperative endeavors. Nixon couldn't pull her aside for an off-color anecdote, talk man to man, or share an alcoholic beverage. In contrast, Paskistani strong men suited him well. He could relate. Not to mention that our country seemed bent on becoming self-sufficient, apparently little interested in becoming slavish consumers of U.S. goods. Thus our tilt towards USSR, out of political necessity, really, with threats from both China and Karachi. Throw in the Afghani connection, and the picture is complete. Instead of flowing through Iran and Turkey, which had become more problematic due to post WWII considerations, opium began to pass through Peshawar, to Pakistani refineries, on its way to lucrative western markets. All of this completely controlled by high ranking military officers to our north. The more cynical here, believe that it wasn't just implicit approval, given by President Nixon, allowing this shift to occur, but that it's part of a cooperative effort in geopolitical expediency. One of the unintended side effects is a dramatic increase in amounts of high grade heroin, not only in Karachi and Islamabad, but also here and in other Indian cities such as Bombay."

So you think drug trade isn't just murky underground figures, constantly evading authorities to push their product on the youth of the world?"

"Of course not! Greed and power are rarely bound by morality. As far as drugs are concerned, we Indians have ample firsthand experience. Great Britain, through the East India Company, in a glorious effort to expand markets for its main product, opium, provoked the Opium Wars with China. A free trade issue they said. Wonderful how they stuck to the principle, isn't it. Ironically, today, the Chinese ex-Kuomintang generals in charge of the Golden Triangle opium trade are losing market share."

"What did they do wrong?"

"Well, to start, they had one strike against them by refusing to flock to Taiwan to rekindle a military counter coup attempt on the mainland, like your country wanted. Next, the convenient cooperative trade effort made possible by the truly massive flow of personnel and equipment between U.S. and Southeast Asia, ended with those desperate souls clinging to the last helicopters above the roof of the U.S. embassy in Saigon. So instead of Bangkok, Hong Kong, New York, it's Peshawar, Karachi, and maybe Panama City, Dallas." This from a twenty-three-year-old aspiring Indian merchant.

"So is there any hope?"

"Surely," he smiled shaking his head ever so slightly back and forth. "Monsoons come every year."

At the zoo the following day, the overwhelming oppression of pre-monsoon conditions captured us all. "They call this stuff air?" said Janet, lethargically hyperventilating.

"It's easier if you just do the breast stroke," I commented, doing a deliberate Johnny Wiessmuller imitation.

"Dad, stop and pop," whined Liam, barely able to lift his finger indicating the nearby stand. Without a doubt, all of us would have run to the streets, to welcome the first rumbles and refreshing raindrops. Later, I read that because of fires, factories, and combustion engines, air here is many times a rare commodity.

The near disaster struck totally unexpected. At the cage of an Asian bear, we absentmindedly cast our languid gaze toward the rear where the furred forest mammal slumbered. As we watched nothing happen, trying to muster the energy for the next step, Conor, desperate for action, any action, had grabbed a small stick and was poking it into the cage, there being no guard rails. We remained blase as the comatose creature was a good ten feet away. Can you imagine how much anger, resentment, and frustration this bear must have built up being in this hell instead of frolicking in the Himalayan foothills like he was supposed to be? The instant, not the stick, but Conor's hand crossed the plane of the bear's barred barrier, occurred a lightning like spring and slash, that in a single instant, had it not been for our simultaneous blood curdling screams and the would be victim's natural quickness, could have provided fresh finger food for this four legged behemoth instead of just raising our collective pulses two or three hundred points and garnishing for himself only a partially skinned twig. Never again will any of us underestimate the world of difference between the reactions of a wild animal and those of mere mortals.

In the morning, we were off, by plane, to the Taj Mahal. Janet and I were reminded of Casa Mumtaz in Gurue whose proprietor had helped us several times during periods of scarcity. This stupendous mausoleum was purported to have been built to assuage a man's grief at having lost his wife, a more famous Mumtaz, in childbirth of their fourteenth offspring, while he was off building the

209

Mughal empire. The guy then proceeded to break the country with a 20 year, 20,000 man project. Gandhi was apparently quite moved by his time spent in the sack when he should have been at his father's deathbed, but somehow this rendering of the Taj story, to my way of thinking, couldn't possibly account for what had happened. Like the race card in Faulkner's "Absalom, Absalom", something deep, dark, and horrific had to have occurred to have provoked such a pathological response.

Hiking through Shahjahan Park, we observed many monkeys frolicking, until finally, we came to what the kids, later were to say, was the highlight of the trip, the Agra Fort. Basically given free run of the huge sprawling structure, they let their imaginations carry them to every nook and cranny, through tunnels, up and down stairways, into dungeons, then to the throne room. At the top were multiple views of the Taj brought into focus by the steady stream of destitute women washing rags in the nearby river.

Our final night in Delhi included a party, where, once again, a vast array of people intermingled. At one point, I was introduced to a certain Mrs. Beig, a local literary critic. We had known her son in Africa. Soon she was making eloquent political pronouncements and I, by now feeling quite Indian myself, entered freely into the fray. The subject matter turned to, as was frequently the case, Indira. My mind wandered as she took off on another expansive commentary. My focus was restored during a lull at the end of a sentence when it appeared that I was expected to make a contribution. Without thinking, I blurted out the following, "What you're saying is quite vituperative." Even now I'm not sure what the word means. I regretted it as soon as I had said it. Pausing for a brief second only, me expecting the worst, she gave me a look that is reserved for those rare occasions just before some cataclysmic explosion, then went on as if what I had said was legitimate, but, at any rate, a misinterpretation of her true motives. Relieved, I took the next opportune moment to excuse myself, and was soon connecting politely with the various people present, listening more than talking, sipping, and not gulping. I didn't want to have to build a Taj Mahal.

The rains came as we boarded our flight to Calcutta, completing our sketchy circle of this richly diverse and endearing land. Two days with Poonam and Rajinder, relaxing, shopping, and posing for pictures, and we were off to the east, ready once again, to engage our previous life.

First day back at basketball, after a prolonged absence, is always an adventure. You can be hot but, more often, it's all thumbs. Defense is the worst, no coordination, lack of timing, poor shape, even if you've been jogging. Only thing you can do is play through it and each day gets better. I'd say within a week you're pretty much back to normal. Getting back to the routine was great, especially the feeling after a good workout. It had been thirty years now, that I'd been playing.

At work, I had received my special federal license, and was in the methadone business for my one patient. Now, within a week's period of time, three more people came in to be started on the narcotic substitute. Heroin addicts, right here in Iowa! As the numbers increased, problems began to arise, as is inevitable. Some of the patients were of color, most were down on their luck and even desperate. My job was to stabilize and rehabilitate, not always a simple matter. There was a minor break in at the pharmacy we used just down the hall in the same building our office occupied. Patients would accumulate, at times, waiting for their dose of medication, causing consternation on the part of other customers. From the beginning it was a public relations nightmare. The kicker came after I was up to twenty some patients and the local hospital bought out the pharmacy, promptly informing me that they would no longer be dispensing methadone.

By then, I had become quite informed on the issue of heroin addiction and its treatment. I was well versed in the work of Vincent Dole, an academic internist at the Rockefeller Institute, who first gained notoriety while doing research on obesity, concluding that the answer to the question why people become fat is not because they overeat. That pat answer, he explained, by its sophist nature, not only diverts attention from the relevant investigation into the unique metabolic and neurophysiologic characteristics invariably found in these people, but easily leads to a conclusion that there is a character flaw involved. Thus, a moral judgment inevitably follows. When asked to take a look at the burgeoning epidemic of opiate addiction plaguing society in the '60's, damned if he didn't try that same old dogged scientific inquiry stuff to jump right past the conclusion that everyone knew to be true: why are these people addicted? Because they shoot dope! He, along with another pioneer, Marie Nyswander, initiated the study of relevant endorphins and neurotransmitters, including serotonin and dopamine, which today has revolutionized our way of thinking, not just about addiction, but about a wide range of conditions previously thought to be "psychological". Repeated use of highly potent neuroactive substances, they discovered, results in recognizable, and many times irreversible, changes in the brain. No cure on the horizon, in a systematic search for a practical tool that could stop the revolving door of treatment, relapse, treatment, relapse, they began experimenting with maintenance therapy using a variety of pharmaceuticals including various opiates. The short acting formulations such as morphine and heroin, left people either too "high" to function, or, within several hours, in a state of ever increasing craving as symptoms of withdrawal arose. Working with methadone, however, provided a startling breakthrough. It turns out that there are a finite number of opiate receptors in our bodies, and when a "blocking dose" of that class of medication is reached, craving stops completely. The slow onset, 36 hour half-life, and excellent absorption of this medication, allowed it to be taken by mouth once a day. Tolerance to any effect on mood, cognition, or motor coordination, developed rapidly, leaving these people, when on the appropriate blocking dose, "normal." Dole was shocked to hear them talking extensively about basketball, for heaven's sakes. What could be more normal? Previously, the talk invariably focused on a single, all-consuming topic, drugs. What a wondrous discovery! Now we had a tool to use for the hopelessly addicted. It made good sense to those afflicted. But hold on, the old paradigm wasn't to be shattered so easily. Society, the media, government, our various moral guardians, weren't buying it. These people are just no good! Don't cater to their needs! It's just another drug! What about the sexual improprieties and miscegenation? They ought to be behind bars!

Frustrated, Dole began to feel the acute sting of having become a pariah. His writings now included more and more material on stigma, ignorance, and prejudice. How quickly logic, academic rigor, and even practicality, disintegrate under the crush of emotional overtones. Over and over, not just Nyswander and Dole, but anyone involved with methadone maintenance, was subject to the old "guilt by association" indictment.

So here I was, not being asked to discuss some issues of concern, but being told, notified, that dispensing would be stopped, period! It was like, would you and your nasty people please go away, disappear. We upright and righteous ones, don't want you! Indignant wouldn't begin to describe how I felt. Had I read about Martin Luther King and Gandhi, and more to the point, had I gone through my Viet Nam war experience and struggled with Cesar Chavez against all odds, to be bowled over by this misdirected injustice? Hardly. I immediately fired off the following note. "In the absence of the initiation of meaningful dialogue on this most important issue, I will, tomorrow at noon, just outside the main entrance of the hospital, be holding a press conference, to publicly air all relevant concerns regarding heroin addiction in the community, and more importantly, racism and prejudice." This being small town Iowa, where such tactics may not be commonplace, the somewhat assertive ploy apparently, while not endearing me to the hospital administration, did manage to get their attention. Within the hour a meeting was arranged to "talk things over."

What followed were a series of discussions where I would bring reams of articles explaining the rationale and efficacy of methadone treatment, and they would stubbornly persevere in their stance that can only be described as enlightened self-interest. Like Dole and Nyswander, I was finding out what it was like to be a "nigger." The same or similar scenarios are played out, time and again, all over the country. Eventually it came down to a public board meeting, press in attendance, with multiple testimonials, several being quite emotional, on all sides of the issue. And, as is nearly always the result with these cases, on the final dramatic vote, I and my patients lost. Out of pity, however, I was given several months to find another solution to the problem.

As I recouped and collected my thoughts, having already contacted every pharmacy in the area and being refused by all, I concluded that I would be better served by searching for an independent setting where I could, as much as possible, control my own destiny. A nice, small but adequate medical office building had just become available several blocks from the hospital. With some adjustments, I would be able to continue my family practice, and run the methadone program, including dispensing medication, from that facility. Actually, the solid brick building was very similar to the office my father practiced out of for many years in Alton. Within the month, negotiations were finalized, and the move was made. It was not, however, without considerable bitterness, as numerous patients, an excellent nurse, and a talented administrative person, accompanied me on the switch.

Several times a year, the four of us would journey across the state of Iowa to the small northwest corner town of Alton to visit my father and step mother. It was a four hour ride, without snow, that is. I had the route down to where all but twenty miles of it could be done on blacktops. This made the trip much more enjoyable, no cops, no traffic, only the occasional tiniest of towns like Dows, Faulkner, Thor, and Laramie, and a good dose of heartland, the farms, livestock, groves and sloughs, all set in analogs of ubiquitous corn and beans. If vision was good, we could move right along, but over a rise, a tractor with manure spreader or worse, a combine could close fast, requiring caution. Deer, also, could pop out at any moment, especially dawn and dusk. For me it was always inspiring. This was the land I knew so well, and the feeling crescendoed the closer we got to our destination, until each town, every road, the buildings, streams, every tree it seemed, had special meaning. These are the memories that anchor one, provide security, like the good automatic Holstein on the path to the barn and stanchion to be milked.

This time was different. Three days earlier, the two of them had walked to church, up on the hill, near the cemetery. Dad hadn't been feeling too well, maybe a cold, prostrate possibly, just a weakness, a feverish feeling. Murphy's typically die in their sixties of coronaries. Occasionally one will hit the seventies. Con was only months from eighty years old. I had firsthand knowledge of his precarious pathological cardiovascular status, having recently assisted on his abdominal aortic aneurysm repair, and being particularly impressed with the amount of atheromatous adipose tissue we had to remove before placing the graft.

Margaret, with years of nursing experience, knew he was gone. Middle finger dipping into holy water for the sign of the cross, the eternal stroll up the aisle toward the red flickering flame, a cough echoing through the nave, like the day thirty years previous with five small children perplexed without their mother and a thousand times hence, flectamus genua, what are you thinking? Kneel. Rest. Silence.

The wake was nothing short of amazing. We children, right in the room with dad, were able to relive his entire life and more as person after person passed through, each with a poignant anecdote, a funny story, some significant remembrance, a hug and a tear. "If you called him in the middle of the night," one farmer told us, "You better get dressed quick, because by the time you got downstairs, he'd probably be turning into the yard." That was the legacy, dedication, compassion, service.

Later, after the funeral, I spent the better part of a day, at Margaret's request, disposing of the old medical files, reading many of the brief notes, each ending in some terminal event, acute coronary thrombosis, renal cell carcinoma, motor vehicle accident, caught in power take off, suicide. A succinct summary of every person's life and the history of forty years in that small community floating page by page into the flames burning within the old well curb dug into the corner of the back yard serving for all these years as a fireplace. Finely finishing the last file, I made one last trip around the friendly yard, listening, touching, smelling, looking up at the same white clouds indifferently resting the sun if only for a brief moment.

"Margaret, the last of the charts is gone," I reported, finding her going over papers in the kitchen. "Sorry I took so long but, you know, dad was such a private person. Those records reflect what must have occupied his thoughts for much of the time. I couldn't help reading some of them."

"Thanks, Danny. I want you to pick out some of his books to take back to Cedar Falls for you and the boys. I know you read to them a lot and your father always preferred a book over television."

Scanning over the shelves, I selected a set of three collected works, A. Conan Doyle, Shakespeare, and Hawthorne. With Liam, I could already start on these, especially the detective stories.

Returning home, one of the first things I did, with the help of Janet's father, was put up a basketball hoop along the side of the driveway. We had bought a home in a quiet neighborhood near the university, not much traffic, and a small winding creek nearby. The height of the rim was adjustable, but before long we had it at ten feet. Many an hour was spent playing h-o-r-s-e, around the world, or just shooting. Both kids seemed to like it almost as much as their dad.

Because of all the time I spent playing at the PEC, I had become familiar with the various coaches, many of whom played in our games at noon. I was always willing to help with pre-season physicals or see injuries so when UNI became Division I in basketball, I was asked to be the team physician. With the position came season passes for my family and the opportunity to travel with the team to special events. So it wasn't unusual, one day after our mid-day workout, to have one of the trainers waiting to ask me to see an athlete. The case, however, was anything but routine.

"What you got, Terry?" I asked as we walked toward the training room.

"One of the starters for the women says she's feeling very tired the last few days, and she's getting bruised up pretty bad the last game or two. Coach wanted you to take a look at her."

Entering the exam room, at a glance I was already concerned. "Melissa, this is Dr. Murphy." Her legs had multiple dark purple bruises. Some appeared to be at least two inches in diameter.

"Hi, how ya feelin'?"

"I don't know, Doc. I just don't seem to have any energy lately."

"What about these bruises? I know you guys play aggressive but this is a bit much."

"Ya, there's a lot of contact, but these just pop up on their own. I don't even remember getting hit for most of 'em."

"Lay down a minute, I want to check your abdomen. You'll have to pardon the sweat, we just finished playing."

As I examined her, I noticed more bruises on her arms, otherwise not much else. "I want you to run over to the hospital for a blood test. No practice for now. We'll talk when the results come back."

Walking out, Terry asked, "What do you think, Doc?"

"I couldn't feel her spleen, and she doesn't appear to be severely anemic, so I'm not betting on leukemia, but I'm worried about platelets. We'll know this afternoon."

"Thanks for seein' her."

About three hours later, the call came from the lab. "Dr. Murphy, this is Peggy at the lab. That platelet count was only 9,000. We did it by hand and double checked it."

"How was the hemoglobin?"

"Hemoglobin 13.6, everything else normal too."

My suspicions confirmed, I had Melissa called to come in to the office, not wanting to tell her by phone.

"You have ITP, " I began, offering her a seat in the exam room. "Idiopathic thrombocytopenic purpura is the full name. Your platelet count is very low, that's why you have the bruises. It's not usually dangerous and we have treatments, but you can't play until you're better. I've spoken with a hematologist at the university who recommends a medicine called prednisone. We'll have to follow you closely and get repeat blood tests. You should be able to stay in school."

The next days were filled with calls from family, coaches, even the press. Although her platelet count responded somewhat, every time we tried to lower the dose of medication, her numbers dropped precipitously. Soon we were back in the room for another talk.

"Melissa, you're not responding as well as we'd like. There's always a chance of internal bleeding, or even in the brain. Your periods could be a problem, and the dose of steroid will definitely lead to complications."

"What are you saying, Doc? Isn't there anything else we can do?"

"Yes there is. I think we have to consider removing your spleen."

"That sounds risky. Aren't there other medicines?"

"Not really. I've read all the latest articles, and talked to three specialists. The consensus is surgery. Mortality would be around 1%, but you're young and extremely healthy. I don't think we have much choice."

The next week she underwent splenectomy, without complication, and her platelet count rose immediately to 500,000 and never dropped again. Her basketball career, however, had ended.

Mine, on the other hand, was still going strong like a seasoned alpha wolf depending ever more on guile and posturing, baring the fang only on those carefully chosen occasions. An example that sticks out in my memory is one Saturday afternoon, as I sauntered into the PEC, searching for a sorely needed run, Terry Allen, one of the assistant UNI football coaches, came up to me saying, "Murph, there's a bunch of guys here who act like they own the place. C'mon over, we got next." Moving over to courtside, we picked up three generics and watched another frustrated five fall. I recognized the winners, who apparently had held court for over an hour. They weren't local, but were a group from Waterloo who got off on coming into a gym, kicking butt for as long as they wanted, then left, ego enhanced. They were some of the most talented around but what stood out more was the way they literally oozed attitude. Terry, in contrast, was the exact opposite, nary a word, but a dogged persistence, driven by a limitless competitiveness lurking behind his expressionless countenance, reminding one of a professional assassin. At only 6'1", he dominated the low post by combining better than average athleticism with an extraordinarily effective use of body density. He could move but in that decisive moment of allowable incidental contact, it was like going against a Central Park statue. The game began with them doing their phi slamma jamma thing, accompanied by the incessant trash designed to humiliate us would be pansies. Taciturn to the tee, we hung around, me making a few outside, but mostly on Allen down low, making room, then finishing with the little power bank. Money! Money! Game is to 15 by one. As we got to double figures, we were still close, and although they had yet to shut up, the quips were more serious, them not wanting to be stung. It was then that they pulled a switch, putting a 6'6" guy on Terry, effectively limiting his possibilities. Realizing, down 13-12, that our best chance now depended on me pulling out something special, I looked my guy off just enough to shift his weight to his calcanei, allowing me to launch a 25 footer dead to silk. Now they're all business, quickly taking it strong to the hole, scoring with superior athleticism, their add. Back to our side, I push off just enough to receive the pass top of the key. Allen gives me a slight nod, leaving his traditional low post spot, coming to a halt about 5 feet to my left. Knowing exactly what to do, my guy being on me like Spandex, I fake right before taking it strong left, effectively rubbing him off on the bone crushing Allen pick, freeing me to blow by the 6'6" guy and finish with the left handed finger roll over the late arriving help "D". Deuce, next hoop wins it. "Just gimme the rock," says my guy, desperately needing to, and dead certain that he can redeem himself. A flurry of quick spin moves and power dribbles takes him past my best efforts and he's elevating at the rim. But no, from out of nowhere, comes T.A. to challenge and get a finger on the ball sending it careening off glass to the awaiting ten man free for all. Summoning all my remaining strength, I leapt as powerfully as I possibly could and somehow came away with leather. These guys don't know me, how could they predict if there's a dagger or from whence it might come. All I see is destiny. Advancing the ball across mid court, using nonchalance as a setup, in perfect rhythm the muscles of the right leg tense imperceptibly as toe touches wood 30 feet from the grail, initiating the near instantaneous release hurtling the spinning sphere toward the now gaping funnel. Swoosh! Finally silence. A dose of humility? Lesson learned? Probably not, but still, not a bad way to get a good cardiovascular workout.

Eldon Miller had become the men's basketball coach at UNI. His previous position was at Ohio State, where he had done quite well, but not well enough to satisfy the exacting standards of the alumni at that high flying Big Ten football powerhouse. A conference championship with a final four appearance might have done it but merely running a clean program, with a high graduation rate while being highly competitive and advancing to post season play regularly, didn't. In his present job, such lofty goals couldn't even be mentioned, just dreamed of. To begin with, how do you recruit in the Hawkeye state. Ever since the advent of electricity, there hadn't been a kid who wasn't spoon fed University of Iowa basketball. First it was WHO radio broadcasting state wide, enriching every farm family's life with fantastic coverage of each and every glorious exploit. Conference champions in the '40's, within a hog's hair of a national championship in the '50's thwarted only by a certain Bill Russell, and routing Wooden's UCLA dynasty in the '60's.

Hell, Ronnie Reagan even got his start talkin' Hawks on WHO. Then TV added the pictures and soon every game was carried live from Sioux City to Davenport. Undefeated Big Ten champs in 1970, then losing to Jacksonville in the NCAA. Ten years later to the Final Four, nipped by Louisville and crushing Notre Dame in consolation. Ever heard of Don Nelson, Connie Hawkins, Fred Brown? If Iowa was full up, then a kid would go to Iowa State, where they've had numerous NBA performers, and better yet people still talk about the time little Gary Thompson from tiny Roland, Iowa, led the Cyclones to a win over Wilt the Stilt's Kansas. And don't forget Drake in Des Moines; they took UCLA to the wire in the Final Four. Where do they get their players? That doesn't leave much for the new kid on the block, UNI.

At any rate, every four years, Div. I programs have the right to an overseas summer pre-season trip. Eldon was generous enough to invite me along for UNI's first ever such experience. For two weeks, we jaunted across Flemish Belgium and Friesland, then France, and finally, Switzerland. Nightly games where anything goes, touring in an all glass walled mini bus, museums, delicious restaurants, and yes, topless beaches, and yes, various pubs and clubs, an Eldon Miller clinic for coaches at the majestic Swiss Olympic training facility, and a thousand interactions with players, coaches, and Europeans including radical Belgian students on King Leopold's role in the Congo, menial workers in Geneva, nearly all Portuguese, on topics from Lisbon to Laurenco Marques, and tall Dutchmen on tulips, hashish, and Huguenots. Overall, the experience could have been considered character building, especially for the players.

Back in Cedar Falls, this group of cohesive Panthers, started off their season with a string of "W's," utilizing a balanced attack keying off a solid go to guy in the middle, Jason Reese. Hardly recruited out of high school in Des Moines, Jason began to bulge and blossom in college, to where he could best be described as a 6'8", 240 lb. Joe Palooka. He always had friendly smile on his face which invariably relaxed his opponent just long enough to allow Reese to get position about two feet closer to the hoop than any decent defense desired. Occupying a double share of real estate, possessing the strength of Charlie Atlas, and having perfected an assortment of moves both left and right, fade, face up, step through, or to the rack with a power dribble, he was no easy assignment. And he could shoot free throws. To top it off, he exuded confidence, especially in the clutch.

Next up was a relative newcomer on the schedule, a team we had never beaten, the Iowa Hawkeyes, perennial top twenty powerhouse. UNI's games were played in the UNI-Dome, a football structure with a canvas roof held up by air pressure like a balloon. If even a door were to be held open too long, theoretically, the roof could collapse. On this particular night, the structural integrity of the place was to be tested. By moving the BB court to the middle of the football field and placing portable bleachers all around, seating capacity was pushed to 22,000. If all would inhale simultaneously, the ceiling would dip, or puff with a unanimous scream. Luckily the loyalty was evenly divided, keeping the barometer out of the danger zone. Long before game time, the place filled, media in full force, mascots, cheers and poms, pep band blaring, players stretching hams and shooting lay-ups, coaches, referees, and team doctors excitedly imagining their particular scenarios. At the opening tip, noise level rivaled that of a U2 concert. Liam and Conor were literally aglow. Having been well prepped for the press and trap, Miller's Panthers somehow held their own on "D" and stayed poised on offense as the lead changed hands frequently while the clock ticked. It was Reese, McCullough, Phyfe, Reese, Reese, Turner, and Muilenburg, hoop after hoop, hanging around. Toward the end, just as hope began to fade, a bench guy, Brad Hill pilfered the certainty from the mighty Hawks with breath taking boards and ice water threes as the place nearly collapsed at 00:00, the Panther swallowing its vanquished avian adversary. Let me tell you, this kind of electricity won't come from a television set.

As the season progressed, UNI continued to do well, although stubbing their toe occasionally, coming finally to conference tournament time, the prize being the automatic NCAA bid. Serendipitously, this year, the site for all the action was what proved to be the Dome of doom for opponents. Illinois-Chicago fell first in a triple OT frenetic, vocal cord paralyzing, paradigm of excitement. Next victim, the fierce and favored Bears of Southwest Missouri State, falling flat and sent to hibernate on a 15 foot Reese swish at the buzzer after a swashbuckling reception of a length of the court assist, a finish even fairy tales can't match. Once again tympanic membranes lose a bit more high frequency capability. All adrenaline exhausted, there were still Bennett and son of Wisconsin-Green Bay, another team UNI had never defeated. Before the game, I was called to the training room to see a player with trouble running. "Doc, this is Tony Bennett, point guard for Green Bay. Could you take a look at his injury?"

"Hi, Tony. What's up with the leg?"

"I hurt it toward the end of yesterday's game. Now every time I pivot, I get pain right here." Pointing to the lateral part of the thigh, he winced as I carefully palpated the quadriceps muscle.

Realizing how important the game was and that this was one of the most competitive kids around, I motioned him over to a chair next to his trainer and said, "I think it's just a minor strain. There's no swelling. We can give you ibuprofen and ace it and you're limited only by whatever pain you can tolerate."

"Okay, then I'm in. Thanks, Doc." Remaining unspoken by anyone, yet of which we were all quite aware, was the high probability that these were potentially precious tissues indeed, as murmurs of NBA draft had already surfaced.

Of course, the game went down to the wire and was a two point affair with a minute to go before perfection from the line sealed the top rung for the high flying Cats as the Phoenix ended up corked like the remains in a memorial urn.

What a three day affair! This was the kind of excitement that inspires one to muse about a magical rendezvous under cover of a vintage bridge. My family was alive, nay, the university, the whole town, all the sports pages, and every conversation pulsated with one more version of said events. I had been able to provide medical coverage for the whole shebang, and it was never too much. Objections overruled, the high level of interest was sustained throughout. Basketball at its best! Yet this was merely appetizer, prelude to the exquisitely prepared entree for only those three score and four who had shown the most insatiable hunger.

"Doc, pack up your bags." It was Eldon Miller on the phone. "We're going to Richmond."

"What kind of medicine do we need, Coach?"

"Tranquilizers, and lots of 'em. Seriously, work it out with Terry Noonan. I want to be prepared for any possibility. These kids deserve the best shot they can give."

"Okay, Coach. And, by the way, congratulations."

Preparations complete, soon we were on the charter heading East toward the former Confederate capital. Beginning uneventfully, the trip became acutely more adventurous somewhere over Ohio where unexpected storms hit like a full court press. At one point we all felt like bungee jumpers caught somewhere between giggles and prayer. Surviving, we were significantly delayed, arriving only to encounter a nonfunctional bus awaiting us. Convinced that we were jinxed or sabotaged, we hit the hotel just before sunrise, scheduled shoot around fast approaching.

Actually, the NCAA tried to do it right. Nice accommodations in the suburbs, several spanking new autos at our disposal, all the proper passes and credentials, per diems, press conferences, etc. It really is a daunting undertaking. Not lost in the hubbub was the minor consideration that opposing us would be Missouri, who, as recently as three weeks previous, had been the number one team in the nation. The only reason they'd even heard of UNI was because their coach, Norm Stewart, had, early in his career, steered the Cedar Falls program. Seeded three, it was a foregone conclusion that they would prevail against a lowly fourteen.

That afternoon, I had arranged to visit a large methadone clinic near downtown Richmond. Leaving my five star digs, I hopped into the fresh smelling Olds, and wound past the spacious light colonial style estates, gradually penetrating into the dark underside to find the beacon within the blotch on the soul of Dixie. Parking, knowingly, atop a hill where a main artery crossed, I did the last two blocks afoot, observing the progressive deterioration while maintaining the deliberate appearance so characteristic of the medical profession. Loitering about the heavily barred and grated, poorly marked house, were groups of nearly all black clients, in twos and threes, discussing tar and white, Jonesing, mandatory drops, and paper. Waiting to be cleared for entry by the armed guard, I observed the faces, looking for similarities to the work I did, not finding much. The clinic director showed me all around, explaining how Richmond was the crime capitol of the South, murder rate exceeded only by D.C. Here it was heroin or methadone by day and coke by night, no jobs, and lots of despair and HIV with little hope. Overworked and underfunded, it was, at best, damage control, rehab being a pipe dream. Exchanging phone numbers and pleasantries, I left thinking of Claude Brown's "Manchild in the Promised Land", realizing that the yawning chasm separating this from middle America would probably never be bridged. For what the insufferable horrors of civil war?

The next day, the game was doing all it could to avoid the preconceived script. Wearing my blazer, I noticed Red Auerbach two rows back, then the packed house, all astonished at the staying power of the pesky Panthers. Anthony Peeler was stinking the place up, partly due to McCullough's tenacity, while Reese et. al. still hadn't realized how intimidated they were supposed to be. Never down by more than a few, UNI actually led much of the way. Finally coming to a frantic finish, it was the Tigers who looked frazzled, the felines from Cedar Falls having just come off of three straight barn burners. Then, twenty-nine seconds left, Jason exited with his fifth, leaving it up to Maurice Newby, subbed in during a time out with ten seconds to go, 71 all, pulling the trigger from deep, over two frustrated, ferocious defenders. It was the shot that was to be shown at least a million times on TV sets everywhere over the next few years. Rain forests tumbled as ink flowed. UNI sweatshirts catapulted past Duke and UCLA. Back home even pre-schools erupted in spontaneous street celebrations. God is good! God is good!

In the locker room, Norm Stewart graciously acknowledged the fine effort as we held our randomly picked players for their mandatory drops. Now the press was ubiquitous and unrelenting, okay for a while but soon becoming bothersome. "Team physician. Well, what did you think of the shot?"

"Personally, I'm a bevel up kind of guy, but it certainly proved efficacious. Just what the doctor ordered."

The next day, one of the assistant coaches, Kevin Boyle, and I, went to see part of an 18-under AAU state championship game nearby. Once again a different reality as we saw lots of talent but were told that only two, of all the players, qualified. Just another bunch of future street ballers, addicts, convicts, and welfare recipients, those whom society fails on a regular basis.

That evening I discovered that I didn't have a shirt for the next day's game. Maybe even I hadn't given us a chance for the win over Missou? The hype of the media glitz and the red carpet NCAA treatment must have really gotten to me as I found myself wandering into a fine boutique, carefully picking out a trendy brand name, and even adding a tie, for heaven's sakes. Where do you find the balance in this topsy turvy world?

The game for the sweet sixteen pitted us against the Gophers of Minnesota. The excitement was sustained at a high level, but after what we had pulled off, we couldn't go back to being nobody again. Arriving early with the team, I spent a few minutes visiting with one of the Minn. assistant coaches, Silas McKinnie, a former Hawkeye running back from the years when I attended med. school. We reminisced about the many times we had butted heads in field house pickup games. It was ghetto versus yahoo, both gaining respect through the intense reverberations of a hard fought game of hoops. Our paths had crossed in the milieu of Iowa City night life, which provided a unique eclectic collage of social interaction, until the horrors of Viet Nam ripped that whole scene asunder. Instead of "Goin' to a go-go," it was "Hell no, we won't go," and "Sugar pie, honey bunch" gave way to napalm, mamma-san, and constructive engagement. Clem Haskins stopped by to say hello, one of the better coaches around.

The game was like a battle of titans, both teams playing well, especially Reese, who ended up with 29 and broke Randy Kraayenbrink's school career scoring record. It took a near perfect night from their Willie Burton, with 36 points, for our northern neighbors to slip by 81-78. End of ride, but what a trip!

The good thing for me was that now, both my kids were very much into the game I thrived on, something we could share many times, and in many ways. Liam, although he participated on school teams and was talented, much preferred unstructured situations. With him, one on one, I faced the classic dilemma: kick his butt, then deal with his anger and frustration, or let him win and stand accused of not giving my best effort. My compromise was to take enough low percentage shots to make each game competitive so it could be,

225

win some, lose some. Still, he saw through the ruse, and the psychological machinations challenged us both. Conor, on the other hand, was more mechanical, structured, disciplined. By fourth grade, we had formed an AAU team with him and his peers from the neighborhood. As coach, I had to push the father thing to the side, just like when delivering my own sons, a task that, too, was to prove nigh unto impossible. More on all of that later.

In my medical practice, such as it was, I was gradually coming to understand the intricacies of opiate addiction in Iowa. As is true everywhere, there exists a well-worn underground network, like the catacombs or the Ho Chi Minh Trail, for the procurement of illicit substances. In times of pain, people go knocking far and wide, seeking to get well. At first I was amazed at how someone from Des Moines would know a Davenport person. Two or three hundred miles was nothing as people chased the poppy dragon. Complications began to surface when a community based, comprehensive alcohol and substance abuse program in the state capital, decided to add methadone maintenance to their armamentarium. Not that there wasn't a big heroin problem there, but the proven successful philosophy of good methadone programs was antithetical to that of the basic 12 step, abstinence approach. Funding, for them, depended on the same state functionaries who had recently been self proclaimed the new State Methadone Authority. Many patients, while desperate for their dose of medication, found the attitudes they encountered at the program, abhorrent. I, on the other hand, being private and having no previous agenda, based my program on a study of the relevant literature and implementation of those practices which had led to positive outcomes elsewhere. Soon sizable numbers of Des Moines patients were transferring to us, despite having to pay modest fees. With each new arrival, resentment and frustration festered like a tropical ulcer, at their previous treatment site, and among their benefactors. Once again, as is so often the case, dialogue was never even a consideration. It was bring on the big stick and skip the speak softly. Coming in the form of the first ever "inspection" by the newly formed SMA, we were immediately suspicious as they poured through the patient records and left with nary a word to us.

Previously, we had been visited periodically by experienced FDA officials out of St. Louis, resolving most of the questionable issues during comprehensive exit interviews.

Our worst fears were realized when the official certified mail letter arrived notifying us that we were found to be "essentially in non-compliance" with state and federal standards, rules and regulations, and that state approval of our federal license to operate was hereby revoked. Immediately I felt that terrible, ice cold rumbling sensation beginning deep down within. Never say uncle, walk alone, into the wind, across the entire tundra, win at all cost, persevere like Gandhi, Dorothy Day, Chavez, Bernadette Devlin, MLK, Marciano, or even Rambo. As a ferocious carnivore, cornered and hungry, paces in its lair, issuing forth barely audible guttural warnings, I retired to my office, mumbling specious invectives, waiting for the seismograph to bottom out. Deep seeded emotion is one thing, while ingenious strategy is another. Trick is to channel the energy of frustration into an effective search for a successful plan of action.

Reading the long list of alleged violations, it was readily apparent that, first, the state was only minimally conversant with the relevant legislative code, and, second, they had failed miserably in their search for proper documentation in the charts they had so painstakingly reviewed. In my letter of response, logically refuting and explaining on each of the issues, I formally appealed their devastating decision. It would have been unconscionable to allow this group of society's most demonized, most alienated, to be slapped back into one of the worst nightmares known to mankind, uncontrolled heroin addiction, by a collection of faceless bureaucrats pushing their political agenda. Some time later, I received another communication from the state placing my case on the agenda of the next quarterly meeting of their parent body in Des Moines.

In the meantime, life went on, meaning basketball. This time it was the Iowa Games state championship, age division 40 and over. Our group of Cedar Falls cronies, used to still playing with the young bucks, rather easily outclassed the field, even winning the gold medal game by twenty. I, personally, had run off a hot string of threes and was awarded the prestigious MVP trophy. Oozing with feigned braggadocio, I turned to my son Conor, who had accompanied me to the game, and declared, "I guess I went around those guys like they were standin' still."

Showing both his wry humor and a growing perception of the nuances of the sport, he immediately retorted, "Dad, they were standing still!" Unfazed by this devastating commentary, I still felt positive enough about my game, that, when I received a call the next week from one of the guys asking me if I wanted to join a team he was putting together for the upcoming national AAU championships coming up in Florida, I immediately acquiesced.

Being made up of the best players around the state, we thought we were hot stuff. As the appointed date drew nigh, the eight of us, highly honed athletes each came together on a Ft. Lauderdale beach to replenish our stores of Vit. D, get our strokes down, and sharpen visual acuity. Then, that evening, held at Hooters, not my choice by the way, but, in the interest of male bonding and team unity, the others feeling it the most appropriate, we discussed strategy while carbo-loading and doing all we could to avert any chance of dehydration on the morrow. I flat out stated, "Look who we got. Greyhounds. All we gotta' do is run the court. Those other old farts won't be able to keep up."

As the night progressed, discussions ranged near and far before finally degenerating to such as, "You know, this town holds a special place in my heart."

"Why's that?"

"It's the place where I first got to use my four years of high school Latin in a real life situation."

"Ya, and..."

"Overzealous Easter bunnies vacationing in college. Got caught in a police dragnet."

"What were the words?"

"Nolo contendere."

By game time the next day, although not feeling our best, we were ready and confident as we faced opening tip off against a team from Buffalo. We didn't get the tip, and, even though I was in good position and had a step on him, the player who received the tip, literally blew by me and proceeded on for the uncontested layup.

Damn, this was going to be a different level of ball! We stepped it up as best we could and stayed in the game but these guys could flat out play, especially the black dude who had shown the juice. Close all the way, we ended up faltering at the finish, losing 114-106. Their flash had lit us up for 51 points, a good amount of it at the expense of my so called "D." Properly humiliated, we straggled over to chat with the victors before heading to the showers to lick our wounds. Approaching the instructor himself, I remarked, "Heck of a game. You must have played college ball."

Before he could respond, one of his teammates jumped in, "That's Randy Smith. You know, as in NBA." Ya, I knew. Twelve-year career. Iron Man. Indefatigable Randy. Just didn't recognize him. OKAY, so that's how it is. Fine, chalk it up to experience, learn from it and move on.

"Good luck, you guys."

"Ya, you too."

We won the next game but never made it out of pool play and failed to advance to the finals. Still a lot of fun. Good diversion.

One of our players was a lawyer from Des Moines, so before the week was up I made a point of asking him about my problem. "Kenny, I'm having some serious difficulty in my work with a state regulatory body. Do you know of anyone in Des Moines who might be able to help me fight these guys?"

"Actually, Dan, while it's not my area of expertise, one of my partners, guy by the name of Mike Sellers, deals with those kinds of issues all the time. He thrives on administrative entanglements, the more convoluted, the more he digs it. I don't think you could go wrong with him."

Back home, I prepared diligently for the fast approaching meeting of the Iowa Commission on Substance Abuse where my case was scheduled to be first on the agenda. This group was made up of political appointees chosen by a conservative governor, all of whom came from backgrounds in community based treatment programs espousing various versions of the twelve step philosophy.

This, plus the obvious fact that they had been well primed on the "circumstances" of my case, may begin to explain why I felt more like I was at the "Inquisition" than at a fair hearing in the democratic home of the free. Cut off at every attempt to explain, treated with obvious disdain, I rapidly realized that this was not to be my forum, and sat quietly brooding, planning subsequent moves, as they arrogantly went into "closed session" before returning to announce, big shock, that the decision was upheld, next case!

How long does it take to learn that, on issues such as this one, you just don't get even a fighting chance? You're dead from the start. Ignorance and prejudice, ignorance and prejudice, all from the emotional side of the brain. Logic and rational thought, move aside. The story never changes. Well, shit, I'm still not going to lie down. "Hello, Mike, this is Dan Murphy. I play ball with Kenny. He told me you might be able to help me."

"Yes, he mentioned something about your difficulty. Let's set up a meeting."

Soon I was wearing out the road to Des Moines, whenever possible on my "days off," while digging deep at work in a determined effort to allay the legitimate fears of patients panicky about the possibility of having the one thing that had given them a life, yanked from under them unceremoniously, like a star witness being released from protective detention. Initially, my tendency was to treat even my lawyer, like nearly everyone else I had dealt with on this issue, with extreme caution and suspicion. It wasn't necessary. His role was that of advocate, and he played it well. In an amazing display, expanding the horizons of human mental capacity, over a short period of time, he digested and absorbed gigabytes of complicated concepts and technical information, all the while integrating it into strategic planning. Data entry included the relevant Federal Register, 25 pages of fine print displaying congressional vicissitude in line after line of Faulkneresque ambivalence mandating a linear process regulating methadone treatment in the hazy maze of a heroin addict's existence. "We will clarify the murkiness of the oozing volcanic exudate, by stirring diligently with a ponderous chocolate ladle." Then an entire chapter of the Iowa code, mostly irrelevant but for the fact that it was the only play ground that our state regulators were familiar with, meaning that they used it repeatedly even though it didn't apply. The book "Addicts Who Survived" in which I had highlighted several passages for his elucidation, Mike devoured, not just the indicated lines but the entire work, in a weekend. Along with the numerous medical articles and local media clippings, it represented a prodigious volume of highly specialized information to become conversant with in a short period of time.

While my approach might have included a sit down demonstration in the state capital by 50 addicts, faces either charcoaled or chalked according to their preference, rigged and ready to inject look alike horse in the antecubital while a straggly band played "Theme from the Man with the Golden Arm", Sellers opted for administrative appeal, followed by district court if needed. Hours, even entire days, were spent preparing and in court, as ill prepared people attempted to unravel the intertwining, often contradictory regulatory layers as applied to our program. Each rule was subject to as many interpretations as there were interpreters. A typical exchange might have been something like the following:

Sellers: {after exhaustively establishing my educational background and experience, questioning Joe Blow, a state investigator} Mr. Blow, may I ask where you received your college degree?

Blow: I don't have a college degree.

Sellers: Well then what about your high school diploma?

Blow: I finished that up with night classes.

Sellers: In other words, a GED. Mr. Blow, as I'm sure you're well aware, in all of the relevant rules, it clearly states that decisions must be made using "best medical judgment."

Blow: Yes.

Sellers: What you're saying, then, is that your medical judgment, with a GED education and absolutely no previous work in the area of methadone treatment, is better than that of Dr. Murphy?

Blow: No, not really when you say it like that.

Etcetera, etcetera.

The irony of the situation was, yes, I had to spend sizable amounts of money to defend the underdog, quite understandable, but the state must have frittered away well over one hundred thousand dollars to keep me from doing work which, not only no one else wanted to do, but that saved the state an estimated sixty thousand dollars annually per patient treated by preventing other medical and social expenses.

Through it all we were able to keep open for services, while the state, frustrated in their inability to accomplish their goals in a straight forward manner, took things personally and adopted a strategy of attrition and siege. Attacked on all fronts, we even found ourselves drawn into state legislative committee hearings after new restrictive statutes were proposed.

State legislator {after two days of nonsensical, garbled discussion during which Sellers, once again, succeeded in making our adversaries look extremely foolish}: Well, at least we have learned something about methadone treatment.

Committee chair: More than we would ever have wanted. I am advising you people to never again bring proposed legislation before this committee until it is competently and professionally prepared and a consensus has been reached by all the parties involved. Hearing adjourned.

Even though it's generally believed a bureaucracy can't be taught a lesson, after a sufficient number of these spankings, the state leashed the hounds and begrudgingly allowed me to struggle along in my work unmolested. Over a period of years, they even began espousing rhetoric strikingly similar to the basic statements I had been issuing from the start, not so remarkable when you consider that none of it was from my head but was based exclusively on what the most eminent experts in the field were saying all along.

I will say that being in the position of David under the constant threat of Goliath provided a very useful therapeutic tool as every patient could easily see how we ran the gauntlet for them over and over. The least they could do was comply with our standards and give rehabilitation a decent effort. In the same vein, the focus brought to our efforts injected favorable publicity for the program into the clandestine communication network serving the state's forever burgeoning opiate addict population. Numbers grew. And it wasn't just heroin. Never underestimate the marketing capacity of the pharmaceutical industry. A typical story might be: "Doc, I'm so strung out, ya gotta help me."

"And why do you come in now, Mrs. Jones?"

"My source just died off. He had cancer and got as many pain killers as he wanted. I'm shootin' six 'purple cows' a day (long acting morphine)."

Or, "It began when I hurt my back three years ago and my doctor gave me Tylenol #3's (codeine). I've had two operations and tried physical therapy and even acupuncture. Nothing helps. I'm in constant pain and now the only thing that helps is Dilaudid (hydromorphone). Still, it doesn't hold me and, out of desperation, the other day I changed a prescription. My doctor found out. He says he isn't going to the authorities but he won't see me again. What am I supposed to do?"

Percodan, Percocet, fentanyl patch
Want another brand, we got something to match
Darvon, Tylox, even Demeral
Runnin' low on samples, give the drug rep a call
Injectable, respectable, Stadol in the nose
Got you a pain, we can bring it to a close
The money, now honey, vision gettin' blurry
The habit, dagnabit, stomach start to churn
Hold on, no worry, we got methadone to burn.

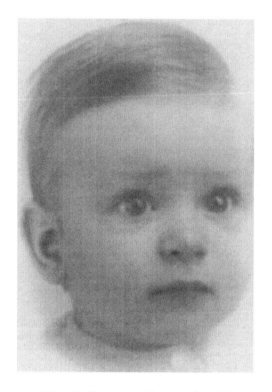

May 1945, me at eight months old

September 1948, presumably on my birthday with my sister Ann,
with whom I share my birthday.

May 1949. (L-R): Mike, Ann, Ethel, Mary, and Dan. Maureen will be born in September of this year, so she is in utero.

Around 1950, this photo was taken on Mary's first communion, thus
the white dress. (L-R): Me, Mary, Maureen, Mike, and Ann

SCHOOL DAYS 1957-58
ST. MARY'S

Eighth grade picture from St. Mary's Academy

1962, the St. Mary's Blue Jay basketball team, my senior year of high school

June 1958, a family trip to Washington DC. We are standing on the
steps of the Capitol with our local congressional representative who
came from our home town. (L-R): Dad, Uncle Mac, Mrs. Hooven
(the representative's wife), Maureen, Mike, Rep. Hooven, Ann, Aunt
Frances, Mary, and me

1970, graduating from the University of Iowa Carver College of
Medicine as the U.S. was deeply into the Vietnam War

1976, "Let's change the world."
With Cesar Chavez. Delano, California

Our first basketball practice was something to behold. These were nine year olds bursting with energy and had very few skills. Dribbling around chairs and practicing two handed chest passes just didn't seem to do it, so early on, one of the other fathers, Reed, and I decided that up tempo fun might be best. We'd start with an equal line of kids at opposite ends of the court, one ball for each line. On "go" each guy had to dribble as fast as possible full court and make the layup or shoot until he did, then pass it back to the next player and continue to see which line finishes first. Anything could and did happen. Kicked balls, travels, lines crossing, double dribbles, kids falling down, and this was only a drill. Or we'd play "burn out" where all the kids begin at the free throw line, the first two having balls. You shoot, run to rebound and shoot again until you make it. Meanwhile the guy behind you can shoot as soon as you leave the line and if he scores ahead of you, you're done. When the ball falls through the net, you fire it back to the next guy up as soon as you can. As the line thins, it gets more and more hectic, finally ending in a frenzy with the last two players scurrying like crazy back to the line with one eventually making the winner amidst high decibel encouragement. Sure, we'd scrimmage, but with modified rules. Only the most blatant travels would be called, and lots of slaps, hacks and bumps had to be overlooked to allow for some continuity. Practices usually went an hour to an hour and a half.

Conor was a better than average player from the beginning. Once at half time of a UNI game, his number was picked, and on the floor he calmly sank four straight progressively longer shots, winning over $100 worth of prizes. Right then I knew that he would probably be a good bet in the clutch.

We did have a few games that year, but what a fiasco. Time after time, I'd see one player with the ball surrounded by nine others yelling for it and trying to grab it. There were turnovers galore and only a rare hoop. And, yes, every so often, in the helter-skelter mix of adrenaline, screams, and shifting directions, a lad's joy would turn to that special frustration and embarrassment that surfaces only when you realize you just scored at the other team's basket. Another highlight was when one of our players who was feeling gangly from a recent growth spurt, or possibly was experienced a spurt at that very

243

moment, actually shot a free-throw clean over the backboard. Amazing! Still, the kids were giving it their all and having a ball. I really don't think it made much difference if they won or lost, they just wanted to play. That endearing aspect of the game, the "gotta win" syndrome, begins subtly and grows sadly with each new level of competition peaking somewhere ahead of apple pie and motherhood.

Normally, at this age, pressing isn't allowed, but we did have one game against a team from across the Mississippi in Illinois, with no restriction. They came out in full court heat. We panicked, choked, collapsed, and folded all at once, yet it was to be one of the most important lessons we ever learned, as we saw a fantastic way to make up for lack of size.

Our winter season lasted from October to March, but it was at about this time in Iowa that organized basketball opportunities began presenting themselves year round. There were still swimming, track, football, baseball, etc., but for many of these kids, basketball became their main passion.

One of my main passions, OB, was being severely threatened, as Sartori Hospital decided to discontinue birthing services. This meant that I would have to go ten miles to the nearest facility for deliveries. This was quite a compromise; you can't check in as often, you get there late, it's more impersonal, and you lose more office time. The clincher came one day at work when I got the following call. "Hello, Dr. Murphy, this is Vickie. I'm starting to have stomach pains, and they seem to be getting stronger."

"But you're only what, six months pregnant?"

"Almost seven. Oh-oh, there's another one."

"You better come in so I can check you. Probably Braxton-Hicks but it's safer to know for sure."

Soon she was in the office and a quick exam revealed six centimeter dilatation with a bulging bag of waters. Now the dilemma. She's going to deliver imminently. That part I can handle, so I think, but do I want a premature baby born in my office with respiratory distress needing incubation that I'm not set up to do? Quickly, I make the call to the Sartori paramedics. "Jay, this is Dr. Murphy. I got a woman here in the office in labor. She's already six centimeters.

Could you and Jeff take us to Covenant by ambulance? Bring the OB kit and throw in the smaller endotracheal tubes just in case, she's only thirty-one weeks. Thanks."

Within minutes we're in the back of the ambulance heading through red lights on our way to Waterloo. Vicki's pains are getting stronger and she's showing those early signs of holding her breath like she's going to have to bear down even though she doesn't want to. Outwardly calm, but inwardly thinking like crazy, I say, "Vickie, I can't think of any professional way to say this, but would you like to take your pants off and lay down on this stretcher? Jay, open the kit and I'll take a pair of number 8's just in case." We're still three miles out and things are rapidly coming to a climax. As we bump over a railroad crossing, the amniotic sac ruptures spontaneously and my heart skips a beat. "Jeff, radio Covenant and have a neonatal ICU nurse meet us with a crash cart outside the ER entrance. We got a double footling preemie breech precipitating on us." Now I need to summon up every bit of calmness and experience I possess. The head of a baby has the widest diameter compared to any other part of the body, but not by much, so that in a full term breech, only a little more squeezing is needed to get the head out after the body delivers, but the more premature a baby is, the bigger the difference in diameter of head relative to body. In other words, big head, and scrawny body, meaning head can stick inside with umbilical cord pinched tight cutting off oxygen rich blood flow to the baby, future ACT scores dropping with each precious second. "Jay, give her four liters, nasal cannula is okay." This must be the bumpiest street in town, I'm thinking, and as the siren takes us through red lights, I observe in rapid succession, the appearance of buttocks, chord, and scapulae. Looking at the diminutive structures, I know how delicate the cranial bones must be offering little protection against trauma. Any added pressure could lead to a tear or bleeding in the brain. Positioning my hands as I had done so many times before, I felt the ambulance swerve around the last turn. Gentle but expeditious. Got to do it just right. "Vickie, it's a boy. Keep panting until I tell you to push. You're doing great. Jay, get ready to give me just a little suprapubic pressure. I want the head to come out smooth and steady." The one thing we had going for us was that this wasn't her first baby, usually meaning tissues open more readily. Both arms

245

came down easily as we came to a stop just outside the hospital. "Okay, Vickie, give us a little push. Jay, help us ever so slightly." As the back door opened, a magical beam of sunlight baptized the just emerged head, a feeble declaration mixing with our ooh's, aah's, and whew's. "Way to go, Vickie! His color's good and he seems strong. About three lbs., I'd guess. Jay, let's just dry him off a little, but I want to leave the chord for a few seconds to give him more blood. You did a great job. Thanks."

It all went well but it might not have. Anyway, that's when I decided to quit delivering babies. I still had plenty to do, especially now with coaching.

Because of their recent notoriety, the UNI Panthers had been among those invited to the upcoming San Juan Shutout. Janet and I decided that this would be a good way to expose our children to another culture and refresh ourselves on the use of Spanish while having some fun with the team so we all packed our swimming suits and stepped onto the plane for the first leg of the journey to Chicago. Liam and Conor, already excited, could barely contain themselves at Midway when up walked the Illinois team, with all their stars and Coach Henson, to join the same flight to Puerto Rico. At first everyone concentrated on looking proud and studly, but soon interactions began. After all, there was that pervasive bond linking each inextricably to the other, hoops. A festive atmosphere pervaded all the way to the Caribbean. Some of the guys were even considerate enough to include the children in their pre-tournament banter.

We stayed in the finest part of the capital, surrounded by luxury and casinos. Even more spectacular was the welcoming banquet, five star in every way. All the teams and delegations, movin' on up and comin' through, unable to keep from noticing the massive chandeliers and fountains tinkling and sprinkling as the bells of bandits punctuated the soft calypso like a fibrillating heart. Only yesterday they were chopping volunteers and baling or low ridin' where people shouldn't go. Handle it, guys! You made your basket!

Served buffet style, the food stretched the width of the hall. Beginning with banana, the fruit section included mango, papaya, lychee, and pineapple, all fresh. Then salads, pastas, vegetables, meats

246

and seafood, topped by innumerable varieties of tangy desserts. Following the caloric deluge, were the politicians, team intros and coaches' summaries, leading up to an excellent sequence of live entertainment. The last group, best of all, had a band accompanied by P.R's version of the Rockettes dressed or undressed in their tropical finest. As the performance progressed the music became livelier before, unexpectedly, stopping abruptly. All eyes watched as the most beautiful performer skillfully twirled and weaved amongst the tables as if searching, before halting at ours and extending a hand to an enchanted Panther, commanding "Vamos bailar." Hesitating for a fraction of a second, Cedric jumped up as the band shattered the interlude with "Oye, Como Va." Cheers and whistles abounded as the two shared the spotlight briefly in a sizzling bump and grind before being joined by successively chosen guests, filling the floor with a frenzy of testosterone flowing to the beat in undulating silhouettes.

Besides attending the games, we took time for the beach, wandering through old San Juan, hiking in a rain forest, and experiencing the exasperation of not being able to get close enough to twenty one. Janet had met a Puerto Rican student at UNI, and on our last day, we were invited to her home for dinner. Not only was the food great and the Latin hospitality exceptional, but the discussion sincere and lively, covering everything from drugs and crime to the independence movement and the pharmaceutical industry. Before we knew it, the time to go was upon us and, after the mandatory pictures, we had to hurry back to the hotel, check out and accompany the team to the airport. Our flight home wasn't as enjoyable for the simple reason that the Panthers hadn't done as well as they had hoped and now faced the possibility of a long and frustrating season.

Back at work, it didn't take long to forget P.R. and once again, circle the wagons and prepare to enter the maelstrom. "Dr. Murphy, I'm sure you don't remember me, but some time ago, you helped me in a time of special need," began the young woman's voice on the phone. "You seemed so non-judgmental and kind. I couldn't have made it without you. What I didn't tell you at the time, because of the obvious contradiction, is about my involvement in the 'right to life' movement. The reason I'm calling is because at our regional meeting you were targeted. Some of the things being said went way overboard. You probably know how zealous people can get. Anyway, I just felt I had to let you know. Picketing begins Monday."

Great, I thought as she hung up. This could be very serious. I could handle it, having been in many tight situations before, but what about my staff and patients? After thinking about it for a minute, I walked out and asked everyone to stay after work for a short meeting. As soon as the last patient exited, we all gathered in the waiting room. All eyes were upon me as this was not a normal occurrence in our office. "I got a phone call today, informing me that Monday we are to be visited by an anti-abortion group. I don't know any details, but you all know what happened in Florida and in various other places. There's a tendency to think, 'This is Iowa. People here don't act like that.' The truth is, people are people, let's not be naive. We're a medical clinic and I'm sure you didn't sign on to have to face this kind of situation, so I want to offer anyone who doesn't feel comfortable, the right to stay off work Monday."

Chj, the nurse who had been with me the longest, spoke up, "Well, Dan, I can't speak for the others, but I think all of us realized that you aren't a run of the mill doctor. You don't back off things just because it might be controversial. We bought into it. Let's face it, the world is messy. All we're trying to do is deal with it. I'm with you."

"Thanks, Chj. I appreciate it." All the rest agreed it would be business as usual. "I don't know what to expect, but there could be name calling, photos, maybe even spitting. Our job will be to remain calm and respectful and not to react. I don't think they're coming for dialogue, so it's probably better to keep our mouths shut."

All weekend I tried to relax but couldn't keep from thinking of all the confusing sides to the issue that was to be on the front burner Monday. My practice included everything from priests, professors, nuns and ministers, to prostitutes, addicts, the homeless, the insane, undocumented workers and hardened criminals. Abortion, to my way of thinking, remained an intensely personal consideration. Just from my own experience, I had seen enough to make me take pause. One of my patients had a condition where her bone marrow stopped making red blood cells when she became pregnant. She had barely survived her first pregnancy by receiving multiple transfusions. During her second, however, her body, having become sensitized, began hemolyzing each and every unit of blood, clogging up her kidneys and leaving her more desperately anemic. Only an abortion saved her life. Another woman suffered from Lupus, pulmonary hypertension and congestive heart failure, and most certainly would not have tolerated a pregnancy. She chose a termination. Just six months previously, I had a patient come in for a menstrual extraction who told a particularly poignant story. Her first child was born with a slowly progressive neurologic condition. Beginning normal, he had progressed to a near vegetative state, with uncontrollable seizures, and never ending medical complications. Now eight years old, he had been seen at the university for the last time, as nothing more could be done. Worse, it had been determined that his condition was genetic and was most assuredly inherited as a dominant trait with a high degree of penetrance. It was then that, despite being on the pill, this mother discovered that she was pregnant again. Who is to tell her what to do?

Arriving at work earlier than usual, I noted the protesters already beginning to accumulate across the street. There were people in religious garb and civilians, busy making signs with all the typical slogans, "Murderers," "Baby Killers," along with various biblical quotes. Inside everyone was nervously attempting to focus on the day's work, but it soon became impossible to ignore what was happening outside. As the first patients began to show up, the marchers, megaphones in hand, crossed over to our side and began marching on our sidewalk directly in front of the clinic main entrance. Several patients turned and left, not wanting to face the confrontation. Squad cars lurked all around, and within less than half an hour, what I hadn't counted on, the media showed up in full force. TV, radio, and newspapers were all amply represented. One particularly bold local anchorwoman entered the office with her cameraman requesting a live interview with Dr. Murphy. Acquiescing, I was soon expounding on how I had always been on the other side of these affairs, but despite my adamant support of freedom of choice, I certainly respected anyone's first amendment rights. Meanwhile, unbeknownst to me, things were getting decidedly more raucous outside. I never was told exactly what occurred, but by

249

the time I had finished my interview, the pickets had left. The most consistent version was that several groups of methadone patients had arrived and one gentle looking woman in particular was accused of probably coming in for an abortion. One of our hardened recovering addicts, looking somewhat disheveled after a trying weekend, walked up wearing his favorite farm cap inscribed with, "Under this hat is one mean son of a bitch." Words were exchanged, and this is where the reports vary, but the upshot of it all was that members of the self-righteous group began to trickle away which then lead to a full scale, somewhat panicky retreat. We were never bothered again.

Late one afternoon at work, one of the nurses told me there was a Tim on the phone who wanted to talk to me. I thought, "Probably another one looking for drugs." But when I picked up the receiver, I was pleasantly surprised as the voice began, "Dr. Murphy, you don't know me but I work in Waterloo at the 'Boys Club,' and I hear you have a basketball team of nine-year-olds."

"Yes I do. What's on your mind?"

"Well, we got a team here too, but it's hard for us to travel and not many teams want to come here. I was wondering if you all would be interested in a game."

My limited experience with AAU basketball had made me aware that the Boys Club was always competitive at every level, but I hadn't really picked up on the total dynamics of the situation. Now I was beginning to understand. Almost all black, coming from poor families, and being on the "east side", they didn't mix well. Iowans are predominantly white middle class and, given the chance, can be every bit as susceptible to intolerant notions as any other group. For me, having lived on the lower east side of Manhattan and having spent six years playing ball on the 'wrong' side of town in California, combined with the chance to put our guys up against some challenging competition, the decision was easy.

"Sounds good, Tim. How's Saturday morning?"

"Ten o'clock okay?"

"We'll be there."

As I hung up, I began thinking, "Jeez, I hope I'm not being too presumptuous. The kids are OKAY but what about the parents?" One of my nurses was from Waterloo, and her husband coached kids baseball, so I decided to ask her about it. She was very reassuring, saying that it wasn't in the worst part of town, just next to the worst part, and that they were a little disorganized but definitely had the good athletes.

That evening I began calling all the parents. None had ever been to the Boys Club and most had never even been to that part of town. A few expressed some concern but there was no outright resistance. We had no blacks on our team, there being almost none in Cedar Falls, but we did have one Mexican-American, and several of Asian ancestry. Many of the parents were college educated, but still, although everyone said they'd be there, I got the feeling that crime and drugs weren't far from people's minds.

Saturday morning we all drove in convoy, arriving at our destination in about twenty minutes. Tim met us at the door. "Come on in. Glad you could make it. Nice to meet you, Doc." Sending the kids out to shoot, I sat down to talk with Tim for a minute. He wanted it to work as much as I did. We decided to just run at each other without keeping score for a while, experimenting with different styles etc., then mix the teams up, putting some of theirs and some of ours on the same team and go skins and shirts, before finally having a real "game" to finish off the session. Looking out on the court, I saw the kids from both sides glancing back and forth, realizing that this was a new experience for all of us. Determined to give it my best shot I called my kids over to huddle. "OKAY guys, we're not going to keep score at first and we're going to sub a lot. When you come out just go to the end of the bench and slide towards me when new guys go in. Pass to the open man and play good man to man defense. Like always, do whatever the refs say and no faces. Just play as hard as you can, all right? Let's go!"

I thought our guys had energy, but theirs, dang, they were all over the place, full court defense, constantly pressuring, gunning and taking it to the hole even if three guys were defending. Balls were flying everywhere, kids going in and out at random, it seemed, spontaneous Brownian anarchy, and always lots of talk. We had worked some on handling pressure "D," but I would have run out of ink here had I kept track of turnovers. Little by little we learned to protect the ball, make sharp cuts, and crisp passes, or it was gone. We even tried some full court defense of our own, and although the kids seemed to like it, I could see it needed more structure to be a plus for us. They seemed to have an unlimited number of players and as the game went on, more showed up and were promptly inserted into the action. Even age didn't matter as all sizes of kids appeared on the floor. Oh well, chalk it up to experience. Nothing really negative happened and the part where we mixed it up was good, the kids spontaneously picking up on each other's names, and working hard to play as a team, somehow putting aside the natural tendency to hog the ball. When it came time for the official game, we were at least familiar enough with their style to keep it respectable but they still kicked us pretty good. No big deal. We all shook hands and I thanked Tim for inviting us over and promised to come again. All in all it had been a very good session in more ways than one. I liked the interracial aspect, and it's hard to overestimate what being used to playing in games with this kind of quickness and intensity can do for you when going up against other competition.

We slowly improved as our kids acquired better skills, and although we didn't even win half of our games that season, we gave a good effort, and by that summer were good enough to win second place in the Iowa Games regional and advanced to Des Moines for the finals. There we got pounded by the River Rats from Hinton, and lost a squeaker to a Cedar Rapids team, thus keeping us from advancing out of pool play. Still, the kids were having fun and we were gaining experience with each new encounter.

My own personal defense was being challenged from time to time, and I don't mean on the basketball court. One day in the office I was seeing a new heroin addict, a dancer/hooker from Des Moines. As I was finishing my interview, I noticed she was subtly changing her position getting closer to me and facing me more directly. At a lull in the conversation, she interjected, "You know, I can't pay but there are other things..." As she smoothly talked, her right hand headed directly for her physician's erogenous zone. Taken off guard momentarily, I recovered just in time to avert an ethical crisis, intercepting her pass by flicking out my right to catch her advancing extremity at the wrist and hold it firmly.

"Uh-uh," I said as firmly as I could, finally releasing her as I stood up to leave the room. To my chagrin, she popped up quick as a misplaced rake, and stood firmly in my way.

"No one does that to me," she said, apparently not used to being rebuffed, or at least being quite comfortable with confrontation. Thinking fast, I tried first my look left, go right move, and then the reverse pivot, but damn, she was a nimble Nellie, cutting me off at every turn. So now I'm beginning to think I'll have to fight my way out of one of my own examining rooms. If she pulls a knife, I could use a speculum to defend myself. As my thoughts wandered from absurd to desperate, suddenly a possible solution came into my sly mind. Stepping back nonchalantly and leaning against the wall, I offered the following: "Okay, let's compromise. I'll do everything I can to help you with your problems, and you do all you can to be fair with us." As I'm talking, unbeknownst to her, I'm leaning on the call button we have in each room connected to the nurse's station.

As Chj opens the door, I breathe a sigh of relief. Deciding to exercise restraint and compassion, I go to my routine line. "We can start her on 30 milligrams of methadone, and if you want to sit down, ma'am, the social worker can come in to start on a treatment plan." Realizing she had no advantage, the patient played along and sat down as I calmly walked out of the room. Back in my office, I explained what had happened and told Chj to be sure to order a full STD screen and to never, ever, leave me in a room alone with this patient again.

Over time, as I got to know this woman, she was one of the more pitiful cases we had. Abused at an early age in every way imaginable, she never had a chance. Having had four children taken from her by the state, she had slipped deeper and deeper into a never ending state of drugged stupor. Through it all, much of her brain had been destroyed, leaving her in such a burned out condition that no amount of illicit substance would now kill her, and even to get high she had to do massive doses. Through it all, she somehow kept a very curvaceous physique, which she displayed flauntingly at every turn. Good with makeup and having a natural smile that could turn on or off to her advantage, she really wasn't qualified for any other kind of work, and how do you convince someone to slave for minimum wage, when they are filled with self-loathing and can reinforce it over and over all night long and come in to see us the next morning with a huge roll of 20's? These are the cases where rehabilitation becomes meaningless and even damage control is difficult to achieve. In this line of work, a person has to keep moving, and eventually she was lost to follow up. But for years afterward, late at night, I would get phone calls that I'm almost positive were from her, never saying anything, just listening to me answer, waiting an extra minute before hanging up. We were the only place she was ever treated with respect.

Because of all this, noon basketball wasn't just fun, it was necessary. Blowing off steam physically was only part of it; the fascination of both observing and being part of the special psycho-dynamics that occur are also therapeutic. Certain match ups are almost sure to be entertaining, like the guy who has a slash to the hoop kind of game against the aggressive, challenge every shot kind of defender. Sparks are sure to fly. How will they handle it? A local sportscaster once coldcocked a guy just for saying something like, "Shit, you can't play it or talk it." I didn't appreciate players who pressed making bad calls right up to the limit. Once this guy who was a thorn in nearly everybody's side, drove on me and in the process of blocking his shot I got a good piece of his arm. He turned to me and said, "Don't you ever do that again." Determined to give him a dose of his own medicine, at the other end, I immediately drove as hard as I could and, being bigger than him, succeeded in getting to the hole, scoring, and, in the process knocking him on his duff. Getting up, with a scowl on his face, he grabbed the ball and fired it at me from close range. Luckily able to block it with my hand, I found the ball bouncing in perfect position at my feet. My spontaneous reaction, and it still seems appropriate, was to kick it full force back at him. Justice prevailed as it hit him squarely between the legs effectively squelching any thought of further escalation. Never did I personally get into an altercation, but once I got close enough that I had to walk off the floor, motioning in a sub, because I was on the verge of explosion. Too much coffee, I suppose.

The unwritten understanding, at least among us regulars, is, say anything you want but nothing physical. Still, in the heat of the game... And then there are always new players coming on the scene. Because of all this, dialogue becomes an art form. One gnarly old professor playing with us had a claim to fame of having faced Hot Rod Hundly in a high school game in some little coal mining town. He still had a beautiful two handed set, and once when an especially long arching one fell through the net, another prof exclaimed, "Clem, it's just not fair to utilize that anachronism."

Someone might yell out, "Traveling!"

"No way!" is the response.

"Well, it's at least attempted traveling." What are you supposed to say to that?

Barry had been playing for some time with us. I don't think he ever played anywhere else in his life but slowly he was developing a shot and that other crucial skill, the strategic foul. Diminutive and always taciturn, he rarely argued and could be counted on to accept his fate without even a frown. He did have a Ph.D. in Sociology, but on the court it was of no help. He had every reason to be at the bottom of the pecking order. So one day he's involved in a play where the call could have gone either way. The other guy is one of those volatile, don't give an inch types, who steps right into Barry's face and says, "Barry, you hacked the shit out of me."

We thought Barry would cave in like always. Well, surprise, surprise; not this time. Hesitating for just the right amount of time, he looks up at the guy and delivers the line that for him was the knockout blow. "All I can say is it's tough to get a call on the road." Perfect! Disarmed the other guy completely making it impossible to continue the confrontational tactic.

One time I was up against this guy who thought he was among the world's elite. Early in the game he got the ball at the free throw line. He was about 6'4" and had real long arms. I just stayed at the dotted line giving him room. "Aren't ya' gonna guard me, Murph?" he asked.

"Just play the game, Brian." I quipped.

"OKAY," he said as he loaded up for the 'J'. But, see, that was the key, loaded up. His shot, with the long arms, went behind his head before finally being released, taking quite a bit of time. Enough for me to step forward, measure my jump, and, as luck would have it on that occasion, swat the ball two courts down.

"What was that you were saying about defense, Brian?"

"Need a toothpick, Brian?" someone else added. Even the great one could only smile, nothing to say for once.

Then, a bunch of us regulars being challenged by five young black guys, the following exchange took place.

"He don't got nothin'," proffered confidently by their apparent team leader as I threw up a three, my guy jumping to defend but not quite getting to the ball.

And, as the ball swishes through the net, "He dooo!" by my defender in a near falsetto voice, face crunched up showing how much he cared and how the blame was somehow on the one who dissed me.

My only response, "I does," shrugging my shoulders and turning to head to the other end.

Which reminds me of the time when Stacy, not a star by any means, took Norm, an ex-NFL player and an excellent athlete, off the dribble, and as he's going by, in a gutsy show of braggadocio, commented, "Where ya'll at?" not noticing that Rich, a tall talented participant, has left his man and is coming over to squash any attempt at a shot. Seeing him at the last minute, Stacey doesn't even break stride, just shifts to the underhanded finger roll off the board from a horrible angle at least ten feet out adding magnificently to the insult as the ball left his hand by saying, "Where both ya'll at?" finishing in time to watch the net accept the improbable offering, and leaving both stars standing with their heads down wondering what had happened as the rowdy cheers reverberated around them. Stacey, wherever you are, that was an all time highlight!

The most blatant attempt to use, or more properly, misuse arrogance, was when this star Div I player, mixing it up one day down at our level, happened to be on the losing team. Anything can happen in a game to 15. The routine is that those waiting automatically come in; in this case there was only one, and then the losing five shoot to see who will make up the rest of the team. Well, this guy declares that he doesn't shoot, he's automatically in. We presume it would be too humiliating to have to shoot with the rest. Anyway, this creates a tense situation since no one comes up there to sit and watch. Still, who will have the balls to challenge him? It didn't take long before one guy can't let it go and says, "Shit, if you're so dam good, how come you ain't on the winnin' team?" Silence. We're all waiting for the explosion. Then one of the mature, peace loving professor types among us, not wanting to see bloodshed, even though he's on the winning team, breaks the tension by offering, "You can take my place. I got a meeting."

Momentary silence. Then, spontaneously, one, two, then everyone, "I got a meeting too."

"Me too."

"Guess we all do."

Funny how a person can run hot or cold for no apparent reason. I've had days where I don't think I could have scored if left alone on the floor for half an hour. But, fortunately the brain locks out those occasions, preferring to focus on the good days. Like the OT game one Sunday at the high school, with all, I mean all, the best players in town participating. You have to win by two hoops, and I was on my game, so they kept giving me the rock, and no matter who they put on me, I delivered. Must have been 15 straight times, and I showed them the whole package plus a few extras just for good measure, until they finally missed a few giving me the chance to finish it, which I promptly did with a lightning quick pull up from 20.

Or there was the day at the PEC when Sam was guarding me. Sam, by the way is an ex-Div I player, no slouch. I later imagined him talking to his buddies: "Sam, how'd ball go today?"

"Not good. I got stuck guarding Murph."

"He light you up?"

"That's putting it mildly. I thought it would be OKAY when he missed the first two, but that was it. From then on, for two games, he hit everything."

"Take you inside or what?"

"Inside, outside, left, right, power moves, fades. I mean some of 'em were from thirty feet. I think he could have kicked it up there today and it would have fell. He's just too athletic and he's definitely not shy when it comes to offense. Pretty amazing for his age."

He was right. Some days, it's almost magical; the body feels like every muscle coordinates perfectly and even the mind senses it and clears itself so no barrier exists, just sweet confidence. Even so, a really good defender can take almost all of that away. That's when you take advantage of picks. What's the chance of running into a whole team of excellent defenders? More importantly, no matter what, I don't care how hot you are, it's still a team game, and people can only put up with so much gunning and still give it their best effort at both ends. At a certain point it becomes counterproductive, and your chance of winning would be better if you distribute enough to keep those types of personalities involved.

Like now, I'm taking a chance here, and I don't want to lose you, but I'm hot, so here's one more story. So my team is holding court and in comes the next group of challengers including a budding new phenom, only a junior in high school, but who had just distinguished himself with a 40 point explosion against one of the top teams around. I, of course, immediately say I got him. Why not? How can something special happen if you don't put yourself in position for it to occur? Besides, you get more exercise if you have to play more intense "D". As the game progresses, he gets me a few times with athleticism on inside post ups, and I'm giving him the "nice move, Zach," and "very good" kind of stuff. Meanwhile our team is doing it's thing well enough to hang in there and actually take the lead at 12-11. Zach is 6'4" but thin, so next time down I play a little more aggressive and deny him that good low post position. He guns anyway and misses, so now it's our turn. I hadn't done much up to that point and he doesn't know me from Adam, so he's giving me space outside. Feeling my addiction coming on, I launch a 20 foot bank from the 45 degree position on the left. He thinks it's luck as it kisses in, not knowing that glass is your friend even that far out if the angle is right. He comes down and forces a "J" that bounces around and falls, still 13-12 us. This time, looking more determined just in case, he's on me respectably close. Giving him an up fake, I go by and finish with a left handed finger roll over help, leaving him consternated in the lurch. They come down and miss but Zach fights by me just enough to tip it back in, 14-13. Now it's game point for us. I start low then burst off a pick to the top of the key, well, not actually top of the key, closer to 25-26 ft. out. He's trailing to get there but as soon as I receive the pass, I hesitate not, letting it fly over his rapidly closing leap, in a perfect parabola to pay dirt. Immediately I go give him the traditional touch. "Nice game, Zach." Sportsmanship, but not really. The other guy doesn't want any part of it. Kind of like getting born again after you become a successful pro.

But now, here's the memorable part. Zach turns to one of his assistant coaches, Pete, who happened to be playing with us, and asks, "What could I do, Coach?"

And the answer, "Nothin'. He's been doin' that to people for years."

Or there was that unforgettable time when I walked up to a game in progress and one of the guys signaled me in immediately since he had to be somewhere. Perfect, no waiting. Then a guy on my team says, "You got to carry us, Doc, none of us can hit anything."

"What's the score?"

"Ten to five, them."

Game to 11, quite a challenge! First possession, I take a 4 foot fade and can it. Then a runner at the free throw line, also good. They don't score so I attempt a 16 foot fade and hit it too. Now I'm getting excited, and everyone knows how I can get. A 22 footer follows, swish time. The last two times down, my teammates didn't even bother to cross mid court. A pull-up from 30 and a Polaris launch with five defenders in my face finished the game.

Confucius taught, "A gentleman is too proud to be arrogant." There's a fine line there somewhere. Strive to achieve excellence, but the ruination of mankind comes as competition leaves a trail of bodies in it's wake. Down with ego. Consensus is the way. Is it compassion or are you merely assuaging middle class guilt? How often must the dragon be killed to vanquish low self-esteem? Yes, my marriage wasn't going well. Poor communication. Isn't it always that? Too busy to work it out now.

Liam was becoming a very good writer. His imagination left him no choice, even when sleeping material was piling up through dreams. Reading incessantly, he was now in the Stephan King phase, but found time to complete a novel size story about the Wild West, and another mind expanding sci-fi thriller. Organized sports were pretty much intolerable to him. That, combined with him being a late bloomer physically, led him down a different path. I coached him in Junior League baseball where he showed the beginnings of a good knuckleball. Others couldn't see it. Who has time for an undisciplined adolescent knuckleballer? Basketball, he could have been something at a smaller school, like the one I went to, but attending one of the largest high schools in the state, translated into pine time for him. Track, he couldn't avoid, simply because he had so much natural talent. First day time trials, he could rip off a 52 second 400, a loping wolf being his prototype. Just messing around one day, he easily cleared six feet in the high jump. I know he could have been a world class triple jumper. But this wasn't him. Having fun, creating, imagining, reading, writing, that was him. Until then, I didn't think those things were me, but a right brain can be nursed along, and our bond was heading in the direction of literature and cinema.

At age 14, after getting his permit, for his first car, we found a classic, a '71 baby blue Hornet. I followed behind him the first time he took it alone to school, because he had refused to practice much and there happened to be a freezing drizzle developing that day. Going up a relatively busy Hudson Road at about 35 mph, I was a little concerned by· the precariousness of the conditions. Concern turned to horror as directly ahead of him I saw a stretch of pavement with that glassy appearance indicative of pure ice. Helplessly, holding my breath, I watched him execute a perfect 360, jump the right hand curb, barely miss a maple, and careen to a halt in two feet of Iowa snow. Carefully pulling off myself, I finally exhaled as I found both him and the insect to be okay. Being a doctor and having to be prepared to go anywhere in all kinds of weather, I always carried a shovel, and within minutes, with the help of a friendly passerby, we were out and Liam drove the rest of the way to school and wasn't even tardy. Until this day, unlike his father and brother, he's a meticulously cautious driver.

Conor, too, was honing his driving skills, but on the basketball court. In the evenings, we'd mosey on up to the PEC, find an open hoop, and begin a workout. Layup right, layup left, reverse right, reverse left, power layup right and left, Isiah right and left (basically a long finger roll as if over a defender from either baseline as in Isiah Thomas), finger roll down the middle, spin right, spin left, pivot off me and finish strong, stop and pop at the dotted line, 45 degree banks, make it and back it out a step further, keep shooting, I'll feed you, now base line "J's," make it and back off, out to the three point line, good, now three's, work your way around the arc, square up and fire, nice shot. Great, now let's do post-up moves, from the right, left, and middle. Turn right, turn left, fade, up fake and step through, c'mon McHale, no, the footwork is like this. You want to, okay, hook shots right and left, Mikan drill first then move out, fine, now jump hooks, hey, lookin' good! Now tip-ins, right, left, middle, need a break? Now rebounds, grab it strong and right back up, now one fake and up, now to the reverse, not too shabby! Okay, you're gettin' the whole package, let's scrimmage. It'd be games to ten, keep it close and interesting, and, at that stage, clean. I could still control things without having to resort to potential foul situations. After each stanza, no rest, right to the line for ten free throws, same routine on each shot, concentrate, follow through. Finally it would be time to go, wait, got to make your last shot. All right! Most of the time, it was fun. We were interacting, doing something positive. Basically, we were alive. That's it. Basketball provides, in a way that's difficult to find anywhere else, a vibrancy, an alertness, a certain mix of expectation, let down, reward, discipline, and frantic effort, all in a setting where physical and psychological share the spotlight equally. Always something new, always a challenge. For me, it was, and still is, quite a habit. The added bonus, at that time: Conor was getting to be an excellent player. Take his blue collar work ethic, combine it with better than average athleticism, and a steady disposition no matter what the situation and you get a player you want on your side.

The AAU team was beginning to take on a unique character. It was, first of all very popular, meaning there were always too many players, and secondly, while kids in other towns seemed to grow like the line on a defense budget graph, ours stayed short like Africans being brought West under the deck. Only logical solution was to run, press, and sub more than anyone else. The key is having a coach who can see through the apparent chaotic frenzy, and recognize the overall advantage. When clicking right, it was a thing of beauty. Even watching you couldn't help but cheer from the edge of your seat or even jump up spontaneously, it was so compelling. In one glorious game in a tournament in the small town of Independence, Iowa, it seemed like every player was determined to have a career performance, giving the scorer a mighty workout. As improbable as it might be, using twelve players more or less equally, and with everyone feeding off each other's energy, we rolled up 58 first half points, and even though we mercifully called off the press midway through the third, no one could do wrong as the century mark fell anyway. The last three or four minutes, with each successive hoop, the fans, even from the opposition, were putting arms overhead and bowing in homage, a special show of appreciation and respect. One hundred and six points in a tournament where the next highest score was 59! What a buzz afterwards! Each kid's face shone bright and the trip back home was filled with chatter and laughter. We had made it to the second day, the final round, and it felt great!

Of course, what goes up must come down, or, at least it could come down. Returning the next day, we faced Iowa City, and nothing, it seemed, went right. We were a step slow, they had good ball handlers, and the ball bounced their way. Our kids fought hard but, in the end, fell short, losing by five. Okay, shake hands, take a deep breath, and move on. You're doin' it, engaged, givin' it what you got. It was a good old battle. We're all right. In fact we're better than all right, we're like a volcano, boiling and churning, waiting to erupt all over some team. Our days will be there, you guys are all great.

After the game, I left directly for Jordan, Minnesota, where I was to meet two of my sisters for a nostalgia party. The agreement had been to rendezvous at 'grandma's.' Sure enough, after having made a wrong turn on a short cut near Belle Plain, I arrived several minutes late, and found the them already reminiscing on the sidewalk outside the sturdy, familiar, two-story structure. "Hey, c'mon, you can't start without me," I blurted, giving each of them a hug. Both Ann and Maureen, had a big spot in their hearts for our mother, gone now for 35 years. Actually, none of us remembered her that well, and had to rely heavily on imagination, making these encounters all the more interesting. Soon we were retracing the lives of our ancestors, walking around the yard, and ambling along the silent streets past the church, school, creamery, and old hardware store.

"You know, we're not that far removed from our roots," offered Ann. "Grandmother's grandparents, the Lonne's and the Beckman's, were among the original settlers from Westphalen, Germany."

"Right, and arriving at Shakopee, where civilization ended, they had to walk all night through Sioux Indian territory to get here," added Maureen.

"Only to have Franz drafted into the Union Army, to help free the slaves, brought from Africa, 'cause those damned Indians, whose land we were taking, wouldn't pick cotton!" I concluded.

"Ironic."

"Glorious legacy."

"Hey, lighten up. We all know they were brilliant people, but they were pawns, mere pawns in the realm of things."

"Ya, Boone, and you've atoned for it by being a draft dodger and working in Mozambique."

"Yes,' added Ann, 'and Maureen and I always vote Democratic, so I'd say we're even."

We had arrived at Valley View, the nursing home where grandma had died, and where Frances, now 95 years old, presently lived. We tried everything we could think of, but she didn't recognize us, even though she had spent nearly six years caring for our family. I switched to a few German phrases, but got nothing. Ann and Maureen did their best, waxing into a toe tapping version of "O, du lieber Augustin," which brought a spark to Frances' eye but she could only say, "Ya, it should be,' and 'you never know." We had fun, and the nurse was entertained, but there was absolutely no meaningful communication.

Later, we picnicked several miles away at the old St. Joseph parish cemetery, where many of our relatives were buried. Blanket spread on a kinsman's grave, we shared a bottle of wine as the stories got progressively funnier and more ridiculous. Suddenly we noticed an old man approaching us from the direction of the church. Feeling as though we had been caught red handed, we quickly straightened up, trying to regain our composure. Noticing his collar, and remembering my days as an acolyte, I stood up, and offered my hand. "Good afternoon, father. We're here visiting a family burial site, and we may have become too loud and frivolous. I offer 'mea maxima culpa' if we've disturbed any one."

"No, not in the least. We don't get many visitors here. Good to have you. I'm Father O'Flaherty, and I'm retired here."

"Well, Father, we're all Murphy's. It wouldn't seem right if we didn't offer you a splash o' wine. Let me help you sit down against this convenient tombstone." Soon we were laughing and hearing all the ancient local lore and more. He was familiar with some of our relatives. "Of course, I'm bound by secrecy of the confessional, but your uncle Alphonse was quite the spirited lad!"

Late that night, I arrived home exhausted, my only regret being that I couldn't really share these experiences with my children. Simply put, they weren't interested. On the other hand, probably the most important part of my fun that afternoon, was sharing what was in common with my sisters, and, in the same way, Liam and Conor were quite good buddies, spending lots of time together, which, in the long run, should bode well for them.

Before going to make rounds at the hospital the next morning, I opened my pocket calendar book and noticed that exactly one month remained before my next special trip. Global Exchange, a San Francisco based organization, in a bold initiative, had put together a journalistic, scientific inquiry into the health care system of the most infamous, heinous, and despicable of international pariahs, Cuba. How could I resist? Talking with Kevin Danaher and Media Benjamin on the phone sealed the deal. We were to test the U.S. embargo, deliver much needed medical equipment and supplies, establish ties, and return to disseminate information. As the departure date approached, collecting materials, again and again, I was treated either as if any attempt to understand why I was going would be a waste of time, or like Columbus, I would most probably disappear off the face of the earth.

I kept thinking, if people could only spend a minimal amount of time outside our beloved motherland, how amazed they would be by the diverse perspectives they would encounter. In both Africa and Latin America, I had extensive interactions with Cubans, and, contrary to local lore, they too are human, and, even more amazing, most of them are very proud of their country and what it has accomplished. Castro is considered by many to be, not only the heroic liberator of his people, but the most dynamic and eloquent spokesman for the nonaligned and impoverished populations of the world. His crime, not that he bends rules to justify ends, or even that he's different, no. It's that he's different and successful. The great fear is that his ideas make so much sense that they might catch on in the minds of others. That's the threat.

All the hoopla over JFK's assassination. To me it was simple; Castro was a hero and one of the few remaining hopes for the world to Oswald, Kennedy tried repeatedly to off Fidel, Oswald took offense, felt justified, and carried out the deed, end of story.

When I hear the Cuban leader say that the idea of Latin America, China, India, and the others, aspiring to become consumers of the world's nonrenewable resources on a par with the U.S., is patently ridiculous and would lead to disaster within one generation, I agree. Or when he explains that to think that ensnaring most of the world's countries into a never ending obligation of interest and debt owed to U.S. banks is a viable plan for a healthy world economy benefiting all is nonsense, I can't help but applaud. When Cuba, with half its population being black, mostly of West African roots, decides to help Angola militarily, to halt the advance of apartheid troops from South Africa, I can understand.

The week before my departure, I try to play my noon ball with special intensity, not knowing if I'll find any games on the trip. Then, silently, I sit on the plane over the Caribbean, thinking of all the places I've been, NY to LA, communist to capitalist, Holland to India, rich to poor. Even though my natural bent, and I hope it doesn't show through in my writing, is to think anything the U.S. is for, I'm against, I can be like Willa Cather describes, my eyes, ears, like tuning forks, burning glasses, catching the minutest refraction or echo of a thought or feeling, perceiving even the deeper vibration, a kind of composite echo, of all that's said, and not said. I will use skepticism and open mindedness. As in treating heroin addicts, pragmatism is the operative word, whatever gives one the most meaningful life, a certain measure of dignity. A doctor shan't be doctrinaire, it's efficacy he seeks. Same for a political system.

Touching down outside Havana, we're welcomed graciously and pass through customs efficiently. On the bus ride to the hotel, I notice, not only the clean streets, but the shoes. How can it be that everyone has shoes? At the hotel, we're told we have two hours before our first event, so I decide to take a walk to get a feel for the capital city. Trying to choose the most crowded streets, I observe the people, especially the small children, looking specifically for signs of malnutrition. Nope, don't see it. And look at all these black people hanging around with whites. What is goin' on? More amazing, why is there no confrontational attitude on display? Must be the tropical climate, or maybe it's all these '50's cars making everyone feel nostalgic and peaceful. On the way back, only three blocks from the hotel, I strike gold, a pickup BB game on a half way nice outdoor court. Chatting with one of the on deck guys, I get the low down on times, rules, etc., and I'm set. "Despues vengo," I assure him, strolling off feeling that this may be a really fun trip.

Soon, our delegation is entering a large hospital specializing almost exclusively on pediatric rehabilitation. Cerebral palsy, congenital anomalies, trauma, etc. I'm struck by the fact that this kind of facility wouldn't even exist in most third world countries. How often had I seen it where these kinds of kids are left to cope on their own, be abandoned, beg, starve, languish and die? Who has decided that this is a priority for allocation of purportedly scarce resources? Our tour is leisurely, giving us plenty of time to question. I find myself off on the perimeter much of the time chatting with patients, mothers, and auxiliary help. Patients came from all over the island and a significant number from other Latin American countries. For Cubans, and many of the others, the care was free and wasn't available to them anywhere else. The families were grateful and spoke of the progress being made with the children. Some of the help didn't seem to have much to do, but a janitor explained that, in Cuba, everyone is employed, and there are always plans to upgrade people's positions eventually. A certain amount of dignity.

Our agenda was flexible. We always had options and could choose from among various tours, spontaneous visits to doctors' offices, hospitals, schools, work sites, neighborhoods, or anything else we could think of. Evenings it might be entertainment or a gab session at a physician's home. Amazingly, Medea seemed to know everyone in Cuba. No one asked to be able to visit with political prisoners, but it probably could have been arranged. Never did it feel like any topic was off limits for discussion no matter what the setting. And we weren't restricted to the capital. I decided to accompany a small group to a remote rural area to get a feel for how health care worked for populations away from the glamorous city centers, knowing that most societies are challenged by this very same distribution of resources difficulty.

How important, you might ask, is health care in Cuba? For an answer, you have only to remember that the co-leader of the revolution was a physician, Ernesto Che Guevara. Much of his time spent in the Sierra Maestra, involved observing the horrid conditions and lack of services available to these people. Everywhere, he did what he could to address the most urgent needs, but in his mind was being formulated, a comprehensive system that would bring meaningful health care to every Cuban. Along with national security, this was top priority. On my visit, I saw the result beginning to blossom. The primary health care system covered the entire island. Every neighborhood, every population group, had a family doctor, who not only saw patients in her office, but emphasized preventative care and periodically visited each home in a valiant attempt at holistic medicine. I use "her" because the majority of post revolution doctors are women. "We are more diligent in our studies," explained one dynamic young rural provider. She told us how she rode on horseback to reach certain families, and outlined the overall approach to health, mental and physical, and impressed us with a summary of just the previous day's work. When asked about her salary, it seemed very modest by our standards, only three or four times what a manual laborer would receive. One of our groups then questioned what kept her motivated to work so hard. "Professionalism," she responded, with just a hint of a smile showing on her lips, while the direct gaze of her eyes toward the inquisitor left no doubt as to her sincerity.

For every group of eight to ten primary care providers, there was a specialty clinic and usually a hospital. Each province had a medical school and a referral hospital, and some of the more sophisticated things were available only in Havana. Schools, factories, even agricultural entities all had doctors tending to their special needs. Internationalism is also important to Cubans. Many of the doctors we met had served in various capacities overseas.

I was surprised to see how complete was the network for the difficult to reach groups, and how sophisticated things were at the top. Kidney and heart transplants were becoming routine. Pharmaceuticals were being produced locally. Even items such as interferon were being made in Cuba with high enough quality to be successfully marketed internationally. At the same time, the use of herbs and local remedies was encouraged, and many of the primary care doctors were involved in clinical research in these areas.

One day, late in the afternoon, I decided to break away from the group, and, as a diversion, avail myself of a little "baloncesta cubana." Arriving at the court, I found a game in progress with mostly teenagers. Another player was waiting and we both went in, making it now five on five, and allowing the game to go full court. Definitely not a high intensity affair, the interaction was fun, and the up and down, with the tropical sun shining, was enough to leave me loose and glistening by the end of the first game. Momentarily catching my breath on the sidelines, I thought I heard someone address me as, "Dr. Murphy." Being so out of context, I didn't even let it register, but the second time I turned around there was no mistake. Speaking was probably the most attractive young Cuban woman I had yet seen. Her white sleeveless blouse accented the smooth bronze skin and athletic cut of her shoulders, while at the same time drew attention to the significant presence of two firm appearing breasts reminiscent of classical Greek sculpture. The designer miniskirt, delicious carmine in color, did nothing to diminish the perfectly proportioned physical portfolio completing her anatomy from the waist down. A silver barrette stylishly swept golden tangerine shaded hair from the mostly indigenous triangular countenance adorned with a warm natural accepting look. "Dr. Murphy, it is you. I'm Cristina, remember? The translator, Managua, a few years ago."

Regaining my poise, I remembered. How could I forget? Not only was this woman palpably attractive, she was even more impressive in her profession. Simultaneous translation is more than a purely mechanical undertaking. It's an art form requiring extensive knowledge of language, slang, colloquialisms, and nuance, all to be kept at the edge of readiness, to be used to transmit substance and sentiment, all the while registering the ongoing delivery or dialogue. Amazed at how effortlessly Cristina had handled complicated technical themes during our Nicaraguan meeting, I had had the opportunity to meet her between sessions, complimenting her on her abilities and visiting briefly about her life and background. "I do remember, but I'm surprised you remember me, even my name."

"In my business details are important, besides, everyone in Managua acted like you were someone special, so I recorded you in my memory bank. But, sport, I didn't know. You got the moves." She gave me this coy playful look, easily enough to put me into a Wilt Chamberlain frame of mind.

"Keep your eyes open," I responded, turning back towards the court. "I can play."

"I'm with you," she quipped, stepping closer to the court. "Teach, Doctor!"

Perfect bounce to the back door. Hmm, this opening pass served notice of a different kind of interaction. Fun but with a potential serious edge. Better be ready. How often does a situation like this happen? Hey, it's just a game.

At first, we moved the ball around a lot, testing the water here and there, seeing how the other side would react. Quite a bit of walking, more like in Europe with the extra steps. My legs were feeling a bit rubbery, but I continued to score points and a glance at Cristina indicated her full attention and gave me all the incentive I needed to press on.

I felt the intensity pick up as it was as if I was lured into the paint, then playfully parried. "Aqui, es mi casa." Fine, I could stay outside but at this point in the game, inside offered a higher percentage.

Soon, as naturally as if it were meant to be, the level of contact increased. It was becoming an all-out effort, with every kind of emotion showing at once. It ended with both sides completely out of breath, but the smiles and hugs showed that everybody was a winner in this one.

"What'd you think, Cristina?" I asked, reaching down to redo the All Stars. "Engaging. That's how the game should be." A bit more bounce in the step as I headed back. A quaint little bar caught my eye several blocks down so I stopped to rehydrate. Sitting off to the side at a small table pondering life and death I saw an elderly patron approaching. "Che," he offered. Thinking he was referring to the historic national hero I replied, "In my heart but just a visitor."

"No, you are in Hemmingway's seat. I thought somehow you had returned." Well, I surmised, I could imitate both.

The next day north to Miami, many questions at customs, then on to my other reality. It had been a memorable adventure, filled with food for thought.

Arriving back in Cedar Falls, I had much to reflect on. Amazingly, other than my family, people in this relatively conservative community, had very little interest in such things. Even Liam, who listened and asked questions, had become skeptical about his father's 'different' views, their being so out of line from those of his peers and their fathers. For sure, it takes a certain leap of faith, to get over being limited by the predominant paradigm that your country, race, sex, church, culture, etc., is automatically the best, even the most moral. For me, that leap had come, irrevocably, with Viet Nam. For many, it never comes; thus lack of appreciation, intolerance, prejudice, hatred, and war.

It was always somewhat of an adjustment getting back into the swing of things in the office after an absence of any length of time. A few athletic physicals, colds, warts, and I begin questioning the meaningfulness of my work. But invariably, just as frustration bottoms, something happens to buoy the spirit, make it all worthwhile. Over the years, I had developed an interest in eating disorders, and had a number of patients with anorexia, bulimia, or a combination thereof. One particularly vexing young woman had taken the illness to new levels. She had been in and out of all the nearby 'programs', failing each, to the point that none would any longer work with her, leaving her fate entirely up to me. My strategy had become to schedule as many visits as I felt she would tolerate, and with each encounter, no matter what, shower this poor soul with positives, encouragement, and even hugs. It hadn't worked, as she continued to spiral downward. With a diet approaching a fat content of zero, protein not much more, and calories hovering just under 500 per day, combined with a steady assist in the form of laxatives and diuretics, her weight had most recently fallen to a mere 56 lbs. Electrolytes were at levels seemingly incompatible with life. No longer could she even open the door to my office without assistance. At the slightest provocation, she would break down wailing in self-pity. Even my nurse, at the last visit, had pleaded, "For the love of God, Dan, have her committed." Each time, I found some way to justify allowing the situation to fester for one more visit, knowing full well that a single virus could probably take her out without even replicating.

So this time, it was not without trepidation, that I entered the exam room, sat down on the stool, and deliberately picked up the chart, as was my way. The number almost knocked me to the ground. Sixty two! Sixty two pounds! Looking up, I saw my patient smiling at me and knew it wasn't a mistake. Immediately getting up and embracing her, I then stepped back and blurted, "What happened?"

"Nothing, I just decided to get better." She then proceeded to expound with a gush of positives, paraphrasing all the things she had heard and been through in her struggle with this hellish curse. And nary a tear. I was shocked, and really had no good explanation for what had happened. Still, a corner had been turned, and all the effort, suddenly, had become worthwhile. She had healed from within.

For Thanksgiving that year, I had planned to visit Alton. Janet, for some reason I can't recall, wasn't able to come along, so after work on Wednesday, the two boys and I piled into the car and headed west. Normally a four hour trip, I began to have a twinge of concern when, barely a mile down the road, scattered flakes of the year's first snow, began hitting the windshield. Like when the Titanic first hit the iceberg, it seemed like only a minor irritation, nothing to get excited about. All the way to Interstate 35, we didn't even have to slow down; the early seasonal teasing, however, never abated, and the size of the flakes was steadily increasing, and, as darkness fell, we were still effortlessly cruising through the curtain of customized crystalloids. Accumulation now began to show, and soon plows with salt and sand began their early efforts to minimize inconvenience. Still laughing and joking with the kids, I began to worry a little as the wind picked up, visibility dropped, and small drifts began to show along the road. Slower and slower we went as cars started to show up where they weren't supposed to be. Not me, I thought. How many years have I battled and cavorted in this stuff? Just have to be careful and know when to goose it and when to decel a little. Look at all those idgeots, teenagers, women drivers, goin' in the ditch. Ain't gonna happen to us.

Down to third gear, we were doing one lane part of the time, now, but still moving. That's the key. Moving, all the time, moving.

271

Very few cars out any more. Well, we're going home. Every town more familiar. We can make it.

Past midnight, all one lane, snow blowing hard, drifting in as fast as you can clear it, blizzard I guess you could say, kids having fun but acting different somehow, keep on truckin'.

Two a.m. and only fifteen miles to go, single lane starting to close. I had to use all my skill and daring to proceed. How fast and at what angle should I clobber this drift to go through and not get hung up? Barely made that one! Some fun though! What's the worst that can happen? Get stuck, dig out, or as a last resort, and clomp over to some nearby farm. No big deal. Oh-oh, this one's too big. No way will we make it. Even I can't bring myself to make the attempt.

As occasionally happens just as all hope is lost, something unexpected comes along and bails you out. This time it appeared in the form of a state plow, twirling amber erasing wrinkles from our brows and beckoning us to fall in for the final leg to the Promised Land. Following our savior we reached Alton at a slightly later than expected 3 a.m. only to have grandma sitting patiently waiting.

"Well, Danny, I can't say that I'm too surprised. I know you well enough to understand that you never allow these petty little inconveniences to get in your way. However, I will say that you've rather outdone yourself this time. Nice job. Let's get these tired angels to bed and then I've got a new bottle of 'Teacher's' I want to show you." Soon we were stationed at the kitchen table, as was our practice, sipping, reminiscing, and gossiping up a storm about family, locals, or any other unsuspecting victim that popped into our heads.

Finally, it was I who had to bring this nonsense to a halt. "Okay Margaret, you win. You may be eighty-three years old, but I can't keep up. In a few short hours, I've got to be ready to attack one of your delicious Thanksgiving spreads. Give me just a few more juicy tidbits and I've got to hit the sack.

In the silence and darkness of my room, I paused for an unknown length of time peering out through the curtains at the swirling storm, before finally crawling under those same covers, eyes blurred, throat thickened, surrendering to fleeting images of a one eyed bear and mother's comforting touch.

Early, awakened by the perfect peacefulness of the morning after, I was drawn inextricably, to the shovel, still in its place. The hated ritual, obligation lifted, now seemed perfectly natural, a privilege in fact. First the steps, beginning at the top, side toward the house. Careful not to step down until the snow is cleared, packs it too tight. Scrape, scrape, scrape, echoes the rhythm in paradise. Job well done.

Late in the day, I took the kids for a stroll outside, eventually heading to the O.K. Cafe for a cherry coke. While sitting in the booth, expounding on the meaning of ancient memories, I halted in mid-sentence as I saw an old farmer in bib overalls approaching us. His face looked vaguely familiar but I couldn't remember a name. Reaching out to shake my hand, he looked me square in the eye. "Afternoon. Some storm, wasn't it?"

"Ya, Eleven inches, I heard."

"Say, ain't you one of them Murphy boys?"

"Yep, I am."

"Sure could play ball. Just wanted to tell ya." That quick he turned to exit.

Amazed, I didn't even think to thank him. Seeing the look of incredulity on the boys faces, I could only blurt out, "I swear I didn't arrange this. I barely even remember the guy." Then as we're walking out the door, "Interesting that they're still talkin' about it though, isn't it?"

Conor's junior high basketball career was just beginning. Practices were at 6 a.m., forty kids out. What a trip! From the start, it was apparent that he was one of the most accomplished performers, and soon plays were being designed with him in mind, and he became the go to guy in clutch situations. One game against East, with mostly Boys Club participants, he tallied an amazing 29 points. Around the school, he was recognized as the star.

Still, lacking was that special fire that we had come to be known for in AAU ball. Deliberateness just wasn't part of my basketball vocabulary. Our season had also begun with a few scattered games and maybe one practice a week as to avoid any conflict with school ball. As their schedule ended, ours picked up and we were back on the weekend tournament circuit. By now we could consistently whip our Cedar Falls female counterparts, something we couldn't do previously because they were so much bigger. I had come to appreciate that quick overcomes big almost every time. I guess quick and big might be another story, but very rarely do you find the two together.

We also handled the Boys Club nearly every time. It was always a battle, especially at their place. The clock wouldn't move, or the score might jump 10 points in their favor, but still the play was fast and furious, and our guys learned to suck it up and do whatever it took to win. Our most potent weapon was becoming an ever more effective full court press, which, many times, helped us pull out wins we had no business getting. Still, against the really good big city select teams, we were a definite level down and that kept us from winning any tournaments. We would many times win our pool and advance to Sunday play, only to get beat by a few of the same teams, over and over.

The Bettendorf Dogs were one of the teams we couldn't get by, so on this particular day, I wasn't overly pleased when I checked the final day match ups and discovered that we would be facing them first. They had a very quick athletic point guard off of whom everything else keyed. In the locker room, just before the game, I outlined a bold new strategy, using one of our quickest guys, basically indefatigable, to disrupt the juggernaut. "Jon, you got their point. Pick him up full court and deny him all you can. If he does get the ball, the next nearest defender go double, even triple if we have to, to make him give it up. You other guys will have to be alert and cover two guys at once. Split the distance. Anticipate. Look for steals and be sure not to let anyone slip behind you for the bunny." As the game got going, the strategy was working. They depended so much on their star that they couldn't establish offensive flow without him being the catalyst. Up 10 at half, we stretched the lead to 14 sometime during the third quarter. After a time out, they finally began attacking aggressively after passing out of the trap, while we hit a frigid spell, allowing them to make a game of it. In the fourth, three of our guys fouled out and we lost the squeaker by a hoop right at the end. Afterward their coach came over and congratulated us on a fine game. "One more basket in the third and I was going to clear the bench. You had us goin'. Nice effort!" Well, we were getting close but hadn't gotten over the hump yet.

Lots of times, instead of another practice, I'd line up a

scrimmage of some sort, usually a challenging one. My theory was that if we learned to play with intensity all the time, we would likely represent ourselves well in tournaments. Even practices had to be fast moving and as high pressure as possible. Each kid needed to be able to develop his skills under difficult circumstances, under the gun, in the fire. We'd practice playing the toughest defense we could with every possible twist: big on little, 2 on 1, even 3 on 1, traps, screens, you name it. No fouls allowed in practice to minimize injuries, perfect clean play and wear out opposition by keeping the clock ticking.

Next up for us was a local tournament sponsored by UNI Athletic Department. In the second game we found ourselves facing the Cedar Falls 8th grade AAU team. We being lowly 7th graders nobody gave us a chance. They're bigger, stronger, cockier and very motivated to avoid the utter humiliation of losing to an inferior bunch of little kids. Our team on the other hand just loved to play. Didn't really matter against whom. As the contest progressed things stayed surprisingly close and we were anything but intimidated. With a few timely steals and 3's near the end of the 4th quarter we actually took the lead by a point. Their greyhound Kinard pushed it aggressively down the court and cut straight into the lane. His imitation teardrop rolled around the rim twice and lipped out. Our Roland managed to sneak in and rebounded the ball and was immediately surrounded. Luckily, with a few deft passes we made it across the 10 second line without turning it over. Now, with them trapping frantically, all we had to do was keep our spacing, hit the open man, and run the clock out. Suddenly, Adam found himself alone with the ball behind the 3-point line. It's true, I always encouraged the kids to take their shots, never be tentative, but not now! Squaring up perfectly, Adam fired, and...and...it fell. Oh my God! But there's still 8 seconds left. They call a quick time. As our team come over, I give Adam a direct look. "Adam,' then I think better of it; this isn't the time, 'nice shot. O.K., we got 8 seconds, up four. Full court man to man pressure, but absolutely no fouls. Slow them up as much as you can. Each pass eats up clock." Hands together we all yell "DEFENSE!" The strategy works somewhat, as they get it in bounds and need two passes before scoring and calling their last time with one second showing. Not wanting to risk a steal and quick shot I instruct all four guys to go clear to the other end of the court. "Girsch, you baseball pass it in to the far free throw line. You four spread out and just be sure to touch the ball if it gets through. Let them intercept it. There's nothing they can do from that far. Whatever you do, don't even get near any of their players. If any of you foul, you're kicked off the team." They seem a little befuddled by our set, but quickly send all but one of their guys deep and try to pressure the inbounds pass with their tallest player. Given the ball, Girsch fakes then heaves a high arcing long ball, spinning perfectly, and followed by every pair of eyes, the moment of truth at hand. Chidester, one of their taller players, leaps high to snag the pass, but then must land, load, and fire. Too late, the horn had sounded. We win! We win! To beat the grade above. Quite a deal. Way to go, dogs.

I had developed the habit of going up into the stands after each game to talk with the parents, say something positive about their son's contribution. On this occasion, everyone was particularly pleased. "Nice job, Doc. You're turnin' me into a nervous wreck."

"I know. Great, isn't it? They all worked hard. Thanks for being here."

Only once did a parent castigate me for not giving enough minutes to his child. My response was that everyone rotates into the game and if they're doing well, they might stay in longer. It's a judgment call and may be based on a particular match up, or setting picks well, or playing the passing lane properly, things a fan might not be looking for. By far, good feelings predominated, even when we lost. Our team never failed to appear to give it everything, and fans appreciated the effort if nothing else.

Conor always started, and probably was the last to be taken out, but he always played well, and in many games, he was the difference. In his mind, he didn't even want there to be any question of favoritism. Adolescents are sensitive and he was no exception. Just having your father as the team coach was, in one way, a problem. How can you be like your peers when your dad's the coach? I will say that I had watched him develop and was very aware of what he could do. I knew the other kids games too, but it's possible that Conor popped into my mind before some of the others during games. A much bigger concern for me was, in tight games, how far could I push the poor lad? Often, as a coach, I felt that if I took him out, we would find ourselves in too deep a hole, and lose a chance at winning the game. Then I would see Conor hustling and fighting with such an effort that it was as if he would collapse from exhaustion on the next play. That was bad enough but I was worried more about what would give us the best chance to win. At a certain point, a player becomes less effective because he's too pooped, no legs, shot's off, reaching instead of moving the feet, not going for the loose ball. Then you're better off giving him a blow. But speaking objectively, I can say, Conor was different. He could, and did, take it to the limit, and beyond, without his level of play falling off. The heat of battle energized him. Jim Brown might have trouble getting up off the ground but hand him the ball on the next play and he'll knock you half way to kingdom come. If you're lucky enough to have a whole group of kids like that you will be a force to be reckoned with.

"Dr. Murphy, this is Jen. She's here to be on the methadone program." Speaking was my social worker, Angela, who was case manager doing intake on opiate abusers. Shaking hands with Jen, I was struck, first by how nice looking she was, but more by her youthfulness. At seventeen, she was part of the new wave of heroin addicts. I listened as Angela presented the history. Drugs and alcohol beginning at fifteen, then, at a party, someone offered heroin, why not, she liked it, and began doing it more and more, soon needed it daily, hooked.

"So, Jen, why are you coming in now?" I asked.

"Well, last week I was on my run into Chicago. I made my connection but there was a misunderstanding and I had to scramble like crazy with them shooting at me as I drove out of there. It's too dangerous. I want out. I know I can't quit on my own, I've tried."

Still hoping she wasn't really in such a desperate condition, I dug a little more. "Tell me how you fix."

"At first my boyfriend helped me but now I can do it easy by myself. I'll run you through my routine. First get everything set up in its place. Put the tourniquet on so the end you tucked in sticks right toward your mouth. Slap the vein three times. Carefully empty the bag into the spoon. Add water. Cook it with the lighter. Put your cotton ball in. I use cigarette filter. I suck it up with the insulin syringe. Hit the vein and see blood coming into the syringe. Release

BREAKAWAY

the tourniquet, and inject. You're off."

Pretty convincing, and she had the tracks to prove it. So now we had a middle class high school kid from Iowa, driving every week to Chicago to get enough heroin for herself and to sell to her group so she could pay. Soon we had many of "her group" on the program too, a whole new wave of heroin addicts, more challenging than ever. I wouldn't really call it insidious. It's simple. The equation has only two factors, the availability of dope, and a vulnerable person. Viet Nam fit. Someone high fits. Someone alienated fits. And merely being immature also fits. So just eliminate the drug availability, you say. It can't be done. Too much profitability. Everyone wants a piece of the action, peasants, refiners, couriers, street people, police, magistrates, DEA, generals, presidents. Laws, to be effective, depend on honest people and must be draconian, leading to fascism and such a limitation of human rights as to foment revolution. Impossible. And we haven't even talked about the ever increasing presence of pharmaceutical opiates in society. Always a new formulation, always more potent, and marketed with the best sophistication money can buy. So forget about that side of the equation. That leaves vulnerability. Fine, eliminate Viet Nam's, good jobs for all, educate, cut the trash and put substance into people's lives, true meaning, down with stress, up with stress management, opportunities, challenges, engagement. Indeed. A tall order. And antithetical to many tenets of the "American way." So we're left with damage control. Legalize, favor low potency opium, tax the crap out of dangerous high risk injectables, support research and innovative treatment for those who run into trouble, eliminate stigma, keep people functional, all the while working to make us more sane, more tolerant, with more genuine opportunities for all. It's a matter of priorities. As long as making money is the dominating principle determining how we live as individuals and as a society, we will continue struggling.

Work, work, day and night, E.R., psych, desperate addicts, tumors and trauma, pathetic patrons from beneath bridges, HIV and PID, baby not feeding, Doctor, she's bleeding, I was beginning to sleep with one hand just above the phone. Noon basketball was no longer a mere compulsion, it had become a biological necessity, physical and mental, my mandatory quotidian milieu therapy. I was

278

driven to go. No injury could keep me away, and almost no emergency. Still, it wasn't enough. I may crack. What is missing? What medicine will make me well?

Brrring, brrring. "Ya."

"There's a doctor on line one."

"Okay." As I press the button, I'm preparing for another, "I have this patient with a bad back who's gotten way out of control with narcotics. I'd like to send him over."

"Hello."

"This is Judith Ladinsky. I'm a doctor in Madison, Wisconsin. Part of my work is with a group trying to improve health care in Southeast Asia, primarily Viet Nam. Recently we have received a grant to begin similar work in Laos. Basically it involves improving primary health care. You come highly recommended by Steve Gloyd from your work in Africa. Can I interest you in a month of teaching overseas?"

What about my patients, my family, basketball, responsibilities? And isn't it dangerous? Tigers, opium lords, counter revolutionaries, mysterious unnamed afflictions causing atrophy of body parts.

"Yes, I'd love to go."

Immediately I began studying Laotian, eating sticky rice, and reading reports and relevant books, even Dr. Doolittle. Several intensive meetings at UW completed the preparation. After the ritualistic passing of the beeper to my right hand nurse, Chj, I anxiously accompanied my family to the airport, hugged everyone and disappeared into the unknown.

Bangkok, I could have done without. It wasn't the predominance of sleazy sex trade, or the questionable political role played in the region, but the face of unfettered capitalist "development" presented. Breathing is out of the question with the belch of one million plus tailpipes. A never ending cacophony assaults the ears at city center, then, escaping out, the olfactory nerve alerts one that the squalid quarters of the displaced masses are nigh. A poor woman on a dilapidated bicycle is hit by a speeding limo as a golden Buddha cries. Thankfully, our business there was completed in three days, and we were able to arrange spots on the weekly flight in an old Aeroflot destined for Vientiane.

Sitting in the sweltering cabin, I noticed that lights didn't function, paint was peeling, no magazines. This was no frills by default. French pilots gave some reassurance, but as we hesitantly bounced airborne, I knew we had entered a drastically different reality. The unbridgeable Mekong River dominated and effectively isolated Laos from other lands, and jungle clad mountainous terrain assured solitude. The capital city resembled more an oversized village than the twentieth century administrative hub of an entire country. Very few vehicles disturbed the easiness of this gentle retreat. The French had done little here, not to say that there wasn't still a lingering resentment easily discerned at any mention of the "colonials." The sprawling outdoor central market provided an opportunity to sample many local foods and artistically produced local items. One of our nurses ventured into a nearby government bank and, without having to show an I.D., cashed a personal check from a bank in LaCrosse, Wisconsin, providing all of us with kip, the local currency. We wondered what type of sophisticated security allowed this primitive appearing country to function in such an apparently cavalier manner.

Meanwhile, our business at the Ministry of Health, didn't go nearly so smoothly. It turned out that no one was aware of our arrival or even had any knowledge of our proposed project. Never mind, we had money, equipment, and medicines. Things could be arranged. Several days later we were accompanied by a high ranking ministry official and were on our way four hours up country where our work was to begin.

First, with the help of several local physicians, we recruited delegates from the surrounding villages who either had some health training or were interested in working in the health related field. We had decided to use the methods of Paulo Freire in an attempt at achieving self-empowerment in health. Of course, we Westerners were highly educated and knew all about illness and prevention. Several of us had even worked extensively in similar third world situations. Forget that. Patronizing lectures by ivory tower saviors won't cut it. Begin by paring off with one of them, learn all about each other, then present a personal bio of your new friend to the group, and vice versa. Next, locals present what they consider to be the most important health concerns in their villages. We are allowed to enter into the discussions and some of our questions may prompt them to ask that something we brought up be added to the list of important issues. As for solutions, each person's input is considered equally. Education may be deemed critical in addressing certain areas of concern. Therefore, we go around the table asking each to relate one important thing that they have learned in their life, and what were the circumstances that allowed them to learn the particular lesson so well. From this could be gleaned a method of education having a good chance of working among these people. Tedious, but according to the theory, the only truly effective way to make a difference. Empowering people to solve their own perceived difficulties.

Our afternoon sessions seemed somehow more enjoyable, but accomplished noticeably less until we discovered that one of the condiments used in the preparation of our noon soup was cannabis. After a close vote, it was decided that rather than ruining the taste of the repast, a lesser amount would be included, so as to avoid alienating locals, not offend the palate, and allow us compulsives to function more effectively.

For us to get a better feel of village life, one day was scheduled for a hands-on visit among the population. Splitting into smaller groups we left early for our destinations. The sun saluted us as we wound our way two and a half hours into the mountains over barely passable roads. Finally arriving we were warmly welcomed by the village leader. In our initial discussions he indicated that things were going well here and that no particular health problems came immediately to mind. But just as he finished telling us this, an old man in only a loin cloth, walking with a staff, approached and beckoned for me to follow him.

Anxious to see as much as I could that day, I broke away from the rest and accompanied my new patron. Within minutes we had left the first group of houses and entered the forest on a well-worn trail. I say forest because the temperature was mild, but a better word may have been jungle. Massive hardwood trees combined with smaller trees, shrubs and vines to form an impenetrable wall of vegetation. It was as if we were in a tunnel, or a long hyperbaric oxygen chamber, the brilliant verdure pointing the way and assisting our every breath. We had heard stories of tigers, so, to be on the safe

side, I kept a lookout for an overhanging limb or vine should I have
to go airborne to escape a surprise encounter. Shortly we came upon
a fast moving stream. My man didn't even hesitate, plunging right in,
water to the waist, using the staff to stabilize against the considerable
current, not even missing a step until he pulled up on the far side.
I'm as adventurous as the next guy, and I know this sounds wimpy,
but wearing shoes and socks, long pants, leather belt, billfold with
documents, dollars, kip and baht, and what if I lost my glasses? I
hesitated. Now what? Instinctively understanding my plight, the
gnarled guide gazed back, smacking me with a superior smile, while
at the same time motioning with his free hand and a nod to a point
just upstream. I hadn't noticed it because of my "civilization," but a
tree had fallen across the torrent, and all the branches trimmed,
forming a perfect bridge. Well, not quite, since there was no hand
rail, and the size was like a telephone pole. Handicapped by our
modernity, we first world types have long lost any meaningful
survival instincts. I didn't want to be so badly shown up by this
unassuming villager so I edged up onto the tree and began to sashay
on over. Balance became increasingly precarious as I got into no
man's land and only with desperate stumble leap did I save any face
at all as I landed with one foot in and one foot out of Asian flow.

Soon we arrived at his elevated house with the loom below. I
waited a minute for my eyes to adjust before examine his daughter
lying on a mat on one side of the room. Cachectic, diaphoretic,
dyspneic she presented little diagnostic challenge but before I was
done in the room 3 more received the Dx of active TB. After the
ritual tea my work completed I descended the narrow ladder without
incident. Quite a crown of what I assumed were curiosity seekers had
gathered. No exactly, one man's pidgin french informed me that
these folks all wanted a consult. Hmm, well let's begin with that
prone young man on a makeshift stretcher. Probably fell getting a
coconut – number one cause of quadriplegia in the tropics – but not
this one. A few tortured questions and steady diet consisting of
polished rice put him at the end of the algorithm in square saying
"dry beriberi." Anemias, congenital blindness, a few leprosies and
partly healed infected wounds later and I was able to exit. This in a
village that had no problems. All depends on what you're used to.

We were learning, each day better able to address the issues at hand. As darkness overtook the Southeast Asian landscape, exhausted, we all retired, hoping to enjoy a refreshing slumber. It was not to be. About midnight, pacific dreams of the glorious days of Buddhist civilization centered in Luang Prabang, were interrupted by the scattered staccato of modern day conflict. I first heard one distant report, didn't think much of it, but then, within minutes, a burst of the same, this time closer. Rumors of counter revolutionaries, raiding from havens amidst the refugee camps across the Mekong, were frequent. Was this it? Eh-eh-eh. Eh-eh-eh-eh. Now closer than ever, exploding right upon us. Diving under the bed, I wonder if this is how I will die. Or could it be our own Rambo's heroically seeking out legendary numerous groupings of MIA's still kept somewhere, maybe here. It doesn't really matter, an AK-47 doesn't discriminate, and neither of those forces would likely appreciate our mission here. Bursts all around. Well, it hasn't been a bad life. Then, what's that, voices, laughter, hey, that one is one of us. Cautiously picking myself up, I made my way to the door.

"C'mon out, Dan. They're just shooting at the full moon. Old custom to ward off evil spirits." Well, I'll be... At least it wasn't something new in the soup!

The next night we had a party with lots of food, a generous supply of lao-lao, a potent fermentation product of rice, with live music and dancing afterward. My opinion is that Laos has much more than their share of attractive women. Females, in an array of primary colors, form an inner circle, while males follow on the outside. Dancing is done as much with the hands as the feet, reminding me of the legend of St. Vitus, arms like seaweed in a slow current, couples politely acknowledging each other with a bow, never touching.

Much later, sitting on the verandah with our host counterparts, I listened intently to their stories of those years that tore both our societies apart. "We operated in caves, by candle light. B-52's incessant. We lived in caves, for years, like rats. To cultivate the rice, we would scurry out at night, do a little work, and hide again as the next wave of bombers approached. Then there were the anti-personnel devices, everywhere. So many killed, or maybe just an amputation. Even now we suffer from this. Women, children, animals, accidentally touch one of them and it detonates. At least we are free. No French, no royalty, almost all the Vietnamese have departed. Finally we have our country; it's up to us to make something of it."

Listening to them talk, I tried to imagine what it must have been like, not just the work of the medical people, but the emotions, the politics, the frustration and resentment. First the U.S. doing all it could to reestablish the hated French in their colonial role. There was Dien Bien Phu, the key being the Thai Dam, actually as much Lao as Vietnamese and no more France. Then the long protracted Americanized portion of the conflict; imperial military might on the side of puppets, royalty, and the elite, in an all-out effort to crush the disenfranchised masses in their liberation movement. It's always the same. Even the spin doctors had trouble rewrapping this one. The high distant rumble, like a physician's beeper in a crowd, whirling steel alerting Radar. Action! Run! The planes loaded with sterile coordinates, coolly calculated somewhere in Okinawa, releasing on this tiny country a quantity of Hell never experienced in all of WWII Europe. So impersonal, so clean, while beneath the evanescent tear filled layer of clouds, Dante and Marquis de Sade gathered material. Added to this were the incursions, the invasion, the exploitation of the Hmong, and, more salient for me, the unofficial role played by U.S. functionaries in the burgeoning heroin business as was so well documented by the meticulous research of Al McCoy in "The Politics of Heroin in Southeast Asia."

Yes, peasants could work the rice paddies and no one was starving, but there was a glaring need for education. Corruption abounded, doctors went months without being paid. This, combined with a lack of any business sense, could be a greater threat than anything previous. Thai, Japanese, and others in fancy clothes were showing up in ever increasing numbers, stealing lumber and other resources for a bribe. The World Bank did its share by providing a dam in Vientiane province, which silted in almost immediately, but did produce enough electricity to provide TV for the surrounding villages. Never underestimate the effect a steady diet of grade B American movies beamed from Bangkok, dubbed in Thai, can have on an idyllic traditional Buddhist culture.

Through all of this, no matter how much lao-lao I imbibed, I couldn't bring myself to ask the question, "What happened to downed American pilots?" One physician who had spent several of those years in Kampuchea related that he had seen hundreds of corpses of U.S. soldiers, but that our government said they had no interest in coming to retrieve them. Politics.

Evenings, I would take time for a run to wind down and stay in shape. Improvising as I jogged, not wanting to lose waning skills, I took to pantomiming basketball as I enjoyed the workout. Dribbling along the jungle trails, defending my way up a mountain, pivoting over pathways, raining virtual pull up J's and hooks all over unsuspecting youngsters as they ran along laughing and yelling, "Russo, Russo." The only Americans in the country at the time were two dedicated Quakers organizing women's cooperatives near the capital.

In the end, it was a good experience, especially the teaching methods we employed. Although forces much greater than anything we could generate were at work, I could see how self-empowerment was ultimately, one of the few legitimate tools that could help save us all.

On the way out, not, in any way, needing another day in Bangkok, I signed up, with little enthusiasm, for an excursion by bus to the river Kwais. It turned out to be quite instructive. Nearly all the prime agricultural land along the way had been usurped by agribusiness. Vast tracts of land covered with export crops such as cassava, explained why desperate slums of the capitol were so crowded. The museum at the bridge contained tape after tape, oral histories of Brits, GI's, Aussies, and locals, relating life and death under the Japanese as they attempted to link Southeast Asia, by rail, to the Indian subcontinent.

Arriving in Hong Kong for a one night layover, I was caught off guard by an attractive young female member of our party who pulled me aside saying she had a special favor to ask.

"Sure, anything."

"I'd like to sleep with you tonight. I mean, in your room. Dr. Ladinsky snores, and I just need the rest. I'd be really grateful."

What a request! Quick, judge the situation. Is she for real, after me, nympho?

"I, ah, ah, okay. Fine, why not?"

Boarding the flight the next morning, she was perfectly rested, while I had maps all over my conjunctivae. Exhausted, I arrived in Cedar Falls. Janet had enrolled in graduate school. Liam showed me a new sci-fi story he had completed. And Conor had broken Fred Hoiberg's record at the Marshalltown tournament by scoring 77 points in three games.

I never had time to adjust after a trip. It was always immediately back into the frying pan. Going in early the first day, I found my desk literally stacked with papers of all kinds, correspondence, journals, lab and x-ray results, and, my favorite, charts requiring only my signature, hundreds of them. By compulsively scanning, scribbling, sorting, reporting, the thousand decisions were made and I was current just as the first of a doubly scheduled appointment book is set up to be seen. "Ready. Set. Go. We have a possible hernia in one, then a new meth patient in two, fever and cough in three, and an M.E. in four. Got your roller skates?"

"You're too sweet, Chj. Just get me out for noon ball or there'll be hell to pay."

"Your sneakers are on the floor of your car with the tongues pulled out so you can step right into them on your way. I know the priorities. Want me to ride along and tie the laces while you drive to the PEC?"

"No, I always tie 'em on the floor, while we fight over teams. Keeps me out of the fray."

Just to get back into the full swing of things, that Saturday I had signed up for a 24 hour shift on E.R. I liked to keep my skills up, especially dealing with the trauma and the seriously ill acute cases. Once again, we were quite busy. Sewing, foreign body in the cornea, croup, fractured radius, appy, migraine, burn, CVA, the usual assortment of cases. Then, just as I got my second wind, the bar crowd warmed to the occasion, Saturday night that is, and the assaults, acute intox's, and coed dumped by boyfriend suicide gestures kept the stream going. Finally, all that's left are the I can't sleep and I'm so lonely people coinciding with the I don't know how much more of this I can take doctor mood. Then dictate the last chart, trudge back to the sleep room, and fall on the bed. Out, dreaming of Star Treck, where the hologram analyzes and fixes everything in an instant.

Don't get too comfortable, "Doctor, we need you right away. Chest pain in one."

Who invented the intercom, anyway? "Right." As I walk up the hall, blinking my eyes doesn't seem to help but entering room one is like an adrenaline shot. It's one of my neighbors. Our kids play together. He's only 49 years old and healthy, I thought.

"John, what happened?"

"I got up to read the Sunday paper and started to feel this ache in my chest and it just kept getting worse. I told Doris and here we are." Even talking, for him, was a chore. The ashen color and the fine diaphoretic droplets combined with the look of apprehension, put all of us into our most serious medical mode.

"He's a 10/10, Doctor, BP 70/50, sublingual nitro didn't help. Here's the 12 lead."

Glancing at the strip, I saw immediately where the stylus had traced out the current of injury anteriorly. Ringers were running and he had O2 at 4L already. "Start the protocol. We need strepto mixed, cardiac lab profile stat, portable chest, and let's give 2 of MS IV. Any contraindications?"

"No, Doctor, but we haven't gone through the whole list yet."

"John, it looks like it's your heart, but we've caught it early and there's a good chance we can reverse it."

Three hits of morphine hadn't put a dent in it. His BP was slowly dropping. The strepto was ready.

"We don't have lab results yet, but we can't wait. Give the enzyme." This was always the moment of truth. Will it or won't it. Will he or won't he.

"It's in, Doctor." Now we wait. I'm reviewing in my mind the various protocols: brady's, tachy's, electromechanical dissociation, arrest. John looks no better. Three minutes have gone by.

Suddenly, his face changes. "We have V-tach, Doctor."

"Bolus lidocaine, 75mg., get a drip ready." It wasn't really necessary. Reperfusion was frequently accompanied by a few cardiac hiccoughs. Before it was entirely in, John was smiling, normal sinus rhythm.

"I feel better. The pain's gone."

"BP 110/70, O2 sat. 95%, monitor looks good." Few things in

287

medicine are more dramatic. His color improved just as if the sun had come up over the horizon, bathing him in life sustaining rays of light

"You're going to be okay, John. We'll have to keep you for a few days for tests, but the worst is over."

"Thanks, Doc."

My shift had ended. Now I could head home, relax, cup of joe, and begin my way through the multiple sections of the fresh smelling Sunday "Register."

Noons remained an epiphany for me. Like Lou Gherrig, or the swallows at Capistrano, when the time came, I had to be there. What can the irregular reinforcement of approximately half a million made baskets do to a Pavlovian subject? If I became brain dead, I'd still show. Patients knew, if you want a leisurely visit, don't get an appointment just before noon. My pulse begins to rise perceptibly around 11 o'clock. I know every possible route, the lights, the timing, even down to what to do if a female driver enters traffic ahead of me on 4th Street. Speed is essential or you miss the first game. The city police know me and what I'm up to. I get slack there, but the University had become an impersonal fascist gulag. I had all the parking scenarios down, but the X factor was the likelihood of a ticket. This car will leave this slot at this time, or I could squeeze in there, back in uptight to that one, have room enough to slip out the door, and still be legal. Or, it's raining, they don't bother, go illegal. Caveat, never in handicapped, too heavy a price. Did I get tickets? Yes. Did I pay? As little as possible. And, well, yes I did get towed, but only once. Ugly scene all around.

Most days, I knew the game situation from the time I entered the locker room, one floor down. Register which cars are in the lot, knowing which guys come on which days and their particular preference for blue or yellow jersey, and then, the crucial ingredient, the tempo of pounding sneakers echoing through the ceiling, direct correlation being between fast paced intense crescendos and nearness of game's conclusion. My big advantage sprung from the 3,000 deliveries I'd done, i.e. I could change faster than anyone.

Something had occurred, however, that was costing me an occasional game. It was the shoes! Black low cut Converse had been my trademark and continued to be long after they had become less fashionable. They were cheap and seemed to work well so why change? Besides, could any other footwear be put on as fast? So, on this day, my Chuck Taylor's had worn through in the sole. I had sent to the factory for new ones but they hadn't arrived. Liam's feet had grown to my size and he had a pair of new high topped state of the art shoes that he had come to dislike stylistically, so, in desperation, I appropriated them. After struggling to loosen the laces, stuff my feet in, tighten laces, and tie, I bounded up the stairs and burst onto the floor, hoping to hit a new game. One can only imagine the startled looks, the unusual commotion caused, and the flat out disbelief generated by this new wrinkle. Time stood still, and then regulars came over ogling and inquiring of my health. It was like the passing of a millennium. In all honesty, my first few trips up and down the floor seemed awkward, as if the shoes slowed me, reduced agility. But the support, the stability, the spring, and the comfort easily outweighed all other considerations and the era was over.

Afterward, in the locker room shower, where a surprising number of important discussions take place, I found myself one nozzle away from Keith, AAU coach of the Conor's age girls' team. "Doc, you taught us a lesson today. Never take anything for granted. I would have thought the sun would fail to come up before you'd change shoes."

"Hey, I'm practical. I can grow. Just today I gave a patient penicillin."

"I suppose next you'll be lettin' the shorts ride just above obscenity."

"Sure, and with a 'coed naked' T-shirt. Never pass up the chance to make a fashion statement. By the way, how's your team doin'?"

"Pretty good. That reminds me, I'm involved in planning an international tournament this summer in Tampa, Florida. It's really shaping up well. You guys should consider coming."

"We've never done anything like that but I would like to do something special with the guys. Do you have more info?"

"I'll send a brochure over to your office this afternoon."

At our next practice, I brought it up with the kids and they were excited. "Now I want all of you to concentrate on growing, they won't cut us any slack down there. Remember, we represent the 'Tall

Corn State' and the land of the free. Pressure's on." Everything was put into motion, forms, fundraising, family preparations, itinerary, etc., and as summer approached, we were organized and ready to roll. To prove that insanity has no bounds, I agreed to drive a sixteen-seat rented van all, the, way, to...Florida, with ten fourteen-year-olds.

As we crossed the Mississippi at the Quad Cities, most of the kids thought we were almost there. Do you know how long Illinois is? I thought surely we must be approaching South America, or at least Dixie, when we finally touched Tennessee. "If one more kid pokes another one, I'm switching from air to heat, and I'm turnin' to country. So shut up! You're supposed to be reviewing plays in your heads anyhow."

"Doc, we ain't got no plays."

"I don't care. Be creative!"

One of my patients, Nathan, who had just returned from a stint in Chile, was my copilot. Not only did he do his share of the driving, but he spoke Spanish, so I was able to blow off steam in words I wouldn't deem appropriate in my native tongue. "Hijo de la chingada madre, como me ha fregado, estos ninos traviesos. Que pendejos."

He would respond, "Bien hecho, caballero. Estamos casi a llegar. Ja mero."

I'd look at him and say, "We just passed Paducah, Kentucky. We still got half the Civil War to go through."

As we crossed into Alabama, I began searching for a typical smallish southern town, and finally pulled over and announced, "Okay easy riders, a taste of what this part of the country is known for. Get out."

I walked up to an elderly black gentleman and asked him kindly where we could find the best barbecue in town. He directed us to a side street out near the edge of town, not to a restaurant, but to a tiny shack with a big old free standing oven alongside. "You'll see the smoke."

As we walked along, the kids wondered at the houses, trees, and especially the people. "Even the dogs are different here," observed Brian.

"Doc, how did you understand that guy?"

"He was speaking English."

Arriving at our destination, I ordered barbecue for everyone. "Eat it or starve." Sitting under a magnolia, soon hands and lips were stained with secret sauce, the best. Fresh picked, chilled watermelon washed down the sticky remains with its own sweetly satisfying nectar. Chickens gobbled up the seeds as we made our way back to the van, still many miles to go.

Into the night, we bypassed Huntsville, and at last, every child dreaming, turned left at the Florida panhandle. On and on to Tallahassee, then south until, twenty-four hours after we left home, we hit Tampa.

Arriving at the beachfront hotel, I was exhausted just as my charges were reviving. The whole situation reeked of danger. Here were adolescents of both sexes, from all over the world, streaming in expecting to find that defining moment, far from parental guidance, in this 'Garden of Eden'. I called a quick team meeting and laid out some rules which no one listened to, and then, in desperation, "Jon, you're the social director and, as such, are responsible for assuring that everyone has a good time, but not a great time. Anything great is probably illegal and could besmirch our reputations. Go get tired. Remember, opening banquet at 7:00." I was about to head to the room to sleep when I ran into Keith who had flown down with his team. Soon he was introducing me to other coaches and tournament people. This was too much. I couldn't pass up the opportunity. Talking basketball from every angle, what fun!

"Who're those guys?" I asked as two towering black kids walked by.

"That one is Damon Flint, and the other one is Dantonio Winfield. They're two of the best high school players out East." Luckily, they weren't in our age group, but, still, it made me wonder if we would be totally outclassed.

Before I knew it, one of my players came up to me wearing a tie. "Where's the food, Coach?" Glancing at my watch, I couldn't believe it was quarter to seven already.

In the huge banquet hall, we were assigned tables by team. Our guys were near the front sharing a table with a women's team from Latvia, sirens all, but unable to speak a word of English. Dick Vitale gave the main address using the word 'baby' exactly 1,000 times, a new record. Nick Anderson of The Magic, was supposed to show but didn't. Still, for the kids, it was a nice event. Immediately following was the dance, at which two of my players fell in love. I had to go to bed at 11:00, feeling as if I had just done ten consecutive deliveries. The next morning I found out that there had been a fire alarm activated suspiciously near our rooms. None of the kids knew anything. All I did was eye Jon intently for a moment. We had a game to play.

Traveling to our venue, I thought I would be satisfied if we could at least make a respectable showing. Realistically, after the trip and last night, avoiding a shutout might be a more realistic goal. As the teams warmed up, I wandered over to meet their coach. Coming from Helsinki, Finland, he spoke English very fluently. He told me how his team had just won the European championship for our age group. His center was later to play for Rick Majerus at Utah. Noting more than a bit of arrogance in his demeanor, I chose humility to counter. "We're just a group of neighborhood kids from a little Midwestern farm town. We'll try to at least give you a workout." Shaking hands we went back to our respective teams.

"Guys, I don't think they're used to our style of ball. Run when you can and let's slash to the hoop at least until we see how they defend. Pressure 'em on the perimeter. See if we get some early turnovers. Aaron, front number 12 inside the dotted line, he looks like he could hurt us low. Let's go!"

As the game got going, they showed vulnerability with some predictable passes absent pace, giving us picks leading to easy breakaways. They could shoot, however, and had a significant size advantage, making us work hard for boards. As half-time approached, it was still a game, and a Corley tip at the buzzer brought us to within one. "How ya feelin', guys. I'm havin' fun. No one's in foul trouble. Just keep doin' the same. They probably very frustrated and gotta come out strong. Be sure to move the feet and keep good position on defense, and good uptakes on shots. They'll hack for sure. We still got our heat we haven't showed yet so stay positive. We just might steal one."

Second half saw them giving it all they had, pounding it inside, crisp passes, and determined defense. We fought back with Reed and Ryan hitting three's, clutch free throw shooting, and then two quick fouls on their star center, one on a reverse by Conor, the other as Jay positioned himself perfectly to take the offensive foul. As he left the floor, I couldn't help noticing a menacing scowl on their coach's face. Six minutes left, down five, I signaled for the full court press. They actually handled it quite well, but did throw one into the crowd, and were called for traveling once, us capitalizing both times with hoops. It came down to five seconds left, our ball, down two, full court to go. They came out with man to man pressure, but Corley set a crushing pick freeing Hulse who took it coast to coast and finished in traffic to knot the score. They tried to call time but were too slow and we were in OT.

In the huddle, as I was trying to come up with strategy, Conor looked at me and said, "Let me jump center, I know I can get it." He didn't often assert himself like that but when he did, he delivered.

Giving up three or more inches, he looked fresh and confident while their guy looked weary and chagrined. We got the tip. Pass, pass, lay-up. Steal by Jay, quick pitch to Danny behind the arc, in the air for three, good! Nothing but net! We're up five! After a time out we trade baskets, then Roland hits a free throw, and I signal for time-out. "OKAY fella's, go four corner, deny three's and hack on layups. We're doin' great!"

They try to press, but they're obviously tired. They have no answer to the delay and we win going away by seven. Not too shabby. European champs. As the kids line up to shake hands, I notice their coach going directly to the locker room, not wanting any part of the real purpose of this tournament, sportsmanship and cultural exchange. All I wanted to say was "welcome to America". That night the kids slept much better.

Next up were the Maryland All Stars, an excellent team, experienced and well coached. However, Conor came up with a phenomenal second half, literally taking over the game. Late in the fourth quarter one amazing move, ending with a driving bank shot from about ten feet executed to perfection with the left hand, caught everyone's attention as pens in the crowd scribbled furiously. Two coaches came up to me afterwards wanting details on who that kid was.

Later that same day, we faced the Irish national team. What a cheerful bunch, really having fun. Later our guys were to spend significant time with 'lads.' Their heroes were all IRA, and they were great story tellers, not to mention the quaint mannerisms and the lilting delivery. Basketball players, however, they were not, and we got to substitute freely, finding it difficult not blowing them out.

Amazingly, we were now 3-0, with next up being none other than the Russian Junior National squad, also undefeated. I had seen a little of one of their previous games. They had a 6'8" center with excellent low post skills. Two other guys were 6'6", one could hit outside, and they were good ball handlers. This would be comparable to traversing the Berlin wall, passing through the eye of a needle, and shucking all the corn in Iowa without losing a kernel. Difficult, yes, and highly improbable, but that's the thinking of a mature, experienced, left brained coach. The kids don't know Russia from What Cheer, Iowa. They do know they're having fun and can't wait for the next game.

Just before introductions, the players exchange gifts. We wowed them with chic John Deere caps, they counter with pins depicting the Kremlin, definitely advantage us.

"Here's our strategy. Ryan, I know you only come up to his knees, but you start on their moose. Pick him up full court and get in his way anywhere he goes like Mr. Twiddle's cat. Nag, bother, pester, anticipate every step and beat him to the spot. No one can withstand such pressure. Conor, you got number 12, he's lights out from the perimeter so make him drive. Aaron, take 32. He rarely shoots so back off. Your main job is to front on Ryan's man if he gets within 10 feet of the hoop. Let's get this one for all the hard working farmers back home."

They got the opening tip and came down for a quick basket, but I noticed that their center wasn't able to leave center circle, Ryan had him surrounded. This was going to be interesting. Our first possession, Matt Hulse swerved his way past his man and through the rest of the timber for the twisting layup. As soon as they turn to go back up court, the big guy forgets and runs right into Ryan. Charge! Quickly they call time-out. Now one of their other tall guys began setting picks for their center and at least he was getting down court but still Ryan, with his gnat defense, kept him out of position half the time, and with Aaron's help, he was basically taken out of the game. Still, their other guys were no slouches, and with such a tremendous height advantage, putbacks and rebounds were killing us. At half time we were down eight.

"I've seen them against the press," I began in the locker room. "But we don't have much choice. They try to stay in good position and pass over the top. Let's start with our tallest lineup and go man to man full court press. Front everywhere, get in the face of the passer with hands up, and make them put it on the floor. That's the signal to double, get them turning, and sneak in for steals."

Our scramble worked somewhat, but we just couldn't score enough and they widened the lead to 11 as the third quarter ended. I did notice, however that they were a little pooped and they had another game to play later the same day. For whatever the reason, they came out in a zone. "Reed, Jay, Jon, Danny, get in there and I want to see 3's. Swing it, reverse it, and fire on anything open at the arc. You're going to have to hack down low, but they're tired, maybe they'll miss a few free throws."

When Jay's first launch from the top of the key banked in, I knew we weren't dead yet. Then Reed drained two more trifecta's, Brian hit a short turnaround, and Danny got a reverse. Suddenly we had ourselves a ball game. They brought back all their starters and went man but now time was getting short and it was still a four point game. Our next possession, Ryan pump faked from the corner, then took his man off the dribble and was soon in paint, surrounded by timber. Looking like he would have to put up a desperate attempt, he knew exactly what he was doing, and without hesitation, no looked it to the cutting Conor for the power lay-up and the foul. The conversion made it down one. Under a minute to go, they pushed it up court and came strong to the hole. Roland stayed in excellent position and challenged the 3 foot leaner just enough to cause a miss. In the battle for the rebound, their center bulled his way in and snagged it. Just as he elevated for the put back, from out of nowhere came Aaron with a very aggressive block/foul. I thought detente was finished but only glares and whispered invective ensued. At the line, the mighty Muscovite sank the first but short armed the second, Corley snagging the ricochet. Time out!

"Twelve seconds left, down two, Guys. Set picks to help each other up court. No set play but I want the shot going up with 5 seconds to go and all five crash the boards." As we inbound, they press, but it's only token and quickly we're across the line. Conor dribbled to the right side, found no opening and handed off to Matt Hulse. Eight seconds. I watch him put it on the floor and head toward the hole drawing more attention with each step. What is he thinking? Surely, they'll rip it or hammer him, and he can't hit free throws. We're done! Six to go, and he surged up as if he were Samson, busting free. Still, there was absolutely no shot there at all. In the air, somehow, he wheeled around and eyed Ryan alone at the top of the key. The dish, and the stat launch. Why does he have to put so much arch on his shots, I thought as our fate begins it's decent toward the rim. Multiple gasps escaped sideline lungs as the sphere clanged off the front of the basket. Three...two...one, but no, the ball had taken a quick vector off the front of orange and fell right into the hands of Reed just in time to fire up an instant 12 footer. Good! It was in! Right at the buzzer!

"Very nice! Good shot, Reed. Now we have 3 minutes of OT. Let's play straight man to man and keep running. Maybe we can pull it off. Don't stop gunning it up." They had become very determined, and executed well as we fell behind, seconds ticking off with each possession. One minute to go, Conor drew a foul, the fifth for their big guy, but missed both free throws. They got every rebound and didn't miss at the line. Down three with twenty seconds to go, we turned it over, and then had to foul. Calmly, their point guard sank two and despite a lay-up by Aaron, we were out of time and lost. Yes, we had come up short, but this was not just any opponent, it was the best of Russia. We had engaged the bear and held him at bay. To vanquish lingered for yet another day.

That evening, all around the hotel, people were commenting, "Hey, I heard you guys almost whipped the Russians," or, "How did you stay with those guys?"

I just kept explaining that our guys don't understand "not supposed to" or "no chance," instead playing the game of basketball with as much heart as you'll ever see coming from deep within each one of them, and combining that with the execution of cold blooded assassins.

Unbeknownst to me, since I retired relatively early thinking that things were going so well for the kids that they wouldn't think of doing anything to jeopardize our chances or reputation, several of my pesky adolescents, who apparently weren't completely in tune with my analysis of the situation, had lost track of time, speaking charitably, and were still wandering out on the beach well after midnight. I didn't hear about any of this until several days later when we were in the van half way back to Iowa. As I had mentioned, Ryan had fallen in love the first night there, and had been unable to find the target of his obsession since being bowled over in that initial encounter. At about 2:00 a.m. or thereabouts, two other members of the team ran into this diva out near the pool, and decided to surprise their friend by showing up at his room with the prize. Naturally, when they arrived at the room, their buddy was, where else, in the shower. Just like I taught them in basketball, you never should feel like you have to stick to a particular script, always be ready to improvise as the situation dictates. Within less than a minute the scene was set. Both directors were out of sight behind one bed, while flirtatious Virginia was tantalizingly tucked under the covers of the other awaiting the cue. Ryan, hair perfectly positioned, wearing only a skimpy towel, opened the bathroom door to emerge in a flood of steam. His happy humming halted ever so abruptly as he looked up to see that which he had dreamed about, close enough to touch, in his bed smiling seductively. "Hi Ryan. I've been waiting for you." As she spoke, our hero saw the covers being turned down with a deliberateness that begged for the definitive response. No one should ever have to withstand such pressure! As fate would have it, the two instigators bailed out their buddy, popping up in peals of laughter, before any foul could be committed. Ryan, declining to reveal all that passed through his mind, would only comment that he would rather have been on the free throw stripe with no time left and the game on the line.

The following morning, we faced the New York City All-stars, winner advancing to the final four. I put two guys back in good defensive position for the opening tip, it being obvious from warm-ups that they could easily out jump us. I began to hear the faint but distinct music of a graceful, long necked, white bird as the Big Apple's best weaved between our token scarecrows soaring high for the slam. General Lee ran off an amazing string, until Appomattox. Yet he remained dignified, respected throughout.

Our next day saw no hardwood but took us instead to Busch

Gardens. Champions we were not to be, but we were accumulating enough experience to move up the ladder more than a little. From then on, no one should have taken us lightly.

As all of this was going on, my relationship with Janet was degenerating from bad to almost nonexistent. Even now it's not something I feel I want to comment on. Everything seemed to be a judgment call, subjective, unresolvable. Certainly, I was not without fault, but seldom are such things so simple. We now had quite a history of mediocrity at best. Even a massive effort to right the ship, it seemed, would have been painful and difficult and, at the same time, highly unlikely to succeed. So when a patient of mine told me one day that she had taken a job out of town and was moving, I perked up enough to ask her what she intended to do with her condo. She told me that it was going up for sale the next week. My mind began to churn. What would be best? The lives of two children were involved, even though they were old enough to hopefully understand and cope. After all, what they were surely picking up on, the way things were now, wasn't exactly the ideal example of how a couple should relate. My final conclusion was that if the demise was inevitable, why prolong the charade?

"Do you have a minute to talk," I began arriving home after work.

"Sure, just let me finish with this salad."

Immediately aggravated, I picked up the sports page but wasn't able to read thinking instead what to say. A few minutes later she came in and sat down, probably realizing that this was to be a serious talk.

"Do you still think that our relationship is a lost cause?" I began.

"Well we basically have no relationship. Still, there are so many factors to consider, the kids, our families, financial things. Why? What are you thinking?"

"A decent condo is opening up across town. A patient of mine is selling it. I could move there. What do you think?"

"I know I can't take much more of the way things are now. Something has to give, or I'll break either physically or mentally. What about Liam and Conor?"

"I was thinking half and half, but basically I think we have to

298

leave it up to them. No question both of us love them and would do anything for them. How does that sound?"

"There's no script, is there? I guess that's as good as we can do."

"Okay, I'll go see if I can buy the condo, then we can talk to the kids tonight."

As I drove off, I wondered what I had done. I alternated between thinking that I was guilty of creating this bungled situation for two wonderful children, to resentment towards Janet for causing half of it, hell, three fourths. Just as it wasn't fair for her to dredge the thing through the coals with her friends ad infinitum constantly reinforcing her position while I said nothing to no one, it wouldn't be right here either, for me to presume to portray the mess without giving her equal space. I will say I did go so far as to grovel when the ship was perilously close to capsizing. She wasn't buying it and, despite the guilt/shame/humiliation, I never hated myself.

"Okay, Carol, it's a deal. I'll move in Saturday." Damn, that was easy! But remember, the incision is only a prelude to the inevitable sweaty mess of removing the inflamed, ruptured appendix and coping with the aftermath.

Supper done, we all sat in the family room. It was like when a patient dies and the family must be told, you just have to say it. Both kids were in high school and were closer than most sibs, making it a little easier. "Janet and I are splitting up," I began. "We've tried to work it out but it just gets worse. I apologize for whatever stress it might cause for you kids, but the stress of us staying together with the problems we have would be worse. None of it is your fault, not even the tiniest bit. I'll be at a condo up near the high school. Both of you are welcome there any time. I'm moving this weekend."

Silence. No response. What could they say? It was a done deal. Janet explained how hard it was for her and that there was no other solution. "Are there any questions?"

"Nope."

"Uh ah."

The hardest part was getting used to the solitude. But then that became a strong positive. Doing dishes turned into a soothing ritual. Cleaning could be ignored and it was no biggie. One price I did pay was that I didn't get to see Liam nearly enough during his whole senior year. I don't think he blamed me for anything, but for him, at the time, it was too big a compromise. Conor, on the other hand, found it easiest to let us decide for him how it should be handled. Thus he was at my place half the time. And when you take into consideration all the time with basketball, Janet probably got the short end of it. We estranged ones got along better than before; just a practical considerate association.

That August, the UNI basketball team was scheduled for another overseas tour, this time Scandinavia. Conor agreed to come along. For ten days we hip hopped around Sweden and, after a relaxing Baltic cruise, Finland. Scenic excursions, playing ball, going to the games, and just hanging out with the players and coaches, filled our days. We even jogged to get Conor ready for the upcoming cross country season, and since we had begun lifting that summer, we searched out fitness clubs where we could pump a little iron. Best of all, instead of spending the few days at the end like most of the others experiencing Norway, Conor and I headed east.

Actually, Helsinki to St. Petersburg is only an overnight boat ride. Pretty convenient location for a German siege, leading me to realize all the more how heroic was the Russian resistance during that desperate time. Winding our way through gypsy beggars, Conor and I entered the magnificent Hermitage museum. Gold everywhere. Entire rooms filled with just Post-Impressionist masterpieces. Two full blocks of this, and all of it was only part of a summer diversion set up for the Czar, surrounded as he was, by impoverished peasants. Is it any wonder a revolution took place? Then a long walk through streets, packed with humanity the entire way, to a large pediatric hospital.

Being a doctor, I walked right in as if I belonged, carefully searching for what I thought would be an appropriate functionary. Finally finding my mark, I walked up boldly, asking, "I'm a doctor from America. Does anyone here speak English?" Smiling politely, the woman signaled for me to wait and walked away. The building was ancient, dank and poorly lighted, with high ceilings above the vast network of hallways and staircases. Having no idea what to expect, I stood patiently, wondering what it would be like for a doctor here. Conor had elected to wait in a small park just outside the hospital, assuring me that he could either beat up or outrun anyone who tried to bother him. Soon I was approached by a very nice looking woman looking very professional and appearing to be in her thirties.

"Hello, I'm the head of surgery here. What can I do for you?"

Very impressed with her perfect English, I answered, "I'm a doctor from the United States here for a brief visit. I wanted to get a feel for the medical system here. Is there anyone who could show me around, spend a few minutes explaining things to me?"

"I'd be more than happy to. Let me show you the hospital."

As we walked towards the post op wards, she asked me about myself, and I gave her a brief summary of what kind of work I'd done. That was all it took for her to warm to the occasion, immediately becoming open and sincere. "Our system and country are in crisis. Greed and corruption are rampant. The hospital is poorly supplied. Any modern antibiotic must be brought in by the patient's family, and many times, even that proves impossible. Here, let me show you a patient I operated on yesterday."

Entering the huge ward, poorly lit, large fan running overhead, we visited a small girl who smiled shyly as we talked about her. The dressing removed, I appreciated the tastefully placed transverse lower abdominal incision. "What was the diagnosis?" I asked, showing more than a little interest.

"I have the x-rays right here." She placed the films on a nearby view box that reminded me of one we had used in California 20 years earlier that was vintage 1940's."

"Well, I'll be...it looks like...but it's so rare."

"You're right. Meckel's diverticulum. She'll do fine."

Just then a nurse came up notifying us of an urgent case in the emergency room. Arriving there, my host was all business. It was a ten year old with head trauma. After seeing the child and ordering tests, she turned to me to explain, "He's a victim of our new society, hit by an automobile. One of the new rich, who exploited 'freedom' to either steal and sell to foreigners, or acquire scarce but much needed goods and put exorbitant prices on them. Soon he must have a new auto, which, of course, he has no idea how to drive. We see so much of this."

"Do you have a neurosurgeon?"

"In reality, no. Only in the special hospital for those with financial resources. I may have to return to do burr holes."

"No CT available?"

"Sadly, no. We are primitive at best, and this is the referral pediatric hospital for 5 million people. I'll have to use clinical judgment on the subdural."

Then we saw two post-surgical thyroid cases. Chernobyl, she explained. Many patients with thyroid tumors, leukemia, aplastic anemia. "It's letting up now," she informed. "But when it happened we were overwhelmed. Here's our library." As we walked in, I took a moment to glance at the shelves. Old appearing volumes in Russian, and only a few journals, none recent.

"I'm impressed," I began as we sat down at a table. "You're a talented, dedicated physician. Tell me, if you don't mind, a little about yourself."

"I work long hours, and I go home to my flat. I have no car. Busses and trolley are inconsistent. I'm not married and spend the rest of my time caring for my mother who lives with me. We are very insecure because her pension and my salary are barely enough to survive. Inflation has left people like us destitute. It's so bad we can't even be sure we'll survive the Stalingrad winter. Yes, I prefer to call it Stalingrad. At least then there was some concern for citizens. Now, what happened in the war, working in the service of others, any idealism, means nothing. There is no dream."

I left the hospital shaking my head. Here was a country with so much talent, so many resources, yet unable to put together any coherent system, basically floundering for the vast majority.

Seeing Conor in the distance, I quickened my pace, noticing a frown on his face as I approached the bench. "Geez, Dad, you took long enough."

"Sorry, what have you been doing?"

"It wasn't too bad. This old guy walked up to me and sat down. He talked for the longest time. All I did was smile or nod every so often. I don't even think he knew I didn't understand a word he said."

Schizophrenia, same the world over. Conor probably made his day.

That night we were on the ship back to Finland. Then, the next morning, a new adventure began, as we ambled through the busy outdoor market to a dock at the far end of the harbor, purchased tickets and boarded the rapid boat to another world. Less than an hour later, having skimmed our way east over a narrow portion of the Baltic, we disembarked at Tallinn. An astounding contrast was readily apparent. Helsinki to Estonia was as if passing through a time warp. Having only a few days, we had decided that what we wanted to see most was the countryside. Walking to one of the main hotels, we were lucky enough to find a car for rent, and soon we were cruising along the sea in a posh Volvo. Stopping at an isolated beach to search for amber, we rested while I read to Conor from a book I had brought along by the same name, *Devils in Amber: The Baltics*, by Philip Bonosky. With this, we began to understand the tragic history of this area, caught between Russia and Germany, pushed and shoved, and now 'independent.' I had patients from Riga who had fled during the war. All their Jewish neighbors had disappeared, along with many other 'partisans' as both sides took turns occupying their land. They survived only by working as virtual slaves in a German war factory, finally escaping and being lucky enough to get to the West. Most paid a much heavier price.

Driving on back roads, we marveled at observing close up, the bucolic yet tragic scenes of farmers making hay with large wooden pitchforks lifting the bounty onto horse drawn wagons. Roadside restaurants had only a few unripened tomatoes and ubiquitous supplies of supersaturated fatty sausage. That night we stayed in a quaint hotel in Latvia. Language was a problem as I finally found that my limited German served me best. Since independence, crime had increased dramatically. We found that the price of gas depended on how the particular country was getting along with Russia at that particular moment. A major issue everywhere was what to do with the many ethnic Russians who lived in the Baltics, had never been well integrated into the dominant society, preferring to remain in their exclusive enclaves, yet had no ties to their ancestral land.

Riga was filled with friendly people, had many nice parks, monuments, and more construction than we had seen up to that point. We shopped for gifts, mostly of amber, for friends and family before heading back north.

There was very little traffic, and, taking the main highway, we made excellent time and soon neared the Estonian capital once again. Not having to reach Helsinki until our ship departed for Stockholm that night at ten, we felt relaxed. We had negotiated a visit to a most unlikely portion of the globe, probed deeply, and, not only avoided disaster, but actually had fun. Seeing a park just ahead, we decided to stop and enjoy the magnificent summer sunshine. For nearly an hour, Conor and I wandered the flower lined paths, sat on benches in little coves, and peered at monuments engraved in a language unlike any I had ever seen. Eventually circling back we emerged from the wooded area to the small parking lot. Conor noticed it first. "Dad, our car's gone."

"What?" For a second I thought it was a joke but the lot was empty. Panic was just beneath the surface. I could see us languishing in an Estonian stalag being fed a diet of borscht and spending endless nights warding off unforgiving insects, ravenous rats, and HIV positive cohabitants coming from behind.

"Maybe there's another lot just like this one. Remember that time along the Baltic when there were three or four identical openings along the shore? You go a minute that way and I'll check this way. Meet you here in two minutes. See the flower shop across the street? We can't get lost."

Nothing either way, we were stuck. "Why not get a taxi, go as quick as we can to the boats, hop on the next one to Finland, and vanish?" suggested my brilliant son.

"I don't know, they've got an imprint of my credit card which they could use to nail me for the cost of the car which is a new Volvo, not exactly cheap, and if they somehow catch us absconding, who knows what we could face, maybe years. You got to remember, I'm probably not high on my own government's list of favorite citizens. Can't expect any help there. I think we got to get the stupid car back."

"Sure, dad, and how do we do that?"

"Let's go ask at the flower place over there. Maybe they saw something." Crossing the street I tried to think like Hercule or Sherlock but kept drawing a complete blank. Walking into the store I went up to the counter and asked the manager if he spoke English. He only shrugged, waiting for my next move. I pulled out my passport, which I kept in a pouch slung over my shoulder, and handed it to him. He looked at it briefly, then walked towards the door and pointed down the street and said something in Estonian. Frustration building, I took the passport back and looked around. The only other person in the place was a girl who looked to be about eleven years old. We had been surprised coming off the boat at Tallinn, when, seeing our American passports, the authorities immediately took us to a separate booth allowing us to breeze right through. Obviously, they were trying to suck up to the U.S. now that they were 'free.' Perhaps English was being taught in the schools as part of the new Estonia. Walking the few steps to where she stood, I began as politely as possible, "Hello."

"Hello." Great, she answered.

"We can't find our car. It was parked right over there and now it's gone. We wonder if the manager saw anything."

"No understand."

I showed her the passport and tried to explain again using pantomime to show what I meant, probably looking very foolish. Then the two of them interchanged a few sentences, with her, after thinking a bit, saying, "He say go..." she seemed at a loss for words, then pointed like he had and added a gesture that looked like the sign of the cross and folding of hands as in prayer.

Oh, I thought, so we should go pray for help. But then she said, "Speak English," as she repeated the pointing down the block.

"Thank you."

"For nothing."

Leaving the store, we began walking the direction they had indicated and, in less than a block, came upon a church. "This is it," I said. "A Catholic church. I bet the priest speaks English. That's what they were trying to tell us." Finding the door open we entered and couldn't find anyone. Even outside, nothing. At the little accompanying flat, no answer.

"Now what? Find the police?"

"Naa, that doesn't even work in more organized countries, fat chance here. Let's start walking towards downtown and see if we can find anyone else likely to speak English." On and on we went. I tried eight or ten different people who I hoped could speak English, and got nothing. About to give up, I happened to see, out of the corner of my eye, off in the distance, what appeared to be a guy in uniform hopping off a motorbike and entering a little pub.

"Let's go, Conor, that might be it."

"What are you talking about?"

"I think that was a Finnish sailor. They speak English almost for sure."

"Okay, you go in and see. I'll wait outside."

"Okay."

Entering the establishment, I took a minute for my eyes to adjust. Slowly I was able to observe maybe ten or more tables. Most of them occupied with what I guessed were sailors, mixed in with a smattering of young women, laughing, smoking and drinking beer. Off to one side was a table where only two guys were seated, another chair being empty. I decided I had to give it a try. "Can I sit down?"

"Sure, why not? Want a beer?" How glad to hear relatively smooth English! As I pulled up the chair, I evaluated the sailor who had spoken. He seemed a little older than the others, kind of tall and had curly brown hair.

"You from Helsinki?" I began, taking a sip from the glass of dark brew he had poured from the pitcher.

"Ya, we come here quite often to relax and have fun. It's cheap and so close for us. You sound American. Don't see many of you over here in Estonia."

"I'm with a basketball team. The Doctor. We've just toured your country and Sweden."

"From Iowa? Then you're the guys that beat our national team a few days ago in Helsinki?"

"Right, it was our best game by far. You guys were pretty good though. Really aggressive."

"My cousin plays on that team. Very hard game, he said. So what are you doing here?"

As carefully as I could I explained our situation and what had happened. He listened closely and then seemed to be thinking for a while before finally saying, "That's very unfortunate. Since independence, it's like anarchy here, lots of crime. But wait here, I have an idea."

I watched as he headed across the room, then bent down to talk to one of the women there. Soon he was back, bringing her along. "This is my friend. She is from here and agrees that there is only one hope for you. A man called Andrej, runs everything in Tallinn, even Estonia. He has no official position, more like, how do you say, Mafia. But he does some good things too. She has a friend who is close to Andrej. We could go on our scooters to meet with her friend. It's the only chance."

"Thank you very much. I really appreciate it. I do have one more concern. I have my young fourteen-year-old son with me outside. Can he stay here?

"It's okay. He can wait here at this table. I'll have them bring some good food for him."

Soon we were off on two scooters, going less than a mile before pulling up to a very nice looking building and entering a third story flat. A very sophisticated looking young woman welcomed us with a friendly smile inviting us to sit in the nicely decorated living room. I observed them closely as they talked either in Finnish or Estonian, trying to guess if the discussion was going to be fruitful for me. After what seemed to be a lot of spirited interchange, my new buddy turned to me and explained, "She knows the scam well. They have been making lots of money off of it. Usually rich, unscrupulous business types. You are innocent. Andrej owes her one because of certain social favors, so she will take you there. I cannot go because of his security."

"Okay, thanks."

"One more thing. She plans to tell him that you were ready to go to the American consulate to complain. That would put him in a bad situation since they have jointly beneficial 'business' arrangements. Just so you know."

Another twenty minutes, all silent, in her car, and we pulled up to a garage under a two story building. Getting out she took a key from her purse and opened the door, then pulled in and closed it before motioning me to accompany her. Inside we were met by two men, one of whom spoke broken English. Neither of them was Andrej, I surmised, as we had to wait while one of the men went to fetch him. I was feeling quite nervous about the whole situation, now more so because of what I assumed to be the unsavory nature of these fellows. Soon, The Man graced us with his presence, embraced my driver but seemed to wince slightly on shaking my hand. After some talk, I was asked through the translator, "So you have problem with car, why we should help you? You go American ambassador?"

All the while I had been looking at Andrej's hand and I was sure of what was wrong with it. I decided to play my doctor card. "Tell Andrej, I am American doctor. I see his painful hand. I can fix hand."

More talking. "He say he take many medicine, no help. What American doctor do?"

Now was my chance. Motioning to Andrej, I instructed, "Sit with your hand on the desk." Pulling up another chair, I glanced at his finger confirming my diagnosis, paronychia, a very ripe, and very tender I'm sure, collection of pus under the flap of skin covering the base of the nail, building up pressure unable to escape. "Do you have a knife?" As he translated, I saw a look of consternation sweep over Andrej's face. I did my best to maintain a calm and confident demeanor. Then, after a tacit nod from Herr Andrej, the translator reached into his pocket and pulled out a beautiful weapon decorated in multicolored amber, pushed the button allowing the blade to spring into position, locking with a definitive click. Handing it to me, I observed just a hint of diaphoresis beginning on my patient's brow, betraying the look of bravado he was attempting to convey with a wry curling of the corners of the mouth.. "Cigarette lighter," I ordered. Immediately, the second man in the room produced the instrument, clearly enjoying the drama. Slowly, I worked the tip of the blade through the flame, knowing that all eyes were watching my every move, and that undoubtedly, firearms had to be present. After a few seconds, I grabbed the back of the blade, about an inch from the end, to show that it wouldn't burn, and then proceeded to use the tip to gently pry up the skin at the cuticle closest to the most inflamed area. Slowly and painlessly, the tunnel was being opened up. Then, ahh, relief, the abscess accessed by gleaming steel, discharging freely a greenish yellow purulence. Andrej's grin turned into a relaxed smile, even sounding a little chuckle. Ms. Tallinn had pulled out some Q tips from her purse, so I proceeded to clean the area and insert a small wick to keep the drainage going for a day or two more. Pushing my chair back away from the desk, I signified that I was finished, then focused my eyes directly at El Jefe.

"Tank you, very mouch." He then barked out instructions to the others present. The translator informed me that the car was already

308

returned. I should go as if nothing had happened. Exiting with my driver, I was soon dropped off at the pub. Conor had just finished eating. Thanking everyone we headed directly to the rental place, found the wayward auto missing nary a bag, and waltzed inside where we were informed that there was no bill. I did ask for my credit card duplicate slip which I looked at, then tore up and put into my pocket. The clerk just smiled, business as usual. Two hours later we were in Helsinki with only 45 minutes to board the ship to Sweden to meet the team for the flight home.

Conor and I laughed about the whole thing, but, deep down, I breathed a sigh of relief, knowing how close we had come to a horrific nightmare. I will say that, in my life as a physician, I've learned to make life and death decisions all the time and it carries over into the rest of life. Still, a blessed existence can only go on so long; how many times can one take it to the precipice without one day falling over?

The first thing I always do on getting back to town is check in with the hospital. On this occasion, I was informed that a ninety-seven-year-old woman had just come in with a stroke. She was new to town, coming to live near her daughter, and had no local doctor. I was Dr. none that week, taking all such admissions. Driving to the hospital, I wasn't very excited about the case, probably senile and worn out. Most difficult would be getting family to decide on living will or, if she survives, nursing home placement. As I stepped into the room, however, I was surprised to find an alert face looking directly at me. Alone with her in the room, I pulled up a chair to the bedside and began to prize out her story. Not feeling rushed, and understanding the privilege of being involved in circumstances where it was entirely appropriate and, at times, critical to get to know someone fairly well, I started at the beginning of her long life and moved forward allowing her to set the pace as we progressed. Rapport is a difficult thing, the trick being getting one to feel that they're special. Having lived so many years, this woman was bound to have had many memorable experiences. She had been telling me about growing up on the farm, always an interesting topic. During a pause in her account, I tried to define her more sharply with the following. "What were some of the most fun things you did back in those years?"

She stared into my eyes, thinking, trying to decide. Then, concluding that we had been thrown into this situation together, and that her very existence had become quite precarious, she decided to share the truth with me, hoping that I would understand. "One perfect fall day," she began. "I walked clear across the section to the neighbor's place." She then hesitated, this time her eyes literally riveted to mine, momentarily continuing, "And made it back home not one minute late for supper." How strange, I thought. This was the defining event of her youth.

Going on with the interview, it soon came time for the physical exam. Her left arm was flaccid but her heart seemed strong. Then carefully covering her middle with the hospital gown, I turned down the sheet to evaluate the lower extremities. Immediately, on glancing at the now paralyzed left leg, I noted the surgical signs of an incompletely repaired pes cavus. She had been waiting for this, and as I looked up, nothing had to be said. Our bond had been formed. Now, no matter what, it would be okay.

And, as it turned out, she didn't do well, difficulty swallowing, aspiration, blood clots, and finally her heart failing. Through it all she remained proud, asking for no heroic measures, dying peacefully in her sleep. That one poignant moment, however, is what I will always remember.

Lifting weights had become quite fashionable and both boys were becoming more interested so I asked a friend of mine to make us a solid bench for the basement. Conor and I took a Saturday afternoon and drove twenty miles to Jesup where there was a warehouse full of wholesale equipment. We picked out a new Olympic bar and 300 lb. of various sized plates. Now we could pump some serious iron! Liam wasn't so diligent but Conor stuck to it and soon we were working our way toward that magical goal, benching the 45's. Finally the day came, and we carefully slipped the big plates onto the bar, centered it perfectly, and tried to decide who should go first. Conor agreed to spot first so I set myself under the bar and slowly knocked off three reps. It felt pretty good. With his turn, I was careful to be ready for anything. He had managed two reps with 42 1/2 lb. on each side two days before, so he should have been able to handle it. Lift off was no problem, and all was steady as the shiny steel came down to kiss his pecs. But then half way up, he hesitated with his triceps quivering ever so slightly. Quickly, I placed my hands just under the bar, but it wasn't necessary. Summoning up additional resources, he was able to put the heaviness in upward motion again, soon locking it out at the top. Taking it from him and setting it on the rack, I reached out to give him five. "Hey, not too shabby," he said. From then on, I couldn't hold him back. By the time AAU basketball arrived, he was definitely ripped.

The first day of practice, I decided to do all I could to step it up a notch. We had had some success the previous year but were still not at that top level of competition. The week previous, as I made the rounds to see who was still interested in playing, I handed out a short philosophical position paper for each player to study.

Murphy on Defense

Basketball is a lot of fun. It's good for both physical and mental health, and you can continue playing well into adulthood. Most agree that winning is more fun than losing. So, how do you go about winning consistently? In a word: DEFENSE! The most important prerequisite to being able to play good defense is aerobic conditioning. If you're not in shape you tend to reach, slap, foul, and generally watch as the game passes you by. The best way to get in shape for basketball is to play basketball, lots of it, full court and intense, whenever you can. Play hard and play to win. So you practice, so do you play in games.

Footwork is the next "must" for any type of defense. Being in the defensive position should become as natural to you as walking bowlegged is to a cowboy. You've got to be able to hold it, shuffle in all directions, and pitter-patter for as long as it takes. This alone will win you games. We will be practicing this!

Another key to defense is quickness. You might say that you either have it or you don't, but that's only partly true; alertness, anticipation, and positioning all help. Jumping rope may do some good. Most useful, however, is taking the other team's quickest, toughest player to guard, and then going on a "mission" to stop him. Do this in every pickup game and you will get amazingly quicker.

Jumping ability, staying focused, knowing your opponent, and understanding when to help out, also play a part in good defense. Mainly it's hard work that will be very rewarding if you want it badly enough.

In man to man defense you start in the basic defensive position as directly as possible on line between your man and the basket. If your man has the ball and is a good shooter, you play more upright, hands higher, and a little closer to him so you can challenge the shot. You don't foul the outside jump shooter; you bother him, keep him off balance, change his shot, and make sure he doesn't get the rebound. If your guy is a driver, you stay lower and wider, ready to move right or left quickly. Make him work hard and go the extra step to get around you. That gives your teammates time to help and rotate. If you get beat, fall back several steps towards the hoop to guard against the easy two. Get back to your original man as soon as you can, especially if there's a mismatch. You can shade your man a half a step one way or the other if he always goes that way. If you're on a player who can shoot and drive well, you can discourage the shot first, and then get help on the drive, or you can go the extra mile to deny him the ball in the first place. Some players get very annoyed when you do that and if they're not in as good shape as you are, they just give up. Search for a weakness. Find a way. If nothing else, do it with sheer determination. Another way to beat a guy who's more talented than you is to use deception; act like you've relaxed a little and then at the last second, flip your hand up and, bingo, you've tipped a pass or even a shot.

In general you try to avoid fouls. Tip at the ball with an upward hand motion rather than downward. Don't leave your feet until the other guy commits himself. Go straight up with your hands straight up; that's all your space to the ceiling. A good way to look at fouling is to be more aggressive when the likelihood of the man scoring on the play is high, and less so on the low percentage shot. There are always special situations like near the end of a game when you're down, when you may have to foul. In that instance you stay in your straight man to man defense and aggressively challenge every pass so that the result is either a steal or a foul. Nothing in basketball looks as foolish as trapping a well-spaced team in a delay game, allowing them to run the clock by easily hitting the open man.

Knowing when to help out is crucial to team defense. The

problem is that a near instantaneous decision must be made, based on calculating multiple factors in each situation. The bottom line is, do whatever is least likely to result in points for them. You don't leave Michael Jordan to help on a bricklayer. You do leave your man to prevent an easy uncontested lay-up. Be aware of the entire court; you might have to help, not only when there's action with the ball, but also when they pick away from the ball or someone beats his man backdoor. Be ready to help at any time, especially if there's a pick or a drive developing. Remember, it's team defense; when someone helps out, you may have to rotate toward the hoop to fill the gap in the defense, or cover the open hot shot. If you do it well, they don't get the easy attempt, and are left with 3-second calls, turnovers, and Hail Mary's.

We will use full court pressure, mostly zone. The idea is to trap early and often, towards the sidelines if possible. They shouldn't be able to dribble through two players. If they start turning their back and reversing the dribble, we should have a swipe. If they pick up the dribble, we pressure the pass with active hands, arms up forcing a high lob. Guys off the ball, front everyone, edging closer to the action according to how distant you are from the ball. Good anticipation will pick off those lazy long skip passes. If they go for a short pass out of the trap, we can trap again, and all of a sudden they have to worry about a ten second call. Weak side must always rotate back quickly in case they do make it up court.

Don't foul on the press. That slows the game down. We want up-tempo so that they tire out and start getting careless. We may not get a turnover every time down but we can make them work their behinds off just to get the ball across mid court.

These are a few of the things we'll be trying to do defensively this year. It should be lots of fun. Good luck!

Later, when I asked some focus questions, I was pleasantly surprised that the kids had taken it as a school assignment, and even understood what we were working at. Very good sign. We still were not big, but we were deep, athletic, smart, and unselfish. No one ever cared how many points they had, and there was never an attitude problem. These kids just worked hard and had fun, whether in games or at practice. It was my job as coach to get the most out of it.

We had a few individual games to start off the season and we looked decent. What was encouraging was the way the kids caught on to the full court pressure game, slowly realizing that we were never out of a game, having only to turn up the press a notch and other teams couldn't stand the heat.

Week three was our first big challenge, the Happy Joe's tournament in Ames. Thirty-two teams were featured from all over Iowa, including every top program. The small town teams were in the B division, while we were among the 16 A division entries. Never had we been able to survive such competition.

Our first pool game Saturday morning was against Newton, a team we should have beat easily. We played the first half in straight man half-court defense, which was adequate, but our offense sputtered. No one could hit, even bunnies it seemed. At half time, down a whopping fourteen points, we decided to come out with full bore aggression, trapping everywhere, and attacking quickly on offense, taking it to the hole as much as possible. How could a town like Newton withstand such an assault? They had a quick guard who had been penetrating quite a bit to hurt us in the first half, but as the second half began, we did a good job of denying him, or, if he got it, making him give it up with traps. Suddenly they were beginning to turn it over, and we were converting more frequently on our end. The third quarter ended with us only down four. I could see our guys weren't tired. In fact they were only beginning to get into it. "Just pour on the coal," I told them. "They're fading fast. Play clean and take it strong. We can't go wrong!"

It was true. They decompensated badly in the fourth, and I was able to give all our guys more or less equal minutes as we won by 15. Afterwards I told them, "Guys, I love the way you build momentum. It was like they were hit by a tidal wave. Matt, Conor, Mike, great job up front on the traps. Shane, you must have had eight interceptions playing deep, excellent anticipation. All of you did good. Let's keep it up."

With two hours until the next game, I took advantage of the glee and announced we were heading to the art museum. Most of the kids had never been to such a place, but I didn't want them running around a mall, using up energy and drinking pop. Besides, a little culture, in a low key contemplative setting would be good for them.

Just as with our first game, the team began the visit in questionable fashion, focusing exclusively on semi-clothed and unclothed paintings and photos in an exhibit of Iowa artists. But true to form, they recovered enough to scatter towards some Remington's and Grant Wood's, and, as our time was running out, they were checking out Andy Warhol, Egyptian pottery, and avant-garde abstract pieces. Telling them how stupefied and pleasantly surprised I was at their eclecticism, I reminded them that we still had more butt to kick at the tournament and soon we were shooting layups and three's warming up for the next battle.

Humbolt had a good team and came out hotter than Hades. We were still recovering from the passion of our diversion, and once again dug ourselves a big hole. When they banked in a three from the top of the key I knew we were in serious trouble. The scoreboard showed us down 18 with still two minutes to go in the half. During a time-out I told them to go to a full court man to man press, with no traps. It worked as I had expected, not that we created turnovers, but they positioned their best three ball handlers up front and mostly dribbled to advance the ball. We scored late and were only down 15 at half. In the locker room, all I saw were gloomy faces, but they brightened considerably as I explained our strategy. "Look guys, they're falling right into our hands. Their only decent ball handlers are up front, and then it's just gangly uncoordinated types. We come out in our zone trap, double their dribblers and force them to give it up, and let's see how their big guys execute the two on one's and three on two's. If those guys try to dribble and run at the same time, go for steals every time. Conor, they got only one guy who does most of their scoring. You take him and don't switch. Fight through every pick and get in his face on those turn around shots in the paint. And, guys, you know I don't have to say it, but keep runnin'. That's our bread and butter."

Funny how momentum can shift in a game. First three possessions for them were travel, bad pass, charge, all by big people. Meanwhile we're flyin' down the court, layups, wide open 15 footers, and an occasional three. Conor is frustrating their star big time. He's getting nothing. Two shots blocked, can't get to his spot, and to add insult to injury, he can't keep up with Conor's inside game, getting faked out over and over. In the fourth quarter, their lead vanished, and, in desperation, they try to press. Sorry, we got too good of ball handlers, too athletic, and with the smell of blood, our attack just becomes more ferocious. With our fans cheering encouragement, we finish strong and notch up our second win.

One more victory and we make it to Sunday. But it won't be easy, next up is the host team, Ames. We don't play until four so we decide to hit a nearby restaurant to rehydrate and maybe a snack, something light. Our mood is positive as we relax at our tables. Even the parents are ebullient. As I'm talking with them, I notice Mike, one of our feistiest players, begin with a banana split and next proceed to an extra-large chocolate Sunday. "Mike," I said. "Light! Do you plan on waddling through the next game?"

"Don't worry, Doc. This is how I eat." I glanced over at his mother who just shrugged her shoulders. So many things can go wrong with a team. That's why it's hard to be a coach. Game plan is nothing. It's all those 'intangibles. '

For the Ames game, we were tired. We had left Cedar Falls at 7 a.m. and this was to be our third tough game today. They were the home team, and had sixteen players on their roster. Doubt if we can wear them out. They didn't look too big so I decided to just play half court ball with them and try to pound it inside. Ryan hit back to back three's to open the game, but then we hit a dry spell. Mike seemed to be clutching his stomach a lot, and Conor traveled twice down low. These refs aren't used to his modified Kevin McHale footwork, I thought, as we fell behind. Everyone seemed to be trying to force things instead of letting the game flow. Ugly would be a charitable adjective for our play the rest of the first half. Now, even I was worried as we entered the locker room down seventeen points. How many times can a team go to the well and come up with a bucket full of miracles? Worse, I didn't have any brilliant ideas. Strangely, the guys didn't seem as depressed as I was, even joking around as we sat there. "Did anyone notice the score," I began. "We're in deep doo-doo."

Danny spoke up, "We're always behind at half, Coach. We still got lots left. These guys aren't that good."

"OKAY, we got a lot to make up. Full court heat, no fouls, and take every open shot you get. Crash the boards hard as you can. Surprise me, guys!'

Just to shake things up a little, I started the second five, instructing them to crank it up full bore. True to form, they played as if possessed, diving for loose balls, in your face "D," and rebounding as if their lives depended on snaring the elusive orb. Gradually rotating in our usual starters, our inspirational effort continued and the deficit narrowed. Ames wasn't able to sub as much as their talent level dropped off after seven or eight players. Early in the fourth, it seemed they were letting self-doubt enter into their minds. Tentative shots and more frequent fouls began to show up. With four minutes left, we were within 5 and they called time. "Crunch time, Fellas. We're looking good, and they're gettin' scared. Now's the time for the dagger. Let's go with Shane, Mike, Matt, Conor, and Ryan. Conor, you're up front on the press. Shane you're back. Take some chances, we need a few steals. You other guys be sure to rotate back. You probably have to hack on wide open layups. They might miss their free throws."

Conor with the left reverse. Shane with the clean pick. Ryan with the good look from the corner. Swish! Ames tried desperately to stem the tide but Matt with the slashing layup and Mike to the right kissing glass perfectly, and they were left with purposely fouling. Four made free throws and our spread delay game and it was over, Cedar Falls 72, Ames 67. "Shake hands, guys. Great game!"

Where do they get the energy? Seems like they always have the little extra. Whatever it takes. Now as I looked over at them. Most were lying on bleachers, or sitting like droopy dachshunds. So unselfish, they had been. Just the game of basketball, giving it all. Proud parents assisted their exhausted warriors out to waiting autos for the two hour trip home. Then, in the morn, a return engagement for the final four.

Over the next twelve hours, although I 'made rounds' twice and answered phone calls about constipation in the elderly, and even slept a little, my thoughts and dreams were hoops, scenarios, strategies. It wasn't just that I was engaged and having fun, I was responsible for providing the biggest dopamine surge possible for everyone involved, kids, families, friends, a kind of collective epiphany.

Two inches of powdery snow had fallen during the night purifying our way. There's a part of the route that passes through the town of Albion, a few houses and a gas station, then curves over a river and down into a beautiful wooded area. On this day, as we passed, the sun poked through directly behind to bless us with a particularly pristine moment before pointing us west on a thirty mile straight shot of blacktop crossing a steady visual diet of Iowa farms. About a mile outside of Ames, I noted a solitary hawk, perched in a lonesome lifeless tree just off the path. Locking our passage in a scrutinizing stare, the proud raptor nodded ever so slightly as if to say, "So this is the team."

As we entered the gym, everyone's pulse rose appropriately. Anticipation is second only to realization. In the locker room, I announced to the kids that we would be wearing white for this game. "But Doc, we're always black," blurted Danny, a dejected look on his face. "You expect us to play good in white?"

"You're just going to have to trust me on this one." They all switched their jerseys. What distinguished our kids was that none of them were bad at all, yet within the context of the game of basketball, they gave no quarter, didn't back off an inch. They saw themselves in black! A lot of kids go for 23. Not ours. First was 13, then 00. Do you know what it can do to another team to go up against such a group of nice boys, who proceed to pick your pocket, reject your shot, and power past you to the hole, all while smiling politely? That's the way we were. That's how we learned to play.

Urbandale is a rich suburb of Des Moines, beautiful school, great facilities, and clones of preppy kids looking for strokes, both on and off the basketball court, but never getting enough. Their center was 6'9". While our team was warming up, I saw him sitting on the bleachers, messing with his shoes. I walked over and sat beside him. "Say, aren't you that big center for Urbandale everybody's talking about?"

"Ya, I'm probably the best player in the metro area."

"Gee, how tall are you?"

"Almost 6' 10". I'm working on my 360 jam. I'll be starting varsity next year for sure."

"Who are you guys playin' today?

"I don't know, Cedar something. Doesn't matter, they're no good."

Walking back to the bench, I realized he didn't even know who I was. Impressive ego though. Excellent material for a pre-game speech.

As the horn sounded, I scanned the crowd and noticed that Mike's sister and her friend had put off heading back to college just so they could be at the game. They said it was the most exciting thing they'd been to in years. Problem was they brought new vehemence to our support network bordering on obnoxious. Nothing intentional, they just had lots of energy. I didn't want anything to detract from our total package, the milieu, the ambiance allowing what could happen to actually take place.

Opening tip went to Urbandale and they came down and ran what looked like a flex offense. Great, I thought, that's so predictable we'll be able to rip it to shreds. They hit a jump shot and we came right back with little bank by Shane and the game was on. Actually we were just messing around with our half-court defense, and as usual, our offense sputtered, and we fell behind a little as the first half progressed. I was busy subbing and studying their personnel for weaknesses feeling that I wouldn't know what to do if we weren't down at least ten at half.

They did have one player who did have some superior skills. About 6'2" and very athletic, he was getting most of their points. What showed most, though, was his attitude. Fancy spin moves when he didn't need to, pouting when he missed or didn't get a call, swaggering in self-aggrandizement when he scored, it added up to a person who needed to be taught a special lesson. It happened late in the second quarter. Guarded by Roland, the most unassuming person you would ever want to meet, he had learned a lesson on the previous trip down the floor as Roland tipped one of his patented curling finger roles, but he hadn't learned it nearly well enough. Taking the ball to the outside and seeing a little breathing room, he thought it would be a good time to exhibit his versatility with the long range jumper. Swat! Instead of going towards the hoop, the ball, deflected in midflight, went straight up in the air about ten feet, having been tipped by Roland as he soared past carefully avoiding any foul. Still, he didn't learn. Having the ball fall serendipitously back into his hands, seeing an open lane to the hole, and realizing that Roland was recovering out near mid court, our man decides to waltz in for the layup. Roland, however, being a robot player, not encumbered by a need to celebrate the good play, was immediately back on track, closing quickly from behind. Just as Mr. I am great peaked his jump to release at the rim, our knight of the round table arrived to send the ball astray again, this time off the glass with authority. After a testy battle for the carom, the cooperative sphere reappears, once again, in the hands of the spankee. This is where all logic is defied. The guy is uneducable. Seeing only Ryan, about 5'6" tall, near him, he elevates to shoot again. Roland, stepping out of the timber, and from behind Ryan, unfolds his Excalibur with exquisite timing, and not just blocks the offering, but snares it himself in a cradle, a la lacrosse, and dribbles nonchalantly to a clearing.

At half-time, we were down twelve, but I turned to Roland and said, "No matter what else, Roland, that was the best I've seen. Three posters in one posesssion. That guy was dissed, shattered, pulverized, and utterly humiliated. I don't see how he can even show for the second half."

We had to come back with the press. What's new? Their big guy screwed up royally, couldn't handle the ball a lick, almost no skills actually, unless you want to count hyperbolic ego. Scott came in for us and hit a three, then two free throws, then a fantastic running jump hook with the left, no less. The fourth quarter saw another team decompensate, Cedar Falls suddenly able to get easy layups, open looks, and charity attempts. It had become our script, fall behind, plug away, work, work, get a spark, then ignite for the kill, leaving a trail of devastation in our wake. Now only one to go. But, oh, that one.

Eby's had dominated our age group for the last few years. Made up of the putative best players from the city of Cedar Rapids, second largest in Iowa with 130,000 people and five class 4A high schools, these handpicked kids had access to a gym any time, played in tournaments all over the Midwest, and were well coached. We had tasted the sting of their lash way too many times, never able to challenge enough to earn even a modicum of respect. Like so many other "good" teams, they wore their cockiness on their lapels, and a particularly obnoxious brand it was. They were like a loaded new car, three talented 6'5" to 6'6" athletes up front, a bevy of gunnin' greyhound guards, and a bench that could win most tournaments by themselves.

We, on the other hand, were nobody. We'd never won a tournament. We didn't have any stars. Just a bunch of mangy junk yard dogs scramblin' for a place to chew on a bone. But I will say this; we had been doing a lot of growing up lately, even in the last twenty-four hours. This pack of hyenas was now learning to charge out of the thicket in the second half, and not let up until satiated.

In the dressing room, thirty minutes before game time, "You guys havin' fun yet? One more hill to climb. It's true, the last two times we played this team, we were crucified, died, and were buried. But you all know what happened on the third day. Think of it like in the "King Kong" movie. There he was lying at the bottom of the Empire State Building. But, wait, his heart is still beating, louder and louder. Only this time, his eyes twitch, he gets up, shatters windows with a yell, beats his chest, and does his thing, vanquishing anything in his path. That's you guys, all heart, never say die. Only I want you to skip the yell part. Eby's will furnish all the blabbin'. You know what crybabies they are. The refs will naturally favor us. Just keep your choir boy faces on no matter what. Give it everything you got, of course, but say nothing. Conor, you start on the bald guy, Hans. He's so volatile anything could happen. Show him a healthy dose of in your face 'D' and let's see how he reacts. Aaron, you got McCullagh. In his face on the turn around. Shane, go with Jones. Main thing is keep him from driving, and block out on every shot. Matt, take Zidicker, and Mike, you guard Sains, force him left. They're good. No doubt about it, but who knows, have fun, play hard, a break here, break there, maybe they stumble."

Soon we were on the main court, last game of the tournament, out of 32 teams, ready to play, all others watching. I felt a certain electricity in the jumble of small talk behind me as I watched the kids follow their routine warm-up, layups right, left, middle, pull up jumpers, a flurry of 3's, and then free throws. The horn signaled the time of truth, but first, something special: each starter introduced over the loudspeaker individually, a nice touch. All present, hands atingle, ears and eyes alert and scanning, helplessly thinking those last second hopes and fears, waiting as he in stripes strides forth to center court. Shaking hands with my counterpart, I return for one deep breath before the opening jump enjoins the battle.

From the beginning, it is as if our play was like a well-oiled machine. The first game must have been the perfect prelude. Loose, yet effective, we unselfishly do our thing and nearly all of it worked to perfection. Shots are fallin', passes crisp, defense solid. I didn't like it a bit. Too easy. That's not our script. You think a powerhouse like Eby's is going to fall over and die. Never! Trouble is, everyone I put in is deliverin' the goods. Eight 3's already in the first half! Meanwhile, our opponents are showing more and more frustration. With two minutes to go in the half, Hans just misses Conor with a vicious elbow. Tweet! His second "T" sends him to an early sprinkle. A couple of minutes earlier he had picked up his first trying to pop the ball with a spike to the floor, succeeding only in sending it back up towards the rafters and giving us two free throws plus possession. During a time out, I couldn't help saying, "Way to go Conor, thought it would take a little longer to get to him." Still, to go into half-time up nine was scary. We'd never been there before. I'd come to prefer being down at least ten at half. How these kids would react, nobody knows.

I made a silly attempt to get the kids to pretend they were down nine, not up. It didn't sell. We came out for the second ebullient. I imagine Eby's half time talk had to have had a generous dosage of bleeps, sarcastic cynicism, and pejorative persuasion. That too, hadn't sold. They were out there screwin' around, figuring they could turn it up at will and whip our behinds.

They did succeed in mounting at least a mini charge. When Jones hit a three and Sains followed it with a steal turned effortlessly into a coast to coast jam, I signaled for a time out. "C'mon guys. This is our day. Let's not get tentative out there. That's not what got us here. We're the ones hitting our shots, so let's be gunning 'em up. They're off their game. Solid 'D' and no more uncontested dunks."

What followed was an amazing stretch of basketball. Roland and Ryan with back to back trifectas, Shane with a put back, Aaron with a beautiful hook shot plus one, and then Conor on an intercepted wing pass streaking down court, only Sains to beat just beneath the dotted line. Instead of angling to one side or the other, Conor freezes him by heading directly at his poised form, like Jim Brown on Butkus. Then, nailing him to the floor with a planted right foot followed by a counterclockwise spin move that would have done Magic proud, he finishes with a feathery little kiss off glass from the right side of the lane. Sains still hadn't moved as their coach yelled for time, the crowd on their feet in frenzied approval. "Hey, don't change one thing. It might get ugly any time now. I'm not sure they can handle this kind of medicine. Remember, it's basketball all the way, even if they try to turn it into football."

With a thirteen point lead, I felt safe. Our consistent play continued into the fourth quarter, and they weren't good at pressing. When they went to the three point attack, we were in their faces. Then it was the frantic foul parade. We countered with cool heads and converted gift shots. Finally, when Scott hit a twelve foot bank with three minutes left, putting us up fourteen, their coach cleared his bench. As the final seconds ticked off, I couldn't have felt more proud of what these kids had accomplished. Every family member there was the same, savoring each moment. Then, out on the floor with the microphone, the tournament director began, "Now for the awards. In second place, 'A' division, from Cedar Rapids, Eby's." We clapped politely as they went out to receive their medals. Somehow second out of all those teams didn't do much for them. It wasn't that they had played badly. We just played better.

"And the champions..." Cheers and applause already mounting. "...Of this year's Happy Joe's tournament..." Noise becoming tumultuous. "The fine squad from Cedar Falls!" Noise now deafening. You can't hold back feeling absolutely exhilarated in such a situation. We all got our medals, oblivious of the multiple flashes, regaling in the moment. As the noise died down, the announcer began again, "Ladies and gentlemen, can I have your attention, please? We now have the presentation of the sportsmanship award." I had forgotten all about this part. It usually went to a team who hadn't performed that well but didn't pout about it. "This award goes to the team that best exemplifies the spirit of friendly competition and demonstrates a healthy respect for the great game of basketball. This year's winner is...Cedar Falls!" Damn! What next, a winning Lotto ticket? Please, someone let some air out of the balloon.

Reflecting on it, which I did, if you win both the tournament and the sportsmanship award, you gotta be doing something right. I swear I was on clouds for a full two weeks. Sex can't do that for you. Not many things in life can. I dreamed about it, woke up thinking about it, relived it in my mind in between patients, and talked about it to whoever would listen. And I was just the coach, never even laced on a sneaker. Probably overkill, but it couldn't be helped. A footnote to the whole thing came several days later when the director of our AAU program, informed me that Eby's had called to pull out of our upcoming Cedar Falls tournament, citing a "scheduling conflict."

Do you ever get the ominous feeling that if things are going really well, an impending disaster can't be far off? Maybe even cataclysmic? Still, the deep voice on the line, at three in the morning, caught me off guard. "Dr. Murphy, this is Officer Williams with the Cedar Falls Police Department. You'd better come down to your office. There's been a break in." Our DEA mandated security system had a direct link to the CFPD. The motion detector in the room where we stored narcotics was so sensitive that one night a helium filled balloon left inadvertently on a desk there, set the thing off as the air conditioning came on. We were only a block from the police station, and although I'm sure they had ambivalent feelings about the work we did, they had always responded promptly when the need arose. I couldn't imagine someone getting in and doing much damage without the police jumping all over them.

Quickly, I threw on some clothes and drove down, only a five minute trip. I found the policemen in the parking lot adjacent to the office, flashlights directed towards a gaping defect, the size of a dog house door, in the last glass block window on that side of the building. The beam reflected off the razor sharp jagged edges. Real precision work. Some desperate fool had used a concrete block to smash his way into my methadone stash paying no cash. Only one minor mistake: he broke into the wrong room. Cautiously I unlocked the front door, politely allowing them to enter first. Turning the lights on, I was horrified to see, not only how extensively trashed the place was, but how significant amounts of blood covered nearly everything as the interior designer executed his touch up. There was even blood dripped down into the computer keyboards. Bloody bloke must have thought he could break the security code through the computer. Anyway, the secure room had never been entered. By then two more of my staff had arrived and, a quick inventory revealed that we were missing a few minor tranquilizers, and, much more disturbing, a prepared individual bottle of methadone that had been left in the refrigerator. What concerned me was that this particular bottle contained a double dose of medication because of the exceptionally rapid metabolic rate of that patient. To someone else, especially a methadone naive person, such an amount could be very dangerous.

The cleanup was bad enough, but worse, much worse, beyond imagination, were the subsequent investigations and reports by regulatory agencies. You'd have thought Ft Knox had been cracked, or the Pentagon. Still, all of this was nothing compared to the shock I felt two days later when I was shown the obituary notice in the local paper. One of my patients, who, in fact had been on methadone until, against my advice several months earlier, had dropped off the program. I had just seen him about a week before the break in. He had been going to the V.A. Hospital in Iowa City, and visiting several other providers to keep himself well medicated, mostly minor tranqs as far as I knew. I had pleaded with him to get back on track, but I don't think his mind was working well enough at the time to understand what I was trying to tell him. They found him cold in his small room in the basement of a house. I understood only too well what a double dose could have done to this guy.

After noon ball that day, I discretely slipped off to a side corridor at the PEC and dialed the coroner, whom I had gotten to know quite well over the years. "Hi, this is Dan Murphy. I have a favor to ask. Anything exciting on the thirty-nine-year-old they found night before last? He was my patient."

"Not really. Preliminary autopsy just came through. Looks like a massive coronary."

"No toxicology yet?"

"No, that will be at least another day, longer for what we sent off."

"Could you let me know if he scores out big on either opiates or minor tranquilizers?"

"Sure, Dan."

"I'll see you at the meeting next week. I really appreciate it."

"Glad to be of help."

"Oh, one more thing. Any fresh cuts or slashes on the arms?"

"Nope. That would have stood out."

"Okay, thanks again."

Geez, I thought, hanging up the phone, sometimes this line of work can be so stressful. One thing I had learned, however, through experience, was that the local authorities don't put much effort into these matters. Once, a patient of mine, shared methadone, along with several other substances, with one of her old boyfriends just released from prison, then discovered him dead in her bed the next morning. Absolutely nothing came of it. Just one less low life to worry about. Good riddance.

Bad P.R. is definitely not needed for methadone programs. They come with two strikes already on them the day they open. It's as if a shroud comes over someone's face when they first tie another human being to a methadone program. Patient or staff, it doesn't matter. The look would be tolerable were it not accompanied, inevitably by an attitude of disdain. What people don't realize, or maybe think doesn't matter, is that active heroin addiction, besides, by its very nature, implying a nonstop daily crime wave, also carries up to a 10% annual mortality rate. Methadone both stops the crime and cuts the mortality figure to well under 1%. Few, if any, treatments of a medical condition have such a profound effect on prognosis. Every addict being human, there's no question on how a service professional should react. As for others with the human condition, at the risk of being preachy, your commonality far outweighs any perceived differences.

What is so taxing is trying to anticipate every possible scenario and be ready to react. Who can you talk to and how might certain things play out? Could we be shut down? Are criminal charges in any way possible? You never know in these things. You try to be cautious, preempt what you can, cover yourself within reason, and not lose your focus on the main reason you're here: to serve the best you can, all those in need.

Nothing more happened this time. Patient load continued to rise. Eighty, 90, 100, 120! These are heroin addicts in Iowa! For a long time I kept thinking that this had to be it. There aren't that many people in this measly state. Now, I just accept that the marketers are sophisticated enough to continuously grind out new victims.

Take Mia for instance. Age twenty-four, grew up in small town Iowa, graduated with honors from an excellent private college, working at a good job in the media. By chance, she was thrown in socially with a group who had begun to dabble with heroin. After resisting repeatedly, one fatal night, for a combination of reasons being particularly vulnerable, she succumbed to the free offer. Then again. Soon her car was being used for runs to Chicago, uncut heroin always left in the glove compartment. Within a month, she was buying an additional $100.00 worth per day. Hooked, trapped, desperate, she came to us. We can help her. But it won't be easy. The trips to Cedar Falls, rules, payments, the pressure of keeping it secret or of facing the near certain negativity if facing it openly, all mitigate against success. Bottom line being she hasn't paid enough price yet, been low enough for long enough, to be able to face the rigors of long term commitment to what would be the most hopeful course of treatment. We'll try our best to work through these things, but most likely she'll drop off, relapse, and reappear several times before we can convince her to do it right. Each time, of course, puts her health in jeopardy; HIV, hepatitis, overdose exacting their toll.

What's wrong with her, you say? The answer is, nothing! The stuff is around. People will use. A certain percentage of us are predisposed genetically, but we don't know which ones. A look at family history may be somewhat predictive, but as with alcohol, cigarettes, tranquilizers, all it takes is exposure in a susceptible one and Pavlov takes over. First contact could be with a prescription opiate. Doesn't matter. Then it's chase the dopamine surge, and wait for the production sites for natural endorphins to atrophy leaving you with an all-consuming beckon shading your every conscious moment for the rest of your life. Not one's worst enemy should be so cursed.

The Cedar Falls tournament was a whole new experience for our team. I saw no one in the field that I thought should be able to challenge us. Not knowing how the kids would react to being favorites, I was pleased to see them come out strong, and breeze through the first day, winning their pool quite readily. Sunday, in the semi's, we sputtered temporarily against a good Parkersburg team, but recovered sufficiently to win by ten. So, once again it was us in the finals on the main floor, for the last game of the day. Facing us was Linn-Mar, a big team with several excellent outside shooters.

The game started off at a slow pace, definitely not to our advantage. One guy in particular for Linn-Mar was on fire, knocking down 3's all over the place. Still, knowing our team the way I did, I continued to rotate everyone in and out, encouraging each player to go hard and do their best. At half-time we were down eight. During the intermission, Tommy, a friend who had been helping me with the team, but had missed the Ames tournament, pulled me aside and, with a look of concern, asked, "Looks grim, doesn't it? What's the strategy?"

"Tommy," I said, with a confident smile. "You missed Ames. There is absolutely no way we can lose this game."

"How's that, Doc?"

"They don't have the athletes. At any time, we go with our five best assault troopers putting on full court heat, and they crumble. I just want to give as many minutes as I can to the other guys."

"Don't wait to long."

"Relax. Everything is under control."

Midway through the third, still down eight, we went to our 1-3-1 trapping press, and what was inevitable, began to happen almost immediately. Soon we were up enough that other kids got to go back in. Linn-Mar rallied with a few clutch shots but never seriously challenged. Once again we were champions! It was good, especially because we were at home, but, like with scoring subsequent to that first hit of dope, it didn't come close to the rush of the Ames epiphany.

Continuing on a roll, the following weekends saw us beat Denver, trounce the Boys Club, and win the New Hamton Invitational. All that was left was the state AAU tournament beginning with the regionals. For this affair, nearly every team was an all-star group or at least had added two or three good players from the surrounding area. I had thought about it in the past, especially adding a good inside guy, but because we had such a close knit group, and more importantly, because what made us good was the way we had learned to play full court team defense together, I had never become convinced that it would help us, not to mention that the kids were never too hot on the idea.

So it was, on a blustery Saturday in March, we headed East on highway 20, about 80 miles, to the town of Dyersville, famous for the "Field of Dreams", seeking to fulfill our own magical wishes. First up was Monticello. This was a town I had barely heard of, invariably meaning they couldn't be that good, and more pertinently, watching them warm up, I could see that they didn't have much talent. We tried as best we could to not embarrass them but, despite our best efforts, still won by twenty.

Next, an hour later was Waterloo West, who had only one good player, and he had an off-day. Four quarters later, we were 2-0, needing only one more "W" to return the next day. That game was to be against a Cedar Rapids bunch, not the Eby's players but mostly kids from Washington High, with a few additions from around town.

With several hours free, I took some of our players and toured Dyersville. Most of the local population was of Luxemburger ancestry. In fact many settlers in my home town of Alton, had come from here first before migrating further West in covered wagons. Stopping to visit the beautiful catholic basilica downtown, I was impressed with both how similar it was to St. Mary's where I had spent so much of my youth, and how many of the surnames appearing on the magnificent stained glass windows, were identical to those of the people I had grown up with; Konz, Mousel, Lichtenburg, Delperdang. Adequately diverted, I drove the boys back to the venue, spouting tales about the "good old days," exaggerating as much as I thought I could get away with.

The game was an ugly affair, but luckily they matched our ineptitude keeping us within striking range. Towards the end of the game, our press took hold and we surged ahead. Conor, Shane, and Matt then proceeded to foul out and it was only a three pointer by Jon at the end of regulation that tied the score and sent us to O.T. In the extra period, Ryan took a charge, Mike stole one and went coast to coast, and Danny drained the big free throws as we squeaked out a victory.

The trip home was so much more enjoyable this way, kids laughing, joking and singing. I had just enough time to go to the hospital, sleep, go to the hospital again, and meet at the high school to head back to Dyersville.

Whisps of snow flew across our way as we tried to put ourselves in the proper frame of mind for the days task. I couldn't help thinking, just a little, of going on to state and, who knows, maybe even nationals. Glancing off to the left, I saw the clustered old solid brick buildings set in an oak grove, Mental Health Institute. Suddenly I could think only of the upcoming game. Facing us would be the host school, Dyersville Beckman, with the addition of the best players from the surrounding small communities. I honestly knew nothing about them other than the fact that they hadn't lost a game yet. On the roster they had a 6'6' and a 6'5' guy but much more important would be if they had ball handlers, quickness. Even then they can't have had challenging experience, playing in these one horse towns, and stars usually don't easily become role players so chemistry isn't right.

Following our usual strategy, we led most of the way but their 6'5' guy was also wide and strong. He did a great job around the hoop and even into the fourth quarter they were within ten points. Using our delay for the last three minutes, the margin never narrowed and, once again, we were in a weekend final.

To challenge us for the right to advance to Des Moines, was Waverly. More interesting to me was that their coach was none other than Randy Kraayenbrink. Not only did we go back a long ways, but he definitely knew basketball and was doing an excellent job motivating his team, consistently winning even though not loaded with exceptional talent. We had a nice chat before the game, but I knew that he wanted to win this one just as much as I did.

As the game opened, just looking at personnel, it seemed to me that we should be in good position, but Randy was the X-factor. Could he be so much more knowledgeable about the game that he could be the difference? I thought not. Gees, I had played, seen, and coached so much basketball that I didn't think anything could surprise me. True, most of the coaches I went against weren't that adept, but during the first quarter, I could see that their team wasn't intimidated and executed their game plan well. A three at the buzzer gave them a six point lead. "No sweat, guys. You can see who their shooters are. Be sure on picks that those two are covered, and watch for the backside cut. You got to rotate to protect the hoop. We're in good shape. They can't stay with us for a whole game."

Second quarter was see-saw, but even though we were down five going into the locker room, we hadn't even showed our main weapon yet. "Doc, let's press," said Ryan.

"Ya, let's pressure 'em."

"Ya!"

"Right."

"Hold your horses, Fellas. I don't want to give it away too early. They got a good coach and he might think of a way to break it. Let's see if we can do it with good old straight up man to man half court. We always got it if we need it."

Second half began with them scoring two quick hoops. Still, I hesitated, but then, knowing that the kids were literally itching to be unleashed, I signaled "the press" for the next time down. Two successive turnovers and Randy called time. From then on they kept the ball in the middle of the floor, spaced their players evenly, and broke to open areas, towards the ball whenever possible. As I had thought, this wasn't going to be so simple. Our traps weren't nearly as effective as usual, but we had succeeded in jacking up the intensity level, where our superior athleticism could show. Gradually, we closed the gap and with two to go in the fourth we were within three points. "Time!" I yelled.

"Aaron, go in for Shane. The press is off. Pick them up at the ten second line and extend the defense in the half court. We still have to force the action as long as we're down. Aaron, you've got to look like you need the ball bad. Demand it to keep your man honest. But I want you on the opposite side from Conor, and stay about 12 feet out. Ryan, Mike, go to Conor down low. No way that guy can stop him inside." I know they were surprised. We always finished close games with our quickest guys. Aaron was 6'5" and, although he ran the floor well, he wasn't quick enough to be effective on the press. What I was looking for was a way to keep their one taller guy away from Conor. They did have a 6'4" player who conceivably could have challenged Conor down low, so I hoped Aaron could draw him away. I hated to call my son's number too often because he thought people might think it was because he was family. There was no doubt in my mind that every player and every parent knew that Conor was our high percentage play. Randy, on the other hand, didn't know our personnel well, and in this game, Conor hadn't shown his stuff much.

First possession down, there's Aaron at the elbow both arms out begging for the ball. Sure enough the big guy is on him tight. Everyone else is clear and Conor goes low on the right block. Ryan flips him the ball, up fake, step through, left reverse, two. They miss and we're at it again. Low to Conor, dribble left, then spin back right, power move and up, hack, whistle, reload in air and off glass for two, and he sinks the free throw for a two point lead. They get fouled but convert only one of two. This time they front Conor, but it's very difficult for a 6' guy to front a 6'2" man. Ali-oop, perfect. Point blank bank, two more. With 20 seconds left they hit a 15 ft. "J" to close to within a point. We come down and they're still fronting but on the pass back side help is coming as Aaron's man left him. Aaron does what he's supposed to and runs to the open spot 4 feet from the front of the rim. Conor soars high to grab the pass, sees Aaron wide and dishes in the air to him. In the confusion both defenders turn to cover Aaron who quickly drops it back to Conor who has space enough to grab and bank it in with one motion. Two, one, bzzz. Game over!

Going through the line, I congratulated Randy as I shook his hand. "Great job, Randy. You really got these kids playing well."

He smiled politely and answered, "Good luck in Des Moines, Doc." Very classy but I know he was frustrated and still wasn't sure what had happened.

On the ride home, I wondered just how good these kids were getting to be. They didn't have overwhelming talent, physically, but playing against them must have been like facing five wolverines. Maybe that's a talent too. As we passed the mental institute, I thought, not yet, maybe someday, but not today.

A message was waiting for me at the hospital when I called in after dropping everyone off. Call Julie C., very important. Earlier that year I had been nominated by Paul Rider to the Cedar Falls Human Rights Commission and was subsequently appointed by the mayor. Now I was in the middle of investigating a case of alleged sexual discrimination. I couldn't believe the number of complaints we received from women about how they were treated in the work place. Some of the situations were subtle, but many were all too blatant. I liked going to the workplace to check things out, and even more interesting was going to people's residences to do interviews.

On one occasion I went to Waterloo to question a Mexican-American co-worker who had witnessed events reported by a complainant. She met me at the door to her apartment and invited me in. I was hoping she would be alone since we had to discuss delicate confidential matters. Forget that, there must have been 15 people in the small apartment. At first I thought there must be a party going on but as I observed more closely it became clear that they all lived here. Children playing, people cooking, some eating, one woman ironing, radio blaring on one side of the room, TV on the other. Spanish spoken by all. Undocumented, no doubt. I had seen this kind of thing in California but hadn't realized that it was happening in Iowa too. Politely asking two people to move, she motioned for me to sit beside her on the couch and we conducted business in the midst of "life," the way all things are done for them, and probably most of the world.

Another time I went to the absolute "worst" section of town for an interview, an area well known for drugs and prostitution. The woman told me she might be several minutes late, and said that it would be better if I waited for her to pull up in her car before I went up to the house. So for about ten minutes I circled the block waiting. Soon I had a squad car following me. I could just hear the radio exchange: "We got a red Chevy, license number 2BAD4U."

"That's Daniel J. Murphy, Cedar Falls, a physician no less."

"Oh ya, he's the methadone guy. Probably gettin' a little on the side. Should have better taste! We'll watch him close."

The car I'd been waiting for pulled up, I did my interview, and left. Nothing happened.

Calling Julie, she said we had to meet so I told her to come to my office. During our initial talk, she had told me how her boss had started with sexual comments about her anatomy from the first week she had begun work. Slowly it had progressed until the previous week he flat out told her that to keep her job she had to "put out." She quit and came to us. Now, she informed me, she had talked to one of the other women who worked there, and she was willing to talk to me about other similar instances. Great! Now we had quid pro quo and corroborating evidence. "Probable cause" seemed likely and I was already thinking of recommending a sizable monetary settlement. The good thing was that I didn't have the burden of "beyond a reasonable doubt," having only to convince myself of what was likely. Either party could always opt for a district court appeal. I looked at it like being a doctor; you did your best and then decide and live with it. Bottom line was society mandated our existence, it was law. To be honest, people don't use it enough; discrimination is rampant and makes many lives much more difficult.

By scrambling, I was able to get the high school gym one night and the UNI gym another for two good practice sessions that week. We were as ready as we could be for state. One serious problem surfaced when the pairings came out showing us playing our first game at 9:00 a.m. Saturday. Because of other commitments, we couldn't go down Friday night and consequently 6:00 a.m. Saturday found us gathering at the high school for the two hour trip to Des Moines. Near Marshalltown snow began to fall and we were lucky to even make it to our destination. As it was we were late and arrived barely fifteen minutes before game time.

All we had time for was a few layups. Our opponent, a Des Moines team, looked fresh and crisp, while we appeared lethargic and bedraggled. Almost immediately the buzzer sounded and we were huddled for final instructions. Digging deep for something inspirational I came up with, "Ryan, tie your shoe. Mike, you got your jersey on backwards. Conor, tuck it in. Basketball, Guys, basketball!" Pointing them towards mid court, I could only hope instinct might take over, or we were in deep trouble.

Our play early bordered on ridiculous. Forget jump shots, we couldn't make layups. Poor decisions, bad passes, sloppy defense, you name it and we took it to a new low. Down five at the end of the first quarter, expanded to down twelve by half no matter whom I put in. I couldn't blame the kids, most of them usually slept until noon on Saturday. Conor, I know, would even get nauseated if he didn't get enough sleep. We talked about pressing for the second half but their eyes still looked glazed and I was feeling more and more like Custer. Half way through the third we went down fifteen and began pressing, and although we showed some signs of life, we were still largely ineffective, and two quick hoops at the end of the third gave them a humungous 17 point bulge. I didn't have much to say figuring it was pretty much a lost cause, and when their point guard opened up the fourth with a three, I was ready to begin putting things into my bag. Down twenty with a little over seven and a half minutes to go made the Alamo seem like good odds. Obviously, the game was over; the Lakers couldn't pull this one out; just kiss it off and move on; sometimes life deals you a bum hand, etc., etc.

This is where all previous bets were swept off the table, reality got seriously challenged, chains fell free, a veil was lifted. I can't say if it was Tinkerbell with the little stars, leprechauns, a time warp, or just a plain old miracle, but somehow we began to play basketball. I mean our kind of ball, taken to the nth degree. It started with Ryan making a steal and instead of taking it all the way for the layup. He pulled up for a three and swished it. Then Conor with a pick off the inbound and a quick bank shot. Shane followed with a gutsy burst of speed on a long pass, barely intercepting the ball at the last moment, throwing a quick pass to Danny up court for a three. You guessed it, nothing but silk. They tried to regain composure, but like when you're caught in a stampede of bison, there's nowhere to turn. They managed a few baskets but our momentum grew like a raging forest fire. Steals, three's, layups, free throws, all in dazzling flurries, and when Ryan drained a twenty footer, I looked up and saw the score tied with nine seconds to go. During a time out I said, "Okay. guys, one more steal. Challenge everything but don't foul unless it's a layup. If we get it back, call time."

They inbounded to half court and thought they had an advantage, two on one, so pushed it for the layup. Somehow, Matt put on a burst of speed and arrived just in time to, not only block the shot cleanly, but send it off their guy's leg and out of bounds. Our ball, five seconds to go! "This is it fella's. Mike, take it in bounds. Matt, start away. Conor set a pick for him coming to the ball and then pivot. Mike, hit one of them. Ryan and Shane, be ready to set screens for them turning up court. Let's try to get a shot from as close in as we can get."

Fate! Oh, fate! Can it be snatched away at the last moment? What does it mean? Mighty Casey swings... Somehow, despite planning, one of their guys stepped in front of Matt and stole the ball. One pass to their big guy, turn and fade from about eight, Conor and Shane both in his face, ball in the air, banks, rattles, and goes into the hoop at the buzzer. No! No! I thought, this can't be!

We shook hands and went to the locker room, shell shocked but still having pulses. Collecting myself, I sat them down and said, "We may have lost that game, but I can honestly say that I have never seen anything like the display you guys put on in the fourth quarter. Down twenty. Do you realize how deep a hole that is? Impossible. But you taught me something, we're never out of a game, never! To make up that many points in under a quarter is, plain and simple, unbelievable, amazing, and you can be proud of it for the rest of your lives."

That was it. Despite winning the rest of our games that day, we came in second in our pool and failed to advance to the final four the next day. Our year was over. We had come a long ways, and were beginning to have a state wide rep, a moderate amount of respect. I would say that we were now, not a great team, but definitely a very good one.

As a coach, I got little credit. Not that I needed any; that's not what it's all about. The kids loved what we were doing, and their parents never failed to tell me how exciting we were to watch, but coaches – real basketball coaches – and I knew lots of them from junior high up through college, saw our play as jungle ball, out of control, helter-skelter, horribly unorganized. At the bottom of most of it was our free flowing offense. Once I overheard two of our kids talking. One asked, "Who do you think would win, our school team or our AAU team?"

The other answered, "AAU, for sure, but it's not a fair match."

"How come?"

"'Cause the school team has to run plays!" Amen.

That's not entirely fair. A perfectly designed and executed play should result in a high percentage opportunity. But what if it's up against a perfectly designed and executed defense? Much too theoretical. Basketball is a game of action and reaction, confidence and emotion, finding advantageous match ups and good decision making.

In my medical practice it was much the same. I got little respect within the profession. I was too unconventional.

"Writes everything generic."

"No drug reps allowed in his office."
"Just drug addicts."
"Weird patients."
"Even makes home visits."

In the "weird patient" circles, I had a good name. My staff knew from the get go that I was a sucker for the underdog, went out of my way for the mission impossible types, the disenfranchised, was constantly on the edge with committees, regulatory agencies, hospitals, insurances, and the establishment community, nearly always because of patient advocacy in one way or another. A significant part of my practice was made up of dysfunctional marginal elements of society.

One woman who lived very close to my office called desperately begging for a home visit. I knew immediately it would be complicated when she met me at the door completely naked. Her problem turned out to be bipolar mental illness self-medicated by repeated ingestion of large quantities of rubbing alcohol leading to episodes of rhabdomyolysis with clogged kidneys. She had a master's degree in art history and was an expert in nineteenth-century cookbooks. Excellent sense of humor. Always fun to talk to.

Another woman came in with a complaint of "hallucinajations." Former homecoming queen and honor student, she began having psychotic breaks as a sophomore in college. Gradually she had become marginalized even from her own family. Unemployed, living alone, few friends, and now unable to sleep. Schizophrenia. Medication helped somewhat, when she takes it, but she's still out of touch with 'reality' most of the time. To me, her poetry and art work are very special.

M. surprised me on his first visit by greeting me in the exam room perched atop the table in a classic Greek model pose, stitchless, of course, asking for surgery to transpose penis and scrotum. A black belt in the martial arts, masters in economics, popular, energetic, and expecting a bright future, he too had been stricken by schizophrenia leaving him a pariah. Many frustrating encounters and a friendship ensued, but finally his eccentricities led to court ordered "tranqs," mandating him to languish in a secluded life of suspended animation. Still, our weekly visits were always uplifting, never failing to add new insight to whatever topic we discussed. On basketball, "Very simple game. Just put the ball right in the middle of your forehead with your hands exactly the same on each side of it and shoot directly for the basket. You can't miss!" And on astronomy, "I'll tell you one thing: the Moon can't go in a circle around the Earth while the Earth goes in a circle around the Sun. It's impossible."

And so it went. Case after case, room after room of 'those kind of people,' the operative word being 'people.' Trying to put meaning into someone's life is what it's all about. Being accepted by the medical community or even society in general just doesn't enter into the equation.

One thing about my chosen profession; variety, challenge, excitement could arise at any moment. I was sitting playing a board game with my sons one Sunday when my beeper exploded with the following, "Dr. Murphy, come to the emergency room immediately. We have one of your patients here with a gunshot wound." Cedar Falls is not New York City. Gunshot wounds don't happen here, I thought as I drove towards the hospital. Walking into the trauma room, I was flabbergasted to find sixteen-year-old Nathan lying on the Gurney with an entry wound near his left hip. His mom was a wildlife rehab specialist, his dad a broker, all of them were vegetarian, compassionate, nonviolent people. How in the hell could he get shot? His story didn't help much. Out jogging on a gravel road, between corn and bean fields, he was barely aware of the car approaching from the rear, and "ping," he's sent rolling into the weeds. The good news, he wasn't in shock and there appeared to be very little bleeding, The bad news, there was no exit wound, meaning lead poisoning and possible surgery loomed. X-rays showed what looked like a .22 slug deep within the hip near the acetabulum, no fracture being evident. Consultation with an orthopedist who had done a year in Nam, and a surgeon who had trained in Chicago, reassured us that an expectant conservative approach was indicated. The lingering question was, why? Who would do such a thing? Here, the police jump all over something like this, and although it took a while, the people were eventually found. Although many questions remain unanswered, the conclusion was that some teenagers were out prowling the countryside shooting cats in ditches, a simply wonderful rural pastime, and, although they denied drinking or drugs, they failed to see Nathan and shot him by mistake. Another innocent drive-by victim, Iowa style.

Track season went well for both kids. I tried to attend as many of the meets as possible. Conor ended the year running a 2:09 half, very respectable for a 9th grader, while Liam finished his high school career at state in a splendid setting in the renowned Drake stadium. Running anchor in the last race of the meet, the 4x400, inspired by the plaque of Jesse Owens in the adjacent tunnel, he received the baton twenty meters back. Knowing this was his final run, he literally shot forward and by the first turn he had nearly closed the gap. At the 200 meter mark, his long loping strides had brought him even with the leader. Around the final curve it was step for step like synchronized swimmers. On the straight-away, his face had a determined set I had never seen before. Then, straining every fiber of his being to finish strong, still neck and neck, five meters from the finish, he had an almost imperceptible break in form that cost him the race by an eyelash. I got his split at just under 50 flat.

That summer, the three of us entered the Gus Maucker 3 on 3 basketball orgy, calling ourselves "The Gene Pool." Supposedly put into categories by a computer based on data from the entry sheets, we found ourselves mixed in with some of the best players around. With Conor's slashing drives, Liam's amazing shot blocking, and my creative calls, we were able to not only survive the early rounds but win even on the second day's games all the way up to the championship match. Here we faced three twenty-some year old guys, all of whom had played college ball, bound and determined to take the trophy. It was a dog fight all the way until, tied 14 all, 15 being game, we left a little space while switching on a pick and their star launched a high arcing prayer over both Liam and Conor's extended hands and made it for two. We were sunk but participating together was a great highlight. I used to think that playing catch on a perfect summer day was as good as it gets. The fluffy clouds, blue sky and green grass, and just the ball going back and forth, father and son, was special in its simplicity. But now I can say that even better is runnin' down court, 3 on 1 or 3 on 2, me, Liam and Conor, knowing we're gonna score, and there's nothing anyone can do about it. That's being alive!

In the fall, Liam, having won writing awards his senior year, was off to the University of Iowa majoring in English. Conor entered high school as a 10th grader, foregoing football, choosing cross country instead, in preparation for his true love, basketball. By the Christmas break, he had proved himself enough to be moved up from the sophomore team to the varsity.

Meanwhile, I invited Liam to accompany me on a trip to Hawaii with the UNI BB team. To entertain ourselves on the long flight to the "Big Island," we both read Conrad's *Heart of Darkness*. Liam had begun to study a more sophisticated variety of literature at Iowa and was sharing all his books with me as he finished with them so both of us were slowly gaining a more critical eye for what was good and what was merely entertaining. *Heart of Darkness* grabbed both of us and sent us spinning. What a masterpiece! Having lived in Africa, and having dealt with many of the issues Conrad addressed, may have been part of it, but nevertheless the subtlety, the metaphor, the multi-layered depth of message, all carried exquisitely by a naturally flowing story line, is, to my way of thinking, unmatched. We still talk about it, years and many books later.

Michener's *Hawaii* described the natural beauty of the archipelago well but being there and driving around the island was another whole experience. Dry on one side, rainy the other, sand beaches and coral, tropical low to snow on high, and even an active lava flow to the sea just for good measure, make the place unique and wonderful. Both of us were inspired. Too much, actually. Attending an all you can eat, and drink, seafood buffet, I got carried away by the 'drink' part and was beginning to wax glib with a table of coaches' wives. Liam, noticing the ominous potential of the blossoming social scenario, creatively used a form of subtle diplomacy to extricate me from the swirling vortex. "Dad, c'mon, let's get out of here." Somehow, the ploy worked, and I accompanied him on a long walk around the seaside portion of Hilo. All in all, a good trip for us, able to relate more than ever, since the separation had taken place.

Back in Cedar Falls, as usual for this time of year, basketball dominated our existence, with both Conor's games and UNI's. There was no AAU for this age group during the school season, leaving only state tournaments in March. All of my players, save Conor, played on the soph. team and had only an average record. Conor got twenty minutes a game on varsity but rarely saw the ball, not to mention taking a tremendous psychological hit day after day in practice, hard core criticism being the order of the day. Losing ugly in the first round of districts ended a spotty season for the varsity, and gave us less than two weeks to get ready for our frenetic run and gun assault on whoever stepped on the court against us in AAU.

By our second practice, I could see the kids reverting back to our style, gaining confidence, having fun, and getting excited to see how we'd do. Three more practices and we were flowing like water, not in the Swanee, more like the upper reaches of the Snake, raging, turbulent, and unforgiving. That Saturday morning, riding to Prarie High, sixty miles south, site of the regional, the kids acted like sled dogs knowing they were about to be released once again to the traces. Traditionally, 10 a.m. is not a good time for us, but it didn't matter on this occasion as we shattered La Salle, a better than average team, by twenty. Our second contest was against Maquoketa, who had won their conference, but was only a 2A school. The game about to begin, I told our guys that I wanted them to start right off with the press because we needed to get back into it in case the need arose. What followed made Germany's takeover of Poland seem leisurely. Hard as it is to believe, in a mere one quarter of tournament basketball, we tallied thirty-six big ones. Yes, thirty-six points in just the first quarter. I mean the scorer had to send out for pencils twice! You simply don't put up those kinds of numbers that quick. Most teams don't get that many in pre-game warm ups. Our opponent seemed like Sebastian after just qualifying for sainthood, yet our quivers were still loaded. I had to call off the dogs. Not because we weren't greedy, but you have to conserve energy in these affairs. Late in the afternoon we shellacked Mt Vernon to advance to Sunday. It was more of the same, as Burlington and Prarie bit the dust for us, paving the road to state the next weekend in Des Moines. One of the parents came up to me afterwards and remarked, "Amazing, Doc, a couple of practices and you got the old magic back. I want to tell you all of us appreciate what you're doing for these kids."

That night I looked at the calendar, then back at the letter I had received. There was no mistake. Having so few opportunities to play now that we were in high school, I had signed us up for both the 16-under and 10th grade AAU tournaments. We had just qualified for the finals in the former, but now I saw that the entire qualifying round for 10th was to be in Des Moines, and here was the kicker, on the same weekend as state for 16-under! What are those people thinking? A few quick phone calls confirmed the scheduling snafu. Both tournament directors, however, said they would work with us, meaning, as far as I could tell, that we wouldn't be expected to play at two places at the same time.

The kids just laughed it off when I told them. "Great, we can O.D. on hoops. Don't worry, Doc, this is what we live for. We can go for forty-eight hours. No problem." Youth, how gallant, how impetuous, how naive. Flesh and blood has its limits. What it meant was that I would have to squeak through each game, juggling players, going away from our style much of the time in an impossible attempt to prevail against the state's best in two simultaneous showdowns.

Talking to the parents led to the conclusion that we should head for Des Moines Friday night and stay in a motel to give the kids a little more rest. Sounded good on paper, but they don't rest. To them it's like going to Disneyland; run around, goof off, lack of sleep.

We could only fit in two practices that week, one bad, one good. We were ready, I thought, until I received the pairings. Turns out we faced the possibility of as many as nine games if, through some unforeseen miracle, we happened to string out the "W's." In addition, the timing for Saturday's games mirrored Madonna in spandex. Richard Petty would have been challenged to comply. We would have to send someone out for food to be ready, have the engines running, not get lost, and avoid speed traps, as we shuttled between Hoover on the west side, and East across town.

One small thing on our side was that two of our players didn't make the cutoff date for 16, so I could give them heavy minutes in 10th, the easier part since it was all school teams. But at the same time that left me with only eight guys for 16-under, which promised to be the much tougher challenge since at the "state" level, every other team was "all-star."

Friday night we made it to the capital without a hitch. The kids said they wanted to relax and take in a movie. I stayed in my room and mindlessly read Nietzche. When they straggled back, I asked what they had seen. "Hoops," they responded. Good god, I thought, can this obsession be healthy? I found out later that two of them even slept in their jerseys!

If you think I can remember all the games the next day, you're worse off than I am. Certain highlights, however, do stand out. Attending one game, against a Des Moines team, was Nick, a friend I had grown up with in Alton, who had been a school principle and was now in insurance locally and was well known by all. Still, sitting in the bleachers, he couldn't help but cheer for us. Little by little, as the game intensity picked up, his acquaintances began to turn on him. Finally, one particularly vehement mother told him if he liked us so much, why didn't he just go over and sit with us. Fine, he told her and strolled over to take a chair next to me on the bench. I really didn't know what was going on, but the game situation called for action since we had somehow fallen behind by fifteen. Unleashing the heat, in an unforgettable spurt of basketball, we went from fifteen down to fifteen up in six minutes of brilliant play. At one point in that run, I dropped my clip board, bent to grab it, and by the time I looked up, we had scored ten more points! Nick turned to me with a big smile on his face and said, "I may lose a few policies, but that's the most fun I've had in years. Great stretch." That game was over; we had taken the heart out of their chest.

Over at East, we faced an all-black, all Des Moines all-star team. Before the game, one of their guys told our guys, "Y'all might just as well walk away now. We got this one without even playing it." We won that one by twenty, while at the same time watching their emotions go from extreme cocky, to frustrated, then angry/vicious, and lastly "who gives a damn."

One team came at us with seven players and a coach that looked about 18 years old. I just chuckled to myself as I saw him trying to fire his guys up. They had absolutely no chance. Up tempo and aggressive slashing offense had their third player fouled out half way through the third. Hard to compete with four.

Against the Dubuque Dunkers, a group much more talented than us, we pulled out a near perfect game, and beat them by ten. Unforeseen construction made the cross town sprints interesting to say the least. Zoom! Zoom! Suck down food and drink. Where's the bathroom? C'mon, let's go! Conor, how's your energy? Aaron, can you jump center? Good work, guys!

Six o'clock Sunday night, the impossible had occurred. Eight straight victories had both qualified us for state in next week's 10th, and brought us to the championship game in 16-under. I don't know what kept our guys going. I was losing my mind, didn't know what to say, barely able to keep my eyes focused. "Okay, five of you guys go out there and do what you do. I'm going to sit over here on this nice chair." We were up against a conference all-star team, "A-P." We had seen them before, and quite frankly they just didn't match up well with what we brought. Our guys started on fire, and midway through the second, we opened up an eighteen point lead. Great! State championship game and we're killin' 'em. Can we go to "four corners" and run it out? Hardly, it's only the first half, Fool. Just keep doin' what got you there. Imperceptibly at first, as their determination gathered strength, our gas gauge was pressing on zero. Shots were coming up short, defense getting shoddy, them getting second attempts, even third. At half, every one of our guys laid out flat in the locker room. Bringing in Kavorkian would have been kinder than to ask them to play more basketball. Our second half brought new meaning to ugly. Nothing worked. No matter who I put in, none could deliver. Our lead was squandered. Gallant though we were, it wasn't to be found. Somehow we mustered up the wherewithal to stay close, and even had a shot to tie at the buzzer, but the wall had rebuffed us big time and we could only dream of what could have been.

Most gratifying for me was the way the kids took everything in stride, no complaining and no sign of arrogance. They were playing a beautiful game in a style that was exhilarating, effective, and absolutely engaging for spectators. Everyone gave it their best and played team ball. We had been doing this since fifth grade; it had become ingrained as if that were the only way to play. The truth is that life doesn't serve you up that many opportunities to experience those special moments. Peak effort, emotion, cooperation, accomplishment, all in one. Go for it, kids. The world is yours.

The next weekend we were back in Des Moines and played well enough to win third place in the state, losing only to Sioux City West in a hard fought battle. Not bad, a second and a third. Still, always more to shoot for.

To keep a certain balance in my own personal life, I had decided to become a docent. This was a program offered by the Iowa State Extension service for anyone interested, as a way of stimulating an appreciation for art in the state. Free of charge, I attended an all-day seminar at the university, showing us exactly what was expected. Covering eight topics, things like modern art, architecture in Iowa, pop art, we were given materials, and were then expected to hold our own sessions around the state. Included was not only studying the works, but also history, theory, and attempting to produce something similar of our own.

What I enjoyed about art was not so much the colors or geometric shapes, but trying to see what was being revealed about the artist, the subject, the history of the time. Reading art history was also fascinating to me; the poetic nature of the lexicon piqued my imagination. Trying to understand the world in general and people in particular was important to me in my profession, and, I suppose is only natural for everyone. Reading history gives you one angle, quite broad, actually, if you include, not just standard texts, but works by people away from the main stream like Howard Zinn. Better yet is chatting with those directly involved in the events. And then art, which many times ties it all together and adds additional perspective.

I had put a signup sheet in my waiting room for the first meeting which was to be on Georgia O'Keeffe. Within several days the sheet was full, reflecting a broad section of the public from PhD's to derelicts. It was mine to orchestrate. With my waiting room full, some even sitting on the floor, we began with a few pages about the artists life and what she was trying to accomplish. We looked at prints of some of her work and discussed what we saw. I made a point of getting opinions from everyone present. Then we all attempted to draw or use crayons to produce something like what we had seen. Looking at each other's work, we saw irises and deserted skulls in various shapes and colors. All in all a very interesting session. I looked forward to doing more.

Before I had time to schedule another group, something more urgent came up. It was late in the afternoon of a busy day at the office. I was in with a patient when my receptionist knocked on the exam room door. "Doctor, could I speak to you for a moment, please?"

Excusing myself, I stepped into the hallway expecting to hear of some crisis at the hospital. "What is it, Ali?"

"A woman from Geneva, Switzerland wants to speak with you. I thought it was important enough to interrupt. She's on line one."

"Thanks." This should be interesting, I thought as I walked to my desk and picked up the receiver. "This is Dr. Murphy."

"Dr. Murphy, my name is Naomi Surratt. I'm calling for The World Council of Churches. As you know, Mozambique is having its first ever multiparty democratic elections later this month. We need competent international observers to lend credibility to the process. We feel it's the best hope to end the violence there. Several of our contacts mentioned you as a person familiar with that part of the world. If you accept, we would like to send you to upper Zambesia as our representative."

Temporarily stunned by the unexpected nature and multiple implications of what was being said, I hesitated momentarily before succumbing to some deep seeded adventurous bent. "I'd like to be a part of that. I'll go."

My head swimming, I finished the last few patients with difficulty and then sat down to collect my thoughts. Mozambique had long since lost its romantic allure. The dream was gone, victim, like so many other emerging countries, to the Western capitalist cabal, by means of its two pronged overpowering assault; unrelenting state sponsored terrorism, coupled with, as desperation mounted, high pressure financial incentives delivered by the IMF and the World Bank. The situation was far from stable, meaning that some risk was involved. I only hoped that my unique knowledge of the people would serve me well. Leaving family and my practice was of concern, but it was tempered by the opportunity to contribute to the peace process and revisit a significant part of my past.

During those short two weeks of preparation, my basketball game took on a special vehemence. I knew I wouldn't be able to play for the duration of the trip, and I wanted to be in peak physical condition, knowing that where I was going, survival could depend on it. Thoughts of impossible terrain, raging rivers, exploited guerrillas and ferocious beasts inspired me to pump out a few extra reps in my lifting routine. Soon documents and guidelines began to arrive, which, along with my own notes from ten years past, I studied assiduously. In almost no time, it seemed, I was boarding the plane, carrying only a small bag and my passport, to once again spring half way around the world.

In the air, out of JFK, the droning of the plane kept me hypnotized in a trance-like state. With each passing hour, as we crossed the Atlantic, East and South, drawing ever closer to the African continent, my thoughts, at first only clouded memories, began to focus as if being brought to light after a prolonged dormancy buried in shadows. Touching down to refuel at Cape Verde, planting my feet, seeing Africans, added detail to my consciousness. Then flying on, destination Johannesburg, I felt as though my head might burst with emerging memories, coupled with emotions as they were. Soon, I was strolling across the modern airport, approaching the gate serving the Maputo connection. Waves of nostalgia welled up into my throat as I caught my first glimpse of Mozambicans and sat down amongst them mesmerized by the soothing quality of their colloquial Portuguese. The short skip to the Mozambican capital served to further engage all my senses as I began to interact, once again with the people I had known so well.

Debarking at Maputo rudely shattered the magical spell, immediately thrusting me into the hubbub and turmoil of a city at crossroads with destiny. A swirl of expatriates, media, and UN personnel, mixing with various local authorities, functionaries, and others, all aggressively seeking something, left me spinning like flotsam under a dam. Then, out of the corner of my eye, I caught sight of the sign, "Conselho Mundial das Igrejas." Several others had arrived from around the world and together we were taken to headquarters for the first of many meetings.

Never had the capital city been like this; so many foreigners, stories of crime and prostitution abounding, political rallies everywhere in a mocking attempt at "democracy." Stores full of goods for those few of means, as capitalism took hold. Even that was false since within two weeks everyone and the flood of foreign currency and per diems would vanish. Peace for such an innocent, long suffering people was a laudable objective, but what I saw reeked of insincerity. UN functionaries told us how they had lost all creditability in sub-Saharan Africa and maybe even the world, when a similar brokered election process in Angola the year before, had ended with the "wrong " side winning, provoking the losing faction to simply resume an all-out military effort as the UN stood by watching helplessly. This time, they had poured so many resources into their effort that it could not fail. Pitiful Mozambicans, like so many pigeons at a park bench, scrambled for the crumbs. To them the concept was as foreign as that of private property. As I observed all the money being thrown around, and remembered the times when I had worked without even an aspirin while fat outside parties orchestrated a nonstop infusion of horror, I could only shake my head at the hypocrisy. What this amount of resources could do, if used properly...

That night I heard gunfire in the distance, bandits or police I presumed. My immediate problem was securing a way upcountry. Calling on all my language and diplomatic skills, I was able to barter for hard to come by tickets for a flight first to Tete, then on to Quelimane. Confusion reigned at the airport and even though the name on my ticket didn't match my identification, I was creative enough to advance. Six hours later we landed in Zambesia. My success thus far, coupled with the familiarity of my present surroundings, instilled me a feeling of growing confidence. From here I could more easily control my destiny and contribute meaningfully.

Quite easily I parlayed a ride to the small Methodist church where the "Council" had headquarters for its provincial efforts. Once again I was shocked to find the office supplied with computers, radio equipment, fax, and even air conditioning. Three Land Rovers were available, a driver, and plenty of local currency. This, in a region teaming with starving refugees. Victims of circumstances, these people seemed sincere. Hearing that I was familiar with the region, I was soon given responsibility for five up country districts, and was to leave early the next day with a young enthusiastic driver, Raul, originally from our assigned area.

That evening was spent visiting old friends now working at the provincial hospital. As emotional as it was reminiscing about the years we had spent working together, hearing details about what had occurred since and the reality of the present situation, struck at my very soul. Too many times the answer to my queries was "dead," "destroyed," "disappeared." Nothing functioned well. Everyone saw the artificiality of the present process but they had long since lost any hope or enthusiasm, survival being the only concern.

Talking late into the night, I finally took my leave and walked the few blocks to my room in a local "moderately priced" hotel, the one decent place being full. Turning out the light, I couldn't take my mind off how horribly we had messed up the world. It wasn't long, however, for that all too familiar "bzzZZZ, bzzZZZ," to get my full attention. Yes, I was in a hyperendemic malarial area, much of it resistant to all treatment, and yes, those were mosquitoes. I tried swatting them, turning the light on, hiding under the sheet which was too small, and finally resigned myself to my fate, like any good African. Early in the morning, little sleep under my belt, I was off on my mission, literally tingling with anticipation.

Along the way, I milked all I could out of Raul, as we passed expressionless people staring silently, here and there observing remnants of what little infrastructure had existed, now destroyed gratuitously during the interminable years of meaningless violence. Half way to Mocuba, we pulled off the road to buy a pineapple from a small boy dressed in rags. He smiled as we left him a few extra escudos. But the taste, oh, the taste, was so delicious. Signposts were lighting up all over my brain. With each new sight, smell, or sound, it seemed, my memories came flooding back. As we gained altitude and began entering Upper Zambesia, I realized that not only had my Portuguese and Lomwe come back to a level of fluency better than ever, but even insignificant details from the charged time of my life spent there previously were now easily accessible on instant recall. Amazing! Packing so many aspects of my previous three years' experience into this fast moving journey, had opened all the memory channels. Our brains are truly remarkable, keeping every bit of minutia imprinted indefinitely. Traveling along, I wondered if genetics and "instinct" were connected to this same process.

Our task was to begin evaluating the situation on the ground. Did people understand? Were authorities ready? Was it free and fair? Between the two of us we knew the area and the people well. Stopping at places large and small, sampling even remote localities, we got a good picture, not only of how the election preparations were going, but also of how the past few years had gone for these particular Mozambican peasants. The picture we were receiving was not pretty. True, the Election Commission, with the help of the UN, had reached nearly every area we visited, a remarkable achievement, but almost no one could tell us who was running, what the issues were, or why all this was taking place. They did know it must be important, since never before had white people come around so much with such amounts of money. This, along with curiosity made everyone want to be a part of it. Suffering, on the other hand, had been common to all. Stories of rape, pillage, kidnapping and torture took little prompting.

As we got closer to Gurue, I began to run into people I had known. Tales of woe now poured forth, and, in addition, I began being asked to do medical consultations. At one distant village, the entire election board lined up to be seen. Mostly it was just taking advantage of the unique opportunity in hopes that some unknown power might improve their existence even slightly. I hadn't brought much medicine, and as each one stepped up complaining of headache, I handed out an aspirin. Ritual at best. The last one, younger than the rest, and obviously more nervous, stepped up hesitantly, and blurted out his complaint. In his confusion, though, he had misspoken, and had uttered the word for venereal disease instead of headache. Immediately the crowd burst out laughing. Worse, there were women and children present. I could see him blush immediately, no small feat for an African. Quickly, I gave him an aspirin, saying that his head would feel better in no time.

At several villages, in powerfully emotional and gratifying encounters, I found the lay midwives I had trained so many years past, still at work. None had escaped the brutality of the hideous turmoil that had engulfed the district. One told of how she had been forced to flee to the bush, as the enemy approached, grabbing only a few things along with her five children including six-year-old twins she had successfully nursed through the critical stages of early life. Luckily, they were not discovered. The village, however, was occupied for more than two months, meaning that she was forced to scrounge for roots and leaves, and live exposed to the elements, hiding most of the time. Slowly, she watched her children's health deteriorate, until, by the time her village was liberated, four were dead, including both twins. All of this was related without any noticeable facial expression. She did, however, allow herself, as she finished her recounting, to gaze for just a moment, deeply into my eyes. That look, so uncharacteristic for an African peasant woman, penetrated my soul, leaving an indelible imprint.

In Gurue town, things appeared much more dilapidated than I remembered. Tea factories were destroyed or nonfunctional. Our old house was run down, trash scattered pell-mell. The Mozambican doctor was off playing politics and hustling dollars. The hospital appeared sadly neglected. Many of the same nurses were there and openly wept, crying for a return to the "old days." All had suffered so much.

Silva, with whom we had left Lucas, invited me over to his house for supper, where he recounted the experiences of the time since we had left. Being of some means and having a large contingency of rural relatives, as the troubles edged ever closer, he found his house inundated with a never ending stream of displaced uncles, aunts, and cousins. Finally he was forced to send his older children, Lucas included, to his brother's place in Nampula province where things were more stable and food was available. Then came the hellish night when Gurue was overrun by Renamo, leaving death and destruction throughout the city. Silva and his family managed to flee just in time and for two weeks lived in the bush along with many others. During that time, as people began to run short on food, Silva, in the middle of the night, crept back into town, moving from shadow to shadow, entered his own yard, slit the neck of his own pig, and then carried it back to the bush, saving the lives of many. Had he been caught, torture and death would have been certain. These kinds of stories were frequent everywhere I went.

The district administrator, although he had never met me, said he had heard much about my work and insisted that I stay at the "Casa dos Hospedes." The next morning, the first day of actual balloting, we left at the break of dawn to observe the process in as many parts of the district as we could get to. Early voting was orderly but painfully slow by our standards. This, coupled with a massive turnout, made for long waits. Very few complained, as all wanted to experience this historic occurrence. The ballots had written names of candidates, party symbols, and pictures of the faces. Still many asked us to help them, saying they couldn't read and didn't recognize the symbols or faces. We could only advise them to do their best, it being improper for us to assist in any way. As we worked our way in the direction of the Malawi border, we couldn't help notice a much more pronounced Renamo influence. By four in the afternoon, we were at Nintulo, one of the friendliest parts of the district when I had worked there, but very isolated and now long under enemy influence. Anathema to me, their signs and banners were displayed all over, and small bands of armed partisans loitered near the election site. I still knew many of the permanent inhabitants, but thought better of any outright displays of familiarity because of both my history and the present operative dynamic. Meanwhile, with peasants patiently participating, the voting was proceeding smoothly; some had walked as much as four hours to execute first time suffrage.

For a moment I found myself back in time. Not far from here I had delivered twins in a mud hut, and just ahead was a trader's dwelling where I had been given my first set of pigeons along with instructions on raising them. How obsessed I was with protein production in those days.

The sun was beginning to dip into the neighboring 'kingdom' of Malawi, when suddenly, in a matter of seconds, the world was transformed. It was as if a veil had come down from horizon to horizon, or a front of icy arctic air materialized from nowhere. Everyone became silent, heads straining, as the curt announcement echoed through our presence from the several blaring radios scattered amongst the crowd. "We repeat, Renamo presidential candidate, Alfonso Dlakama, has just renounced the election process and has withdrawn his party from consideration. He will be returning to the bush to resume his military campaign. We will announce further developments as soon as they occur."

A million thoughts flashed through my mind at once, the most urgent being how people would react right here, right now. Quickly, I began to formulate a speech, which, if I could pull it off, might possibly prevent a blood bath. At the same time from the periphery of my visual field, I searched for the nearest cover and possible escape route. Eyes darted to and fro, and for a moment no one moved. Just as I felt I had to step forth to speak, an elderly man, presently second in line, dressed in traditional garb and leaning heavily on his walking stick, turned toward the nearby table where sat the local election board to declare, "From before sunrise I have walked to get to this location, then waited many hours in the heat for my turn. I am old and have never been asked to vote before and may never have another chance. Those voices from the box mean nothing. I will put my mark today!"

Beautiful, I thought, as many others nodded in accordance. It wasn't what some unseen announcer said, or what an unknown politician declared, or even what any brash young cold blooded counter revolutionary might think, but a centuries old tradition of respect for elders, now there's a powerful force. The line began moving again, less than an hour left until polls closed. Nevertheless, Raul and I both understood how precarious our situation was, and as soon as the hour had passed, we graciously thanked everyone and took our leave. I went out of my way to shake hands with the man who had spoken, thanking him in his own language as a sign of regard.

Two hours later we were back in Gurue where the town was buzzing with rumor and speculation. Late that night it was announced that a resolution had been found, and that instead of two days of balloting as had been planned, now there would be three. Local UN observers, however, with access to their own two way radios, told us the real story. Dlakama had received reports that the election was going badly for him, and felt he had to play his "Angola" card. To a certain extent, it worked, as in a tense meeting with chief UN representatives, after multiple calls to New York, a large amount of money changed hands, and the "democratic" process was a "go."

The next day progressed uneventfully as we checked out the voting ritual both near and far. Towards the end of the day I told Raul that I would like to be left off at Nicorropali, the most isolated section of the district. He was scheduled to return to Quelimane that night, but I elected to remain for the extra day to be able to accurately reflect the entire process for the "Council." Having been there several times in the past, I was able to direct him to an almost invisible turn off from the main road seeming to head into nothing but trees. There was, however, a faint path, and I assured him that there was only one river to cross which was never deep at this time of the year. An hour later we were at the village and the election board proudly explained to us how well everything was going. After a delicious bowl of chili spiced sorghum gruel offered by a woman I had helped during my tenure as chief medical officer, Raul departed and I settled down to watch and take notes. This area was so remote that neither Renamo nor Frelimo had much influence. I felt good about being there as I was sure no one else, probably in the entire country, would cover such a location.

Feeling completely comfortable, knowing that the likelihood of political danger here was nonexistent, I was about to doze off when a completely unexpected challenge of an entirely different nature arose. The voting booths were situated near the edge of the village, and about thirty feet away, just under a large tree, were the table and chairs for the election board. Sometimes things happen that can stretch credulity to the limit, but, remember, this was Africa, primitive and fantastic, a land of animism and little understood atavistic forces.

As I gazed across the open space separating me from the proud board members facing me, I saw, crawling from the dense foliage at their backs, a snake, not a large snake, just average-sized, maybe six feet. Still, slithering slowly toward us, it seemingly posed no imminent threat, and not wanting to disrupt the election, I was content to watch closely and say nothing. This, however, was apparently no ordinary reptile, but some sort of creature on a mission. Without the slightest hesitation, the prescient intruder advanced directly towards the unsuspecting table. I felt compelled to act; within less than a minute it would be within striking distance. Arising and walking deliberately towards the table, I raised my hand pointing behind them and said as coolly as possible, "Disculpa, esta a vir uma cobra." It was as if I had announced incoming mortar rounds. Pandemonium, panic, instantaneous scattering, papers flying, voters and villagers fleeing, distinguished board members scampering like rabbits. Adrenaline animated all, we observed from a more than healthy distance. I don't assume to be able to explain what happened next; many may not believe it but it did occur thus. Never changing course or speed, this mesmerizing messenger, proceeded directly to the table and climbed, not just any chair, but that of the president of the election board. It then raised its head above the table, peered out at us mortals and began swaying back and forth, tongue flickering as if delivering a critical directive.

The effect on those present was equally unnerving. Everything was being said at once, all ominous and baleful. Even I thought this could be Dlakama, appearing simultaneously at every site, mocking such a pitiful attempt at changing destiny. Finally, a brave soul, in an act of monumental courage, circled around, and with a good sized cane, smacked the serpent from behind, flinging it into a nearby tree with one foul swoop. Fine, I thought, that's that; now we can proceed with the election. Foolish man! After such an occurrence, do you believe people will continue as if nothing had happened?

Fascinated, I listened to the ensuing discussion. Absolutely no one thought it meant nothing. Some, however, interpreted it as a positive sign, ancestors giving approval to the voting. After nearly an hour of animated discussion, a compromise was reached. The booths and table had to be moved to the other side of the village, and most finished their civic duty. A sizable number, however, had vanished, foregoing their chance to participate in determining their own future, choosing to distance themselves from the site of such an inexplicable, yet certainly powerful harbinger.

The last day was spent in and around Gurue town, finishing the task at the local secondary school where I was to monitor the all-important "count." Gathered at the rear of the large classroom, we anxiously awaited the unfolding of the first ballot. "Joaquim Alberto Chissano." The name reverberated throughout the room. Personally, although I was in a neutral roll, I couldn't help feeling somewhat satisfied. Chissano was honest, intelligent, dedicated, and hard working. I had met him on several occasions and he was always very cordial and likable. The job of president of Mozambique was, of course, impossible, having to resist the full force of international capitalism. Fifteen straight times the name echoed until finally some chump's vote came up for Dlakama. Who could possibly choose that evil hired villain? Final count was 666-88. Shallow victory at best. The stranglehold now was economic, just as effective, just as cruel, merely slower.

I did my best to file an objective report, hoping, in some small way to help avert the slide back to violent encounter. Personally, I had never seen such widespread persistent suffering. Just before leaving, I emptied my pockets, billfold, and suitcase, leaving all to friends. Now ready for the long bumpy trip down to the coast at Quelimane, filled with emotion, I stood alone waiting for my ride. Suddenly, from behind me came a woman's voice speaking broken Portuguese, "Doctor, Doctor." Turning, I faced a middle aged middle aged Mozambicana, hair nicely wrapped in a brightly colored scarf, spotless capulana around her waist, and even shoes. I immediately realized she was dressed for the occasion, but why? What does it mean?

Reaching out to shake her hand, I politely responded, "Sim?" thus giving her permission to continue.

"Doctor, you probably don't remember me, but you might recall my daughter. When she was born, you called her a miracle. She didn't even fill one of your hands she was so small, but you promised to do all you could for her."

Yes, I did remember, and, yes, her chance for survival was slim indeed. "What happened to her?" I asked, half expecting to hear another horror story.

"Here she is." Turning and extending her hand, she waited proudly as a beautiful budding adolescent, also dressed in her best, came forward. The two of them stood side by side, with near identical smiles. For a moment I was paralyzed. There were no words for what I felt. Then, reaching out, I shook her hand, holding it for an extra second. My ride had come. As I turned toward the Jeep, I heard the mother say, "Doctor." Looking back at the still smiling faces, I accepted the single parting word, "obrigada."

Jumping into the vehicle, we were off. For a long way, I couldn't get those two out of my mind. How far had they come? To what lengths had they gone? Doesn't matter. That alone made my trip worthwhile.

"Hey, Doc, where ya' been?" It was my first day back at noon ball. Even the ritual was fun. Run in, go to the cage, greet Ross and Jack, get your stuff, strip fast as for a delivery, damn the socks for slowing you down, bound up the steps and hit the floor, hoping to have timed it right for the next game.

"Africa."

"Bet it's hot, huh?" What a probing inquiry. Is it just Iowa or are people in general becoming exclusively interested in their own lives?

"Just like my game," I answered, throwing up a hook shot, banking it home.

"We got ten. Let's get it goin'." I grab the ball and stand at the top of the key, hoping people will divide up into teams so we can start. Little groups are still chatting.

"Ball in," I yell pointedly. Everyone else comes up blue. I'm yellow, always.

"You wanna go one on nine, Doc?"

"We could do that, Ward, but why don't you give me Norm, Marlin, Scott, and Clem, and we got a game?"

"Shit, Doc, that ain't gonna work and you know it. We'll take Norm and you got Barry."

"No way. I been gone two weeks. It'll be brick city."

"Right. We saw that hook you just threw up."

"Pure slop. C'mon, let's go!"

Sounds like a lot of silliness, doesn't it. But it's not. If you lose, you sit. At least get the players that will give your team a good shot. The trick is to know what to say to whom to get your way. That involves knowing the personalities involved, how they might react, and being able to spontaneously deflect whatever ploy they may dream up. Hurting someone's feelings by seemingly not wanting them on your team had long since been dropped as having any part in the considerations. There is one exception. There are a few guys, maybe one out of a hundred or even less, who are so little fun to play with that it's worth being a huge underdog just to avoid the distinct frustration of being on their side. Of course they're all ball hogs, but it's more. When people start referring to you as "black hole," you've arrived. Adding to it the invariable nasty self-serving attitude completes the loathsome package. Better to have a few molars pulled without anesthesia. What's really strange is that some of these guys seem normal, even nice off the court. It can go both ways. One thing for certain, a good hard game of basketball will definitely reveal another side of your makeup.

"Wait a minute, Doc. Shoot for outs." It's Dick speaking, not wanting to lose an advantage.

"Go ahead," I quip, knowing he can't shoot a lick.

"You can do it," he responds, certain that my ego will convince me to accept.

He was right but he had only tricked himself, confusing winning the argument with getting an advantage.

"You never learn, do you," as I swish it from the top of the key.

Then, before starting, it's the match ups, probably the most important part of the game. No way can you allow an aggressive scorer to match with a poor defender. Height, quickness, none of that stuff matters if the opponent is the type who never looks to score. There are innumerable little strategic ploys that can be used. I might choose to guard a certain player knowing that I can eat him up on the other end and that his stubbornness won't allow him to switch even if I score ten in a row. I'll even give up first outs if it means I can get that advantage. Some guys you will hardly ever win with. A really bad defender you can usually hide on a non-scorer, but what do you do with the guy who thinks he's a great shooter but hits around ten per cent? Worse yet are players who think every pass should be a highlight, translating into multiple T.O.'s. Sure, you try not to give them the ball, but a certain number of times, by chance, it bounces their way. Then there's the guy who doesn't like to be told what to do. More often than not, he's the same one whose thinking just doesn't make good basketball sense. So you're left with delicate diplomacy, tricky maneuvers, or back handed compliments intended to achieve the desired match up.

We do actually get to the game. All this other posturing etc. only takes a few moments. Then it's the action. The physical component, the exercise, is the reason we're all there. Like my son Liam says, "I think of myself as an athlete. I like the feeling of my body in motion. I'd even say it's essential." The running, the quick moves, the frantic leaps, and the fierce battles for position all exhilarate. Then there's the aesthetics; I once made a move that was mentioned as resembling ballet. The perfectly timed block, the glistened look of the hard-working competitor, the unintended freaky occurrences, all add to the enjoyment. When you mix it with the mental gyrations, the gamesmanship, the quips, and emotional outbursts, what's not to like?

This guy never makes a call so I can play him really tight. That one doesn't argue. He prefers to be the victim. All day dreamers, fudge a point or two on the score. Get him frustrated and his game goes to hell, use it! Take it down low with this one. He doesn't like contact, won't challenge much at all. Compliment Billy on the shot he made, for sure he'll miss the next three or four. Hack! Careful now, got to give up the call early to be more likely to get it late.

"Doc, at least wait on the shot 'til there's rebounders."

"You got to come up with something better than that, Norm; doesn't make me feel bad enough, I'll still gun." Friendly banter, with an edge. Play continues.

"Hack!"

"No way was that a foul."

"Bullcrap, you were all over my arm."

"No worse than what you did to me down there."

"I'm makin' a call."

"I don't know how you sleep at night."

"I can sleep, and I might want to know how your mother is but I'm not asking. Now gimme the ball."

"OKAY, I can play like that."

"Bring it!" Has to be game point. So many times win or lose comes down to debating skills. Pays to have a lawyer or two on your team, even a judge if you can get one.

Interestingly, no matter how barbed the comments, when you hit the locker room, all is forgotten. Hop in the shower, a few laughs, maybe some business talk, and out the door.

Speaking of showers, guys don't seem to look at each other much. Oh sure, there's always the one who's especially well-endowed, can't help but be noticed. Others got it almost all pulled up inside. One guy seems like he's got no ass at all. He can run pretty well though. Then there's the few who pick a locker in a back row, hidden from view, and emerge with a towel around their waist all the way to the shower and even in the shower, keep their back turned most of the time. What are they hiding? Or maybe they were abused as children. Hmm. And some guys got to scrub their entire body every time. What's up with that? Can you imagine the soap they go through? Way back, I saw a medical student wash right on his anus with suds. When you think about it, not a bad idea. After all we don't have bidets, and what is it, they say – don't stain the Hanes. Ya, I do it too. Enough!

Jade was sitting on the exam table in room two when I entered with the chart. "Possible UTI" the nurse had written. Born in Thailand, this copper colored child had been adopted as a three year old by long standing patients of mine, and had thrived up until now, both mentally and physically. I hadn't seen her for some time and she had grown considerably. A urine test had revealed "4+" blood. Carefully, I began to tease out the history. This was the fun part of medicine. Solve the mystery. One week of headache, neck pains, loss of appetite, chills, stomach ache, diarrhea. Then, last night, temp up to 105 degrees. Could be anything. History wasn't going to give me the answer. Neither was physical exam, I thought, until I got below the diaphragm. Laying her down and raising her blouse to expose her abdomen, I needed only one look to put me on full alert. At first glance she appeared to be five to six months pregnant! But she's only ten years old, I thought, showing no change in demeanor, and she's smiling, happy, and well-adjusted. I don't even feel I should bring up what I'm thinking. My head ran through many possibilities as careful palpation confirmed something the size of a cantaloupe in the lower abdomen. This would have to be handled both delicately and scientifically, to achieve the desired outcome. "You can sit up," I said returning to my chair.

"What do you think?" asked Lu Ann, Jade's mother.

"I'm not sure, but I'm considering distended bladder or, more likely, something with an ovary. We'll have to do tests." I explained to Jade what would be involved in a cath U.A. and culture, one of the things I would order at the hospital, along with a blood test. They left, but as I continued seeing patients, I couldn't help wondering what the future might hold for young Jade.

About an hour later, I got a call from one of the nurses at the hospital speaking in unusually hushed tones. "Dr. Murphy, I don't know how to tell you this, but you have to know. On your patient Jade, we had trouble getting the cath U.A., and one of the surgeons was on the floor, so we asked if he would help. We probably shouldn't have, but it's done. Anyway, that's not the problem. We got that done, but then he started checking the abdomen and now he's ordered tests. I think he's planning surgery. We don't know what to do. The family is asking what's going on."

I couldn't believe my ears. Here I'd been trying to summon up all my skills to do the job right on a tricky case, and now it's not just a problem of diagnosis and treatment, but I've got to drop everything and defend against shameless general surgeons.

"Hold off on all new orders. I'll be right there."

In some people's minds, there exists a hierarchy among doctors with the more specialized at the top and the primary care physicians at the bottom. Lowest of all would be a GP with no residency training, and if he took care of mostly the poor and marginalized, well who cares? It's almost as if he doesn't exist. This patient's parents worked at the university, i.e. they had good insurance. Pounce! Move over ambulance chasers. Watch a real pro operate. This was too brazen. If he was counting on me being intimidated into compliance, that had no chance. But it wasn't about us frail and arrogant doctors, the patient wasn't well served by this course of action. Bubba shouldn't be the one to tinker with the rocket engine.

Arriving at the nurses' station, I found everyone on edge. An X-ray and ultrasound had already been done. My cohort wasn't present. Calling the radiologist, I was told that they saw a large pelvic mass, partly solid, partly fluid, containing calcium deposits. Hanging up the phone, I turned to the nurse, "C'mon, Holly, let's go straighten everything out."

In Jade's room, we found both parents with concerned looks on their faces. "Jade, Tony," I began, nodding at them. "Sorry for the misunderstandings. The important thing is doing what's best for Jade. It looks like what we're dealing with is a growth on an ovary. It seems to have come on quite rapidly, which is worrisome. There may be other complications. This is definitely not an everyday problem. With your permission, I'd like to call the University of Iowa. If they recommend a referral, I think we should arrange it as soon as possible."

"Sounds fine. Thanks for your help."

Speaking with a pediatric oncologist confirmed what I had been thinking, and soon Jade and her parents were on their way to Iowa City. The following day a team of surgeons removed the tumor, along with a "subtotal omentectomy, left oophorectomy, and partial resection of the right ovary." Pathology revealed a grade III malignant teratoma. What followed was a rocky course of chemotherapy, hair loss, low blood counts, further surgery, and finally, success. No sign of recurrence, Jade is living a normal life.

I had been working diligently on a paper called "Opiate Addiction in Iowa." My goal was to raise the level of awareness for Iowa physicians not only about how easily they can be inveigled but also about treatment options now readily available. I was pleased when it was accepted for publication in "Iowa Medicine" and felt even better when it received the "Albert Lasker Award" for best scientific achievement. What was disheartening however, was the near total lack of response from Iowa doctors, even locally. Everyone reads that journal. Still, only one comment from a peer. Had to be the subject matter, just not appropriate for a real doctor. About of as much concern as leprosy. Oh, ego, why art thou so persistent? Know thee not yet that your concerns are as nothing here? Except basketball, that is. Cuts across all lines, draws attention, and makes a statement like nothing else.

Conor's junior year saw him starting varsity, big man on campus. He was stronger, more confident. Could be a good season. And they did win their first four games.

Liam, home for Christmas break, came up to play with us at the PEC. He had gotten a lot tougher, mentally and physically. I didn't realize how much until he started showing his stuff. A rebound isn't usually considered a glamour play, but on this occasion, it actually stopped the game cold. On what was just a routine shot, Liam, definitely not imposing at 6'1", 160 lb., stepped into the middle sprang skyward with such alacrity and vehemence, achieving an altitude easily surpassing anything gravity had previously allowed, and snatched the ball somewhere near the ceiling. It was as if he had come off a trampoline. Every player stopped to ponder what had happened. There was nothing, just a rebound, but what a remarkable rebound. After the game I asked him how his jumping had been. "Pretty good," he said. "Let's see."

Stepping over to the wall where the basketball team had marks taped on the wall with heights up to eleven feet, he casually pogoed up vertically, touching his hand somewhere above the high end of the tape. If I wasn't convinced the kid could jump then, the next Sunday playing with him at the high school erased all doubt. Coming down the lane dribbling, he split two defenders while cradling the ball, left the planet at the dotted line, and on reentry brought thunder to the cylinder in an amazing display of athleticism.

Now, when the three of us would show up at a court, people took notice. All we had to do was pick up two generics and we owned it for as long as we wanted no matter who challenged.

Just after New Year's, while Liam was still on break, he and I headed North for a bonding session. We had done Hawaii previously but now intended to plunge deep into the opposite climactic extreme. Leaving just after noon ball on a Wednesday (I try to do that whenever possible since it's my standard afternoon off. I miss less work that way), we had only to make the Twin Cities by evening. Hurtling along, taking in the frozen Iowa landscape, we probed each other's minds in an in depth discussion of Jack London's *Martin Eden*, which he had just studied as part of a literature class and I had read somewhere in the distant past. Both of us had been impressed by the stinging social commentary, and who could forget the powerful suicide scene at the end? Our imaginations then carried us to consideration of London's many depictions of struggles for survival in the Yukon. Crossing into Minnesota, we were able to get more personal. Yes, he drank at college, and yes, his breakup with his girlfriend had been rough. We were getting closer to a more meaningful interaction. Then snow began to clutter our progress. Soon we were in the throes of a full blizzard. "This is good, Liam. It's like a warm up for what we'll face up there."

"But Dad, I can barely see the road. Is it safe?"

"Would Buck and White Fang worry about such trifles? Sure it's safe, pretty much. Let's listen to the radio and see if they give a weather report." We didn't have to wait long, that's about all they talked about. Western Minnesota had received twelve inches already and counting, with wind gusts up to forty miles per hour. We tried tagging along behind semi's whenever possible but there were times of total whiteout that were of definite concern. Still, we continued to move. When the governor announced that he was declaring half the state a disaster area and pulled all plows off the roads, even I had trouble maintaining my stance of denial.

"What do you think, Buck? Should we look for a doghouse?" But then the veil of swirling crystals seemed to lift just enough for us

363

to enter Minneapolis and less than an hour later we arrived at my sister's.

Sitting around the fireplace we talked long into the night, and at the break of dawn, the storm having abated, we were back on track, destination Duluth. Sailing up Interstate 35, invigorated by the 15-below crisp post storm stillness, we passed near where my father had grown up, now seeing less farm land and more woods, all freshly decorated in a flawless wavy white like a seven-year-old parading up the aisle for his first communion. Coming upon the port, we ducked under the spiraling streamers atop the scattered stacks while gazing out over Superior, still wet and hazy. Erroneously thinking we were close, our anxiety levels increased as we hit the North Shore Drive, catapulting in the direction of Thunder Bay. Passing Two Harbors, we could sense the growing solitude, seeing only occasional signs of civilization. Finally, Grand Marais, stop for food and fuel, before attacking the last leg, a foreboding strip of tar known as the Gunflint Trail penetrating deep into wilderness. Near the end of the line we searched through the early night and after missing the turn at first, corrected ourselves in time to reach the lodge still open. Checking in we arranged equipment, studied maps, and wearily climbed into bed to dream romantically of the coming adventure.

"Yurt to yurt" is what it's called. These structures, somewhat more substantial than tents, are scattered out among the wolves and moose, connected by a tangle of old Indian trails, used for skiing this time of year. Arising early, we nervously downed as much breakfast as possible, dressed up, and received our final instructions. "Weather is supposed to be good, just above zero and no snow, but be ready for anything. You never know up here. Stick to the trails, they're well marked. Careful with your packs, you may need everything in them. I'll be going out by snowmobile later today to supply the first yurt with food and sleeping bags. Don't screw around on too many side trips or you won't make it by nightfall. Shortest route is still over 20 kilometers so you got to keep moving. Have fun!"

"What about menacing carnivores?" I asked.

"Bears are sleeping, and wolves don't bother anyone. You'll hear 'em at night though."

It had taken me fifteen minutes just to get my skis on. I had never gone cross-country skiing before. Liam had only minimal experience, but I figured that since we were both in decent shape and well-coordinated, it wouldn't be too hard to move our legs back and forth. About ten falls and less than a kilometer later, I began to seriously question my own sanity. Liam was doing much better, spending much of his time laughing at his bedraggled father. The surroundings were marvelous, and between calamitous dumps I was able to feel a bit of the inspiration provided by the passing pristine environs. Just as I was catching on to the subtleties of negotiating never ending hills and curves on skis, we hit our first lake crossing. Suddenly wind was a factor, this time helping as we sailed across the frozen glass like a schooner running wing and wing. Near the far shore, however, a protected bay was covered by a layer of snow. Liam passed over fine but somehow, as I attempted to traverse the final few feet, my skis broke through a crusted layer of deceptive frosting and I was up to my ankles in slush. I managed to step right out. The lakes are frozen six feet deep this time of year, but later I was told that cracks can form allowing water to seep up occasionally. No big deal, I thought as I came ashore and attempted to hit my stride again. Curses! I could barely move. Almost instantly ice had formed on the bottom of my skis. Mixed in with snow and slush, the rough surface just didn't slide. I tried chipping and scraping but no luck. It has to be smooth throughout or you simply can't glide. Through pure chance we were still close enough to civilization that there was a cabin just ahead. Serendipity! Inside was a fire and soon we were back on the trail, wiser but still so far from our destination.

Every hour got better and better, falls becoming the exception, as we followed the sun westward. My legs, however, were paying a huge price, mostly because I had to tense my muscles much of the time just to keep balance. It was nearly dusk when we came to the final junction with a wooden sign inscribed with the delightful words, "Yurt 1 Km." A short time later we arrived at a high spot from where we could see the opening down below near a still gurgling stream. That must be it, we thought, as we triumphantly advanced over the last few feet of level terrain. Another quaint carving hung from a branch. "Two Fall Hill" it warned. Liam and I looked at each other, hesitated, and shrugged our shoulders. What choice is there at that point? I elected to go first and thought it was a ruse until I rounded a bend and came immediately upon the most precipitous drop we had yet encountered. There was no time to prepare. I was right into it, gaining speed faster than I cared to think possible. Slam, bam, crash and tumble. I eventually made the bottom, but make that two a four, or was it five. Worse, Liam soon arrived with a hoot and holler, and not a flake of snow on his wraps. We had made it!

Soon a fire was heating up the yurt, thawing our ice covered faces. After hanging up our clothes to dry, we ate our food and crawled into the sleeping bags, being sure to leave plenty of fire wood near the stove for the duration of the night. Neither the echo of not too distant howls, nor the busy scampering of friendly rodent cohabitants, kept us from curling up into a cozy slumbering repose, as the indomitable darkness accompanied us towards the next day's dawn.

At the first blue jay's reveille, I scurried forth to heave three sizable logs onto the shrinking coals in a vain attempt to modify the reality indicated by the thermometer, minus twenty. Diving back into the womb, I waited for combustion to work it's magic. "Liam, I don't know if it's the cold or those last falls, but I hurt."

From inside a closed fluffy mound, "Are the mice gone?"

"Ya, they went outside to warm up in the snow. I'm beginning to appreciate how Sam McGee felt."

Within minutes it was considerably more tolerable. Having no choice, we emerged, dressed, and made the mandatory trip to the nearby outhouse. Micturition sounded like ball bearings bouncing below, and defecation, well defecation reminded me of a single ear of fresh picked corn coming off a silent elevator in slow motion tumbling to some precarious resting place; a rather glorious rendition of what in summer would be merely so much ignominiously splattering scat. Even the smell had been instantly sealed within by the plunging mercury.

Within less than an hour we were on the trail. In the first ten minutes, despite two pairs of gloves, I was sure I would at least lose fingers to frostbite, but soon, just like the day before, I realized that I had overdressed again, perspiration peppering my brow. Two layers below the waist and three above was about right for -20.

Now loose, we were able to progress with much less effort than the previous day. Liam looked like Michael Jackson moonwalking over finely sprinkled flour. I was beginning to feel like a tall lithe breaststroker flowing rhythmically along in untouched waters. Hitting "The Banidad," a relatively straight shot all the way to Ely, we were in a hypnotic groove. Two feet of recent snow, no bugs, perfect stillness, and not a cloud in the sky, gliding through uninhabited wilderness, each passing scene outdid the previous. Moose tracks were frequent, and once we stopped to examine where a single wolf had crossed the path not too long before. Wide open on the down slopes and skating on the up hills, we could easily have covered thirty kilometers that day. For hours at a time we saw no one, making the adventure even more romantic.

By the third day I had become a Siberian soldier heading west to meet the Germans. Jumping into my skis was second nature, falls a thing of the past. Almost, that is. We had arrived at an area where a maze of groomed trails had been painted into the hills. Experimenting, we survived several of the less challenging side runs with nary a difficulty. Looming ahead, however, was a sign marked in red. Hmm, what could that color indicate? Stopping to read the inscription, we both chuckled politely. "Don't even attempt this trail unless you have previous world class experience."

"What do you think?" I asked, looking at the flushed face of my companion.

Liam has an unrestrained opinion of his own physical abilities, but, ironically, he tempers that with a definite caution when danger may enter the equation. "The way I read it that sign is meant to be a warning. I promised Mom I wouldn't do anything too risky." Immediately realizing how fatuous that sounded, and totally ignoring the fact that my judgment had proven to be perilously inadequate in similar situations in the past, he quickly blurted, "I guess it can't hurt to at least take a look."

"Let's go," I said, quickly striding out before he could have second thoughts. Rounding the first bend, we started what was to be a steady diet of steep ascents. Several we even had to side step up. Where in the hell did this mountain come from, I thought. We're in the boundary waters; it's supposed to be flat.

"I guess this is how people get VD," I said as we finally reached the top. "Once you get started, it's just too hard to stop."

"Very funny, Dad. How do you propose we get down?"

"We could take off our skis and walk, but I for one, will probably never be here again, so I'm going to let it fly. You and Conor split everything if I don't make it, all right?"

It started off with a continuously curving gradual downhill that was so smooth and beautiful that by itself it made the whole trip worthwhile. But then, after a brief interval of level trail, I came upon a scene that took my breath away. Waiting for Liam to appear, we both stared at a long narrow segment of such a grade that even in deep snow, it seemed life and limb, would be on the line. Now what? Without even a word, I pushed off with my poles, accelerating almost immediately beyond anything I had previously experienced. You don't traverse on these trails, and, as far as I know, there's no way to slow down even a little. Just relax and ride it out. Easy to say. Trees were flying by blurry as beside a Japanese monorail. I became weightless as I hit mach I and continued hurtling toward my uncertain destiny. Somehow, of all times, I kept my balance, my torso as a gyroscope atop two madly bouncing shock absorbers perfectly adapted to the grooves. Seconds seemed as years before I hit bottom, only to find a hellacious curve rapidly approaching. That I took with one ski about three feet off the ground thinking surely now, catastrophe must come. Miracle of miracles, I came to a halt still standing, suffering only a pulse rate in the range of 200.

Turning, I went back to where I could see Liam's run. Seeing what I had done, he edged closer to the precipice and slid into motion. About three quarters of the way down, having achieved a speed near that of someone jumping off the Golden Gate Bridge, he lost it. I saw tumbles, cartwheels, bounces high and low, snow flying like from a giant egg beater, then silence. Nothing moved. Slowly, an arm arose, then another. He sat up. "You okay?"

"Ya!" he yelled back. Completing the descent without incident, he looked like a yeti when he got close up. One minor problem, however. In the tumultuous acrobatics, he had fractured a pole. Fortunately we had only ten kilometers to go, without many hills. About six o'clock we pulled in at our destination. For our final night we had chosen to end at an isolated cabin overlooking a frozen lake. Here we had electricity, a sauna, beds, and a twelve pack in the fridge. What a finish! We enjoyed it all, feeling like we had just conquered the world. The next day left only a 5K ski out to our car and we were heading home.

Arriving in Cedar Falls in record time, we were able to quickly change clothes and still make the evening pick up BB game at the high school. My first shot was a running left hook from twelve feet which I converted. Next was a dipsy-do to a finger roll from the baseline with a gravity defying hang time. I was literally bounding up and down the floor. My leg muscles had been primed beyond any imaginable programmed workout. On one play I posted up, got the pass, and effortlessly deposited the turnaround. "Three seconds!" lamented Floyd.

"Ya, in the air," was the retort.

Liam felt the same, spending most of the game above the rim. If a person plays hoops enough, he might be able to put together quite a list of variables he could control to give his game a boost for a special occasion (more later).

At the office, heroin addicts continued to appear, sometimes in groups of three or four, meaning that a source dried up, as in dead or prison. Another common scenario, in Iowa at least, is an addict who uses prescription opiates from either a cancer patient or someone with AIDS. Because of both the aggressive marketing of the pharmaceutical industry and the unwitting compliance of hospice groups, these patients can easily obtain amounts of pain killers that would normally never be given. The extra is then sold, borrowed or taken by the addict. It can be quite lucrative, easing the "pain" of the patient by enabling him to meet inevitably burgeoning expenses. Many addicts have told me that they can breathe a sigh of relief when a friend or family member gets cancer, because then they have an almost sure place to "cop" for the duration. Of course, most of these preparations are dissolved and injected, contributing to the spread of all those little microbes bankrupting our health care system. And it's only getting worse. Marketing of pain relief pervades not only the medical literature but also the mass media, invariably accompanied by the rejoinder that, if taken for pain, these medicines are not addicting. On my side of the equation, day in and day out, I deal with the devastation wreaked by the literal flood of the ever escalating number of new formulations, invariably more potent, readily available on the streets. At the same time purity and quantity of heroin is at an all-time high and prices lower. It's a battle for market share between the pharmaceutical corporate giants and the "smack" industry. I often wonder if it couldn't be just two heads of the same monster. After all, only a relatively simple chemical reaction separates morphine from heroin.

The other all too common problem is the patient with chronic pain also cursed with a high tolerance to pain medication. At a certain point, doctors get skittish with amounts of narcotics needed to alleviate suffering. These patients may have never done anything illegal in their lives, but when that arbitrary line is crossed, they get dumped cold or are referred to Dr. Murphy. I then struggle to pick up the pieces and give these people as good a life as I can. But invariably there is stigma, and it can be devastating. It's not just family and friends. Routinely I hear of how, when being seen at another health facility, a patient is treated with the utmost respect and consideration, until it is discovered that he or she is on methadone or a sizable dose of narcotic. Immediately resentment is apparent, every statement is doubted and abruptness rears up, anathema at its worst. Health care suffers greatly. Demonization has succeeded so pervasively, demonstrating again human frailty. What's so frustrating is the irrationality of it all. Logical arguments, evidence based studies, physiologic explanations carry no weight. Better to send the neurosurgeon a drawing of a stick man holding a morphine tablet, tears streaming from his eyes.

Sometimes, it seemed that all I saw anymore were people needing opiates. But wedged in, here and there, were a sizable number of patients with other problems. This day, Chj, my nurse from the beginning, who, by the way is so good she knows what I'll do before I do, came up to me and said, "Go see four first. I don't know what it is but she definitely has something." Great, I thought, a challenge. Do your thing, Hercules. Entering the room, I was greeted by a middle-aged woman with the most plethoric countenance I have ever seen. Immediately thoughts of carbon monoxide, nitrites, emphysema, and right to left shunts came to mind. She had only felt poorly for two or three weeks, just tiredness and no energy. Like many of my patients, this one was schizophrenic and on major tranquilizers. Then it clicked. Buzzing for Chj, I had her bring the patient's mother's folder. Ten years before, I had treated her for a condition called polycythemia vera. She had died of an unrelated condition. Blood tests confirmed my suspicion, hemoglobin being twenty-four grams with normal being twelve. Twice a week, Chj turned vampire, until eighteen phlebotomized units later, our patient's ennui vanished as tests turned normal. The two of us went out for a beer that day after work, laughing and joking about all the crazy things we had seen. I realized that I wasn't the easiest doctor to work for. Not that I was mean or stingy, but my mix of patients never failed to try us in one way or another. At least we weren't bored, and most of these people had no access to other providers. My policy was to welcome all comers, the more difficult, the better. Chj seemed to understand, but the rest of my staff just assumed that I was a little tweaked upstairs. At least they all did an excellent job at making sure that nothing, bar a near death situation, kept me from my noon ball.

Meanwhile Conor was having a nice year in his inherited game of passion. In one contest, he treated fans to an eye popping spurt of offense, tallying twenty points in three minutes. This, on a team that plays deliberate slow down basketball. They won their share, but lost more than they should have and came up a few points short in the game that would have taken them to state. Making all-metro and making second team all-conference were nice for Conor, but other problems were creeping into his life.

Part of it was that at each progressively higher level of basketball, it's less fun and more win at all costs. A lot of his identity centered on being one of, if not the best player around. But sadly, the positive returns were just not there as much. Trying to branch out, he decided to run for student body president, a bold decision in a school of more than 1,200 students. Janet and I backed him all the way. He was very popular, belonged to no cliques, and was a natural leader. But the way it works is that the votes are counted secretly and then a committee of teachers and school officials picks from among the candidates whom they feel would best represent the school. This is where it gets complicated. Conor, like his parents, was not religious. And while he didn't throw it into the faces of others, neither did he hide it or feel ashamed in any way. Every other bio contained numerous references to membership, and even leadership roles in various church groups. When the committee named another candidate, Conor felt cheated. He had worked hard and felt he had received the most votes. Then came trouble in track when, despite having run on the 4x800 team the entire season, when they qualified to run at state, he was informed that he would be replaced by one of the coach's sons who had never beaten Conor at any time during the year. My saying that life isn't always fair seemed empty. Gradually drugs and alcohol found their way into his life. I can't say how much, but both Janet and I had our nights, sitting up or being awakened by the noise and then the encounter with our obviously intoxicated son. It wasn't that he got mean or nasty; he just didn't set limits well. We worried about health and safety, talked a lot and seriously considered commitment for treatment. Through it all, he managed to remain functional and out of trouble. Still, options were compromised, opportunities narrowed.

That summer a bunch of the varsity players, including Conor and several others of my guys, asked me to coach them in the Iowa Games, 18-under division. I readily agreed but with less enthusiasm than I would have had for our old bunch of scrappers. We didn't practice much because the juniors were in two summer leagues and attended multiple team camps so were in excellent shape.

The set up that year called for the top two teams from each regional to advance to Ames for the finals. As the weekend approached, I felt we had as good a chance as anyone just on individual skills. Saturday's games proved me right as we went undefeated in our pool heading to Sunday. First up was Waterloo West, who played way above their heads, making us reach deep to finally win in the fourth quarter. Now the finals were, in a way anticlimactic since both teams advanced. Facing us was Hank's Huddle, an assortment of players hand picked from as far away as Des Moines by Hank, a friend of mine who frequently played noon ball with us. Surprisingly, despite the fact that he had quite a few quality participants, we held our own, and only by a desperation last second basket did we lose the game.

Two weekends later, in Ames, we survived the first round by whipping Indianola 76-61. Only four teams left. Next for us was a conglomerate team with players from Ft Dodge, Algona, and Humboldt. As the August air got hotter, it seemed our shooting did the opposite and I thought we were cooked. Fourth quarter heroics by several of our players, however, saved the day as we squeaked out a "W." Advancing through the other side of the bracket without skipping a beat was Hank's Huddle. The stage was set for the rematch. This time we knew we could play with them.

Outside the gym on the track, many other events were taking place. The Iowa Games was a celebration of a wide variety of sports and had become quite a happening. I had borrowed Liam's spikes just in case the schedule allowed me to enter a few races. Having just turned fifty and being in good shape, I figured I could be competitive. We had two hours before our championship game so we wandered out to see what was taking place. Looking down the schedule, I saw that the only event that would fit was the 50-over men's 200 meter dash. As I signed up I noticed all these lean mean guys with farmer tans, stretching and loosening up. Well whoop-de-do, I thought, while they were chasing plows, I've been playing full court race horse basketball, should be a piece of cake. At the starting line, I quickly decided to forego the use of blocks, having never been in them before and fearing I might get tangled up somehow in the darned thing. At the gun I took off flying and by fifty meters I had already made up the stagger. Whew, what fun, heading into the straight away, me in the lead, cheered on by my loyal hoopsters. Then the strangest thing happened. It seemed as though, just as I was able to focus on the finish line, not only did it fail to come closer, but it seemed to be fading away from me as I pushed harder and harder. Damn, what can I do about that? Before I could react, guys passed me and the whole thing was over. They told me I finished fourth. Somehow, I decided, that even though the whole thing was mysterious, strategy may have been an important factor.

Before heading back into the gym, I wandered over to the high jump pit and was told that it was going slow and would probably be several hours before the 50-over competition. At least I'd done that one before in high school.

Back inside, it had to be a hundred degrees, horrendously humid, and even with all the doors open, not the slightest movement of air. Just sitting on the bench was enough to send streams of sweat down my face. Watching Hank's team score the first ten points added nervous sweat to my already drenched shirt. "Time-out!" I yelled.

"Don't let it get to you, Guys. Start to get a little angry.

Remember, we had this team beat in the regional. Do it with defense. Pick 'em up half court and make them execute. They'll tire in this heat. On offense, don't pass up any open shots. Let it fly and look to rebound. We're just getting started here. Let's go!" Sure enough things began to get better. Our shots started to fall and they got sloppy. So much so that by half time we were up six. Now our guys were relaxed and confident but at the same time determined not to fail.

Second half began with Hank trying to press full court. Quickly putting in our best ball handlers, I watched contentedly as we silently ripped their best effort to shreds. Not only were we getting numerous layups but our threes were goin' and defense was solid. With six minutes to go in the game we were up twenty and they gave up, thus assuring the win for us. Shaking hands with Hank, I gave him the polite "good game." He hit me with his best Clint Eastwood and delivered the line, "Next year, it's ours."

Medal presentation and pictures followed. Everyone felt so good that I decided to ask Conor if he would mind staying for a while to allow me to see if I could still do the high jump. There had been a certain friction between us of late, all tied in with his perfunctory feints into adulthood and the accompanying search for meaning in life. Happily he agreed to come with me to the pit, and he was sincere; there was no trace of it being a compromise by him, making me feel like we were bonding, doing something together, an occurrence that had become less frequent of late.

As we arrived on the infield, the bar was just being set for the competition to begin. They added my name to the list and I quickly changed shoes and did a few stretches, enjoying the wafting fragrance of Ben Gay. One fellow wearing a knee brace failed on three attempts at the opening height of, don't laugh, three feet even. You can step over that, I thought, as I sailed over the bar without even trying. "Way to go, Dad. You cleared that with at least two inches to spare," said Conor laughing. Not wanting to exhaust myself, I passed all the way up to four feet and then another two inches. The field was narrowing considerably. A little nervous, Conor turned to me advising, "Don't you think you should jump, it's getting up there a ways?"

"I did six feet, don't worry."

"Ya but that was, what, thirty-five years ago? Maybe you've lost a little."

Being in a conciliatory mood, I gave in. "Okay, Coach, I'll hop in at 4'4"." I cleared the bar easily with my patented scissors, the only way I knew since we never had a pit where I'm from. Other guys were doing Texas rolls and an occasional Fosbury Flop. Finally, it came down to me and one other competitor at the prodigious height of 4'10". Both of us missed our first two tries bringing the entire competition down to one jump apiece. Up first, he gave it his all, and looked like he had it with his perfect form, but nicked the bar with his trailing foot and could only lay on the foam as the long thin triangle alighted on his defeated form.

"This is what it's all about," grinned my erstwhile mentor. "Don't hold back."

Summoning up every ounce of energy, I attacked the bar like never before, hoping I could time it right and that my left leg wouldn't give way as I planted to spring upward. I only remember kicking my right foot high into the air as I released all my force vertically. For just a moment I thought I was in orbit, then quickly, feeling nothing, landed on sponge. People were clapping. Glancing up, I saw the bar still balanced on the standards. Jumping up, I power walked over to Conor for a high five, then shook hands with the second place guy and the judge.

Walking back to the car, I told Conor, "Well, we both got gold, but really 4'10" isn't much."

"No, you did good. There's still some ups in those legs." Before we got out of Ames, he was asleep. To me, the corn and beans never looked better.

Before school started, Liam, Conor, and I had planned to take a long weekend in Kansas City. Nothing special, just catch some music, movies, maybe a ball game. We left Cedar Falls about 4 p.m., stopped in Des Moines to eat, and headed south on Interstate 35. Conor drove all the way to the Missouri border before tiring and, during a gas stop, turned the wheel over to me. Darkness had begun to envelop the busy freeway so I was careful to flick to low beam as we pulled back into the flow in the direction of K.C. Chatting with the kids about how different this state was from Iowa, I noticed the many trucks on the four lane asphalt path dug into the farmland.

Now cruising at 70 mph, we hoped to be at our destination sooner than expected. It was not to be. In a matter of five seconds or less, this trip was to be terminated.

Concentrating on traffic, I failed to see the lurking amorphous threat materializing like an obscene chunk of ice indifferently barricading our progress. In an instant it was deer, not one, not two, but wall to wall. I let up on the accelerator and plowed into the gaggle, decelerating as if plowing into knee deep water. A near simultaneous series of sickening thuds, shattering glass, brown corpse over the top, another crushing my door, then silence. No motor, no lights, only crickets.

"Are you two all right?"

"I'm okay."

"Me too."

"Both of you jump out and push the car off the road. The next semi could squash us. Hurry!" Shoving it into neutral, I was able to steer the destroyed vehicle well onto the shoulder before the uncanny lull in traffic abated.

We stayed at the Eagle's Landing truck stop that night. Janet came to pick us up the next day. One moment of terror was all we had to show for our efforts.

We seem to be a fairly resilient genetic line. I myself never miss work. Injuries? That's a different story. As I type this document, I can see visible deformities in approximately half of the joints of my fingers. Four extensor tendons have been ripped off the backs of my fingertips. Sprains and strains, cuts and bruises, one slight concussion, traumatic vitreous floaters, two broken ribs, nails ripped off and stomped off, tendonitis, sacroileitis, hip pointers and groin pulls, all part of the game. Creative taping and a strong dose of denial and I can still play. I may have to shoot exclusively left for a while, guard a non-scorer, avoid paint, contribute more with attempts to obfuscate the tally, but rarely not play. Some things heal faster than others. I messed up a rotator cuff overdoing above the head weight lifting one day. It took nearly a year to heal, and that's with me doing active rehab. On the other hand, just as that shoulder was getting better, I foolishly dove for a loose ball, not recommended for a 50 year old, and felt a dull pop. Getting up, I couldn't move my other shoulder. Although I'd never had it before, I knew it was dislocated.

I asked one of the guys to pull on it hoping to quickly return it to the socket. No such luck. Quickly trudging down to the training room, I had Terry, head trainer at the university, hand me a twenty pound weight for traction as I lay prone with the shoulder over the edge of the table. Still nothing.

"Okay, Terry, let's go old fashioned on this. Take your right shoe off," I said as I got off the table and lay on the floor facing up.

"It's your shoulder," he responded, kicking off his loafer.

"Get down on the floor, grab my wrist with a towel, put your heal in my armpit, and slowly increase the traction. Great. Bring it in a little." *Thwap!* "Got it! Damn, that felt good. Nice work, Terry."

The point is, even with that, the next day I played. Well, sort of. Up and down the floor, at least. And in two weeks I made my first jump shot. Soon it was as if it hadn't happened. The human body has an amazing capacity to heal. If you quit being active, you just set yourself up for another injury. Push it, stress it, prime the pump, and you will be quick to mend.

Even though I play ball partly to get away from it all, a doctor never totally escapes. I have to see all the cuts and injuries on the spot. Some I meet afterwards at the office or in the ER. Once I had to put two dislocated fingers back into place during a single game to fifteen. Guys throw tough questions at me right during the flow of play. While we're running up and down the floor, the guy I was guarding tells me his dad had to go see the doctor. I ask what was wrong and he told me the man was forgetting things, confused. For how long, I continue. Just yesterday, he responds, very unlike him. But they didn't find anything wrong, he says. Well, I told him, he either has kidney infection or his oxygen level is low. Have the doctor check both. Next day I found out it was the oxygen. I did balk when one player wanted me to check him for a hernia in the shower after we played.

Certain days everything just seems to be magical. For example, there was the morning, after a particularly satanic run of problems at the office, when, already late, I rushed to change and scurry to the court, only to find us two players short. "Well, where's Marlin?" I asked of no one in particular. As if asking would somehow make him appear. Damned if at that very instant, Marlin didn't stride through the door. Everyone smiled politely. Instinctively, pushing my luck, I followed with, "How about Vorland?" Before I could close my mouth, in walks Vorland.

Now they were all commenting. "Pretty impressive," "I don't believe it," and "How does he do it?" Then Dave, one of the regulars, pipes up with, "All right, here's the test. Michelle Pfeiffer." And...

That, I couldn't do. But I had picked up a few medical tricks through the years. One afternoon Mrs. Brown came in all excited over Jr. "Doc, you got to do something. He stuck a kernel of corn up his nose and it won't come out!"

"Calm down, Hattie, we can get it." Looking closely I saw the troublesome seed way up inside, nothing easy to grab with forceps.

"You'll have to help me with this maneuver. I'm going to stand behind his head and close off the other side of his nose. You love Jr. now, don't you?"

"Yes."

"Good. I want you to put your mouth over his and blow air into his mouth. Get a good seal. It has to be pretty hard. Don't be shy."

It worked perfectly. Jr. helped by resisting and even forcibly exhaling at the same time. Out popped the displaced portion of state bounty on the first try. Only complication was the mess on momma's cheek.

Conor's senior year began with him surprising everyone by deciding to go out for cross country on the day of the first practice. He had been searching for meaning anywhere he could find it and had temporarily settled on a philosophy that nothing mattered. I knew it wouldn't do any good for me to talk to him. It was at the point of where, not only would he refuse any advice from a parent, but very likely might do the opposite just out of spite. I had presumed he wouldn't participate. Of course he wasn't in running shape but in the second meet of the season, still on the J.V. squad, he came into his own. With eight hundred meters to go, ten runners back, he took off in a full sprint. Sure he would run out of gas, I watched in amazement as he passed man after man, never letting up, and nipped the last guy at the finish line to win the race. His time put him at varsity level and his courage caught the coach's eye. A month later, in freezing rain and snow at Mason City, against nine teams, he finished 12th overall, running 17:10. I realized that, like me, he was a cold weather runner. His coach told him he was varsity from then on, but Conor, still stinging from his 4x800 slight, said he would rather remain on the top seven only as long as he got a top seven time each meet. I know I should be proud of him for making such a decision, and I am, but more often than not, I think of what might have been. In the last meet of the regular season, a hot day, a young JV runner had a time several seconds faster than Conor's varsity posting. So, as agreed, he ran districts, which Cedar Falls won, and state, while Conor became first alternate. Still, the big all Iowa show down couldn't have been more exciting. Held in what was now late fall in Ft Dodge, the temperature was near freezing with blasts of wind challenging any nose to stay dry. The final polls had not even placed our team in the top ten. It was to be a battle to the finish between Dubuque Senior who was very good, and Iowa City High, also very good, but with the despicable reputation of wearing their superior attitudes plainly visible on their singlets. In another twist of fate, it was at their meet where my beloved son, along with several teammates, had got caught returning Iowa City moonings, costing him a two day in-school suspension during which he discovered Herman Hesse which he says changed his life forever. No last minute injury or sickness occurring, Conor, like me, observed the race from the frozen sidelines. In such weather, in perfect condition after doing every step of the taper with the team, I knew he could have run low 16's. If, if.... *Blam!* The report sent the hoard sprinting off the line. The course took the runners, after the initial mile, into a wooded loop out of our sight for the second mile. Hope very much alive, we anxiously shifted our eyes from watches to woods, until finally the lead runners sailed from the distant trees. C. F. had chosen special never before worn white outfits for the occasion. Imagine the excitement as, just behind the first two colored shirts, came a sizable collection of participants significantly peppered with brilliant white. Only a mile to go, the runners quickened their pace. At the finishing gate, I couldn't help being caught up in the impending drama. Here came two Dubuque harriers, the clock only registering in the 15's, then a few scattered colors, followed rapidly by three straight whites just after the sixteen-minute mark. More Dubuque's and, yes some frowning Iowa City reds, and before long, white number four and finally, white number five. There is so much action at the end that you can't be absolutely sure about team results, but as the numbers went up on the board, our guys were ecstatic. Dubuque, number one all season, had finished first, that was a given. But Cedar Falls, unranked coming into the race, had roared into second, edging Iowa City by six points. What a thrill! The entire team, beaming with pride pushed their way through the throng to the platform to accept their trophy, the culmination of months of hard work, sweat, and struggle. Now number two in the state, it was quite a payoff. For Conor, a mixed bag of messages for sure, each a component of character being forged.

The next day, in the best shape of his life, he began senior year basketball, where he, undisputedly, was to be the man. As practices progressed, he knew no one could stop him. He could outrun anybody. He could post up anyone. Nothing mattered. By himself, length of the floor, ten flailing arms in his wake, it was sure money in the bank. Three's, free throws, never before seen creative moves, and on top of it all, the best defender! Glory, all state, Mr. Basketball, there for the taking. He even compromised and got contacts, allowing him to see the length of the floor. Then it would be on to Div. I, and, who knows, possible NBA. Why not? A really good 6'3" white guy wasn't unheard of at that level. Of course they hadn't even played their first game yet.

Overlooked were the unmistakable signs of looming detours. A certain tediousness with each successive practice session, a psychology laced with negativism, the 'wrong' mix of players moved to the front, and a purported plan for up tempo play thinly covering the same old deliberate patterns of the past. Conor was the man, but this game was about X's and O's, designs and patterns, intricate blueprints beautifully planned, not individuals, not "Conor's."

Winning their first few games, things were still all right, because, even though they weren't impressive wins, they were victories. Scoring in the 60's, or maybe in the 50's, wasn't exactly up tempo, and left lots of opportunity for less talented teams to sneak back into games with a few lucky breaks. Then a loss. The glitter was beginning to fade. Conor's line would be something like seven for eleven from the field including a few three's, and a hand full of free throws. Two or three of those field goals inevitably were on layups just from beating everyone down the court. But his shape was waning, frustration was accumulating like mold on a fine loaf of Wonder Bread improperly attended. Three losses by Christmas, alcohol and drugs sneaking back into the now more jaded scene, resignation, indifference, even depression began to surface.

Liam came back for the holidays, and he too was having problems, lack of motivation, disillusionment, anxiety, all self-medicated with generous doses of fermented barley. We had some fun games of basketball together, but mostly, Conor was with his team, having less and less fun.

Liam and I decided to celebrate his twenty-first birthday by mounting an assault on a nearby gambling casino. Carefully attending to even the smallest detail, we headed east toward the Mississippi dressed in 20's garb, hoping to execute the perfect plan and return rich. After the requisite stop at the ATM, we anxiously crossed the plank onto Diamond Joe's posh milking machine, floating innocently on the muddy surface. Reconnoitering, we got the feel of the establishment and, as planned, finished our second beverage, before turning in our $300.00 for custom chips and heading for the busy two dollar minimum black jack tables. Choosing table, dealer, and seat, based on frivolous intuition, we felt confident as we sat down to outsmart the house and win big. Alternating play, we worked as a team, warming up and getting used to the inevitable distractions in such an action packed engagement, defying concentration through multiple attempts at sensory overload. Our plan was foolproof. We couldn't loose, if we executed properly, stuck to our guns, and didn't succumb to the inevitable pressures. Simply stated, what we purported to do was begin with a two dollar bet, and if we won, start over with another two dollar gamble, while if we happened to lose, merely double the amount to four for the next hand, keep doubling until we won, then immediately back to the minimum bet again and start the process anew. It was perfect, so sensible, and early on seemed to be working, the only drawback being that it was at best tedious, being so mechanical. Arbitrarily, we had decided that if the dealer had any chance of being busted on one more card, we would stick on fourteen or above, letting him self-destruct. An hour in, we were up a good hundred bucks, feeling quite invincible, when we began to receive our unavoidable spanking. It began innocently enough with losses at $2, $4, $8, and $16, but sweat began to accumulate as the lousy cards continued and we gave up $30, then $64, and yes, $128 in rapid succession. How long can a bad string go on? It's against the odds, isn't it? Hands shaking, we watched $256 swept away indifferently by the sneering dealer as he exacted his punishment for those so bold as to challenge the well-oiled profit mill. Quickly I snatched up the remaining chips and distanced myself from the table. In hushed tones, Liam and I steadied ourselves and attempted to logically dissect the situation.

"I don't know, I'm a doctor but these stakes are getting a little high."

"Way out of my range," said Liam. "But what about the plan?"

"Right, we can't keep losing indefinitely, but it's already way past what I thought was even very likely. A couple more bad hands and I might crack, lose nerve, whatever."

We discussed it from all angles and finally took out all our chips and money and decided to put the whole works into one last glorious do or die attempt. "Gunfight at the O.K. Corral," for the world championship, win or lose we walk.

Striding confidently back to the tables, we found our seat taken. In fact every low stake seat was occupied. At the far end of the room was a lonely female dealer at an abandoned $50 dollar minimum table.

"Should we?"

"Why not, odds are that we're due to win, right? Doesn't matter what table or dealer."

Why did my mind keep thinking that that deck didn't know that we were due to win. Each card had a one in fifty two chance to come up, nothing else mattered.

Glad for the action, the young dealer shot into gear showing off her various shuffling techniques before asking Liam to cut. With a sigh, I put the $512 grubstake on the spot waiting for the flip of fate. A queen, nice. Could have been a lot worse. Slow down, let us savor this. She got a seven. Looking good! A quick glance at Liam. The moment of truth. Can't stop it now. It's a.... I can't believe it! It's an ace! Yes, an honest to goodness ace! Praise the gods. Mercy me! Incredulous, we watch as the author of good fortune matches the pile, then half again. High five, tip a ten, and then sweep the spoils, cash in and we're on the road. Mission accomplished. And, I might add, lesson learned.

The rest of Conor's BB season was much of the same, winning more than losing, but falling far short of what had been dreamed of. True, the conference they played in was the best in the state, but indelibly imprinted in the memories of all was the long history of AAU ball in which we had faced these same teams and come to consistently dominate all of them save the Cedar Rapids bunch known as Eby's previously, and now Jefferson. The difference was no secret. In AAU, all ten guys rotated in, playing like road runners full throttle, winning by being hot, exhausting the opponent, or, if needed, by the all-out full court trapping defense, at which they were the best I had ever seen. Heaven help the other side when the hounds were unleashed, executing like cold blooded professional assassins. The prep style, in sharp contrast, was characterized by sparing substitution, painfully deliberate tempo, and absolutely no use of all out pressure. This transformed an exciting well-oiled win machine into a lukewarm 'good' team. The former never even worried until they were down 15, while the latter had no way to make up even a 6-8 point deficit. The question is how to provoke a momentum shift, and then how to maximize the effect. I believe it's as much emotional as physical.

Still, individually, Conor, had some amazing games. At home, against C.R. Jefferson, rated number one in the state, time after time he found a way to score including 5 three's mostly in the second half keeping the game close. But then, down one with possession and twelve seconds to go, he never saw the ball as victory eluded them again.

As the regular season ended and tournament play began, I received word that Margaret had been taken to the hospital in Sioux City with a stroke. I had been on the phone a lot with her of late, as swelling in a leg became a clot, then a question of pulmonary embolism, followed by blood thinners, and now slurred speech and paralysis on one side. Up until then, this was a woman who, although well into her 80's, remained vital and dignified. This was also someone who had played a significant role in Conor's life, even becoming his prime care giver during the time Janet was ill. Mixing in trips across the state with district BB games was not the easiest. The team managed to win and got to the point of needing only one more victory to go to Des Moines. Up next was number one, Jefferson. I had just returned from Sioux City, having spent hours both laughing and crying with Margaret. She was a nurse and knew she was slipping. "To be honest, Danny," she told me. "I have no desire to go on. I've had more than a full life, and wouldn't feel right being a burden." I suggested the possibility of returning to her home of the last thiry years in Alton with full time nursing care but other members of the family rejected the idea since it involved giving up the last hope for recovery. Death with dignity is a difficult concept for our culture.

Now, two days before the big game, Margaret died. All the family flocked to the old house probably for the last time. Somber at times, but mostly celebratory, everyone pitched in to bring fitting closure to Margaret's long life. Conor had to leave after the wake. The following morning, at the funeral, it was as if Ethel's final requiem were being repeated, "Dies Irae" still echoing through the stoic nave. This time, however, modern liturgy provided opportunity for a more positive expression. Asking if anyone present had a remembrance to share, the priest was pleasantly surprised as person after person arose to recount an anecdote, read a poem, bring back some poignant moment. "No one had ever said anything before," he told us later.

Not long after the funeral, I excused myself, having to drive straight through to make the big game that night.

The game did not come close to living up to its hype. Neither team played well; Conor, in particular, gave a lackluster performance as Cedar Falls ended their season losing by eight points in another low scoring affair.

Later he told me that his desire to have the season over with far outweighed any other considerations. What all was going through his mind at the time, I can't say, since our communication had become more difficult. Not that it was negative, but there was a certain distrust, maybe of all adults. Busying himself as a budding bohemian, he plainly didn't have time for any 'serious' concerns. Being named all-Metro, all conference, and honorable mention all-state didn't help.

"Do you think all I want to be known as is a basketball player?" he said one day.

Delving into Buddhist thought, he attempted to minimize the role of ego in his life. Meanwhile I wrestled with the notion that, although having expectations for a son may be unavoidable, being unconditionally supportive must be the dominant persuasion.

We did still relate on other levels. For instance, to complete a school project for extra credit, he chose to review Conrad's *Lord Jim*. We alternated reading the entire book out loud, discussing as we went. At first Conor had his doubts, but eventually became convinced, and courageously analyzed the author's "brilliant and daring portrayal of a young man's epic struggle with his sexuality." His teacher was amazed at the result, sensing something special in Conor's work, effusively praising and challenging him to pursue further literary interests. Nevertheless, a void had taken hold in his mind, the search for meaning only just begun.

Two weeks after the BB season was the AAU 18-under regional. Yes, I had asked the old group of guys if they wanted to play and they agreed, but I sensed a somewhat diminished enthusiasm. We were only able to practice once and after winning a few early games, got whooped up on by Hank's heroes, eliminating us from the picture. Was the magic over? Can the Phoenix rise up to fly again? Can it? Hmmm.

Succumbing to the expectation thing, both Janet and I tried to engage our son in meaningful conversation about the future, as in college. Treading lightly, we would say, "Conor, deadlines are coming up. What do you want to do next year?"

"I don't know, I'm thinking."

He would vacillate from day to day, mentioning schools all over the country, even Alaska. Meanwhile Division III coaches from many colleges were actively recruiting him. One in particular, Grinnell College, maybe the best academic institution in the Midwest, had him as their number one recruit. "They play the ultimate up tempo style," I vainly tried. "And they stress academics. All their graduates get a wide range of opportunities."

"If I see myself playing basketball, it's in Division I." But he wasn't sure about basketball, and he wasn't sure about a rigorous academic school. He wasn't sure about anything.

385

"No Division I coaches are after you. I have contacts in Iowa City. I could inquire into walk-on possibilities, you know, the gray team. Or we could try to market you to other Div. I programs; I can write a letter and we can go over the list of places and decide where to send it, see if they want tapes."

Reluctantly, he agreed to the latter, so I put together the following letter:

Dear Coach _____,

My son, Conor, is considering attending your school. I'm writing to see if you think he might fit into the basketball program. I have coached him in AAU since fourth grade, over three hundred games.

He is 6'3" and weighs 165lbs. He has run 2:02 in the 800, 17:10 for 5k, high jumped 5'8", and benches 200 lb.

His ACT is 27, and he has a 3.2 GPA.

As a player he is eminently coachable even by his father. He has always been given the toughest defensive assignment except for the strongest post-up type opponents. He's a better than average shot blocker and anticipates well to get steals. Usually he plays up front on the press.

On offense, he is very unselfish and doesn't take bad shots. This year he averaged 20 points per game on 10-12 shots plus free throws. He uses a quick first step for strong moves to the hoop as his forte, many times scoring plus getting fouled.

He is very adept around the hole being equally creative with right or left, especially reverses and power layups.

On 3 pointers he hits 40%, getting 1 or 2 per game, normally preferring to drive. However, against the #1 team in the state, Conor did manage to go 5 for 8 from the arc.

He has a pull up "J," used occasionally, and he can dunk. Free throw percentage is 70-80.

In one game he was able to score 20 points in just over three minutes.

Ball handling and passing skills are good as he plays 2, 3, and 4 positions.

Playing in the 4A division (largest) in the most competitive conference in Iowa, he made all-Metro his last two years, second team all-conference last year, and first team all-conference this year.

In AAU, he's been all-tournament at two state tournaments and last year's team won the Iowa Games. Two years ago he broke Fred Hoiberg's Marshalltown record, scoring 77 points in three games. In an international tournament in Tampa, Conor led us to a win over the European champions from Helsinki and took us to overtime against the Russian Junior National team.

He always hustles and loves basketball. I feel he would be an asset to any team.

Sincerely,
Dan Murphy

Mighty impressive, but it was never sent! Insecurity, indecisiveness, lack of direction, motivation, whatever, it was all we could do to even get the application for matriculation at Iowa filled out and sent in on time. By default, it appeared that was where he would go.

Emblematic of how life was going for him at the time, is the recounting of the prom. Having just broken up with one young woman, there was initially a question of whether even going would be appropriate. Then as the day dangerously approached, it seemed two or even three maidens either thought they were the one or were perilously dangling in wait for his moment of decision, a frightful position for all involved but particularly for him, now practicing such a deliberately existential life style. Finally, through the dynamic use of some variation of both daring and dreadful diplomacy, the field was narrowed to the correct number. Then the compromise of

BREAKAWAY

interminable prosecution of frivolous detail in preparation for the actual event. Tux, corsage, non-sneaker foot ware for him, hair, nails, makeup, gown for her, all contributing to the perfect occasion. She was to drive since his car had been trashed way beyond anything mere cleaning could address. As the appointed time drew nigh, both of us sat about joking absentmindedly as he intermittently fidgeted with a tie or flower, awaiting her glorious arrival. Jokes became less as five, then ten minutes fled past the predetermined hour. Conor, anxiously rising to glance out the window, began taking to tugging at various parts of his attire. "How do they make these things so uncomfortable?"

"Are you sure she was supposed to drive?"

"Yes, I'm sure, dad."

Five more minutes go by.

"Maybe you'd better call her."

No answer.

"Where are her parents?" I ask.

"Her mom lives in some other state, and her dad lives in an apartment across from her. But he's almost always in China."

"So she's a junior and lives in an apartment by herself?"

"Yep."

"Oh."

I asked when he had last talked to her and he said not in the last day or two. She had been too busy, and they had never been able to connect. But he was sure he had everything planned.

Forty five minutes late, the phone rang. Conor took it in his bedroom. All I could hear was a scattering of emphatic remarks like, "What," "No way," "I never," and "Fine with me." Strolling back into the living room, pulling off his tie, he rather unceremoniously announced, "The whole thing's off!"

That begged for more explanation but I didn't want to provoke any more serious reaction. As he stripped off the entire outfit and threw it on the couch, I finally took the chance.

"What happened?"

She was waiting out back the whole time, 'til she finally got ticked and went home. Then she starts right off raggin' on me. Screw it. It was a stupid idea in the first place."

Is there any doubt about why kids have trouble? I thought.

Sorely lacking were any semblance of coping skills or communication. So, determined not to pout, Conor slipped a movie into the VCR, "Dr. Giggles" if I'm not mistaken.

About an hour later the phone rang again. To the bedroom for the answer. Five minutes later, emerging as if all this were normal, my so recently scorned socialite began donning, once again, the hated monkey suit.

"We're going again. All we missed is the dinner which would have been lousy anyway, so we're heading straight to the dance."

Just the way I would have planned it! Out the door and I didn't see him until around noon the following day. No details were ever offered but I did count two arms and two legs on his return.

For me, hopelessly mired as usual in recurring thoughts of basketball scenarios, as weather warmed, Iowa Games parked itself ever more prominently in my consciousness like scag in someone locked up with a Jones. Wracked with nostalgia, I very well knew that this would be the last hurrah for "the guys" since they were destined to be scattered here and there in the fall. I wanted to do it but I knew Conor was, at best, ambivalent. The day before the entry deadline, without being pushy, I somehow got a decision from him and several of the other mainstays of our beloved team through the years. It was a go! They only wanted eight people on the roster so everyone would get minutes. Fine, I agreed, recording the names they mentioned in my memory, and later filling the same onto the forms to quickly stuff into the mail destined for Ames.

School out, graduation completed, summer here, we now had six weeks to get ready. Only two of the kids had opted for track that spring, so shape for the rest, including Conor, was abominable. Determined to have at least two good practice sessions a week, I was able to procure the UNI full-length college practice court for evening use. One of Liam's friends, Ryan, had put together a pretty competitive team for the open division, and had agreed to work against us as much as possible. The fact that he asked Liam to be a part of his team was also very special since never before had my older son participated in any meaningful way on a team in an official competition. And he was picked, not because of friendship, but because he had become a respected, sometimes dominant force on the court. Several of UNI's better players who were around for the summer also asked if they could work out with us. So with me busting my butt to keep people on task and be sure that we got the most out of each session, the kids got challenged over and over, in multiple fast-paced full court scrimmages against a high level of talent. Most of them also played at other gyms when they could. Fascinated, I watched as they all seemed to get bigger, stronger, and more mature with each passing week. And, as always, they had fun at what they were doing. No bitching, no attitude, just up and down, doin' their thing the way it should be done, one hundred percent hustle and live with what you get. After a couple of practices, I was pleasantly surprised at what our team was becoming, not just holding their own, but even managing to win more than a few of the hard fought battles. By the time the regionals rolled around, we were as ready as we could be.

It didn't take a genius to see how things might play out. We were at the top of the brackets and looming on the bottom was, once again, Hank. The 18-unders were scheduled to do it all in one day and more than likely we would clash in the finals, this time one team only advancing to Ames the next week. Rumor had it that Hank, still smarting from the previous year's spanking, had pulled out all the stops, putting together an all-Iowa dream team said to be the best ever in Iowa Games history.

But that's a bit premature; we still had a few games to play. First up was a conference all-star team built around champion Grinnell's three best players. Not to worry, as experience had taught us so many times, a star in a town of five thousand people just can't match with our big battle hardened storm troops. Our worst practices had an intensity level they had never seen before.

There was an interesting sideline to this encounter though. One of their players hailed from Mozambique. Sneaking up on him during warm ups, I drummed up my best imitation of that country's street jargon. "O que e que esta a fazer?"

Taken aback, he turned to face me. Quickly, I introduced myself and we agreed to chat after the game. Shaking his hand I issued a "boa sorte," before returning to my team. It was not a close game as virtually none of their players matched up well with ours. Sadly, the game well out of reach, several of their players, lost their poise, and at one point an ugly physical confrontation was narrowly averted.

Afterwards I complimented Mike for not pulling the trigger when he had the hammer cocked and ready for action. With only eight players, we could hardly afford a suspension.

Next up were a group of Cedar Falls seventeen-year-olds. Used to tougher play, they could have presented a challenge if it weren't for the fact that they were more than a little short on talent and also tended to respond to adversity with burgeoning attitude. We won handily, but paid a heavy price when near the end of the game, Danny, the Korean flash, went down with a severe ankle sprain. Although only 5'8", he was probably the quickest member on our team, tough perimeter defender, excellent penetrator and creative finisher with either hand, and a good tree point shooter to go along with sure ball handling and rarely miss free throw skills. Now down to seven, we had to suck it up and play better than ever.

Between games I had a chance to observe part of a contest between Montezuma, our next opponent and Hank's team. Early in the second half, Hank was relaxed and laughing as his quintet was up 38, and basically scoring at will. His players were the ones seen in the sports pages all the time. I overheard someone say that they were scheduled to play in some prestigious tournament in Las Vegas the next week. I couldn't take watching much of such a slaughter and quickly returned to where my guys were sitting relaxed, taking in one of our practice partner's games featuring Liam and Ryan. Surprisingly, they were holding their own against the last year's open division champs made up of mostly ex-Iowa State Cyclones. Liam played valiantly and Ryan was nothing short of sensational, but in the end, the other guys were too much and our buddies came up short, eliminating any chance of advancing to play the next week.

Still half an hour before game time, I wandered up to the top row of seats to take in the whole picture. It was like being in heaven, the huge domed structure, big enough for football, now teaming with basketball games galore, all ages male and female represented, each seeking perhaps a bit of glory. The cacophony of yells, whistles, applause, buzzers, bounces, clangs, and squeaks played a hypnotic tune, mesmerizing yet stimulating. All this plus perfect climate control, you couldn't ask for anything more. Except for one small detail...

Back down on the floor, it was time to warm up. The guys felt good, a little tired maybe, but confident and ready to take the next step. Layups left, right and down the middle, pull up jumpers still in line, more balls for threes around the arc while two players rebound and feed the rest, five to go it's free throws. This is the routine. This is how you do it. And it works, automatically leading to a win. Can't miss.

"Listen up. Run if it's there, but if we're doin' good, save a little energy. Never know when we might need it." I could just as well have been talking to a cornfield. These guys only have one speed. Early in the game it looks like the Indianapolis 500, 3 on 2, 2 on 1, to a trailer for a 3, zip, zap, in your face. I make sure I use every time out. Montezuma, not in a good mood from their still fresh shellacking, helps us out by channeling their frustration into the creation of a hackathon, pausing the contest for repeated trips to the charity stripe. By mid second half, the game is out of reach for them, and all that's left is for us to coast out the remaining minutes. Then disaster struck. Driving hard to the hoop, Matt, quarterback on the football team and our strongest player, is literally mauled from the side by one of their forwards who probably, on top of getting up on the wrong side of the bed, came from a broken home, was always the neighborhood bully, and had just been dumped by his girlfriend. As Matt hit the floor, immediately grasping his right arm, that sickening look on his face, I knew exactly what was wrong. Motioning Shane into the game, I quickly instructed, "Go four corners and eat the clock, no retaliation, just stay cool." As they finished out the game, I took Matt behind the bench and carefully reduced his dislocated shoulder. He was fine but was obviously done for the day. Six players left!

Egads, we had made it to the finals undefeated, but at what a cost. Our ranks had been decimated, our coach was mentally fatigued, and the remaining warriors were flat out exhausted. "Go get a drink and lay down somewhere, we got one hour. I'm gonna go check the board."

This tournament is set up to showcase the 18 year olds. These are the top preps now making the big jump to the college level. All our games had been on the two college-sized courts. We were assigned the best refs, and drew the most attention. As I wandered around the side courts, many already into their last games, it seemed like I knew everyone there. Many were my patients. Others were die hard BB people like me.

"How ya doin', Doc?"

"You and Hank's Huddle for the championship?"

"Wouldn't miss it for the world."

"Good luck to you."

Arriving at the board I checked Hank's scores. The closest was 35 and their last game they had won by 60. Randy, father of our Ryan and in charge of scheduling, saw me studying the board. "What do you think, Doc?"

"I don't know, Randy. Even at full strength it would have been a stretch for us, but without Danny or Matt, I guess you'd say we're like a newborn lamb surrounded by starving wolves."

Ten minutes to game time, as other courts finish, players and fans gravitate to the main UNI college floor, shiny and cool, waiting to tremble with the final contest of the day. I get encouragement from virtually everyone. We couldn't be more favorite. Wracking my brain for any plausible strategy, all I can come up with are seemingly desperate ploys. Court side, I quickly put into effect maneuver number one: fill our bench with three other guys looking as much as they can like they're part of the team. Along with Matt and Danny, we fill the spots. Maybe Hank won't notice we got only six left. Otherwise, all he has to do is push the tempo and we're dead meat. It just might work 'cause he is busy still coaching his 16-under group on another court. I tell the guys to skip warm ups to add to the effect. Fine with them, two are lying flat on the floor and the rest look like wet towels draped over the chairs.

Watching them get ready was a real treat. Dunk after dunk, each more fantastic than the last. What a group of athletes! No less than seven of the ten were to go Division I. Their center measured 6'8"and 250 lb. Heading for Iowa State to play both football and BB, he occupied the entire low post area just by himself. Then it was 6'7", 6'6", and 6'5" on down the line. All state, all state, all state. There's the all-Iowa scoring champion. And look at those guards! Three, three, three. Do they ever miss?

And who do we have? There's Conor, 6'3" without a haircut, humble, unrecruited by "D-I's", seriously questioning the game of basketball. Shane, 6'4", a solid consistent performer for me, but a kid who was lucky to get any minutes on the high school team. Ryan, 5'7" tops, streaky shooter, but how's he gonna stop any of their guys? Mike, 6'2" and primarily a football player, prone to foul difficulties. Then there was Roland, 6'4", timid and unassuming, hadn't even gone out for BB his senior year knowing he wouldn't leave the pine. And finally Ben, 6'3" and still eighteen even though he had already completed one year of college at a NAIA Div.II school.

In my heart, I gave our guys no chance. Runnin' on empty, shorthanded, over matched at every position, we would be lucky to keep it competitive for even the first minutes of the game. Just before game time Hank made it to court side and I went over to shake hands.

"Good luck, Doc. I hate to say it but I'm afraid we got the horses this time."

"Well, take it easy on us, Hank. None of this sixty point crap, okay?" Smiling, he strode back to his bench, and as I returned to mine, I tried to think of something inspirational to say. Luckily, our guys weren't into analyzing the situation like me; they just wanted to play ball. Still, I had to play the role.

"This is it, men. Did you notice the attitude on those guys? Must be tough to be that good. They can't throw anything at us we haven't seen before. Just play solid ball, hit the open man, and good position on defense. We can't afford foul trouble. Roland, you sit. The rest of you get us off to a good start."

As the game began, I couldn't believe my eyes. They were coming at us with a zone, no press, no up tempo. Great, I thought as we proceeded to knock down a few treys and execute some neat back door cuts to the hoop for easy tallies. We didn't exactly stop them but, between more than a few errant passes and ill-advised I'm-the-star type of shots. We stayed with 'em. Twice Roland stuffed their big guy cold, and Shane was rebounding like a man possessed. Ben and Ryan were distributing the rock beautifully, keeping everyone involved or knockin' it down themselves if given space. Conor and Mike had the toughest defensive assignments and were gettin' it done, until late in the half Conor picked up his third foul forcing me to call a time. "Damn, Conor, these guys on the bench are fake. You can't foul!"

"Don't worry about it, I can play clean. I swear I won't get another foul."

Less than a minute later he picked up his fourth. Quickly, I got him out, saying nothing. A closing surge including a Ryan three and a nifty put back by Roland and we were actually up one for the intermission.

"Way to go, you guys. So far so good. Everybody needs drinks."

"Doc, can you bring me something?" It was Mike plopping down on a chair. "I'm too tired to go for a drink."

"Here, you can have some of mine," piped up Ryan handing him a bottle.

Almost immediately it was time for the second half. Looking around, I saw that every other final was finished and no one had left, all crowding around the main court entranced by what was taking place. Off to the side, Hank was lecturing his guys, a look of concern contorting his previously jolly countenance. Pulling Conor to the side, I gently reminded him, "They might not even know you got four. I'm puttin' you back in. Go as long as you can, but take one of their outside guys to avoid contact. Just do your best."

As the second half began, they seemed poised and determined, actually playing team ball. A couple of nice moves, a three, and two straight thunder dunks and all of a sudden we were down seven. Oh well, I thought, at least we stayed with 'em longer than anyone expected. I can't take anything away from the way our kids performed.

Once again, I was out of touch with my minions' mind set. Unfazed, they calmly stepped it up a notch. Didn't matter who they were playin', just do it! Ben for back to back three's, Conor on a breakaway, a Shane jumper, and two free throws for Ryan, and we're back in the lead. Time out, Hank. While our guys are smilin' and feelin' good, we hear Hank reamin' his entire team. They return the ream and as they trudge back out he issues a parting shot, "I don't care how you do it. Just win the s.o.b."

By this time the crowd is going bonkers with every play. The only ones not screaming for our side besides Hank were the parents of his players. For us, adrenaline is barely keeping ahead of lactic acid, allowing long spent players to perform well. They try a press, but Ryan and Ben cut it to shreds much too easily, giving us easy hoops. Back to a straight man, they begin doing better. By pounding it down low where they have a definite advantage they stay close. A fade away by Conor gives us a three point lead with two minutes to go. They score quickly cutting it to one then Roland tries a tricky back cut pass and has it intercepted. Without changing his expression, he turns to head up court, but no, as if with eyes in the back of his head, he reverses himself just as the new thief begins his motion to heave the ball ahead to a streaking teammate. Up with the fly paper and in an instant Roland has possession again. At the same time Mike sees an open lane and sprints down the right side of the court catching the quick pass from Ro as he blasts directly toward the hoop. From the left comes their two sport behemoth, determined to prevent any easy attempt. If there's one thing about Mike it's that he doesn't even recognize the word fear. A strong safety in football, he would pop his own mother to prevent a completion. The collision took place in the air about three feet from the basket. Going to the right is money for Mike but usually there's not a barn in the way. His knees hit the defender at about mid sternum, followed closely by a hip and various other body parts. The huge mound didn't give, but raised arms couldn't wrap up before mighty Mike bounced off, reloaded and canned a nifty bank shot. A furious flurry of whistles accompanied the consequent crash to the floor. Near pandemonium clutched the crowded court side. Feisty principals were held apart momentarily but the quickly assessed foul and Mike's swished free throw sent the action back into high gear. Under a minute now and they come down and after two passes feed the post once again. Collapsing all around, our defense forgets a man deep in the corner. Boom, the ball sails out and a high arching three is launched just over Ben's fast closing swat. Anxiety mounts as the silk adapts to the spinning seams. A single point lead is all we got, thirty-four seconds to go. Hounded everywhere we manage to advance the ball across the ten second line and proceed to spread the floor. With them desperately overplaying, Ryan sees an open alley and darts into the paint catching the picture perfect bounce two steps from pay dirt. As he elevates, a defender materializes as if from nowhere forcing him to change the shot. A sure two becomes a rebound them and we're racing the other way. My pulse soars above the danger point as much too quickly, one of their generic D-I's sticks a twelve-footer giving them a fragile one point advantage.

Signaling our last time out, I gather the beleaguered boys around, twelve ticks 'til destiny. All cling to their thighs, too pooped for even a facial expression. All they want is a right line, a direction, assurance so they can execute what they know must be done. "Conor, take it out. Ben and Ryan up front, Mike and Shane at half court. Mike run up to back pick for Ben and Ben, you go long. Maybe we'll catch them denying too much. Everyone keep your spacing and break to the open area. Any decent shot, pull the trigger and crash the boards."

Nice plan but Hank had his team picking up at half court. Ben wisely let the ball bounce a few times before grabbing it and dribbling across the line and pushing to the top of the key. A quick pivot and suddenly he's in the lane threatening to score. All the attention comes his way, allowing Conor to step open to the left. The quick pass, the shot, no good! But somehow Shane is there to snare the carom. And he's fouled, they fouled him, no doubt, hacked across the arms! Six seconds to go and we got bonus!

As Hank calls time, I try to think of what to say, especially to Shane. Minimal varsity high school experience, a genius in math, practical joker, always a grin on his face, he defied any read. His play was consistently good for me so I decided to minimize the moment and get on with business. "No time outs left, guys. If we're ahead one, just pressure 'em to slow it down, no foul. Ro, challenge the inbound. If we're behind, it's a steal, foul situation. All right? Put 'em in, Shane." Everyone standing and straining, referees poised in their positions, Hank consternated, me feeling as though a delivery were imminent, the stage was set. The man of the hour steps to the line. The referee checks the positions on both sides and begins to hand over the ball. Wait! Hank has jumped out on the floor screaming for another time out! I look over at him and yell, "C'mon ,Hank! What's with the double ice? Let's finish it!"

A boisterous two minute interlude and then Shane alone in the world, ball in hand. What could be going through his mind? Nothing, everything, who knows. Swisheroo! Tie game! Again poised, this time he takes a few dribbles. What are you doing, Shane? The routine, don't break it now! Kaboom! Just like the first! Jubilation ready to erupt! They have it looking deep, arm back, ten people scrambling for all they're worth, the throw...it's tipped!

Roland got a piece of it! Mike has it at mid-court! The clock is running. Ross has started the clock! In amazement I see Michael, without hesitation, whip the sphere skyward, freezing all eyes up, and up, and still higher. Only in the dome! Three...two...one. That ball may still be flying. Chaos ensued, players mobbed, mothers crying, high five's everywhere, retired farmers dancin' to a yipeekyay, so much good feeling the roof could have popped. Then the shaking of stunned hands. Nice game, good game, good hustle, nice try, until finally, it's me and Hank. Putting my hand out, I see only a sullen vacancy. No words, just a quick grasp and back to our teams. Ten minutes later the noise hadn't abated. No one had left. Our guys still on the court, unable to use up the savored miracle. The baby had delivered and was fine!

There had never been such an underdog. This stretched it as far as it could possibly go. Everyone wanted to be part of it. Comment after comment like, "That's the best game I've ever seen," or, "What a win!" and "Absolutely incredible!" As I looked at the players faces, I saw total exhaustion, like they had just taken Iwo Jima or gone 15 with Sonny Liston, but each had a continuous smile reflecting something akin to stepping through the pearly gates. I don't consider myself emotional, but regions of my right brain that had lain dormant for generations were emitting all sorts of spontaneous impulses, and for quite some time I was on clouds I had never even seen before.

For days it was wonderful. Even Eldon Miller came up to me and asked, "How did you guys do that?"

Trying to avoid pretension, I answered, "Team ball, positive attitude, and hustle." What else is there? A bunch of rag-tag nobodies, or better said six rag-tag nobodies, and a wistful country doctor, had whipped the best players in Iowa.

Two spirited practices and we were in Ames for the final four. Anything would be anticlimactic after what we had already accomplished but it wouldn't sit well to blow it now. And there was adversity; Mike had a charity benefit football game that same day in Des Moines, Danny was limping and Matt couldn't raise his right arm above shoulder level. That left five solid players who I felt could match up well with anything we would face.

First up was a group made up from various schools in the Des

Moines area. They were big, and cocky. Must it always be so? It seemed like we were the only group that just played the game, none of the posturing, bragging, put downs or trash. Basketball, pure and simple. Consequently, we got no respect, 'cause we didn't hot dog it or act like we were superior, until it was too late and another team was stung, humble lesson delivered.

The game began rather slowly, baskets traded, score near even, until about five minutes into the contest when one of their guys decides to drive the lane and show the finger roll. Coiled in the timber is Roland, who proceeds to smite the rock to smithereens, directing it to near mid-court before it first bounced. Anticipating the monumental shingling, Conor had taken off sprinting and now swept up the rejected object in full stride and proceeded to dribble twice and plant the left sneaker at the dotted line going airborne from there to finish with the tomahawk. He'd never done that before and the crowd went nuts. Now the "mo" was ours and we proceeded to run off a substantial string of scoring plays which, along with solid defense put the game virtually out of reach by the end of the first half. The most amazing sequence of all occurred in the second half when Ryan made a steal and flipped it ahead to Conor, who, once again was first in transition. Seeing that the pass was high, he leaped skyward with such explosiveness that he rocketed right out of one shoe, and still couldn't get to the pass. This is where things get hazy and also how legends are made. Being a meticulous dresser and a purist on proper basketball decor, he first crouches down to slip the sneaker back on before racing after the errant assist. By then the ball was heading toward the far corner and threatening to go out of bounds. Utilizing an all-out sprint and a finishing dive he was able to corral the darned thing and, while still in the air flattened out well over the base line, flip it behind his back perfectly splitting two oncoming defenders to arrive untouched in the hands of Danny at the hoop for the uncontested layup!

What can I say, other than the loss of a little skin, Conor was having fun, and the team was not to be denied. Winning by 20, we went out for a light lunch, having two hours before the championship game. Everyone had played well and no one even thought about individual stats. It was just a real pleasure being part of this swan song. Now all that remained was to finish it off.

As was my custom, between games, I took the opportunity to visit with various groups of parents present for the festivities. Without fail, each was appreciative, excited, and proud. Roland's father and mother, both from impoverished Mexican families in San Antonio, were especially effusive and poignant in their comments. "Doc, this next game doesn't matter. If nothing else happens, we can't begin to thank you enough for what you've given our son. Being a minority is never easy and you know very well Roland's story. He's a very quiet boy, or *was* would be a better description. We had to be out of town last weekend. After your last game, he called us and Doc—it was as if it wasn't him. He was so excited, telling us all about it. He couldn't help it, on and on with the details. Rita and I were laughing and crying at the same time. Now he's proud and confident. I don't think he'll ever be the same."

Damn, I thought, it was just a basketball game. But in my heart I knew they were right. Everyone there had been affected, some more than others. I know my calluses were thinning and my hat size was up a little. Imagine for those whose lives may not have been as fortunate. In a way, even an NBA title didn't carry the same significance. At that level you're supposed to be good, you're not sneaking up on anybody.

I reverted back to Spanish for my response. "Bueno, su hijo esta a jugar mejor que nunca. Ojala que se pueda enfrentar todo los desafios en su vida con el mismo valor."

Back on the floor, while we were warming up for the big one, I took stock of the opposition. Twelve deep, a few big guys, and a coach that looked about two years older than the players. They were from Clinton and although I had never seen any of them play before, I knew they couldn't be any better than us. The number 12 did concern me slightly, but our guys were in excellent shape and didn't foul much. Besides, if they got deep into their bench, most certainly their talent level would fall off and we could rip them to pieces.

Sure enough they came out in full court pressure with multiple substitutions. It wasn't that they were so effective but we just weren't hitting well at all while they happened to score some nice hoops and by half time we found ourselves down four. In the locker room, "I like this, guys. This is our kind of scenario. Always better to be behind at the half. You're not doing anything wrong, just keep

400

gunnin'. No way can we go a whole game like this. Hit the streak and ride it."

Back on the court, I knew something was up when Conor asked me if he could jump center. I hoped it meant he was ready to take over the game. When he easily out jumped their 6'6" post man tipping it to Ben who pulled up to can a three, I knew I was in for a show. In rapid succession it was Ryan for three, Conor for two, and Ben again for three. From there on we never looked back. Everyone started hitting, except for Conor that is. Conor went beyond hitting. He entered a groove rarely found in basketball, not even having to think about shot selection. Penetrate, the "J" for three, spin left or right, fade, it didn't matter, everything fell. Reminded me a little of his dad. In no time the game was out of reach. We didn't try to show them up but it still ended up us by twenty. As always no one thought of individual stats but I found it within myself to estimate the number 40 following Conor's name. How any coach could have seen that demonstration and not wanted to recruit him I'll never know. Anyway we were state champs. Out on the court, pictures, medals, fanfare, it was great. Hank, who was there with his 16-under team, was one of the first to come up to congratulate us. This was it, the end of an odyssey, an eight year fun run, a generation come and gone.

The next day we were off to Ladakh! Liam, Conor, and I in flight east to Chicago, then Amsterdam, on what Conor had picked, for high school graduation, as his dream trip. All three of us were in excellent shape and, although not knowing exactly what to expect, were ready to prove our mettle. In the ultra-modern Dutch airport, Liam and I gambled guilders and guzzled carafes of tapped domestic while Conor practiced painting the porcelain fly yellow before boarding the 737 directed towards Russia. Arcing high over Moscow, we took advantage of global spin and met the subcontinent just as Delhi came under us.

Touching down we sought our bags and prepared for the rigors of customs. For light reading, I had planned to bring Salman Rushdie's *The Moor's Last Sigh*, but changed my mind when Janet asked, "Are you nuts?" In my suitcase, however, were a number of instruments of the trade, to be left at appropriate places along the way. The stainless steel caught the attention of the official and I was obliged to open up and display the hardware.

Grabbing one of the shinier items, the pesky bureaucrat asked, "And this?"

"Dental forceps," I answered making a gesture with my own hand near my mouth. Immediately he began to describe a problem he had with a decayed molar, literally hoping I would pull the offending ivory on the spot. Seeing no wisdom in such a course of action, I declined as inoffensively as possible hoping to avoid confiscation or detention. A flurry of comments from the waiting line behind us may have helped. The only word I caught was "dacoit" which couldn't in any way be construed as complimentary, but nevertheless we were then perfunctorily passed through.

Having only one day in the Indian capital, we were able to experience only bits and pieces of the grimy sweltering hell swarming with hoards of petulant mendicants hoping desperately to exploit our differentness. Early the following day, after several key bribes by our chosen intercessor, we were on the small Indian jet skimming over Rajasthan, then Punjab before beginning the steady climb above the chronically disputed state of Kashmir. Far above the once beckoning capital of Srinigar, we distanced ourselves further from the turmoil and approached what may be the most spectacular sight on earth, the Himalayas! In azure we were soon wending our way amongst a vast array of 20,000-plus snowcapped pinnacles as far as the eye could see, enraptured in dreams of Tin Tin and the Dali Lama. K-2 to the west, Annapurna and Everest to the east, our craft hung still before attempting a final swoop into the valley of Leh. With the skill of a bush pilot we were brought to a halt at 12,000 ft. atop the world, exiting into a wondrous land of fresh thin air and a scattered culture untouched by modern contradictions.

"Dr. Murphy, jullay, welcome." It was Norboo, greeting us in perfect English. 'Tonight you will acclimate in the hotel before beginning the trek in the morning. This is the most beautiful time of the year. I have planned many things but just let me know if other ideas come up. We can make any adjustment you wish along the way." Hopping into the jeep we began the short drive through the outskirts of the ancient town before penetrating to the bustling center en route to a tiny family establishment part way up a mountain overlooking the city. Every sight was new and wondrous setting us all atingle as we checked into our room and sat down to a deliciously spiced vegetarian dinner; or was it a lack of oxygen? All that night I slept not. How could I, compelled as I was to take a deep inspiration every third or fourth breath just to stay alive! Anxiously clutching the bottle of acetazolamide I had brought along just in case, I kept wondering why those two were out like babies while I was tied up doing my own vitals the whole time. I never succumbed to taking the medicine and by sunrise I was at least no worse.

An early breakfast and we were on our way availing ourselves of the one sure road closely adapted to the upper reaches of the Indus river, gray and daunting as it carved its way through the foreboding landscape. Pulling over frequently to allow convoys of tank trucks to pass, we were told of the upcoming winter, long and harsh, and the fuel needs of the ever vigilant Indian military, threatened here by both Chinese and Pakistani hegemony. Ladakhi's, like most other peoples, want only to be left alone, content in their ways developed over the millennia. This was the high Tibetan plateau, firmly embedded in a rich Buddhist tradition more important than ever now that Lhasa had been gobbled up by its most populous and aggressive neighbor.

Turning off we began a steady ascent and finally came to the end of the road surrounded by snowy peaks. "From here we walk. In four hours we will come to our campsite. There is a monastery nearby which we can visit if you wish. Each of you take a pack and we will begin." Midday, the temperature near eighty, our shoulders properly weighted, we were trekking! The contrast between here and Delhi couldn't have been more acute. From the acrid plethora of grunge in the seething sauna below we had advanced to a position alone atop the globe where vestiges of thin dry gasses patiently awaited their first contact with human hemoglobin. Marching east along the centuries' old path, we worked our way towards the first of many passes. Beads of sweat were already forming on my down turned brow as from that perspective we could have been in the western U.S., until glancing up to the level of the horizon, that is. What magnitude of geologic collision could the subcontinent have provided for the creation of such prodigious buckles? Then the well-deserved pause at the acme of the pass where in addition, we three novices were treated to a sight as wondrous as any we had ever before encountered. In brilliant sunshine, just before us, and stretching up an entire mountainside, was the most perfect carpet of uniform flowering vegetation imaginable. Clearly enjoying our reaction as much as the scene, Norboo chuckled. "Lavender," he informed. The richness of color alone took what little breath we had away. Is there any doubt why this plant has such a magical calming effect? The smell was like freshly cut alfalfa mixed with that of a million just sharpened pencils. This trip was going to be all we had hoped for and more.

At our campsite, along one of the innumerable clamoring streams originating under some distant glacier, we rested briefly before going pack free to the aforementioned monastery. First a glorious stroll down a deep gorge lined by cliffs soaring too far off meetings with the sky. Eagles seemed to float immobile in the blue, surely ruling their magnificent kingdom. After three or four miles, it was off into a grand valley which we followed to the far uppermost reaches of the blind pouch where the sprawling man made structure lay against the mountainside.

Thinking of the construction alone was humbling, but the demeanor of the monks was even more impressive. Painstakingly patient, supremely dedicated to their lifestyle, these caretakers of the Buddhist path graciously answered all our questions, as we delved into the fascinating philosophy unchanged here for so many centuries.

Our first experience with butter tea was less than positive. All I could imagine was that the fat content, over the generations, by its high caloric value, had given a survival edge to those who partook most of this somewhat vile tasting concoction. Quickly we mastered the technique of placing our outstretched hand over the partially filled cup.

We had learned about and seen prayer wheels, deep meditation and guttural chants, but now it was time to depart. Looking up at the sun, Norboo informed us that more time had elapsed than he had anticipated and that we would have to take a shortcut to avoid darkness. Great, I thought, shorter would be fine since I was already more than exhausted. Never have I been more foolish!

Instead of going down the valley, we headed straight up the

mountain behind the monastery. Assured that this was the way the monks always took, we were soon using hands more often than not as we proceeded where even a goat would have been challenged. Finally reaching the summit we then angled off onto a windswept pointed ridge climbing at a steady upward grade soon lined by drop-offs on either side which, if one should fall, were of such a slope and height to, in my eyes, preclude survival. Added to this concern was the fact that now each step was preordained by centuries of repeated use, no trail being present, only footprint after footprint, none anywhere near the size of our inflated American feet. The kids seemed to be doing fine but not me. Trailing farther and farther behind, I began to feel a chill in my bones as my leg muscles screamed for relief. Rest was out of the question as every imaginable position offered no stability. Like walking on the railroad track, up on the iron rail, your best bet is to keep moving forward, except here we were going uphill and a slip meant at least a thousand foot tumble. Temperature dropping, wind picking up, oxygen debt steadily gripping my soul, I began to seriously question both my physical and my mental state. Just as I was about to enter into the final acceptance of my fate, I came over a rise and there were my companions resting on a safe plateau. "Kinda tough, huh?" remarked Conor as I draped myself over a convenient boulder. Recovering mentally, I stood back up only to face the horror of seeing no way to advance other than a gigantic slope of sand and pebbles at about a 70 degree grade dropping maybe three or four thousand feet before leveling off.

"What do we do here?" I asked stupidly.

"Jump!" was the single word answer, as if my question had been rhetorical. Right, I thought. And how many monks are buried at the bottom? Septuagenarians in saffron sailing salaciously. Well, hell, there's no way I'm going back the way we came.

"I'll go first," I volunteered throwing caution to the indifferent wisps of air dancing by our lightened heads.

Although wanting to look brave, my good judgment got the better of me, and my initial leap was a bit timid. It didn't matter as the forces of gravity made each successive bound more legendary than the last. There was no stopping, or even slowing down, just dig in the heels and try to maintain balance as you are pulled into the next Hulk-like hop. *Wham...wham...wham...* Air flying by, arms flailing, every cell invigorated, eating up real estate in a grand and glorious fashion! Less than thirty seconds later it was over. Standing on flat ground I turned and waved, feeling great. One by one the others tried their luck. Hoops and hollers echoed off granite as each finished off the necessary task with youthful vigor. Only Liam got a little carried away and ended up in some bushes just beyond the landing strip. No harm done, we brushed ourselves off, laughing as we started up the now shortened trail, the kids leading the way.

That night I slept as well as anyone could ever sleep, covered by a billion extra stars.

At sunrise we were up, ready for more punishment. After eating, we embarked on an undulating four hour stroll, several times meeting herds of goats heading higher in search of vegetation. Each animal had its own personality and prided itself on its unique look. There's Lincoln, and Van Dyke; over there, God himself.

On one high pass, as we inched along a narrow ledge, solid cliff on one side, abyss on the other, a flirt with certain death was once again perilously interjected into the precarious prosecution of our path. Coming around a corner, not ten feet away, was a huge yak, going where we had just come from. There was no discussion of right of way, or even hesitation on his part. We all exhaled simultaneously, pancaking ourselves to the cliff. Glistening nares, lance-like horns, bulging cervical sinews, and deadly hooves passed within inches of our frail and frightened forms. Never a prayer wheel when you need one, I thought as we continued on and reached a broad plain. Our guide pointed to a distant rim, telling us that just below it was a village. Nearly there we came upon a hole in the ground, maybe 15-20 ft. deep. "Wolf trap," explained Norboo. "Put a goat, or better yet, a wolf pup in the hole and the adult wolf will jump in."

Advancing on, we reached the edge and were treated to a visual delight. Scattered dwellings filled the valley, mingled with a variety of fields and fruit trees, all bathed in glorious green thanks to an age old irrigation scheme. Beginning with the mountain cataract entering the valley high on our left, hand crafted stone arteries began diverting the precious liquid commodity and continued to do so all the was down, assuring sustenance to even the smallest garden plot in this

BREAKAWAY

beautiful arid land.

Entering the bountiful space, we came upon women alternately pounding wheat, and then flinging it into the air with half shell thatched baskets, singing as they worked. "What do they sing?" I asked.

"They ask that the breeze continue soft and steady, to remove the chaff and keep their work easy."

"Why do they seem so happy?"

"Because the land is theirs. All brothers of a family must marry the same wife and share her. It's worked for thousands of years."

Norboo knew everyone. I was impressed by the absolute lack of reticence among the Ladakhi people at each house we visited, even children, so different from other cultures I'd been in. As usual, when told I was a Western doctor, people asked for medical help. Soon my meager supplies of antibiotics and analgesics were being depleted. At the school, after being entertained by renditions of several local songs, each accompanied by a meticulously choreographed dance step, I treated a child with a particularly nasty infection swelling one ear completely shut. I hoped the penicillin I had would do the job.

We were given fruits, vegetables, and various grain preparations, invariably accompanied by the ubiquitous butter tea. Already we had had enough of that to last a lifetime. Mentioning it to Norboo, magically, from then on we were also given cups of local brew, much more satisfying.

At one point Liam questioned a well weathered village elder about snow leopards. "Yes, I shot two in my youth, hunting high in the mountains."

"You must have been quite a marksman," I added.

"Plenty of practice on Pakistani's," was the retort as he flashed a toothless grin.

Expecting to hear about yeti, we listened to more tales, many quite realistic, about "little people" far above, who seemed to be able to vanish at will.

The high point of the visit for me was an encounter with the local "amchi." Trained in Tibet, this primary care giver patiently explained his holistic approach to health. One entire room was filled with roots and herbs, all collected and prepared according to detailed ancient methods outlined in his much worn thick Tibetan texts.

Astrological charts played a key role in decision making, as did family structure. Acupuncture was used extensively. Minor surgery could be performed. Various diets were either pre- or proscribed.

Pulse was mentioned so I asked if he would take mine. Having me lay down, he lifted my arm up, grasping my wrist, fingers lightly measuring the impact of blood bounding through the underlying radial artery. Assuming what had to be the classical pose, he closed his eyes, focusing exclusively on Harvey's pivotal discovery. After a long several minutes he said, "I detect a strong heart and significant recent ingestion of butter tea." Laughing, he put my arm down and asked if I wanted to see some projects he was working on. First we went to an adjoining room where he pulled a string and a light came on. Amazed, I followed him to the window where he pointed to the nearby stream. He had put in a paddle wheel connected to a generator and now had electricity. Next was a greenhouse covered by solar panels. "Solar energy for another crop each year," he proudly mentioned. Before we departed, I gave him dental forceps, other instruments, and a small supply of medicines.

Over the next several days we visited more monasteries and villages, hiking twenty to thirty miles a day. Even though we were steadily gaining altitude, because of our good conditioning we were able to make better time than anticipated. That evening, camped far from any humans, we observed the now dramatically amplified heavens. Falling stars seemed to appear every few minutes. No wonder, I surmised, so much importance is placed on these scintillating oracles. Here, more than anywhere, night after night, people were reminded that they are only part of a dynamic universe, vast and eternal. Respect, mindfulness, and detachment flow so naturally from such a stage.

"We have an extra day. How would you like to spend it?" Our guide, Norboo already seemed like a close friend.

"Did you have something in mind?" I asked.

"There is a glacier not far from here. I wouldn't even suggest this for any other group but I've seen how strong the three of you are. Would you like to go there?"

Without hesitation or consultation, I jumped at the opportunity. "We came for adventure. Let's do it!"

"All right. I have never been there myself, but I know it's

accessible this time of year; herders take yak there to graze. We'll pack light and leave before dawn."

"Oh, Norboo," I asked hesitantly. "What's the altitude there?"

"Probably 20,000 feet."

My god, I thought. We're at fourteen now, how difficult might it be to ascend six thousand and return in a day? Crawling into my sleeping bag, I hoped I would be up to the task. My legs felt good. What I needed was a solid night's rest.

It was not to be. Conor had lost the sun screen lotion, and up this close, I had developed sizable areas of first and second degree burns. Worse, the "you need more air" syndrome was back. Not as bad but enough to force me into an inspiratory prolongation every six or eight breaths.

By the time the dimmest gray dabbed at the eastern horizon, we were moving. Direction wasn't a problem. Basically we were following a stream to its source, only occasionally cutting a corner if we saw the channel doubling back. Terrain was another story. Clambering and climbing describes it best, most taxing being the incessant ascent skyward. Midmorning we got to a cluster of maybe eight primitive dwellings on a broad plateau. I was sucking for wind on every breath, closer and closer to the slippery slope of the oxygen disassociation curve. It wasn't like when you've pushed too hard in a close BB game, but more of a vague feeling that you're not getting air and that a deeper breath should help. Well, if it did, the change was almost imperceptible.

A woman there invited us in for food and tea. Clearly impoverished, uneducated, and more primitive, she nevertheless attended us most graciously. How far to the glacier? A ways. She hadn't been there but her ten year old son was there now with the yak.

On we went, hill after hill, rise after rise, always seeing our destination but seemingly not gaining on it. How deceptive perceptions are in this diffuse attic of the world! Pausing to sit on a rock with a view, I now saw no plants. So this is the Aeolian zone, I thought, only crustaceans, bacteria, fungi, and a few insects.

The combination of radiant UV waves and the constant exertion minimized the steadily dropping temperature. I was sweating profusely. When Norboo told us of a majestic lake awaiting us at the foot of the massive ice pack, I, fool that I am, pledged to jump in if we ever got there.

Nice sentiment but I doubt it added to our motivation any. In fact it didn't as atop one of the more challenging swells, once again not revealing a direct path to our destination, Liam flat out quit. Sitting down, he stated that he was done, not a step further. None of us were thinking straight and just accepted it as if it mattered little. "Catch you on the way back," and we trudged on as if walking in syrup. Looking back later we saw him straggling along like a lonesome puppy.

We did get there, but it took much longer than anticipated. Even the prodigal son drew near as I stripped down to skivvies poised to fulfill my promise. The lake was nice but not near what we had anticipated. The actual glacier was still above us and to touch it would be another two hours of difficult climbing.

Putting my hiking shoes back on to protect my feet from cuts, I stood on a large rock, like an Olympic diver, poised for takeoff. The gathered audience of one small boy and assorted yak looked on in anxious expectation. Degree of difficulty, zero point zero, or so I thought.

High into the thin air for a dramatic feet first plunge, push off bottom and exit as quickly as possible. The perfect plan. As the murky water closed over my head, I realized that something horrible was amiss. It was as if mind and body came unglued, an unimpeded thrust into the state of suspended animation. My first notion was that water shouldn't have the right to be this cold. But that wasn't it. My feet had become embedded up to the ankles in a semi-congealed muck at the bottom of this nondescript nameless pond. What ignominy! Was it to be death by quick freeze or drowning? Or would I gradually sink into the primordial ooze to be preserved there in perpetuity? Not a bad fate. No! Not yet! Remember lifesaving. Sink and think! Sink and think!

I had the sink part down pat; I was sunk. And as for the think, I wasn't doing real well on that one either. Luckily I had taken a deep breath on jumping. Actually, my last ten thousand breaths had been deep. And my metabolic rate was surely plummeting. I probably had all of thirty seconds before total blackout. Okay, here's the plan: I'll curl my toes up, sweep my arms down, and at the same time leap with all my might to liberate my encased appendages. If all else fails, I'll reach down and untie the laces and just leave the puppies planted here. Better to die half way down the mountain of overwhelming blisteritis.

A quick "Om Mane Padme Hum" and.....*Ssshlloopp*! My shoes had come free! I would live! Yes! In seconds, without touching bottom, I was up on shore. "My feet were stuck," I reported.

But in the time I was down, the world had changed. Sleet was falling. Mega-chills wracked my weary bones. And my skin was the color of fetid plumbs. A wave of nausea hit me as I struggled to dress myself. While the others ate lunch, I tried to decide which of the two glaciers was real. Twenty thousand feet above sea level, hypothermia, old age, exhaustion, take your pick. I chose to say nothing. Does that tell you anything? Finally, as we were about to begin the descent, I quietly asked Conor if he would be so kind as to take my pack and let me walk ahead of him for a bit. Life is full of compromises.

My survival may have still been in doubt but even after the first two down hills, I could already feel the difference. A few thousand feet more and I had a bounce back in my step. As daylight evaporated, we came within sight of camp and soon were cooking over the gas burners. What we had accomplished was, in my mind, nothing short of prodigious. Never would I attempt it again.

The day before we were to return to Leh, a man came up to talk to Norboo in hushed tones. The look on their faces implied something was up but even in my wildest imagination would I have guessed what it was.

"There has been a bombing of a Buddhist shrine in the city. Military curfew is in effect. The Indian soldiers are paranoid and unpredictable. I have a friend nearby who may be able to sneak us in after midnight by a back road. Wait here and I'll go seek him out."

Wonderful, I thought, now we have to struggle with political intrigue and face impetuous young idealists, overloaded with deadly technology, lurking in every shadow. It would make a great movie. Too bad it was real. No, don't worry kids. It's just some group of fundamentalist fanatics trying to make a point. That's the way things are here. We're Americans, they won't bother us. Even they laughed at that one.

Deep into the night we were slowly approaching the troubled town. The last part we did without lights, reaching the hotel just before dawn without incident. I had asked Norboo to see if there was a way he could get me to the hospital in the morning and about eight o'clock he arrived by scooter saying he thought he could get me there if we avoided the main roads. Almost no one was on the streets as we took the roundabout route through poorer neighborhoods to arrive at the sizable medical facility.

After being introduced to the head physician, I asked if I could accompany him on rounds and see some of the hospital. He was very accommodating, even anxious to show me everything. Although Ladakhi, he had studied in Delhi, and spoke excellent English. Not only that but he proved to be a very competent dedicated government health worker. We saw the usual TB, leprosy, and pediatric pneumonia cases, but also more rheumatic hearts than I expected, and an entire ward of men on oxygen. "These are all impoverished Bihari's, recruited by private construction enterprises as cheap labor. Arriving here one day, they are immediately taken by lorry to the site at 15,000 feet. Many, of course, go into pulmonary or cerebral edema and are just dumped at our door. Not only do they deplete all our oxygen and medicines, but we then have nowhere to send them. It's a very frustrating situation."

All in all, I thought the quality of care was quite high. Of course most of the population lived in remote areas and had no access to such modern facilities. Still, I enjoyed seeing the cases and discussing all the issues. Before I left I presented my new colleague with a state of the art stethoscope and all the accessories I had brought along for just such an occasion.

Back at the hotel, Liam and Conor told of how they had ventured out just a few blocks when suddenly an explosion took place up on a mountain. Instantly the street was filled with uniformed men toting automatic weapons. Ducking into a doorway, they waited until the street cleared and quickly returned to the hotel. Egads, kids! Where do you get such notions?

At the airport the next morning, everyone was extremely anxious, security up the wazoo. At least the plane was supposed to show. As our wait in the line approached the intolerable level, I noticed an elderly Frenchman ahead of us gradually get more ashen.

412

Finally he began to slump to the ground as I hurried to assist if I could. Head down and feet up, all I could think of to say was "tres bien." His pulse was approximately forty, with fine droplets of moisture appearing on his forehead. Probably fainted, I surmised, but couldn't rule out some sort of cardiac event. Then a woman appeared speaking like a physician, perfect French, but with a cigarette dangling from her lips. I stepped back and allowed her to take over. Minutes later he was able to lean up against a bench, only a little pale, but probably in much better shape than I had been several days earlier.

Eventually the plane arrived. Loading quickly we were soon in the air and back in Delhi by noon. The kids were against it but somehow I convinced them that rather than waste our last hours we should hit Old Delhi and check out the rich cultural diversity and pulsating hoards of humanity.

The only way to do this, of course is by bicycle rickshaw. I hopped in the first one while they hesitated before reluctantly climbing into the second to follow. The place was absolutely vibrant. Every space occupied, we alternated between streets crowded with various types of vehicles and narrow alleys filled with scurrying children, industrious urchins, women in sari's and burkha's, humble Hindu's of all castes, turbaned Sikh's in full regalia, proud looking Muslim's, and jabbering Jain's all doing business simultaneously at the innumerable stalls selling anything imaginable. Stopping to eat at a Muslim restaurant, we then went to the Red Fort and the zoo before ending at the hotel for a few hours' sleep. At 4 a.m. we took the limo to make the early flight to Amsterdam. Then on to Chicago and finally Waterloo, still intact, and rich in possession of the impressions, scars and memories we had won.

My first day back at noon basketball was less than memorable. I was, however proud to display my badge, the shoulder scabs of the pack. Conor left for the University of Iowa, and I began to think more seriously of going back to work in the third world.

One night the phone rang and I was pleasantly surprised that it wasn't the usual "I'm in pain, anxious, depressed, and can't sleep, can you help me" kind of call. It was Craig, a basketball buddy. "Doc, you want to play for the world championship?"

Craig was actually as much, and in some ways more of a BB

junky than me. I mean I was pretty sure that there was more to life than hoops. He wasn't. Take a couple days, or even a week off work to go to some obscure hick town for a "really good" three-on-three championship; let's do it, he'd say. Plan your whole life around it; this is the big one. For the last two years we'd participated in the first ever Cedar Falls Seniors Festival basketball extravaganza. These were half court games where with any new possession you clear it to the 3-point line and go. We hadn't just won all our games, we dominated. Our closest challenge was a thirty point squeaker. If there was ever a perfect guy to play with, it was Craig. At 6'5", even tempered, all he did was run the floor, rebound, and play, not just good, I don't hesitate to say, excellent "D". He'd routinely take their top scorer out of the picture. Two on one, even three on one, with him back, advantage us time after time. And the few times he did look to score, it was a high percentage shot. Anyhow, in the aforementioned games, he'd just rebound or block a shot, flip it to me and I'd score. Ain't no fifty-year-old can stop me. I can stop myself, but they can't. The referees for those contests were the UNI women's BB players, which made it more fun. I must have averaged 45 at least, and in one game, when I really got smokin', I swear I canned a good twenty "3's." To top it off, I had won the 50-55 50-meter dash at 7.1 seconds, while Craig and I tied for the high jump title. So my light was shining bright. Craig's perception was that the rest of the field was definitely coming back to us. No reason we couldn't win anywhere. Back to the phone call.

"Okay Craig, where's this one, Pocatello, Idaho?"

"No, but close. I'm talkin' World Senior Games, St. George, Utah."

"Not AAU?"

"No, we're not messin' with just U.S., this is world. Russian Olympic team of '72, Brazil, Canada, they're all coming. This is it, the ultimate challenge, for all the marbles. What do you say?"

"Well, putting it that way, I guess I can't pass it up."

"Good, I already sent your name in!"

"One more thing—who we got so far?"

"Never fear, Phil and I are combing the countryside, telephone, internet, obscure YMCA's. It'll definitely be a dream team. I'd say we got the gold."

As I hung up the phone, I was already castigating myself. Do I really want to spend a week doing this? Shouldn't I be with the kids more, or at least off somewhere like Honduras doing health care? How can I justify it? What kind of weakness is it that sucks me into these things every time? But we might win! So what? It's a game. Five over the hill reruns, hideous in their skimpy shorts, out in public playing mock basketball, desperately trying to do the impossible, assuage the insatiable ego.

Meanwhile work at the office intensified: 16 year old dentist's daughter with a year and a half heroin history, bronchogenic ca. coughing blood, and fractured pelvis lost in irreversible shock, Guillain-Barre on the vent, adult varicella, HIV, SIDS, suicide, and psychosis. Fight in the waiting room, staff discord, failed M.E., money missing, computer down, another subpoena, I need basketball!

"Dad."

"Hey, Liam, what's up?" Kind of funny him calling at this hour. Must be something unusual.

"Ryan's father died. Jack and I are coming up to be with him."

"Jeez, he wasn't that old. What happened?"

"I don't know. We just found out. There's something more about it but we haven't heard what it is. Ryan's not talking, so Jack and I are on the way."

"Okay, I'll see you tonight."

Ryan was one of Liam's good friends, Conor's too, actually. All the last summer we had played BB together, Liam and Ryan getting their team ready while at the same time providing tough practice competition for our Iowa Games team. Ryan's dad, a two sport star in college, had even played a couple of years in the NFL. I had heard, somewhere along the line, he had developed an alcohol problem, but I wasn't close at all to the situation. As soon as I finished my last patient, I drove over to their house.

Opening the door for me was Thad, Ryan's best friend. The dark room was filled with the most somber faces I'd seen in a long time. Walking up to Ryan's mother and putting my hand on her shoulder I said, "Sorry to hear about your husband."

"Thanks for coming, Dr. Murphy."

"Where's Ryan?" I asked, not seeing him in the room.

"Did you hear what happened?"

"No, I haven't heard anything."

Taking me into an empty bedroom, she proceeded to pour out one of the most heart wrenching testimonials conceivable. "Ryan's been to the police station," she began, grabbing even more of my already heightened attention. "I was out of the house. My husband had been drinking, and apparently he and Ryan got into some sort of disagreement. There was a tussle, not a fight, more like a minor confrontation. Anyhow, Ryan's dad fell. He said his side hurt but he got up and made it to the couch to lie down. It wasn't long before Ryan saw that he just didn't look right so he called "911." The ambulance came and right away transferred him to the hospital but the police had also been contacted and they took Ryan to the station for "questioning." While he was downtown, his dad died. He lasted less than 30 minutes. Ruptured spleen and alcohol. Ryan's lying down in his room. He won't eat, drink or sleep. He barely says anything."

If ever a situation screamed out for compassion and empathy, this had to be it. A young boy's father was dead, bad enough in itself, and then all the circumstances, the past, the problems, the way it happened, and the possibility of criminal charges. Too much! Too much for anyone to handle.

Let me say this right off: Ryan was the most even-tempered kid I knew. In basketball, with his quickness, he went to the basket a lot, which led to numerous fouls, some of which were anything but subtle. Never did he come even close to losing his composure. What he was feeling that evening, I couldn't imagine, but I was sure he needed as much support as he could get.

"Can I see him?"

"Sure, I'll take you in."

This is what doctors are supposed to do, talk to people in need, explain things, provide comfort, and make things a little easier. As we entered the room, I had no idea what I could say.

Lying perfectly still on the bed, Ryan looked like a shell of himself, his face drawn and drained, as if he'd been lobotomized.

"Hello, Ryan."

Looking up, it was all he could do to utter a faint, "Hi, Doc."

Sitting down on the edge of the bed, I began, "Your mom told me what happened."

No response.

"Ryan, this has to be worse than any nightmare you could ever think of. But it did happen, and you're right in the middle of it. I'm here to help if I can. Tell me how you feel."

Slowly, he turned a bit, took a breath, and began speaking. He felt nothing, everything, frustration, guilt, anger, despair. There was only the slightest push off as his dad had come at him. Now, how could he face anyone, do anything at all?

I tried to let him say all he wanted, draw it out so he could begin to deal with it. At the end, "Ryan, I'll come back tomorrow. No one should expect you to say anything, but if you do choose to respond, remember, there are only two simple points: You loved your dad, and what happened was an accident. Tell yourself that over and over."

No charges were brought and Ryan ended up majoring in psychology.

Craig and I took off on a Saturday from Des Moines to Las Vegas. Up and over the puny Rockies, we dropped down into the air-conditioned neon, tempted by the legalized harlotry, keno, and overwhelming ambiance of debauchery. But this was serious; world championship, c'mon! Securing our 4-door Cavalier rental, cool 12 in hand, we zoomed up the hill, barely stopping for the Joshua tree forest, arriving higher in St. George. Our version of "Fear and Loathing," now that I think of it.

Graciously greeted and attended at the motel by one of the ubiquitous perfect Mormon women, we were off to reconnoiter. First, tournament headquarters. Requisite T-shirts, check the all-important pairings, free body fat analysis, by impedance no less, 11% me, 9% Craig, well he's had more fluids, off to the venues.

At Dixie High, we find a pre-tourney 3 on 3 warm up about to begin. By chance, one of our Internet teammates is there forlornly loitering around. We meet and enter the fray, but no! They won't let us enter, too late. "Look," I said. "Rotate the brackets, shift Idaho over here and move Brazil up two slots and you got the same number of games on the same courts with no more refs, just New

York and Bill's Baldies get one less game apiece." You won't! Well, to heck with you too. Anal-retentive yahoo!

Desperately scrounging the community, summoning up that intuitive sense of chronic gym rats, we score a pickup game, where else, on a nice indoor court behind the altar of a small Mormon church. We got a good run in, all we wanted, but my play was pitiful, atrocious. A step slow, plodding, couldn't hit, couldn't defend. Part of it was that I was matched up against a guy that I later found out was a junior college all-American. On the positive side, after that you're almost for sure due to be hot.

The rest of the guys had showed up back at the motel so we had our first chalk talk over suds and pretzels. Help on "D" and take what you can get on "O," is all I remember. Afterwards, a few of us moseyed on over to the shooting contest. I knocked down thirteen of fifteen from the stripe and three of the five from the circle and won nothing. These old dudes could shoot! Guess defense and running will have to carry us.

Next day, our first game was at the armory against Indiana. I'd done my meditation and yoga ritual and was ready to roll. I won't say we played great but we did well enough to pull it out in the second half. Our center was this 6'8" guy from Rapid City, S.D., who could bang pretty good and even had some semblance of touch left. With him, Craig, and Phil inside and us gunners hittin' a few from downtown, we got it done.

"Hey Doc, we're 1-0. Not too shabby! Gotta rehydrate. How about that Quick Trip? Pabst all right?"

"Damn, Craig, my liver can't take this steady assault. Think of the team."

"You're right. I'll just get a six. Then let's find a place to eat."

Out he comes with a twelve, soft jazz on the radio, we cruise for a restaurant. After much irrelevant discussion having to do with superstition, tradition, and the effect of chili on the jump shot, we pull into this primitive looking Mexican establishment, a shack, really. My accomplice shows an ever so subtle recalcitrance. "No, Craig, this is where you get the authentic stuff. We don't want no Tio Taco gringo fare. You watch, tomorrow will be lights out."

This was the place. Straight from Guanajuato, el padre had left his sixteen-year-old hijo in charge. Soon, using my best campesino

Spanish, I was back in the kitchen helping cook the tasty repast. Jalapenos, extra Jack, and a few Coronas, and we were doin' fine.

As the week went on, we kept winning. Between games, Craig and I did it all: saluting the "three patriarchs" at Bryce, entering amongst the hoo doo's at Zion, peering over the north rim of the Grand at dawn, searching genealogies at the LDS computer center, contemplating petroglyphs, even spending one unforgettable afternoon in search of the elusive desert tortoise. Dodging determined deer hunters on back roads, our Cav was pressed to the max more than once.

Meanwhile the vast field narrowed to four. Utah, gone; Portland, gone; Russian '72 Olympians, eliminated. In the semi's we faced Chicago. We got an inkling of how it was going to be, one minute into the game when our center along with theirs, were given the early shower. Still, these pick-up refs allowed an unbelievable amount of contact. Picks were loaded up and delivered with nitroglycerin. We could play physical but this was beyond where we had ever gone and it cost us. Down fourteen late in the first half, even though guarded by a former NBA veteran, whom we were told was either Wally or Jo Jo, I decided to take it upon myself to try to bring us back. Looking him off ever so slightly, I let fly with a three. Swish! Next time down, he's on me like flies to feces. Dribbling to the corner, I think I have a slight opening and pull up for the "J." But damn, this guy's got ups, and suddenly he's in my face. In the air, adjusting for all I got, pulling it back and releasing it nearly straight up with all the extra wrist and finger stroke I could find, I get it over his hand and wait with the others for it to return to earth. Silk again! That really wasn't fair, but we'll take it. Now his teammates are on him, "Ain't you gonna guard him?" and "Where's the 'D'?"

Pride on the line, he now makes the pledge, "That's it, you history." I don't respond but I can feel an incredible amount of juice flowing. I don't care who he is. He doesn't know what mystical forces can be brought to bear in these situations. Soon we got it again and I'm bouncin' the rock across the half court line. He's waiting, grim faced, to pick me up eight feet past the arc, hands only part way up. I never get there, popping a lightening-like launch from thirty.

"Pffft! That ain't got no chance," he announces, only to have to eat the words as another trifecta stretches chords. Finally they shut up. But there's still twelve seconds until half time and they're pushing it up the floor to give us payback. Suddenly Craig steps in to swipe a pass and we got a two-on-one goin' the other way with our "hero" being the one. I got the ball, so I'm gonna keep it until he commits to me, then dish. But he's quick and knows exactly what I'm thinking. Reacting perfectly, he's on my teammate almost as soon as he receives the ball. In doing so, though, he had taken his eye momentarily off of me. Seizing the opportunity, I quickly slip beyond the arc, get the return, and fire as he charges my way. Buzzer and swoosh coincide as the crowd fills the air with noise. The four three's put us back in contention but they were not gonna go down easy. I wished we could have foregone the half time but figured I could hold the heat through the intermission if I had to.

Five minutes shouldn't make much difference but when you're over fifty, stiffness sneaks up frighteningly fast, not a full blown Parkinsonian rigidity but just enough to take the edge off of that well-oiled perfectly smooth running machine feeling. That plus heightened recognition meant my run was over. Luckily teammates stepped up with solid contributions, especially Phil and Craig reaching deep for focused "D," rebounding with zest, and hitting free throws. They tried to press in the last stages but we avoided turning it over and even utilized the spread delay to protect the lead. Winning by six, we were now headed to the finals.

Not wanting to change anything, we celebrated with 3.2's but not in excess. For me, the concession was token since by this stage of the tournament, the reinduction of my hepatic enzymes was complete allowing me to metabolize etOH as fast as I could twist off, tip, and whack it back.

Having already done most of the big name attractions, Craig and I decided on an unstructured afternoon closely in touch with what nature had to offer in this inspirational setting. Up past Snow Canyon and off the beaten path, we finally stopped in the most isolated spot we could find. "Give me thirty minutes," I said, getting out of the car.

Climbing up the canyon wall, I found a perfectly quiet ledge with a thicket of shrubs forming a natural chair back to sit down and lean against. A distant eagle soared over the vast panorama tantalizing my imagination. Settling into a meditative state of sorts, I allowed the senses to register randomly, renewing my awareness of being irrevocably connected to all that exists. Slowly, clarity entered my consciousness. Clocks and watches became just so many atoms. White clouds formed and reformed, then disappeared. A chickadee visited, feeling as I did. Renewed, then down to the resting car.

Tomorrow's game would be as a metaphor for life. I would look to enhance the experience of those around me. The play, picks, the assist, all in the natural flow of the action. The drama would unfold as it will. Yes, it is for the putative world championship, but what value has it if not accomplished with the appropriate class?

That evening the preparation began in earnest. Meaningless ritual? Psychobabble? Superstitious foreplay? Hardly! I'm talking tried and proven performance enhancing techniques. First the nails. Normally I clip thumbs Monday and progress to pinkies every Friday over cutting ever so slightly to give myself a full week of touch with minimal risk of a disastrous torn edge. Years of experience have taught me the exact range of acceptable length almost guaranteeing the feel needed for a high percentage. The final adjustment on any shot is with the finger tips, and for me both hands are involved, so not one nail can be too short or the oversensitivity throws the stoke off. Pulling out all the stops, I proceeded to trim all ten to the precise predetermined length. I know, it was a big risk, but taking into consideration the overarching magnitude of the contest, I felt it was justified.

Then, around 9:00 p.m., I head to the local weight room. Any amateur lifter can verify the next day pump derived from a good workout against the bar. That effect is amplified if you can go, say two weeks without lifting, and then hit it hard, blasting those striated fibers through the stratosphere. I had gone seven days. Too heavy could theoretically affect touch, but probably not in a regular lifter. Besides, my effort the next day was going to be predicated on defense and rebounding so do it big. Actually, my plan was to go for slightly higher reps and less poundage because of the aforementioned concerns, but there's something about a successfully completed set that drives one to add plates for the following effort. Restraining myself mentally, I was able to stick to the plan and hurry the steel along thus giving the fast twitch component a vigorous kick, not stopping until each body part was vanquished. Finishing with deads and crunches, I felt primed, satisfied that my body would do the rest as I slept.

Game day, 6 a.m. breakfast of granola with sliced banana bathed in O.J. Read quietly, *The House of Mirth*, by Edith Wharton. Somehow, I glean motivation out of the biblical quote on which the work is based: "Sorrow is better than laughter; for by the sadness of the countenance the heart is made better. The heart of the wise is in the house of mourning; but the heart of fools is in the house of mirth."

Then exactly two hours before 12-noon game time, one and one half cups of caffeinated jo. Another swallow would risk jitteriness, and more dreaded yet, an episode of exercise induced PAT which took me to near syncope every time, requiring a good five minutes rest to resolve. Once again, planning ahead, I had gone a week without, and knew I'd get a nice edge from the stimulant.

Peaceful meditation followed by a yoga routine designed to loosen and stretch, completed the preparation. Let's do it!

Our opponent was Team Colorado, excellent shooters, a seven-foot center, and an extremely physical style of play. Warm ups, introductions, "Star Spangled Banner," the crowd all a blur; it's only the game, poised, center court, and the tip.

We started off okay even scoring a few easy ones. They on the other hand, were firing on all pistons, cooking, knockin' down everything. I had their toughest guy but they ran him off pick after pick like in a gauntlet. Their roll was scary but I knew it couldn't last. Already I had two assists and my body felt good, no pain, runnin' the floor at will. Then, as I flashed under our hoop, the ball is passed to me in perfect position and instinctively I put it up and in with the left reverse all in one motion. Soon, on a long rebound, I find myself ahead of the pack and get the pass for the layup. Next I'm posting up a much shorter guy for the five-foot turn around. An immense pressure is beginning to assert itself deep in my central nervous system. These shots haven't been amazing but I'm scoring and I haven't missed. Always, always I ride these things out, take it as far as I can. Isn't this now my duty to the team. It has nothing to do with pride, arrogance, hot doggin'. A wide open three, squeeze the trigger, ch-ching. Pull up "J" from twelve, it's in! Killer cross over to the stop and pop, kaboom! I am hopelessly mired in the middle of a one man dominating hot streak. Swish, count it, nothin' but net, facial, bank's open, yes.

At half time Murphy had twenty-four points on an assortment of moves, inside and out, free throws, and break away layups, leading his team to a seven point lead.

"Hey, do you ever miss?" It was one of the referees.

"Just lucky today," I answered showing a humility that my game had definitely not demonstrated even the slightest little bit of.

In the second half, we trade baskets, then gain a few, and gradually extend the lead to twenty with seven minutes to go. I had barely sat so I take myself out thinking the game's pretty well over. World championship. Wait a minute, these guys aren't dead yet. Pushing the tempo like crazy, they score five straight times down the floor while our side of the scoreboard is stuck. "Doc, get back in there!"

A perfect bounce pass from Phil and I caress a feather high off the glass going full throttle for a deft two. Seconds later I receive it at half court with a step on my guy and push it to the hole finishing as he swipes my head from behind. Converted free throw completes the conventional three. Keep runnin'. Down the left side with the outlet, got the angle, push it, no, he's cuttin' me off- shovin' me out of bounds, leap-whistle-release from behind the board a la Bird, it drops! It dropped in! Free throw for the three. Hustle, truck it, they miss, two-on-one us, got it at the arc, launch.... Swisharoo! This is insane, call Sparky.

Looking up, one whole minute had come off the clock and I had put in eleven counters. Now it was over. They looked crushed, vacuous stares on drained countenances, energy spent, tired oldsters contemplating AARP.

I sat for the rest, myself dazed by the fantastic flurry. The last minutes floated by, rescued by the gracious buzzer. Every hand had to touch mine, players, kids, fans, old timers. The scorer came over and knelt for a moment, arms overhead in obeisance. World champs, all tournament, MVP, it was the whole caboodle.

You know, I was born in '44, and that has always been my favorite number. At my request Phil had given me jersey #44. It's even my coat size, but never, ever, in my wildest imagination did I

BREAKAWAY

dream that in the world championship match, I would ring up, you guessed it, forty-four points. Astrology, Ouija board, Tarot cards, I don't know, but there has to be something with that number!

Craig and I couldn't linger. We had a flight to catch. Floating down the mountain, gold in hand, we announced our joy to Arizona, then Nevada before vanishing over the Rockies, now standing at attention.

Once again that cold Siberian wind is blowing, not in bursts but a steady howl, unchanging, dark and sad, whispering its reassuring message. Collar upturned, leaning into icy flow, I gladly trudge the treadmill. Now in stasis, I think how fulfilling it's been, medicine, my kind of medicine; basketball, also my brand; family; life itself. Yet somehow there's an ultimate futility to it all. Then the tundra, always the tundra.

All I have is a carry-on, a stethoscope, and a basketball in a mesh cinch bag. Tired and frazzled, I'm finally scheduled to connect in twenty minutes. Stepping outside the primitive building, I see him. Maybe nine-years-old, bouncing a rubber ball off the nearby wall. But that's not it. He's wearing a tattered jersey with the number 23. Pondering, very deliberately I remove the ball from the bag turning it a few times in my hands. On cue he looks at me. I bounce it over, drop the bag, and walk back into the Denpasar airport. Seeing the single phone free, I try my luck and connect almost immediately. "Sister Joan. Yes it's me. We're taking off shortly.

"Great. I'll meet you in Dili."

424

ABOUT THE AUTHOR

Dan Murphy is a product of nowhere. Well, almost nowhere; it appears on the detailed maps of Iowa. Intelligent and athletic, he found meaning in battling over and over for dominance on the hardwood and for good health where it is scarce.

From nowhere he has gone everywhere, dribbling, engaging, and consulting...and now taking up the pen.

Recognition has come in the form of MVP awards, Distinguished Alumnus designation (of University of Iowa Carver College of Medicine), and a plethora of expressions of gratitude coming from the disenfranchised in little known lands.

He continues to do battle in Dili, Timor-Leste, where he is known affectionately as Dr. Dan. Rumor has it that he can be sometimes seen late at night on an abandoned court announcing the game as he plays.

Made in the USA
San Bernardino, CA
06 December 2015